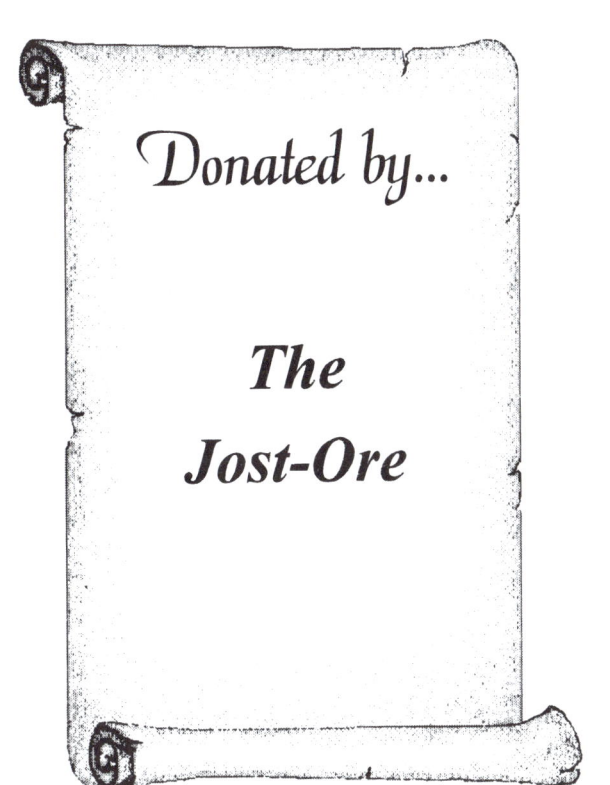

Donated by...

**The
Jost-Ore**

T.S. ELIOT
Critical Assessments

T.S. ELIOT
Critical Assessments

Edited by
Graham Clarke

VOLUME II
Early Poems and *The Waste Land*

CHRISTOPHER HELM
London

Ft. Wayne
May, 1991

Selection and editorial matter
© 1990 Christopher Helm Ltd
Christopher Helm (Publishers) Ltd,
Imperial House, 21–25 North Street,
Bromley, Kent BR1 1SD

ISBN 0-7470-0419-6

A CIP catalogue record for this book
is available from the British Library

All rights reserved: No reproduction, copy
or transmission of this publication may be
made without written permission.

No paragraph of this publication may be
reproduced, copies or transmitted save
with written permission or in accordance
with the provisions of the Copyright Act
1956 (as amended), or under the terms of
any licence permitting limited copying
issued by the Copyright Licensing Agency,
7 Ridgmount Street, London WC1E 7AE.

Any person who does any unauthorised act
in relation to this publication may be liable
to criminal prosecution and civil claims for
damages.

Frontispiece: Portrait of T.S. Eliot by
Wyndham Lewis (courtesy of Eyre and
Spottiswoode Ltd)

Typeset by Leaper & Gard Ltd, Bristol, England
Printed and bound in Great Britain by Biddles Ltd,
Guildford and Kings Lynn

Contents

Prufrock and Other Observations (June 1917)

61	The New Poetry ARTHUR WAUGH	3
62	Drunken Helots and Mr Eliot EZRA POUND	6
63	Anonymous review	9
64	Recent Verse ANONYMOUS	10
65	Shorter Notices ANONYMOUS	11
66	Divers Realists CONRAD AIKEN	12
67	Prufrock and Other Observations: a criticism MAY SINCLAIR	13
68	Another Impressionist BABETTE DEUTSCH	17
69	A Note on T.S. Eliot's Book MARIANNE MOORE	19
70	Recent United States Poetry EDGAR JEPSON	20

Poems (May 1919)

71	Not Here, O Apollo ANONYMOUS	25
72	Is This Poetry? ANONYMOUS	28

Ara Vos Prec (February 1920)

73	The Eternal Footman JOHN MIDDLETON MURRY	33
74	A New Byronism ANONYMOUS	36
75	An Ironist ROBERT NICHOLS	39
76	New Poets, T.S. Eliot DESMOND MACCARTHY	42

Poems (February 1920)

77	Perilous Leaping MARION STOBLE	49
78	T.S. Eliot E.E. CUMMINGS	51
79	Anglo-Saxon Adventures in Verse MARK VAN DOREN	54
80	Irony de Luxe LOUIS UNTERMEYER	55
81	What Ails Pegasus? RAYMOND WEAVER	59
82	Studies in the Sophisticated PADRAIC COLUM	60

Contents

The Waste Land (1922)

83	Review of *The Waste Land* and notice of first issue of the *Criterion* ANONYMOUS	65
84	Books and Authors ANONYMOUS	67
85	Comment ANONYMOUS	68
86	The Poetry of Drouth EDMUND WILSON	71
87	T.S. Eliot GILBERT SELDES	76
88	Disillusion vs. Dogma LOUIS UNTERMEYER	81
89	Mr Eliot's Slug Horn ELINOR WYLIE	84
90	Notes for a Study of *The Waste Land*: An Imaginary Dialogue with T.S. Eliot HAROLD MUNRO	87
91	A Contrast HARRIET MONROE	92
92	Waste Lands JOHN CROWE RANSOM	96
93	Waste Lands ALLEN TATE	103
94	A Fragmentary Poem ANONYMOUS (Edgell Rickword)	106
95	T.S. Eliot CLIVE BELL	109
96	Poetry J.C. SQUIRE	113
97	The Waste Land F.L. LUCAS	115
98	Waste Land and Waste Paper HUMBERT WOLFE	120
99	The Esotericism of T.S. Eliot GORHAM B. MUNSON	123

Studies of *The Waste Land* and Other Poems

100	T.S. Eliot EDMUND WILSON	133
101	From *The Coming Struggle for Power* (extract) JOHN STRACHEY	154
102	T.S. Eliot F.R. LEAVIS	159
103	The Bloody Wood T.H. THOMPSON	188
104	From *Archetypal Patterns in Poetry* MAUD BODKIN	195
105	Herbert Read; D.H. Lawrence; T.S. Eliot GEOFFREY BULLOUGH	201
106	*The Waste Land*: Critique of the Myth CLEANTH BROOKS	212
107	T.S. Eliot as the International Hero DELMORE SCHWARTZ	237
108	A New Interpretation of *The Waste Land* JOHN PETER	244
109	T.S. Eliot: The Death of Literary Judgement KARL SHAPIRO	263
110	The Defeatism of *The Waste Land* DAVID CRAIG	278
111	Eliot: The Poetics of Myth ROY HARVEY PEARCE	290
112	T.S. Eliot: The Retreat from Myth LILLIAN FEDER	309
113	Maps of the Waste Land BERNARD BERGONZI	321
114	The Word Within a Word DENIS DONOGHUE	326
115	*The Waste Land* as a Dramatic Monologue ANTHONY EASTHOPE	340
116	A Handful of Words: The Credibility of Language in *The Waste Land* JONATHAN BISHOP	356
117	*The Waste Land*: A Sphinx without a Secret MAUD ELLMANN	377

Prufrock and Other Observations

June 1917

61
The New Poetry*

◆

ARTHUR WAUGH

Cleverness is, indeed, the pitfall of the New Poetry. There is no question about the ingenuity with which its varying moods are exploited, its elaborate symbolism evolved, and its sudden, disconcerting effects exploded upon the imagination. Swift, brilliant images break into the field of vision, scatter like rockets, and leave a trail of flying fire behind. But the general impression is momentary; there are moods and emotions, but no steady current of ideas behind them. Further, in their determination to surprise and even to puzzle at all costs, these young poets are continually forgetting that the first essence of poetry is beauty; and that, however much you may have observed the world around you, it is impossible to translate your observation into poetry, without the intervention of the spirit of beauty, controlling the vision, and reanimating the idea.

The temptations of cleverness may be insistent, but its risks are equally great: how great indeed will, perhaps, be best indicated by the example of the 'Catholic Anthology', which apparently represents the very newest of all the new poetic movements of the day. This strange little volume bears upon its cover a geometrical device, suggesting that the material within holds the same relation to the art of poetry as the work of the Cubist school holds to the art of painting and design. The product of the volume is mainly American in origin, only one or two of the contributors being of indisputably English birth. But it appears here under the auspices of a house associated with some of the best poetry of the younger generation, and is prefaced by a short lyric by Mr W.B. Yeats, in which that honoured representative of a very different school of inspiration makes bitter fun of scholars and critics, who

> *Edit and annotate the lines*
> *That young men, tossing on their beds,*
> *Rhymed out in love's despair*
> *To flatter beauty's ignorant ear.*

* *Quarterly Review* 226 (October 1916), p. 386.

Early Poems and *The Waste Land*

The reader will not have penetrated far beyond this warning notice before he finds himself in the very stronghold of literary rebellion, if not of anarchy. Mr Orrick Johns may be allowed to speak for his colleagues, as well as for himself:

This is a song of youth,
This is the cause of myself;
I knew my father well and he was a fool,
Therefore will I have my own foot in the path before I take a step;
I will go only into new lands,
And I will walk on no plank-walks.
The horses of my family are wind-broken,
And the dogs are old,
And the guns rust;
I will make me a new bow from an ash-tree,
And cut up the homestead into arrows.

And Mr Ezra Pound takes up the parable in turn, in the same wooden prose, cut into battens:

Come, my songs, let us express our baser passions.
Let us express our envy for the man with a steady job and no worry
    about the future.
You are very idle, my songs,
I fear you will come to a bad end.
You stand about the streets. You loiter at the corners and bus-stops,
You do next to nothing at all.
You do not even express our inner nobility,
You will come to a very bad end.
And I? I have gone half cracked.

It is not for his audience to contradict the poet, who for once may be allowed to pronounce his own literary epitaph. But this, it is to be noted, is the 'poetry' that was to say nothing that might not be said 'actually in life—under emotion,' the sort of emotion that settles down into the banality of a premature decrepitude:

I grow old . . . I grow old . . .
I shall wear the bottoms of my trousers rolled.
Shall I part my hair behind? Do I dare to eat a peach?
I shall wear white flannel trousers, and walk upon the beach.
I have heard the mermaids singing, each to each.

I do not think that they will sing to me.

Here, surely, is the reduction to absurdity of that school of literary license which, beginning with the declaration

Prufrock and Other Observations (1917)

I knew my father well and he was a fool,

naturally proceeds to the convenient assumption that everything which seemed wise and true to the father must inevitably be false and foolish to the son. Yet if the fruits of emancipation are to be recognised in the unmetrical, incoherent banalities of these literary 'Cubists,' the state of Poetry is indeed threatened with anarchy which will end in something worse even than 'red ruin and the breaking up of laws.' From such a catastrophe the humour, commonsense, and artistic judgment of the best of the new 'Georgians' will assuredly save their generation; nevertheless, a hint of warning may not be altogether out of place. It was a classic custom in the family hall, when the feast was at its height, to display a drunken slave among the sons of the household, to the end that they, being ashamed at the ignominious folly of his gesticulations, might determine never to be tempted into such a pitiable condition themselves. The custom had its advantages; for the wisdom of the younger generation was found to be fostered more surely by a single example than by a world of homily and precept.

62
Drunken Helots and Mr Eliot*

EZRA POUND

Genius has I know not what peculiar property, its manifestations are various, but however diverse and dissimilar they may be, they have at least one property in common. It makes no difference in what art, in what mode, whether the most conservative, or the most ribald-revolutionary, or the most diffident; if in any land, or upon any floating deck over the ocean, or upon some newly contrapted craft in the aether, genius manifests itself, at once some elderly gentleman has a flux of bile from his liver; at once from the throne or the easy Cowperian sofa, or from the gutter, or from the oeconomical press room there bursts a torrent of elderly words, splenetic, irrelevant, they form themselves instinctively into large phrases denouncing the inordinate product.

This peculiar kind of *rabbia* might almost be taken as the test of a work of art, mere talent seems incapable of exciting it. 'You can't fool me, sir, you're a scoundrel,' bawls the testy old gentleman.

Fortunately the days when 'that very fiery particle' could be crushed out by the 'Quarterly' are over, but it interests me, as an archaeologist, to note that the firm which no longer produces Byron, but rather memoirs, letters of the late Queen, etc., is still running a review, and that this review is still where it was in 1812, or whatever the year was; and that, not having an uneducated Keats to condemn, a certain Mr. Waugh is scolding about Mr. Eliot.

All I can find out, by asking questions concerning Mr. Waugh, is that he is 'a very old chap,' 'a reviewer.' From internal evidence we deduce that he is, like the rest of his generation of English *gens-de-lettres*, ignorant of Laforgue; of De Régnier's 'Odelettes'; of his French contemporaries generally, of De Gourmont's 'Litanies,' of Tristan Corbière, Laurent Tailhade. This is by no means surprising. We are used to it from his 'b'ilin'.'

However, he outdoes himself, he calls Mr. Eliot a 'drunken helot.' So called they Anacreon in the days of his predecessors, but from the context in the 'Quarterly' article I judge that Mr. Waugh does not intend the phrase as

Egoist 4, no. 5 (June 1917), pp. 72–4.

Prufrock and Other Observations (1917)

a compliment, he is trying to be abusive, and moreover, he in his limited way has succeeded.

Let us sample the works of the last 'Drunken Helot.' I shall call my next anthology 'Drunken Helots' if I can find a dozen poems written half so well as the following:

[Quotes 'Conversation Galante'.]

Our helot has a marvellous neatness. There is a comparable finesse in Laforgue's 'Votre âme est affaire d'oculiste,' but hardly in English verse.

Let us reconsider this drunkenness:

[Quotes 'La Figlia Che Piange'.]

And since when have helots taken to reading Dante and Marlowe? Since when have helots made a new music, a new refinement, a new method of turning old phrases into new by their aptness? However the 'Quarterly,' the century old, the venerable, the praeclarus, the voice of Gehova and Co., Sinai and 51A Albemarle Street, London, W. 1, has pronounced this author a helot. They are all for an aristocracy made up of, possibly, Tennyson, Southey and Wordsworth, the flunkey, the dull and the duller. Let us sup with the helots. Or perhaps the good Waugh is a wag, perhaps he hears with the haspirate and wishes to pun on Mr. Heliot's name: a bright bit of syzygy.

I confess his type of mind puzzles me, there is no telling what he is up to.

I do not wish to misjudge him, this theory may be the correct one. You never can tell when old gentlemen grow facetious. He does not mention Mr. Eliot's name; he merely takes his lines and abuses them. The artful dodger, he didn't (*sotto voce* 'he didn't want "people" to know that Mr. Eliot was a poet').

The poem he chooses for malediction is the title poem, 'Prufrock.' It is too long to quote entire.

[Quotes 'Prufrock' 'For I have known them' to 'leaning out of windows'.]

Let us leave the silly old Waugh. Mr. Eliot has made an advance on Browning. He has also made his dramatis personae contemporary and convincing. He has been an individual in his poems. I have read the contents of this book over and over, and with continued joy in the freshness, the humanity, the deep quiet culture. 'I have tried to write of a few things that really have moved me' is so far as I know, the sum of Mr. Eliot's 'poetic theory.' His practice has been a distinctive cadence, a personal modus of arrangement, remote origins in Elizabethan English and in the modern French masters, neither origin being sufficiently apparent to affect the personal quality. It is writing without pretence. Mr. Eliot at once takes rank with the five or six living poets whose English one can read with enjoyment.

The 'Egoist' has published the best prose writer of my generation. It follows its publication of Joyce by the publication of a 'new' poet who is at least unsurpassed by any of his contemporaries, either of his own age or his elders.

It is perhaps 'unenglish' to praise a poet whom one can read with enjoyment. Carlyle's generation wanted 'improving' literature, Smiles's 'Self-Help' and the rest of it. Mr. Waugh dates back to that generation, the virus is in his blood, he can't help it. The exactitude of the younger generation gets on his nerves, and so on and so on. He will 'fall into line in time' like the rest of the bread-and-butter reviewers. Intelligent people will read 'J. Alfred Prufrock'; they will wait with some eagerness for Mr. Eliot's further inspirations. It is 7.30 p.m. I have had nothing alcoholic to-day, nor yet yesterday. I said the same sort of thing about James Joyce's prose over two years ago. I am now basking in the echoes. Only a half-caste rag for the propagation of garden suburbs, and a local gazette in Rochester, N.Y., U.S.A., are left whining in opposition.

(I pay my compliments to Ernest Rhys, that he associates with a certain Sarolea, writer of prefaces to cheap editions and editor of 'Everyman.' They had better look after their office boys. I like Ernest Rhys personally, I am sorry to think of him in such slums, but it is time that he apologized for the antics of that paper with which he is, at least in the minds of some, still associated. His alternative is to write a disclaimer. Mr. Dent, the publisher, would also have known better had the passage been submitted to his judgment.)

However, let us leave these bickerings, this stench of the printing-press, weekly and quarterly, let us return to the gardens of the Muses,

Till human voices wake us, and we drown.

as Eliot has written in conclusion to the poem which the 'Quarterly' calls the *reductio ad absurdum*:

I have seen them riding seaward on the waves
Combing the white hair of the waves blown back
When the wind blows the water white and black.

We have lingered in the chambers of the sea
By sea-girls wreathed with seaweed red and brown
Till human voices wake us, and we drown.

The poetic mind leaps the gulf from the exterior world, the trivialities of Mr. Prufrock, diffident, ridiculous, in the drawing-room, Mr. Apollinax's laughter 'submarine and profound' transports him from the desiccated new-statesmanly atmosphere of Professor Canning-Cheetah's. Mr. Eliot's melody rushes out like the thought of Fragilion 'among the birch-trees.' Mr. Waugh is my bitten macaroon at this festival.

63

ANONYMOUS REVIEW*

Mr. Eliot's notion of poetry—he calls the 'observations' poems—seems to be a purely analytical treatment, verging sometimes on the catalogue, of personal relations and environments, uninspired by any glimpse beyond them and untouched by any genuine rush of feeling. As, even on this basis, he remains frequently inarticulate, his 'poems' will hardly be read by many with enjoyment. For the catalogue manner we may commend 'Rhapsody on a Windy Night'.
[. . .]
Among other reminiscences which pass through the rhapsodist's mind and which he thinks the public should know about, are 'dust in crevices, smells of chestnuts in the streets, and female smells in shuttered rooms, and cigarettes in corridors, and cocktail smells in bars.'

The fact that these things occurred to the mind of Mr. Eliot is surely of the very smallest importance to any one—even to himself. They certainly have no relation to 'poetry,' and we only give an example because some of the pieces, he states, have appeared in a periodical which claims that word as its title.

Times Literary Supplement, no. 805, (21 June 1917), p. 299.

64
Recent Verse*

ANON

Mr. Eliot is one of those clever young men who find it amusing to pull the leg of a sober reviewer. We can imagine his saying to his friends: 'See me have a lark out of the old fogies who don't know a poem from a pea-shooter. I'll just put down the first thing that comes into my head, and call it "The Love Song of J. Alfred Prufrock." Of course it will be idiotic; but the fogies are sure to praise it, because when they don't understand a thing and yet cannot hold their tongues they find safety in praise.' We once knew a clever musician who found a boisterous delight in playing that pathetic melody 'Only a Jew' in two keys at once. At first the effect was amusing in its complete idiocy, but we cannot imagine that our friend would have been so foolish as to print the score. Among a few friends the man of genius is privileged to make a fool of himself. He is usually careful not to do so outside an intimate circle. Mr. Eliot has not the wisdom of youth. If the 'Love Song' is neither witty nor amusing, the other poems are interesting experiments in the bizarre and violent. The subjects of the poems, the imagery, the rhythms have the wilful outlandishness of the young revolutionary idea. We do not wish to appear patronising, but we are certain that Mr. Eliot could do finer work on traditional lines. With him it seems to be a case of missing the effect by too much cleverness. All beauty has in it an element of strangeness, but here the strangeness overbalances the beauty.

Literary World 83 (5 July 1917), p. 107.

65
Shorter Notices*

ANON

Mr. Eliot may possibly give us the quintessence of twenty-first century poetry. Certainly much of what he writes is unrecognisable as poetry at present, but it is all decidedly amusing, and it is only fair to say that he does not call these pieces poems. He calls them 'observations,' and the description seems exact, for he has a keen eye as well as a sharp pen, and draws wittily whatever his capricious glance descends on. We do not pretend to follow the drift of 'The Love Song of J. Alfred Prufrock,' and therefore, instead of quoting from it, we present our readers with the following piece:

[Quotes 'The Boston Evening Transcript'.]

This is Mr. Eliot's highest flight, and we shall treasure it.

New Statesman 9 (18 August 1917), p. 477.

66
Divers Realists*

♦

CONRAD AIKEN

Mr. T.S. Eliot, whose book 'Prufrock and Other Observations' is really hardly more than a pamphlet, is also a realist, but of a different sort. Like Mr. Wilfred Wilson Gibson, Mr. Eliot is a psychologist; but his intuitions are keener; his technique subtler. For the two semi-narrative psychological portraits which form the greater and better part of his book, 'The Love Song of J. Alfred Prufrock' and 'The Portrait of a Lady,' one can have little but praise. This is psychological realism, but in highly subjective or introspective vein; whereas Mr. Gibson, for example, gives us, in the third person, the reactions of an individual to a situation which is largely external (an accident, let us say), Mr. Eliot gives us, in the first person, the reactions of an individual to a situation for which to a large extent his own character is responsible. Such work is more purely autobiographic than the other—the field is narrowed, and the terms are idiosyncratic (sometimes almost blindly so). The dangers of such work are obvious: one must be certain that one's mental character and idiom are sufficiently close to the norm to be comprehensible or significant. In this respect, Mr. Eliot is near the border-line. His temperament is peculiar, it is sometimes, as remarked heretofore, almost bafflingly peculiar, but on the whole it is the average hyperaesthetic one with a good deal of introspective curiosity; it will puzzle many, it will delight a few. Mr. Eliot writes pungently and sharply, with an eye for unexpected and vivid details, and, particularly in the two longer poems and in 'The Rhapsody on a Windy Night,' he shows himself to be an exceptionally acute technician. Such free rhyme as this, with irregular line lengths, is difficult to write well, and Mr. Eliot does it well enough to make one wonder whether such a form is not what the adorers of free verse will eventually have to come to. In the rest of Mr. Eliot's volume one finds the piquant and the trivial in about equal proportions.

*From *Scepticisms: Notes on Contemporary Poetry* (New York, 1919), pp. 203–5. Originally published in the *Dial* 63 (8 November 1917), pp. 453–5.

67
Prufrock and Other Observations: a criticism*

MAY SINCLAIR

So far I have seen two and only two reviews of Mr. Eliot's poems: one by Ezra Pound in the 'Egoist', one by an anonymous writer in the 'New Statesman'. I learn from Mr. Pound's review that there is a third, by Mr. Arthur Waugh, in the 'Quarterly'.

To Mr. Ezra Pound Mr. Eliot is a poet with genius as incontestable as the genius of Browning. To the anonymous one he is an insignificant phenomenon that may be appropriately disposed of among the Shorter Notices. To Mr. Waugh, quoted by Mr. Pound, he is a 'drunken Helot'. I do not know what Mr. Pound would say to the anonymous one, but I can imagine. Anyhow, to him the 'Quarterly' reviewer is 'the silly old Waugh'. And that is enough for Mr. Pound.

It ought to be enough for me. Of course I know that genius does inevitably provoke these outbursts of silliness. I know that Mr. Waugh is simply keeping up the good old manly traditions of the 'Quarterly', 'so savage and tartarly,' with its war-cry: 'Ere's a stranger, let's 'eave 'arf a brick at 'im!' And though the behaviour of the 'New Statesman' puzzles me, since it has an editor who sometimes knows better, and really ought to have known better this time, still the 'New Statesman' also can plead precedent. But when Mr. Waugh calls Mr. Eliot 'a drunken Helot,' it is clear that he thinks he is on the track of a tendency and is making a public example of Mr. Eliot. And when the anonymous one with every appearance of deliberation picks out his 'Boston Evening Transcript', the one insignificant, the one negligible and trivial thing in a very serious volume, and assures us that it represents Mr. Eliot at his finest and his best, it is equally clear that we have to do with something more than mere journalistic misadventure. And I think it is something more than Mr. Eliot's genius that has terrified the 'Quarterly' into exposing him in the full glare of publicity and the 'New Statesman' into shoving him and his masterpieces away out of the public sight.

For 'The Love Song of J. Alfred Prufrock', and the 'Portrait of a Lady' are masterpieces in the same sense and in the same degree as Browning's

---

*Literary Review 4 (December 1917), pp. 8–14.

'Romances' and 'Men and Women'; the 'Preludes' and 'Rhapsody on a Windy Night' are masterpieces in a profounder sense and a greater degree than Henley's 'London Voluntaries'; 'La Figlia Che Piange' is a masterpiece in its own sense and in its own degree. It is a unique masterpiece.

But Mr. Eliot is dangerous. Mr. Eliot is associated with an unpopular movement and with unpopular people. His 'Preludes' and his 'Rhapsody' appeared in 'Blast.' They stood out from the experimental violences of 'Blast' with an air of tranquil and triumphant achievement; but, no matter; it was in 'Blast' that they appeared. That circumstance alone was disturbing to the comfortable respectability of Mr. Waugh and the 'New Statesman'.

And apart from this purely extraneous happening, Mr. Eliot's genius is in itself disturbing. It is elusive; it is difficult; it demands a distinct effort of attention. Comfortable and respectable people could see, in the first moment after dinner, what Mr. Henley and Mr. Robert Louis Stevenson and Mr. Rudyard Kipling would be at; for the genius of these three travelled, comfortably and fairly respectably, along the great high roads. They could even, with a little boosting, follow Francis Thompson's flight in mid-air, partly because it was signalled to them by the sound and shining of his wings, partly because Thompson had hitched himself securely to some well-known starry team. He was in the poetic tradition all right. People knew where they were with him, just as they know now where they are with Mr. Davies and his fields and flowers and birds.

But Mr. Eliot is not in any tradition at all, not even in Browning's and Henley's tradition. His resemblances to Browning and Henley are superficial. His difference is twofold; a difference of method and technique; a difference of sight and aim. He does not see anything between him and reality, and he makes straight for the reality he sees; he cuts all his corners and his curves; and this directness of method is startling and upsetting to comfortable, respectable people accustomed to going superfluously in and out of corners and carefully round curves. Unless you are prepared to follow with the same nimbleness and straightness you will never arrive with Mr. Eliot at his meaning. Therefore the only comfortable thing is to sit down and pretend, either that Mr. Eliot is a 'Helot' too drunk to have any meaning, or that his 'Boston Evening Transcript' which you do understand is greater than his 'Love Song of Prufrock' which you do not understand. In both instances you have successfully obscured the issue.

Again, the comfortable and respectable mind loves conventional beauty, and some of the realities that Mr. Eliot sees are not beautiful. He insists on your seeing very vividly, as he sees them, the streets of his 'Preludes' and 'Rhapsody'. He insists on your smelling them.

[Quotes 'Rhapsody on a Windy Night', 'Regard that woman' to 'rancid butter'.]

He is

> *aware of the damp souls of housemaids*
> *Sprouting despondently at area gates.*

And these things are ugly. The comfortable mind turns away from them in disgust. It identifies Mr. Eliot with a modern tendency; it labels him securely 'Stark Realist', so that lovers of 'true poetry' may beware.

It is nothing to the comfortable mind that Mr Eliot is

> *. . . moved by fancies that are curled*
> *Around these images, and cling:*
> *The motion of some infinitely gentle*
> *Infinitely suffering thing.*

It is nothing to it that the emotion he disengages from his ugliest image is unbearably poignant. His poignancy is as unpleasant as his ugliness, disturbing to comfort.

We are to observe that Mr. Eliot's 'Observations' are ugly and unpleasant and obscure.

Now there is no earthly reason why Mr. Eliot should not be ugly and unpleasant if he pleases, no reason why he should not do in words what Hogarth did in painting, provided he does it well enough. Only, the comfortable mind that prefers So and So and So and So to Mr. Eliot ought to prefer Hogarth's 'Paul Before Felix' to his 'Harlot's Progress'. Obscurity, if he were really obscure, would be another matter. But there was a time when the transparent Tennyson was judged obscure; when people wondered what under heaven the young man was after; they couldn't tell for the life of them whether it was his 'dreary gleams' or his 'curlews' that were flying over Locksley Hall. Obscurity may come from defective syntax, from a bad style, from confusion of ideas, from involved thinking, from irrelevant association, from sheer piling on of ornament. Mr. Eliot is not obscure in any of these senses.

There is also an obscurity of remote or unusual objects, or of familiar objects moving very rapidly. And Mr. Eliot's trick of cutting his corners and his curves makes him seem obscure where he is clear as daylight. His thoughts move very rapidly and by astounding cuts. They move not by logical stages and majestic roundings of the full literary curve, but as live thoughts move in live brains. Thus 'La Figlia Che Piange':

[Quotes 'La Figlia Che Piange'.]

I suppose there are minds so comfortable that they would rather not be disturbed by new beauty and by new magic like this. I do not know how much Mr. Eliot's beauty and magic is due to sheer imagination, how much to dexterity of technique, how much to stern and sacred attention to reality; but I do know that without such technique and such attention the finest imagination is futile, and that if Mr. Eliot had written nothing but that one poem he would rank as a poet by right of its perfection.

But Mr. Eliot is not a poet of one poem; and if there is anything more astounding and more assured than his performance it is his promise. He knows what he is after. Reality, stripped naked of all rhetoric, of all ornament, of all confusing and obscuring association, is what he is after. His reality may be a modern street or a modern drawing-room; it may be an ordinary human mind suddenly and fatally aware of what is happening to it; Mr. Eliot is careful to present his street and his drawing-room as they are, and Prufrock's thoughts as they are: live thoughts, kicking, running about and jumping, nervily, in a live brain.

Prufrock, stung by a longing for reality, escapes from respectability into the street and the October fog.

[. . .]

His soul can only assert itself in protests and memories. He would have had more chance in the primeval slime.

> *I should have been a pair of ragged claws*
> *Scuttling across the floors of silent seas.*

As he goes downstairs he is aware of his futility, aware that the noticeable thing about him is the 'bald spot in the middle of my hair'. He has an idea; an idea that he can put into action:

> *I shall wear the bottoms of my trousers rolled.*

He is incapable, he knows that he is incapable of any action more momentous, more disturbing.

And yet—and yet—

> *I have heard the mermaids singing, each to each.*

> *I do not think that they will sing to me.*

> *I have seen them riding seaward on the waves*
> *Combing the white hair of the waves blown back*
> *When the wind blows the water white and black.*

> *We have lingered in the chambers of the sea*
> *By sea-girls wreathed with seaweed red and brown*
> *Till human voices wake us, and we drown.*

Observe the method. Instead of writing round and round about Prufrock, explaining that his tragedy is the tragedy of submerged passion, Mr. Eliot simply removes the covering from Prufrock's mind: Prufrock's mind, jumping quickly from actuality to memory and back again, like an animal, hunted, tormented, terribly and poignantly alive. The Love-Song of Prufrock is a song that Balzac might have sung if he had been as great a poet as he was a novelist.

It is nothing to the 'Quarterly' and to the 'New Statesman' that Mr. Eliot should have done this thing. But it is a great deal to the few people who care for poetry and insist that it should concern itself with reality. With ideas, if you like, but ideas that are realities and not abstractions.

68
Another Impressionist*

BABETTE DEUTSCH

A slim little book, bound in pale yellow wrapping-paper, 'Prufrock' invites inspection, as much by the novelty of its appearance as the queer syllables of its title. The individual note which these suggest is even more emphatically pronounced in the poems between its covers.

The initial one, which gives its name to the volume, is 'The Love Song of J. Alfred Prufrock.' Mr. Prufrock, as he explains in his amorous discursions, is no longer young; his hair has perceptibly thinned, his figure has lost what Apollonian contours it may have possessed. He is self-conscious, introspective, timid. In a-metrical but fluent lines, embroidered with unique metaphor, he draws himself; his desires, his memories, his fears. 'Do I dare,' he asks,

> *Disturb the universe?*
> *In a minute there is time*
> *For decisions and revisions which a minute will reverse.*
>
> *For I have known them all already, known them all—*
> *Have known the evenings, mornings, afternoons,*
> *I have measured out my life with coffee-spoons . . .*

In the end, he does not presume.

The method used in this poem is typical of Mr. Eliot's work. Impressions are strung along on a tenuous thread of sense. A familiar situation: the hesitating amours of the middle-aged, the failure of a certain man to establish the expected relation with a certain woman, is given in poetic monologue. The language has the extraordinary quality of common words uncommonly used. Less formal than prose, more nervous than metrical verse, the rhythms are suggestive of program music of an intimate sort. This effect is emphasized by the use of rhyme. It recurs, often internally, with an echoing charm that is heightened by its irregularity. But Mr. Eliot, like M. Géraldy, of whom he is vaguely reminiscent, is so clever a technician that the rhymes are subordinated to afford an unconsidered pleasure.

*New Republic 14 (16 February 1918), p. 89.

In these 'observations' there is a glimpse of many slight but memorable things: of dirty London streets, crowded with laborers, dilettantes, prostitutes; of polite stupidities in country houses; of satiric fencings; of the stale aroma of familiar things. Mostly they are impressions of a weary mind, looking out upon a crowded personal experience with impartial irony. They have the hall-marks of impressionism: remoteness from vulgar ethics and aesthetics, indifference to the strife of nations and classes, an esoteric humor thrown out in peculiar phrases. Something of Eliot's quality may be got from 'The Boston Evening Transcript,' whimsically suggestive of that fragment of Sappho's: 'Evening, thou that bringest all that bright morning scattered; thou bringest the sheep, the goat, the child back to her mother.'

[Quotes 'The Boston Evening Transcript'.]

69
A Note on T.S. Eliot's Book*

MARIANNE MOORE

It might be advisable for Mr Eliot to publish a fangless edition of 'Prufrock and Other Observations' for the gentle reader who likes his literature, like breakfast coffee or grapefruit, sweetened. A mere change in the arrangement of the poems would help a little. It might begin with 'La Figlia Che Piange', followed perhaps by the 'Portrait of a Lady'; for the gentle reader, in his eagerness for the customary bit of sweets, can be trusted to overlook the ungallantry, the youthful cruelty, of the substance of the 'Portrait'. It may as well be admitted that this hardened reviewer cursed the poet in his mind for this cruelty while reading the poem; and just when he was ready to find extenuating circumstances—the usual excuses about realism—out came this 'drunken helot' (one can hardly blame the good English reviewer whom Ezra Pound quotes!) with that ending. It is hard to get over this ending with a few moments of thought; it wrenches a piece of life at the roots.

As for the gentle reader, this poem could be followed by the lighter ironies of 'Aunt Nancy', the 'Boston Evening Transcript', etc. One would hardly know what to do with the two London pieces. Whistler in his post-impressionistic English studies—and these poems are not entirely unlike Whistler's studies—had the advantage of his more static medium, of a somewhat more romantic temperament, and of the fact that the objects he painted half-hid their ugliness under shadows and the haze of distance. But Eliot deals with life, with beings and things who live and move almost nakedly before his individual mind's eye—in the darkness, in the early sunlight, and in the fog. Whatever one may feel about sweetness in literature, there is also the word honesty, and this man is a faithful friend of the objects he portrays; altogether unlike the sentimentalist who really stabs them treacherously in the back while pretending affection.

---

* *Poetry* 12 (April 1918), pp. 36–7.

70
Recent United States Poetry*

EDGAR JEPSON

But the queer and delightful thing is that in the scores of yards of pleasant verse and wamblings and yawpings which have been recently published in the Great Pure Republic I have found a poet, a real poet, who possesses in the highest degree the qualities the new school demands. Western-born of Eastern stock, Mr. T.S. Eliot is United States of the United States; and his poetry is securely as autochthonic as Theocritus. It is new in form, as all genuine poetry is new in form; it is musical with a new music, and that without any straining after newness. The form and music are a natural, integral part of the poet's amazingly fine presentation of his vision of the world.

Could anything be more United States, more of the soul of that modern land, than 'The Love Song of J. Alfred Prufrock'? It is the very wailing testament of that soul with its cruel clarity of sophisticated vision, its thin, sophisticated emotions, its sophisticated appreciation of a beauty, and its sophisticated yearning for a beauty it cannot dare to make its own and so, at last, live.

This is in very truth the lover of the real, up-to-date United States:

> *In the room the women come and go,*
> *Talking of Michelangelo.*
>
> *And indeed there will be time*
> *To wonder, 'Do I dare?' and, 'Do I dare?'*
> *Time to turn back and descend the stair,*
> *With a bald spot in the middle of my hair—*
>
> *Do I dare*
> *Disturb the universe?*
> *In a minute there is time*
> *For decisions and revisions which a minute will reverse.*
>
> *For I have known them all already, known them all—*

---

*English Review 26 (May 1918), pp. 426–8. This is an extract from a longer essay.

> *Have known the evenings, mornings, afternoons,*
> *I have measured out my life with coffee spoons;*
> *I know the voices dying with a dying fall*
> *Beneath the music from a farther room.*
> > *So how should I presume?*

And then the end:

> *I have heard the mermaids singing, each to each.*
>
> *I do not think that they will sing to me.*
>
> *I have seen them riding seaward on the waves*
> *Combing the white hair of the waves blown back*
> *When the wind blows the water white and black.*
>
> *We have lingered in the chambers of the sea*
> *By sea-girls wreathed with seaweed red and brown*
> *Till human voices wake us, and we drown.*

Never has the shrinking of the modern spirit from life been expressed so exquisitely and with such truth.

Consider, again, that lovely poem, 'La Figlia Che Piange':

> [Quotes 'La Figlia Che Piange'.]

How delicate and beautiful in the emotion! How exquisite and beautiful the music! This is the very fine flower of the finest spirit of the United States. It would be the last absurdity for such a poet to go West and write for that plopp-eyed bungaroo, the Great-Hearted Young Westerner on the make. It seems incredible that this lovely poem should have been published in 'Poetry' in the year in which the school awarded the prize to that lumbering fakement, 'All Life in a Life.'

Poems

London, May 1919

71
Not Here, O Apollo*

ANON

In spite of the interest now taken in poetry, and the diverse and interesting experiments made in writing it, it still suffers from two defects which troubled it in the Victorian age, namely, that it contains either too little of the content of the writer's mind or much that is not the real content of his mind. Either the poets have a great difficulty in saying anything at all or else they say anything too easily. Mr. Murry, in his 'Critic in Judgment,' says so much, and so easily, that we find it hard to discover what he is writing about. His metre, blank verse, sways him with its memories of past masters—Shakespeare, Milton, Browning, Tennyson. They seem almost to dictate to him what he is to say, so that, as we read, we fade out of one poet into another, aware only of changes of manner, the matter itself escaping us. The Critic, whose purpose and character are always vague, begins in the style of Browning and then passes into Tennyson. It is Browning who says:—

> *Let him put up that scribble on the wall*
> *To worry old Belshazzar, till he tired*
> *With all the tiredness of a lesser man . . .*
> *And you, eternal Toby, bark outside*
> *Weary beside a lamp-post, while the shadows*
> *Torment me for the thousand millionth time*
> *There on the wall.*

It is Tennyson who follows, soon, with this:—

> *In them do I believe.*
> *Nay, you but mock me. How could they believe*
> *who felt no doubt? How can I not believe,*
> *Flung up upon the stage by unseen hands*
> *To unheard music, speaking lines unknown*
> *Into a void of darkness?*

Then there are echoes of Swinburne:—

---

* *Times Literary Supplement* no. 908 (12 June 1919), p. 322.

*Not thus may mine eyes sleep, not thus mine arms
Slacken, nor thus broken lips receive
The kiss of mortal death desirable.*

Then beginnings of Miltonic periods:—

*Thou art not he
Foretold, that should speak comfortable words—
Sweetest most bitter thine, and tongued with fire.*

Then early Shakespeare or Marlowe:—

*My name is Helen and my spirit is love,
By fame once Menelaus' bride ravished
By bowman Paris across the Aegean sea
To be the doom of ships and many men
Imbattled on the plains of Ilium.*

Then this passage fades again into Milton. As for the lyrics, they too turn from style into style. One begins pure Swinburne:—

*Life holds not any higher thing than love
  Nor shall men find another rose than this
And be immortal, not in the heights above
  Nor in the deeps, save only where love is.*

But the next four lines are like an Elizabethan song:—

*For him who seeks believing
Love hath no weary days,
Love hath no thorny ways
But joys beyond receiving.*

   It is a very curious case of writing made almost automatic by unconscious influences; or are they conscious? Does Mr. Murry mean all these imitations? We do not know, and we are still uncertain of the aim of his poem. But we do know that the fading of influence into influence makes it very hard to read. The very fluency lulls the mind to sleep; and at the end we are left only with the impression that the writer has read many poets, and that they will not let him reach what he has to say. It is like those dreams in which one is continually prevented from packing up and catching a train. These ghosts from the past make Mr. Murry speak with alien jaws, distract him from his purpose, whatever it may be. His task is to forget them.
   Mr. Eliot's case is the opposite. We may guess that he is fastidiously on his guard against echoes. There shall not be a cadence in his few verses that will remind anyone of anything. His composition is an incessant process of refusing all that offers itself, for fear that it should not be his own. The consequence is that his verse, novel and ingenious, original as it is, is fatally

impoverished of subject matter. For he is as fastidious of emotions as of cadences. He seems to have a 'phobia' of sentimentality, like a small schoolboy who would die rather than kiss his sister in public. Still, since he is writing verses he must say something, and his remarkable talent exercises itself in saying always, from line to line and word to word, what no one would expect. Each epithet, even, must be a surprise, each verb must shock the reader with unexpected associations; and the result is this:—

> *Polyphiloprogenitive*
> *The sapient sutlers of the Lord*
> *Drift across the window-panes.*
> *In the beginning was the Word.*
>
> *In the beginning was the Word.*
> *Superfetation of* τὸ ἕν,
> *And at the mensual turn of time*
> *Produced enervate Origen.*

Mr. Eliot, like Browning, likes to display out-of-the way learning, he likes to surprise you by every trick he can think of. He has forgotten his emotions, his values, his sense of beauty, even his common-sense, in that one desire to surprise, to get farther away from the obvious than any writer on record, be he Donne or Browning, or Benlowes even. We say he has forgotten all these things, because there is no doubt of his talents. They are evident in 'The Hippopotamus,' and even in 'Sweeney Among the Nightingales,' where he carries the game of perversity as far at least as anyone has ever carried it. But poetry is a serious art, too serious for this game. Mr. Eliot is fatally handicapping himself with his own inhibitions; he is in danger of becoming silly; and what will he do then? Or else he is in danger of writing nothing at all, but merely thinking of all the poems he has refused to write; a state which would be for a poet, if not hell, at least limbo. He is probably reacting against poetry like that of Mr. Murry. But you cannot live on reactions; you must forget them and all the errors which past writers have committed; you must be brave enough to risk some positive follies of your own. Otherwise you will fall more and more into negative follies; you will bury your talent in a napkin and become an artist who never does anything but giggle faintly. The final effect of these two little books is to leave us all the more melancholy because of their authors' cleverness. If they were nothing, it would not matter; but they are something, and they are very laboriously writing nothing.

72
Is This Poetry?*

ANON

The 'ordinary man,' the ghostly master or terror of most writers, would certainly ask the same question about Mr. Eliot, and answer it with a decided negative.

> *Polyphiloprogenitive*
> *The sapient sutlers of the Lord*
> *Drift across the window-panes.*
> *In the beginning was the Word.*

Thus begins one of Mr. Eliot's poems, provocative of the question and of the jeering laugh which is the easy reaction to anything strange, whether it be a 'damned foreigner' or a Post-Impressionist picture. Mr. Eliot is certainly damned by his newness and strangeness; but those two qualities, which in most art are completely unimportant, because ephemeral, in him claim the attention of even the serious critic. For they are part of the fabric of his poetry. Mr. Eliot is always quite consciously 'trying for' something, and something which has grown out of and developed beyond all the poems of all the dead poets. Poetry to him seems to be not so much an art as a science, a vast and noble and amusing body of communal feeling upon which the contemporary poet must take a firm stand and then launch himself into the unknown in search of new discoveries. That is the attitude not of the conventional poet, but of the scientist who with the help of working hypotheses hopes to add something, a theory perhaps or a new microbe, to the corpus of human knowledge. If we accept, provisionally, Mr. Eliot's attitude, we must admit that he comes well equipped to his task. The poetry of the dead is in his bones and at the tips of his fingers: he has the rare gift of being able to weave, delicately and delightfully, an echo or even a line of the past into the pattern of his own poem. And at the same time he is always trying for something new, something which has evolved—one drops instinctively into the scientific terminology—out of the echo or the line, out of the last poem of the last dead poet, something subtly intellectual and spiritual, produced by the

*_Athenaeum_ no. 4651 (20 June 1919), p. 491.

careful juxtaposition of words and the even more careful juxtaposition of ideas. The cautious critic, warned by the lamentable record of his tribe, might avoid answering the question: 'And is this poetry?' by asking to see a little more of Mr. Eliot than is shown in these seven short poems and even 'Prufrock.' But, to tell the truth, seven poems reveal a great deal of any poet. There is poetry in Mr. Eliot, as, for instance, in the stanzas:

> *The host with someone indistinct*
> *Converses at the door apart,*
> *The nightingales are singing near*
> *The Convent of the Sacred Heart,*
>
> *And sang within the bloody wood*
> *When Agamemnon cried aloud,*
> *And let their liquid siftings fall*
> *To stain the stiff dishonoured shroud.*

Yet the poetry often seems to come in precisely at the moment when the scientist and the science, the method and the newness, go out. A poem like 'The Hippopotamus,' for all its charm and cleverness and artistry, is perilously near the pit of the jeu d'esprit. And so scientific and scholarly a writer as Mr. Eliot might with advantage consider whether his method was not the method of that 'terrible warning,' P. Papinius Statius. We hope that Mr. Eliot will quickly give us more and remove our melancholy suspicion that is the product of a Silver Age.

Ara Vos Prec

London, February 1920

73
The Eternal Footman*

JOHN MIDDLETON MURRY

Here is Mr. T.S. Eliot, and here once again is the question: What are we to make of him? It is not a question that even the most assiduous (assiduity is demanded) and interested (interest is inevitable) of his readers would care to answer with any accent of finality. For Mr. Eliot, who is a connoisseur in discrepancy between intention and achievement, is likely to be himself an example of it. Nothing so sharpens one's sensitiveness to false notes in life at large as experience of them in oneself; so that there is more than a remote chance that even in regard to 'Ara Vos Prec' and while we hold it in our hands Mr. Eliot may whisper deprecatingly:

> *That is not it at all,*
> *That is not what I meant, at all.*

Yes, it seems to us sometimes that the inmost vital core of Mr. Eliot's poetry, the paradoxical impulse of his expression, is his determination to be free to whisper that refrain in our ear; its seems that he is like the chameleon who changes colour infinitely, and every change is protective. True, the range of variation is not truly infinite; there are colours which the chameleon cannot compass. But the chameleon, if he were an artist, would make it an essential of his art not to be lured against a background which he could not imitate.

The question for the critic is to determine whether Mr. Eliot—a conscious artist if ever there was one—has at any moment allowed himself to stray beyond his functional limit. That limit is set in the case of Mr. Eliot at the point where discrepancy ceases between intention and achievement, between soul and body, man and the Universe. At a crucial moment in his beautiful—we insist, precisely beautiful—'Love Song of J. Alfred Prufrock,'

> *The Eternal Footman snickers.*

Since that day Mr. Eliot has fallen deeper and deeper into the clutches of the Footman, who has come to preside over his goings out and his comings in.

---

*Athenaeum no. 4686 (20 February 1920), p. 239.

The Footman has grown into a monstrous Moloch. All that Mr. Eliot most deeply feels is cast into his burning belly—or almost all.

Yet consider the case of men, and of their more perfect exemplars who are poets. It is only when the Eternal Footman has given notice, when no longer

human voices wake us, and we drown.

when we pass out of the limbo of discordant futility, that there comes to us all the crash, the collapse, the ecstasy, the peace of surrender. Mr. Eliot is like us, terribly like us, for all that he is much more clever; the difference is that the Footman clings to his service longer. With the truly aristocratic, as we know, the Footman will stay for fifteen shillings when he would leave Mr. Bleistein and fifteen guineas; and we admit the implication that Mr. Eliot is truly distinguished. Another implication is that it is difficult for Mr. Eliot to talk to us, and difficult (as the present essay proves) for us to talk to him.

The future question arises—we continue to speak in parables on a matter hardly susceptible of discussion otherwise—whether we are to accept that Footman or not. Is it polite of us, have we a right, to seek an interview with Mr. Eliot when the Footman is not there? The rightness of an action is fortunately not measured by its ease of execution, but neither can we accept the dogma that the difficult is necessarily the virtuous path. Have we a right to say in our turn: 'It was not that at all,' to insist that the Footman in the long run makes everything impossible for us also, to gather up tell tale accents that have escaped, bubble-clear and bubble-frail, from under the Footman's all-regarding eye? May we, for instance, perpend

The notion of some infinitely gentle
Infinitely suffering thing.

and seek in it a solvent to the icy brilliance of an all but inexpugnable society manner? May be proceed thence, following a tenuous and evanescent clue, and ask not whether 'Gerontion' is solidly and definitely anything, but what it was that brought him to his premature old age? Is there anything other than that which we found (if indeed we found it) cowering beneath the strange notion, which would be apt

To lose beauty in terror, terror in inquisition?

The Footman snickers audibly. But do we care? Rather, do we care now? We, who have lost with the capability the desire to be respectable, can stop our ears to him when there is a chance of hearing something that is all important for us to know, whose sub-terrene tremor is not wholly lost.

Think at last
I have not made this show purposelessly
And it is not by any concitation
Of the backward devils.
I would meet you upon this honestly.

Ara Vos Prec (1920)

I that was near your heart was removed therefrom
To lose beauty in terror, terror in inquisition . . .

Assuredly we are not tempted to think it was purposelessly made. The conviction of purpose remains whether we accept the Footman or reject him. True, we should prefer that he were dismissed, partly because his going (or our sense that he is gone) makes elucidation (or what we think elucidation) easier, but also in part because he can never be wholly abolished. The sense of the Footman belongs to a generation; he is our *datum*, our constant. But by an effort of imaginative will he can be compressed within the circle of our vision to less than a bogey-size. Mr. Eliot, more ably than ourselves, can stand apart from the Footman and his victim both. It is necessary that he should turn himself into a bigger Footman still, and yet a bigger when that one too has been compressed, and a bigger *ad infinitum*?

Nowadays it is consciousness that makes cowards of us all. The complexity of our enemy is indicated by the fact of Mr. Eliot's determination that it shall make a brave man of him. But is it possible really? At least, Mr. Eliot would admit that it is a super-cowardice; he would claim that, indeed, as his exact intention. To make virtues of our vices is a good way of disarming them; but is it the best? Surely it cannot be unless with it is preserved the instinction that it must be abandoned when it begins to prey upon the vitals. *Impavidum ferient ruinae.* We do not doubt it for one moment with Mr. Eliot; but we have a notion that in the last resort the ruins will count for more than the impavidity that marks his unflinching diagnosis.

[Quotes 'Gerontion', 'After such knowledge' to 'our impudent crimes'.]

74
A New Byronism*

ANON

The death of Swinburne marked the end of an age in English poetry, the age which began with Blake. It was impossible for any poet after Swinburne to continue the romantic tradition; he carried his own kind of versification and the romantic attitude as far as they could be carried, and both died with him. Now our poets have to make another beginning, to find a method of expression suited to their different attitude; and of this fact they are almost overconscious. They have indeed often been led into an obvious error by that over-consciousness; because they must find new ways of expression and because they react differently to the great facts of life, some of them appear to think that the very subject-matter of their verse must be different. This was the error of the eighteenth century; it sought for a new subject-matter and chose one more suitable for prose than poetry, with the result that it developed a style suited for neither, the style which ended in invocations like—'Inoculation, heavenly maid, descend—' and was parodied in the Loves of the Triangles,.

The romantic movement itself was at first a return to the proper subject-matter of poetry and to a poetical technique. In its decline it narrowed the subject-matter of poetry to themes which seemed obviously and easily poetical, and its technique also became obviously and too easily poetical. So the young poets of to-day are apt to insist that they will make poetry of what they choose; but their choice is not always so free as they think. It is conditioned by reaction, disgust, *ennui*; they want no more of La belle dame sans merci, or of King Arthur or Pan or Proserpine, just as they want no more of rhythms such as

> By the tideless, dolorous, midland sea—

so they choose themes and rhythms the very opposite of these. Often they seem in their poetry to be telling us merely how they refuse to write poems and not how they wish to write them. It is like the bridge-movement of the

---

* *Times Literary Supplement* no. 948 (18 March 1920), p. 184.

Choral symphony; a continual rejection of themes and rhythms, but without anything positive to follow.

Mr. Eliot is an extreme example of this process. His cleverness, which is also extreme, expresses itself almost entirely in rejections; his verse is full of derisive reminiscences of poets who have wearied him. As for subject-matter, that also is all refusal; it can be expressed in one phrase; again and again he tells us that he is 'fed-up' with art, with life, with people, with things. Everyone for him seems to be a parody of exhausted and out-of-date emotions. To read his verse is to be thrown deliberately into that mood which sometimes overcomes one in the streets of a crowded town when one is tired and bewildered, the mood in which all passers-by look like over-expressive marionettes pretending to be alive and all the more mechanical for their pretence. In such a mood one is morbidly aware of town squalor; everything seems to have been used and re-used again and again; the symbol of all life is cigarette ends and stale cigarette smoke; the very conversation is like that, it has been said a thousand times and is repeated mechanically; in fact all things are done from habit, which has mastered life and turned it into an endlessly recurring squalor.

[Quotes 'Portrait of a Lady', 'You will see me' to 'ideas right or wrong?']

'Recalling things that other people have desired'—Mr. Eliot's verse is always doing that; and, like jesting Pilate, he will not wait for an answer to his own question—'Are these ideas right or wrong?' He asks it and goes on to something else with a hope, that is too like despair, that something may come of it. But nothing does come—

> *And I must borrow every changing shape*
> *To find expression . . . dance, dance,*
> *Like a dancing bear,*
> *Cry like a parrot, chatter like an ape.*
> *Let us take the air, in a tobacco trance—*

That may be satire on some one else, but it does exactly express the effect of his own verse, not once or twice but all the time. The habit of those whom he describes has got into his own technique, into his very way of experiencing; he, like the lesser romantics, has found too easy a way of functioning, and he functions and functions just as narrowly as if he were still writing about the Holy Grail:—

[Quotes 'Preludes', Part II.]

This might be a prelude to something, some passion or reality that would suddenly spring out of it; but with Mr. Eliot it is not. Near the end, after an enumeration of all the squalors he can think of, he says:—

> *I am moved by fancies that are curled*
> *Around these images, and cling:*

> *The motion of some infinitely gentle*
> *Infinitely suffering thing.*

That being so, why does he not tell us about it? It might be interesting; but no. After this momentary relenting, this flicker of natural feeling, he ends:—

> *Wipe your hand across your mouth, and laugh;*
> *The worlds revolve like ancient women*
> *Gathering fuel in vacant lots.*

But if that is so, why write verse about it; why not commit suicide? Art presumes that life is worth living, and must not, except dramatically or in a moment of exasperation or irony, say that it isn't. But Mr. Eliot writes only to say that it isn't; and he does not do it so well as the author of Ecclesiastes, who at least keeps the momentum and gusto of all the experiences he pretends to have exhausted. For Mr. Eliot—

> *Midnight shakes the memory*
> *As a madman shakes a dead geranium.*

There we are reminded a little of his countryman Poe, and 'The Love Song of J. Alfred Prufrock' is like Poe even in its curious and over-conscious metrical effects. They seem to be, as so often in Poe, independent of the poem itself, as if the writer could not attain to a congruity between the tune beating in his head and any subject-matter. In this poem he is really, with the poet part of him, questing for beauty, but the other part refuses it with a kind of nausea:—

> [Quotes 'Prufrock', 'Shall I part my hair' to the end of the poem.]

So it ends. Human voices for Mr. Eliot drown everything; he cannot get away from his disgust of them; he is 'fed up' with them, with their volubility and lack of meaning. 'Words, words, words' might be his motto; for in his verse he seems to hate them and to be always expressing his hatred of them, in words. If he could he would write songs without words; blindly he seeks for a medium free of associations, not only for a tune but also for notes that no one has sung before. But all this is mere habit; art means the acceptance of a medium as of life; and Mr. Eliot does not convince us that his weariness is anything but a habit, an anti-romantic reaction, a new Byronism which he must throw off if he is not to become a recurring decimal in his fear of being a mere vulgar fraction.

75
An Ironist*

ROBERT NICHOLS

Mr Eliot is known to the world at large through the columns of the 'Athenaeum' as a widely erudite critic possessed of a natural distinction in style and such a mordant perspicacity as is hardly to be matched in British or North American letters to-day. To some few else he is known also as the poet of 'Prufrock.' The Ovid Press has now gathered up 'Prufrock' and the later 'Poems,' and displays them to the world in one of the most beautiful productions of the modern press. The paper and printing (with initials and colophon by Mr. E.A. Wadsworth) are superb.

Let me say it at once: Mr. Eliot is, more especially in his later work, emphatically not an 'easy' poet. Nor is the reason far to seek. Mr. Eliot mostly does not deal with what are popularly considered the main streams of emotion. Not for him the generalised joys or sorrows of a Whitman or a Shelley, nor such rhythms as roll the consenting reader he scarcely knows whither upon the bosom of the flood. No; Mr. Eliot is not going to appear to lose his head or suffer the reader to lose his. Mr. Eliot, like the poet in 'Candida,' muses to himself and the world overhears him; but not before he wishes it to; no, not by a long chalk. For, you see, the stuff of his musings is complicated, and Mr. Eliot does not pretend it is easy. 'The primrose by the river's brim' is for Mr. Eliot most emphatically neither a simple primrose nor a possible ingredient in a Disraelian salad. It is primarily something that someone else has written about, and which has thus become invested with such associations as can but destroy the innocence of Mr. Eliot's eye and apprehension. The pity is, he seems to hint, that there have been so many poems and, yes, it must be confessed, so few really satisfactory salads:—

[Quotes 'Prufrock', 'And I have known the eyes' to 'how should I begin?']

It is, perhaps, this sense of everything having happened a trifle earlier in the day that gives me an impression of there being a preponderance of afternoons in Mr. Eliot's poetry:—

[Quotes 'Portrait of a Lady', 'Among the smoke' to 'left unsaid'.]

* *Observer* (18 April 1920), p. 7.

Or, if not of afternoons, of early evenings:—

> *Let us go then, you and I,*
> *When the evening is spread out against the sky*
> *Like a patient etherized upon a table.*

Ah, that patient etherized upon the table! It is not the evening only lying there in such lassitude; it is Mr. Eliot's perpetual spectator; it is the wistful and ironic evocation of all super-sophisticated persons; it is, alas! our cultured selves at this late and almost, it would sometimes seem, deliquescent stage of civilisation. Under the spell of Mr. Eliot's gentle and wavering rhythms we become slightly etherized, and when the spell has sufficiently o'ercrowed our animal spirits we proceed, at once investigator and investigated, to inspect our emotions 'as if a magic lantern threw the nerves in patterns on a screen'; a doleful piece of introspective dissection, a lamentable appraisement. Our scientific precision but informs us the nature of our trouble:—

> *You will see me any morning in the park*
> *Reading the comics and the sporting page.*
> *Particularly I remark*
> *An English countess goes upon the stage.*
> *A Greek was murdered at a Polish dance,*
> *Another bank defaulter has confessed.*
>
> *I keep my countenance,*
> *I remain self-possessed*
> *Except when a street piano, mechanical and tired*
> *Reiterates some worn-out common song*
> *With the smell of hyacinths across the garden*
> *Recalling things that other people have desired.*

And when the scientist has done the artist steps in with his comedian melancholy to draw this conclusion:—

> *Though I have seen my head (grown slightly bald) brought in upon a*
>   *platter,*
> *I am no prophet—and here's no great matter;*
> *I have seen the moment of my greatness flicker,*
> *And I have seen the eternal Footman hold my coat, and snicker,*
> *And in short, I was afraid.*

The irony of things-as-they-are haunts the poet as it haunted his forerunner Laforgue and levies board-wages upon all his emotions. Yet the poet has his moments:—

> *I am moved by fancies that are curled*
> *Around these images and cling:*

Ara Vos Prec (1920)

The notion of some infinitely gentle
Infinitely suffering thing.

The moment, however, will not last, and I cannot but puzzle whether it is not that capacity for enjoying the quintessential emotions precipitated from the still of literature which Mr. Eliot so superabundantly possesses and cultivates, that has vitiated his taste for those distractingly heterogeneous emotions which are the material offered him as an artist by Life itself. Irony is a good servant, but a bad master; the Footman, however eternal, should be kept in his place even if one is only the perennially passing visitor to the earthly mansion. Mr. Eliot has a taste for the more terrible realities—if he would only indulge it. He has the power of evoking 'the still, sad music of humanity' from the most quotidian, sordid, and apparently unpromising of materials. Here is an interior—as unqualified in statement as a Sickert, but in addition informed with something of the understanding and compassion of a Rembrandt:—

[Quotes 'Preludes', Part III.]

It is a pity, I feel, that Mr. Eliot seems in his later poems to have acquired a habit of sheering away from so immediate and poignant a reality in order to make remote and somewhat generalised fun about 'The Boston Evening Transcript,' the visit of a Cambridge intellectual to New England, the editor of the 'Spectator,' and the Established Church.

76
New Poets, T.S. Eliot*

DESMOND MACCARTHY

When two people are discussing modern poetry together the name of T.S. Eliot is sure to crop up. If one of them is old-fashioned, and refuses to see merit in the young poets who attempt to do more than retail 'the ancient divinations of the Muse,' the other is sure to say sooner or later: 'But what about Eliot? You may dislike *vers libre* (I admit it is easy to write it badly) and attempts to manipulate in verse the emotional coefficients of modern experience, still what do you think of Eliot? You cannot dismiss him.' And the other (I do not think I am attributing to him an unusual amount of sensibility or judgment) will reply: 'Well . . . yes . . . Eliot . . . I grant you there seems to be something in him.' I wish to try to find out here what that 'something' is which recommends the poems of Mr. Eliot, if not to the taste, at least to the literary judgment of even those who think the young poets are, for the most part, on the wrong path.

Mr. Eliot, like Mr. Ezra Pound, is an American. This is not a very important fact about him, still it has its importance. Both poets resemble each other in two respects, one of which I will deal with at once, in connection with their nationality. When either of them publishes a book, they publish at the same time that they are scholars, who have at least five languages at command, and considerable out-of-the-way erudition. The allusions in their poems are learned, oblique, and obscure; the mottoes they choose for their poems are polyglot, the names that occur to them as symbolic of this or that are known only to book-minded people. In short, they both share the national love of bric-à-brac. A half-forgotten name, an echo from a totally forgotten author, a mossy scrap of old philosophy exercise over their imaginations the charm that the patina of time upon a warming-pan or piece of worm-eaten furniture does upon their more frivolous compatriots. Both poets are illegitimate descendants of the poet Browning, in whom the instinct of the collector was equally strong—with a difference I shall presently mark. Both share with Browning a passion for adapting the vivid colloquialism of contemporary speech to poetic purposes. It has not

*New Statesman 16 (8 January 1921), pp. 418–20.

been grasped so far as I know by critics, that linguistically Browning stands in the same relation to Victorian poets as Wordsworth *thought* he himself did as a poet, and in a measure truly, to the poets of the eighteenth century. Mr. Eliot has woven a very remarkable literary style, composed in almost equal parts of literary and erudite allusions and crisp colloquialisms, in which to clothe the emotions he wishes to express. Let me make here at once the most adverse comment I have to make on his work, namely, that he is always in danger of becoming a pedant, a pedant being one who assumes that his own reading, wide or narrow, is common property or ought to be, so that any reference he makes is of general validity and bound to wake the same echoes in his reader's mind as it does in his own. Collector of bric-à-brac, mystificator, mandarin, loving to exclude as well as to touch intimately and quickly his readers, he would be lost as a poet were it not for his cautious and very remarkable sincerity. When a reader seizes an obscure reference he is flattered; it gives him a little thrill. But though this thrill may seal him one of the poet's admirers, it is not an aesthetic thrill. In the same way even the verbal obscurity of a poet may tell in his favour, once he has convinced us that his meaning is worth grasping; in the effort to get at his meaning we may actually get his phrases by heart, and the phrase which sticks always acquires merit in our eyes. I do not say that Mr. Eliot's reputation owes much to these causes, but that they have helped it in some quarters I believe. Certainly he is a poet whom to admire at all fervently marks one down as among those who are certainly not a prey to the obvious.

FitzGerald did not like Browning (partly because he knew Tennyson very well perhaps), and in one of his letters he throws out a phrase about 'that old Jew's curiosity shop.' Now Browning's curiosity shop is a huge rambling place, cobwebby, crammed, Rembrandtesque, while Mr. Eliot's reminds one rather of those modern curiosity shops in which a few choice objects, a white Chinese rhinoceros, a pair of Queen Anne candlesticks, an enamelled box, a Renaissance trinket or two, a small ebony idol are set out at carefully calculated distances on a neat cloth in the window (one sees at a glance they are very expensive—no bargains here); but there is behind no vast limbo of armour, cabinets, costumes, death-masks, sword-sticks, elephants' tusks, dusty folios, gigantic cracked old mirrors, sedan chairs, wigs, spinets, and boxes, containing pell-mell, watch-keys, miniatures, lockets, snuffers, and tongue-scrapers. The man who keeps the shop is not a creature with a Rabelaisian gusto for acquisition, whose hand shakes with excitement as he holds up the candle, expatiating volubly, but a sedate, slightly quizzical, aloof individual—a selector, perhaps, rather than a collector to whose maw the most indigestible treasures are delicious nutriment. Such is the difference between Browning's and Mr. Eliot's attitude towards the harvest of erudition.

I have compared them so far only to differentiate them, moreover Mr. Eliot's subject is always the ingredients of the modern mind and never, as was often the case with Browning, of the minds and souls of men and women who lived long ago. But it is instructive to compare them also at points in which they resemble each other, always remembering that the temperament of the elder poet is hot, responsive, ebullient, and simple, while that of the younger is subtle, tender, disillusioned, complicated and cool. Both are possessed by the passion of curiosity to a greater degree than is common with poets; in both the analytical interest is extremely strong. Consequently, Mr. Eliot, too, loves to exploit that borderland between prose and poetry which yields as much delight to the intellect as to the emotions—if not more. Most of his work is done in that region, and the most obvious thing to say about it as a whole is that even when it is not poetry it is always good literature. Reread 'The Love Song of J. Alfred Prufrock' or 'Portrait of a Lady'; it will be obvious that he not only owes much to the diction and rhythm of Browning, but that he is doing the same thing as Browning for a more queasy, uneasy, diffident, complex generation. Here is the opening of the 'Portrait'.

[. . .]

'The latest Pole transmit the Preludes, through his hair and finger-tips'—is not that pure Browning? Like Browning, too, Mr. Eliot's favourite form is a soliloquy of the spirit or monologue. Many of his poems thus fall between the lyrical and the dramatic form; they are little mental mono-dramas, broken now and then after the manner of Browning by a line or two of dialogue or by exclamations such as are common in Browning's poems ('Here comes my husband from his whist'), or by asides to the reader; but these asides never have the argumentative, buttonholing quality of Browning's. There is nothing of the impassioned advocate, so characteristic in Browning, in Mr. Eliot. He is rather a scrupulous, cool analyst of extremely personal and elusive modes of feeling, and his method (this is his most distinctive characteristic as a writer) is to convey an elusive shade of feeling, or a curious, and usually languid, drift of emotion, by means of the rapid evocation of vivid objects and scenes. He does not care whether or not there is a logical or even a casual association between these objects he presents to us one after the other. He is like a dumb man who is trying to explain to us what he is feeling by taking up one object after another and showing it to us, not intending that we should infer that the object is the subject of his thoughts, but that we should feel the particular emotion appropriate to it. This makes his poems hard even when they are not (and they often are) too obscure. The reader is always liable to dwell too long on these scenes or objects which he evokes so skilfully, instead of just skimming swiftly off them, as it were, an emotion they suggest, and then passing on to the next. A poet who thinks in pictures and allusions, and expects us to understand his mood and thought by catching one after the other the gleams of light flashed off by his phrases must often be obscure, because compact phrases (Mr. Eliot's are extraordinarily compact) are apt to scatter refracted gleams which point in different directions. Indeed, we are often expected to catch not one of these flashes but several. First, however, let me give an example of his method of thinking in pictures or symbols. Take one of his later poems, 'Gerontion.' The whole poem is a description at once of an old man's mind, and of a mood which recurs often in Mr. Eliot's poems, namely, that of one to whom life is largely a process of being stifled, slowly hemmed in and confused; to whom experience, truthfully apprehended, gives only tantalisingly rare excuses for the exercise of the lyrical faculty of joy within him. His (Mr. Eliot's) problem as a poet is the problem of the adjustment of his sense of beauty to these sorry facts. His weakness as a poet is that he seems rather to have felt the glory of life through literature; while his reflection of all that contrasts with it has the exciting precision of direct apprehension. 'The contemplation of the horrid or sordid by the artist,' he says in one of his criticisms, 'is the necessary and negative aspect of the impulse towards beauty.' In him this impulse in a negative direction is far the strongest of the two.

[...]

Mr. Eliot has something of the self-protective pride, reserve and sensibility of the dandy—like Laforgue. His impulse is not to express himself in poetry, but to express some mood, some aspect of life which needs expression. He sets about it coolly, like a man making up a prescription, taking down now this bottle, now that from the shelf, adding an acid from one and a glowing tincture from another. He belongs to that class of poets whose interest is in making a work of art, not in expressing themselves; and the fact that his subject-matter, on the other hand, is psychological and intimate, makes the result particularly piquant. But even the works of the most detached poet, if he is not imitating old poems, have an affinity to each other which has its roots in temperament. The temperament, as in Laforgue's work, which shows itself in Mr. Eliot's is that of the ironic sentimentalist.

> *But where is the penny world I bought*
> *To eat with Pipit behind the screen?*

he asks, after concluding that he will not want Pipit in Heaven.

> *Where are the eagles and the trumpets?*
>
> *Buried beneath some snow-deep Alps.*
> *Over buttered scones and crumpets*
> *Weeping, weeping multitudes*
> *Droop in a hundred A.B.C.'s.*

The contrast between peeps into glory and the sordidness of life is never far from his mind. (It is in literature that he himself has seen the eagles and heard the trumpets—not in life.) His style has two other marked characteristics. His phrases are frequently echoes, yet he is the reverse of an imitative poet. They are echoes tuned to a new context which changes their subtlety. He does not steal phrases; he borrows their aroma.

> *Defunctive music under sea*
>   *Passed seaward with the passing bell*
> *Slowly: the God Hercules*
>   *Had left him, that had loved him well.*
>
> *The horses, under the axletree*
>   *Beat up the dawn from Istria*
> *With even feet. Her shuttered barge*
>   *Burned on the water all the day.*

Just as 'weeping, weeping multitudes' in the other poem quoted above, is an echo from Blake, so 'Defunctive music' comes from 'The Phoenix and the Turtle' and 'Her barge burned on the water' of course from 'Antony and Cleopatra.' But the point is that the poet means to draw a subtle whiff of Cleopatra and poetic passion across our minds, in order that we may feel a peculiar emotion towards the sordid little siren in the poem itself, just as he also uses later a broken phrase or two from 'The Merchant of Venice' for the sake of reminding us of Shakespeare's Jew, compared with the 'Bleistein' of the poem. His other characteristic is the poetic one of intensity; it is the exciting concision of his phrasing which appeals especially to his contemporaries:

> *I should have been a pair of ragged claws*
> *Scuttling across the floors of silent seas*
>
> *. . . the smoke that rises from the pipes*
> *Of lonely men in shirt sleeves, leaning out of windows.*

He is master of the witty phrase, too,

> *My smile falls heavily among the bric-à-brac,*

and is, to my mind, the most interesting of 'the new poets.'

Poems

New York, February 1920
(The American edition of Ara Vos Prec)

77
Perilous Leaping*

MARION STROBLE

Mr. Eliot evidently believes that a view from a mountain cannot be appreciated unless the ascent is a perilous leaping from crag to crag. At least the first pages of his latest book (an American reprint, with a few additions, of 'Prufrock and Other Observations,' published in 1917 by the London 'Egoist') are filled with intellectual curios—curios that form a prodigious array of hazards leading up to the big poems. Lovers of exercise will find their minds flexed, if not inert, after following the allusions and ellipses of 'Gerontion.' It is as though, in this initial poem, Mr. Eliot went through his morning callisthenics saying: 'This, my good people is a small part of what I do to give you a poem;' or more accurately perhaps: 'Come—work with me—show you deserve true beauty.' And with a 'Whoop-La'—for he is in beautiful condition—he swings from romance to realism, to religion, to history, to philosophy, to science, while you and I climb pantingly, wearily, after him, clinging to a few familiar words, and looking from time to time at signposts along the way to reassure ourselves of the fact that this does lead us to true beauty.

The poems guaranteed-to-produce-white-blood-corpuscles-in-any-brain come before page 37 (a specific hint for the faint-hearted). Fortified by a dictionary, an encyclopedia, an imagination, and a martyr's spirit, even these may be enjoyed. They are certainly remarkable for their mystifying titles, their coy complexities of content, and their line-consuming words. What, for instance, could be more naive than the introduction to Sweeney in 'Sweeney Erect':

> *Paint me a cavernous waste shore*
> *Cast in the unstilled Cyclades,*
> *Paint me the bold anfractuous rocks*
> *Faced by the snarled and yelping seas.*
>
> *Display me Aeolus above*
> *Reviewing the insurgent gales*

*Poetry 16 (June 1920), pp. 157–9.

> *Which tangle Ariadne's hair*
> * And swell with haste the perjured sails.*
>
> *Morning stirs the feet and hands*
> * (Nausicaa and Polypheme).*
> *Gesture of orang-outang*
> * Rises from the sheets in steam. . . .*
>
> *Sweeney addressed full length to shave. . . .*

However, in among these stepping-stones to the poems that are worth a great deal of trouble to get—through one resents being reminded of the fact by Mr. Eliot himself—are one or two resting-places, such as the whimsical pathos of 'A Cooking Egg,' the gentle crudity of 'Sweeney Among the Nightingales,' and the sophisticated humor of 'The Hippopotamus.' And I must further acknowledge that Mr. Eliot's humor is the cultivated progeny of a teasing spirit of fun and a keen audacity—the mixture of the Zoo and the True Church in 'The Hippopotamus' will tickle the palate of the most blasé epicurean.

And now, feeling that the ascent has been long and hard, we reach the summit, and are repaid by reading 'The Love Song of J. Alfred Prufrock' and 'Portrait of a Lady.' These two poems are so far superior to the gymnastics that precede, and to the interesting versatilities that follow them, that they must be classed alone.

'Prufrock,' which was first published by 'Poetry' in 1915, is a psychological study of that rather piteous figure, the faded philandering middle-aged cosmopolite; a scrupulous psychological study, for the pervasive beauty of the imagery, the rhythms used, and the nice repetitions, all emphasize the sympathetic accuracy of the context. For instance the three lines:

> *I grow old . . . I grow old . . .*
> *I shall wear the bottoms of my trousers rolled.*
>
> *Shall I part my hair behind? Do I dare to eat a peach?*

In 'Portrait of a Lady' we find a like startling acuteness for details, with a dramatic ending which is a fitting example for the definition, '*L'art est un étonnement heureux.*'

And possibly—possibly—it is wise to work up to 'J. Alfred Prufrock' and 'Portrait of a Lady,' and to slide pleasantly down again on the humor and ironies of the poems following; for we might become dizzy if we found ourselves on a mountain without the customary foundations.

78
T.S. Eliot*

♦

E.E. CUMMINGS

The somewhat recently published 'Poems' is an accurate and uncorpulent collection of instupidities. Between the negative and flabby and ponderous and little bellowings of those multitudinous contemporaries who are obstinately always 'unconventional' or else 'modern' at the expense of being (what is most difficult) alive, Mr. T.S. Eliot inserts the positive and deep beauty of his skilful and immediate violins . . . the result is at least thrilling.

He has done the trick for us before. In one of the was it two 'Blasts' skilfully occurred, more than successfully framed by much soundness noise, the 'Rhapsody' and 'Preludes.' In one of the God knows nobody knows how many there will be 'Others', startlingly enshrined in a good deal of noiseless sound 'Prufrock' and 'Portrait of a Lady' carefully happened. But 'this slim little volume' as a reviewer might say achieves a far more forceful presentation, since it competes with and defeats not mere blasters and differentists but τὀ ἐ ν-s and origens and all that is Windily and Otherwise enervate and talkative.

Some Notes on the Blank Verse of Christopher Marlowe are, to a student of Mr. T.S., unnecessarily illuminating:

> . . . this style which secures its emphasis by always hesitating on the end of caricature at the right moment . . .
> . . . this intense and serious and indubitably great poetry, which, like some great painting and sculpture, attains its effects by something not unlike caricature.

Even without this somewhat mighty hint, this something which for all its slipperyness is after all a door-knob to be grasped by anyone who wishes to enter the 'some great' Art-Parlours, ourselves might have constructed a possibly logical development from 'Preludes' and 'Rhapsody on a Windy Night' along 'J. Alfred' and 'Portrait' up the two Sweeneys to let us say 'The Hippopotamus.' We might have been disgracefully inspired to the extent of projecting as arithmetical, not to say dull, a classification of Eliot as that of Picasso by the author of certain rudimentary and not even ecclesiastical

---

* Dial 68 (June 1920), pp. 781–4.

nonsense entitled 'The Caliph's Design.' But (it is an enormous but) our so doing necessarily would have proved worthless, precisely for the reason that before an Eliot we become alive or intense as we become intense or alive before a Cézanne or a Lachaise: or since, as always in the case of superficial because vertical analysis, to attempt the boxing and labeling of genius is to involve in something inescapably rectilinear—a formula, for example—not the artist but the 'critic.'

However, we have a better reason. The last word on caricature was spoken as far back as 1913. 'My dear it's all so perfectly ridiculous' remarked to an elderly Boston woman an elderly woman of Boston, as the twain made their noticeably irrevocable exeunt from that most colossal of all circusses, the (then in Boston) International. 'My dear if some of the pictures didn't look like something it wouldn't be so amusing' observed, on the threshold, the e.B.w., adding 'I should hate to have my portrait painted by any of those "artists"!' 'They'll never make a statue of *me*' stated with polyphiloprogenitive conviction the e.w.o.B.

Sway in the wind like a field of ripe corn.

Says Mr. Eliot.

In the case of 'Poems,' to state frankly and briefly what we like may be as good a way as another of exhibiting our numerous 'critical' incapacities. We like first, to speak from an altogether personal standpoint, that any and all attempts to lasso Mr. Eliot with the Vorticist emblem have signally failed. That Mr. E. Pound (with whose Caesarlike refusal of the kingly crown we are entirely familiar) may not have coiled the rope whose fatal noose has, over a few unfortunate Britons, excludingly rather than includingly settled, makes little or no difference since the hand which threw the lariat and the bronc' which threw the steers alike belong to him. Be it said of this peppy gentleman that, insofar as he is responsible for possibly one-half of the most alive poetry and probably all of the least intense prose committed, during the last few years, in the American and English languages, he merits something beyond the incoherent abuse and inchoate adoration which have become his daily breakfast-food—merits in fact the doffing of many kelleys; that insofar as he is one of history's greatest advertisers he is an extraordinarily useful bore, much like a rivetter which whatever you may say asserts the progress of a skyscraper; whereas that insofar as he is responsible for the overpasting of an at least attractive manifesto, 'Ezra Pound,' with an at least pedantic warcry, 'Vorticism,' he deserves to be drawn and quartered by the incomparably trite brush of the great and the only and the Wyndham and the Lewis—if only as an adjectival garnish to that nounlike effigy of our hero by his friend The Hieratic Buster. Let us therefore mention the fact. For it seems to us worthy of notice—that at no moment do T.S. Eliot and E.P. propaganda simultaneously inhabit our consciousness.

Second, we like that not any of 'Poems'' fifty-one pages fails to impress us

Poems (February 1920)

with an overwhelming sense of technique. By technique we do not mean a great many things, including: anything static, a school, a noun, a slogan, a formula, These Three For Instant Beauty, Ars Est Celare, Hasn't Scratched Yet, Professor Woodberry, Grape Nuts. By technique we do mean one thing: the alert hatred of normality which, through the lips of the tactile and cohesive adventure, asserts that nobody in general and someone in particular is incorrigibly and actually alive. This some one is, it would seem, the extremely great artist: or, he who prefers above everything and within everything the unique dimension of intensity, which it amuses him to substitute in us for the comforting and comfortable furniture of reality. If we examine the means through which this substitution is allowed by Mr. Eliot to happen in his reader, we find that they include: a vocabulary almost brutally tuned to attain distinctness; an extraordinarily tight orchestration of the shapes of sound; the delicate and careful murderings—almost invariably interpreted, internally as well as terminally, through near-rhyme and rhyme—of established tempos by oral rhythms. Here is an example of Eliot's tuning:

> *Apeneck Sweeney spreads his knees*
> *Letting his arms hang down to laugh,*
> *The zebra stripes along his jaw*
> *Swelling to maculate giraffe.*

Here is a specimen of his compact orchestration:

> *I have seen them riding seaward on the waves*
> *Combing the white hair of the waves blown back*
> *When the wind blows the water white and black.*
>
> *We have lingered in the chambers of the sea*
> *By sea-girls wreathed with seaweed red and brown*
> *Till human voices wake us, and we drown.*

Here is Eliot himself directing the exquisitely and thoroughly built thing:

> *His laughter was submarine and profound*
> *Like the old man of the sea's*
> *Hidden under coral islands*
> *Where worried bodies of drowned men drift down in the green silence,*
> *Dropping from fingers of surf.*

To come to our final like, which it must be admitted is also our largest—we like that no however cautiously attempted dissection of Mr T.S.'s sensitivity begins to touch a few certain lines whereby become big and blundering and totally unskilful our altogether unnecessary fingers:

[Quotes 'Rhapsody on a Windy Night', 'The lamp hummed' to 'a paper rose'.]

At the risk of being jeered for an 'uncritical' remark we mention that this is one of the few huge fragilities before which comment is disgusting.

79
Anglo-Saxon Adventures in Verse*

MARK VAN DOREN

But the most amazing man is T.S. Eliot, whose first formally collected volume, long awaited by those who think they recognize downright, diabolical genius when they see it, is distinctly and preciously an event. It is not known how long the author of 'The Hippopotamus,' 'Sweeney Among the Nightingales,' 'The Love Song of J. Alfred Prufrock,' 'Rhapsody on a Windy Night,' and 'The Boston Evening Transcript' will remain in England, whither he went two years ago to set up as a critic. Whatever happens, it is hoped that he keeps somehow to poetry. For he is the most proficient satirist now writing in verse, the uncanniest clown, the devoutest monkey, the most picturesque ironist; and aesthetically considered, he is one of the profoundest symbolists. His sympathy and his vision travel together, striking like bitter lightning here, flowering damply and suddenly like mushrooms there.

*Nation 110 (26 June 1920), 856a–7a. From a longer review.

80
Irony de Luxe*

LOUIS UNTERMEYER

For two or three years the poetry of T.S. Eliot has been championed warmly by a few protagonists and condemned even more heatedly by many who suspected the young author of all things from charlatanry to literary anarchism. Those who have read it have talked of this product, not as poetry, but as a precipitant, a touchstone; they pronounced 'Eliot' as though the name were either a shibboleth or a red flag. Controversy was difficult. For, with the exception of two longish poems and half a dozen scattered verses, this native of St. Louis continued to publish his occasional pieces in England and threatened at the age of thirty-one to take on the proportions of a myth. This volume then, is doubly welcome, for it enables one not only to estimate Eliot's actual achievement but to appraise his influence.

The influence, although exceedingly limited, is indisputable. And it is even more remarkable when one perceives that the present volume, including all of Eliot's poetical works, contains just twenty-four examples, five of them being in French. In these two dozen pieces there can be heard, beneath muffled brilliancies, two distinct and distinctive idioms. The first embodies the larger curve, to more flexible music; in it are held the shifting delicacies and strange nuances of 'The Love Song of J. Alfred Prufrock' and the sensitized 'Portrait of a Lady.' It is the idiom which Conrad Aiken has exploited (and amplified) in 'The Jig of Forslin,' 'Senlin,' and 'Nocturne of Remembered Spring.' The second accent is sharper, swifter, more obviously sparkling. A far more definite tone of voice, it lends itself so easily to imitation that it has quickly captivated most of the younger British insurgents. Osbert Sitwell, whose anti-war verses are still remembered, frankly models his new quatrains on the plan of 'Sweeney Among the Nightingales' and gives us (in part) such experiments in satiric futurism as:

> *The dusky king of Malabar*
> *Is chief of Eastern potentates;*
> *Yet he wears no clothes, except*
> *The jewels that decency dictates.* . . .

*Freeman 1 (30 June 1920), pp. 381–2.

But Mrs. Freudenthal, in furs,
From Brioche dreams to mild surprise
Awakes; the music throbs and purrs.
The 'cellist with albino eyes

Rivets attention; is, in fact,
The very climax; pink eyes flash
Whenever, nervous and pain-racked,
He hears the drums and cymbals clash.

Herbert Read, another of the younger poets, echoes the strain with slight variations in his recent 'Huskisson Sacred and Profane.' Even Robert Nichols, turning from his precise Shakespearian sonnets, his academic nymphs and correctly English fauns, indites 'The Spring Son,' the quatrains of which run like:

Sinclair has bought a new top hat,
  A jetty coat and honey gloves,
A cane topped by a glass-eyed cat,
  And Sinclair goes to meet his loves.

Sinclair would make his muslin choice,—
  Spring and his father say he must:
Corah has ankles and a voice,
  Nancy has French and a neat bust.

It is but a step to the more acerb original. Here are two illustrative segments from Eliot himself:

Apeneck Sweeney spreads his knees
Letting his arms hang down to laugh,
The zebra stripes along his jaw
Swelling to maculate giraffe . . .

Grishkin is nice: her Russian eye
Is underlined for emphasis;
Uncorseted, her friendly bust
Gives promise of pneumatic bliss.

It is this vein that tempts him most—and is his undoing. For irony, no matter how agile and erudite— and Eliot's is both—must contain heat if it is to burn. And heat is one of the few things that can not be juggled by this acrobatic satirist. With amazing virtuosity, he balances and tosses fragments of philosophy, history, science, tea-table gossip, carelessly screened velleities. There are times when he discards his flashing properties, changes his vocabulary of rare words for a more direct irony which is not only amusing but incisive. 'The Hippopotamus,' that audacious whimsicality, is an example.

[. . .]

But at least two-thirds of Eliot's sixty-three pages attain no higher eminence than extraordinarily clever—and eminently uncomfortable—verse. The exaltation which is the very breath of poetry—that combination of tenderness and toughness—is scarcely ever present in Eliot's lines. Scarcely ever, I reiterate, for a certain perverse exultation takes its place; an unearthly light without warmth which has the sparkle if not the strength of fire. It flickers mockingly through certain of the unrhymed pictures and shines with a bright pallor out of the two major poems.

These two are the book's main exhibit, its jewelled medallion. Medallion, too, in the sense that both of them complement each other, obverse and reverse. The 'Portrait of a Lady,' the franker and more easily communicable, is a half-sympathetic, half-scornful study in the impressionist manner of the feminine dilettante, the slightly-faded *précieuse* hovering tremulously on the verge of an abortive 'affair.'

[Quotes 'Portrait of a Lady', 'Among the smoke' to 'the conversation slips'.]

'The Love Song of J. Alfred Prufrock' is even more adroit though less outspoken. Sensitive to the pitch of concealment, this is an analysis of the lady's sexual opposite—an inhibited, young-old philanderer, tired of talk and the eternal tea-tables; a prey to boredom that breeds its own revulsion, a victim too sunk in himself to escape it. For him, eternally, it seems that

In the room the women come and go
Talking of Michelangelo.

Prufrock would shatter the small talk, pierce the whispered inanities, cry out!

But he can neither discharge his protest nor find words for it. He listens politely; he accepts the proffered cup; he chatters on aimlessly. It is the quiet tragedy of frustration, the *revolté* buried in the gentleman.
[. . .]

Yet Prufrock is not all psychology. Eliot can be delicately fantastic and purely pictorial when the mood is on him. He can speak of early morning with

. . . the damp souls of housemaids
Sprouting despondently at area gates.

He hears the laughter of Mr. Apollinax (who sounds suspiciously like Bertrand Russell) 'tinkling among the tea cups' and he thinks of

. . . Priapus in the shrubbery
Gaping at the lady in the swing.

He watches the fog rubbing its back upon the window-panes.
[. . .]

But these are the exceptional moments. For the most part, Eliot cares less for his art than he does for his attitudes. Disdaining the usual poetic cant, he falls into another tradition; he leans towards a kind of versifying which, masquerading under the title of 'occasional' or 'social' verse may be found in many a *Lyra Elegantiarum.* Pliny had in mind this type when he wrote: 'These pieces commonly go under the title of poetical amusements; but these amusements have sometimes gained as much reputation to their authors as works of a far more serious nature.' And some two thousand years later, Locker-Lampson described their qualities again: 'The tone should not be pitched too high; it should be terse and rather in the conversational key; the rhythm should be crisp and sparkling, the rhyme frequent and never forced . . .' Both Pliny and Locker-Lampson might have been reviewing Eliot's conversational ironies. For Eliot's gift is seldom the poet's. His contribution is related to poetry only at rare intervals. His lines, for the most part, are written in a new *genre* or, to be more accurate, in a modernization of a surprisingly old one. They are, primarily, a species of mordant light verse; complex and disillusioned *vers de société.*

81
What Ails Pegasus?*

RAYMOND WEAVER

The 'Poems'—ironically so-called—of T.S. Eliot, if not heavy and pedantic parodies of the 'new poetry', are documents that would find sympathetic readers in the waiting-room of a private sanatorium. Clinically analyzed they suggest in conclusion one of Mr. Eliot's lines: 'After such knowledge, what forgiveness?' As a parodist, Mr. Eliot is lacking in good taste, invention, and wit. Compared with Rudyard Kipling, Thackeray, and Phoebe Cary (among the most accomplished parodists in the language) Mr. Eliot is prodigiously labored and dull. General incomprehensibility and sordidness of detail (defects not difficult to imitate, but excessively difficult to parody) are Mr. Eliot's distinguishing traits. He is usually intelligible only when he is nasty. His similes are without humor and without point:

> He laughed like an impossible [sic] foetus.

> Midnight shakes the memory
> As a madman shakes a dead geranium.

> The world revolves like ancient women
> Gathering fuel in vacant lots.

Mr. Eliot may cynically have perpetrated this slim volume in order to glean from the tributes of his admirers material for a new 'Dunciad'.

---

* *Bookman* 52 (September 1920), p. 59.

82
Studies in the Sophisticated*

PADRAIC COLUM

To give prose the precedence of verse in a review that deals with both is possibly wrong, but there is an excuse for it in the present case. The 'Instigations' of Ezra Pound deal in many places with the poems of T.S. Eliot. Some of these passages make the best introduction that could be written for the poems. They are eulogistic, and at least in one passage, possibly extravagantly eulogistic. Mr. Eliot's form is compared to Ovid's form in the 'Heroides,' and to Browning's form in 'Men and Women.' 'The form of "Men and Women" is more alive than the epistolary form of the "Heroides,"' Mr. Pound says, and then he goes on to suggest that the present-day poet has made a certain advance on Browning's form—'Browning included a certain amount of ratiocination and of purely intellectual comment, and in just that proportion he lost intensity.' Mr. Eliot has stripped away the ratiocination and the intellectual comment.

His first volume has been published in the present year—a small collection of twenty-four pieces, four being in French. Had Mr. Eliot excluded such pieces as 'The Boston Evening Transcript,' 'Hysteria,' 'Cousin Nancy,' one would be able to judge his poetry without making a reference to The Smart Set. That he has included these is evidence that he is not amongst the super-sophisticated.

I do not know if these poems mark the beginning of a cycle in poetry, but I am sure that they mark the end of one. Twenty years ago Mr. Yeats published 'The Wind Among the Reeds.' He brought a new set of symbols into poetry. He heard 'the Shadowy Horses, their long mains a-shake, their hoofs heavy with tumult.' Today Mr. Eliot sees that 'The red-eyed scavengers are creeping from Kentish Town and Golder's Green.' The cycle is complete: the vague and visionary territory has become defined as points on a subway, and municipal employees have taken the place of creatures out of a myth.

And the truth is that our imaginations are put at no loss by the change in

*New Republic 25 (8 December 1920), p. 52.

symbols. Mr. Eliot, like the Mr. Yeats of 'The Wind Amongst the Reeds,' is a symbolist. He, too, has his Aedh, his Hanrahan, his Michael Robartes. But he calls them Sweeney, J. Alfred Prufrock, Mr. Apollinax. The Hippopotamus of the Zoo takes the place of the boar with bristles and the deer with no horns. The change, of course, would not be real if there were no poetry transmitted through the symbols. Poetry is transmitted. In such poems as 'Gerontion,' 'The Love Song of J. Alfred Prufrock,' 'Portrait of a Lady,' 'Cooking Egg,' we get a glimpse of the visions and tragedies that are in the soul—it does not matter that the soul in these situations has to look out on restaurants instead of on temples, and on 'rocks, moss, stonecrop, iron, merds,' instead of on the mountains and the sea.

Mr. Eliot has learned from Jules Laforgue how to make modern settings as well as how to parade a mockery of the literary allusion. This by itself would serve to put him with the modernists. But he is modern in a way that is more significant. He has the modern approach to the soul, or, let us say, to the psyche—to the soul that is not an entity but a collection of complexes—the soul that is at once positive and reticent, obscured and clairvoyant. The poet is well aware of the tragedy that is marked by a yawn, and the dreadful dismissal that is in a cliché repeated. His art is indeed achieved when he can give us such revelations in the medium of verse.

For a generation there have been attempts to do this kind of thing in English, and verse in which ennui turns upon disillusion has gone the rounds. But now that Mr. Eliot has published we see that in this verse there were only approaches. Mr. Eliot's work is complete; he has adapted a modern technique, and his personae are stabilized into types. The group in the workshop were aware that he was completing a tendency, and for that reason they were speaking of him with Ovid and Browning before he had published a book. I have said that if he does not mark the beginning of a cycle he certainly marks the end of one. This poetry of his will act in the body literary like those tremendous fellows, the corpuscles in the blood that seize upon and devour the de-vitalized corpuscles. Romantic poetry, in its spent stages, will encounter Sweeney and Prufrock and will not know what has happened to it. But that comparison is wrong: the poetry of Mr. Eliot, in spite of its being so well exercised and so well disinfected, belongs after all to Byzantium; the shadows of a long decay are upon it all.

The Waste Land

Criterion, London, October 1922, vol. i, pp 50–64;
Dial, New York, November 1922, vol. lxxiii, pp. 473–85;
first edition, New York, 15 December 1922

83
Review of *The Waste Land* and notice of first issue of the *Criterion* *

ANON

If we are to judge by its first number, the 'Criterion' is not only that rare thing amongst English periodicals, a purely literary review, but it is of a quality not inferior to that of any review published either here or abroad. Of the seven items which make up this number there are at least five that we should like to see preserved in a 'permanent' form. And of these five there are two, the long poem by Mr. T.S. Eliot called 'The Waste Land' and Dostoevski's 'Plan of a Novel,' now first translated into English, that are of exceptional importance. We cannot imagine a more untidy plan for a novel or anything else than this one by Dostoevski, and yet, even on a first reading, one has a confused impression of having passed through an exciting and significant experience. To the student of Dostoevski this so-called 'plan' will reveal much; it is full of hints of spiritual discoveries which, we may be confident, Dostoevski would have fully revealed. And it is very interesting to see how entirely the *points d'appui* of a Dostoevski novel consist of such flashes. Of orderly planning in the ordinary or even in the Jamesian sense there is no trace. He must have found composition extremely difficult. There is no machinery of which the momentum carries him on. He had to create every page.

Mr. Eliot's poem is also a collection of flashes, but there is no effect of heterogeneity, since all these flashes are relevant to the same thing and together give what seems to be a complete expression of this poet's vision of modern life. We have here range, depth, and beautiful expression. What more is necessary to a great poem? This vision is singularly complex and in all its labyrinths utterly sincere. It is the mystery of life that it shows two faces, and we know of no other modern poet who can more adequately and movingly reveal to us the inextricable tangle of the sordid and the beautiful that make up life. Life is neither hellish nor heavenly; it has a purgatorial

---

* *Times Literary Supplement* no. 1084 (26 October 1922), p. 690.

quality. And since it is purgatory, deliverance is possible. Students of Mr. Eliot's work will find a new note, and a profoundly interesting one, in the latter part of this poem.

Of the other items in this number we may single out an excellent short story by May Sinclair, an interesting literary study by Sturge Moore, and a maliciously urbane and delightful article on 'Dullness,' by George Saintsbury. What literary school, then, does this new quarterly represent? It is a school which includes Saintsbury, Sturge Moore, and T.S. Eliot. There is no such school, obviously. It becomes apparent that the only school represented is the school of those who are genuinely interested in good literature.

84
Books and Authors*

ANON

The annual award of the 'Dial,' amounting to $2,000, has been given this year to T.S. Eliot, the American poet living in England. This award, which is not presented as a prize, but in recognition of able work, was given last year to Sherwood Anderson, the novelist. Thomas Stearns Eliot, to give him his full name, is a Harvard graduate and a writer who may be regarded as the poetical leader of the Younger Generation. His volume, 'Poems,' containing such unusual efforts as 'The Love Song of J. Alfred Prufrock' and the 'Portrait of a Lady,' appeared several seasons ago. A new volume from his pen, 'The Waste Land,' a single poem of some length, is shortly to be published by Boni & Liveright. Mr. Eliot's work is marked by an intense cerebral quality and a compact music that has practically established a movement among the younger men.

*New York Times Book Review (26 November 1922), p. 12.

85
Comment

◆

ANON

The editors have the pleasure of announcing that for the year 1922 the 'Dial's' award goes to Mr. T.S. Eliot.

Mr. Eliot has himself done so much to make clear the relation of critic to creative artist that we hope not to be asked whether it is his criticism or his poetry which constitutes that service to letters which the award is intended to acknowledge. Indeed it is our fancy that those who know one or the other will recognize the propriety of the occasion; those who know both will recognize further in Mr. Eliot an exceedingly active influence on contemporary letters.

Influence in itself, however, is no service, and what makes Mr. Eliot a significant artist is that his work, of whatever nature, is an indication of how ineffective the temptation to do bad work can, for at least once, become. Few American writers have published so little, and fewer have published so much which was worth publication. We do not for a moment suspect Mr. Eliot of unheard-of capacities; it is possible that he neither has been pressed to nor can write a popular novel. But the temptation not to arrive at excellence is very great, and he is one of the rare artists who has resisted it. A service to letters peculiarly acceptable now is the proof that one can arrive at eminence with the help of nothing except genius.

Elsewhere in this issue will be found a discussion of Mr. Eliot's poetry, with special reference to his long work, 'The Waste Land,' which appeared in the 'Dial' of a month ago; in reviewing 'The Sacred Wood,' and elsewhere, we have had much to say of his critical work, and may have more. At this moment it pleases us to remember how much at variance Mr. Eliot is with those writers who having themselves sacrificed all interest in letters, are calling upon criticism to do likewise in the name of the particular science which they fancy can redeem the world from every ill but themselves. As a critic of letters Mr. Eliot has always had preeminently one of the qualifications which he requires of the good critic: 'a creative interest, a focus upon the immediate

* *Dial* 73 (December 1922), pp. 685–7.

future. The important critic is the person who is absorbed in the present problems of art, and who wishes to bring the forces of the past to bear upon the solution of these problems.' This is precisely what Mr. Eliot has wished, and accomplished, in his function as critic of criticism. It is impossible to read the opening essays of 'The Sacred Wood' without recognizing that it is from these pages that the attack upon perverted criticism is rising. The journalists who wish critics to be for ever concerned with social laws, economic fundamentals, and the science of psychoanalysis, and never by any chance with the erection into laws of those personal impressions which are the great pleasure of appreciation, would do well to destroy Mr. Eliot first; for it is from him that new critics are learning 'that the "historical" and the "philosophical" critics had better be called historians and philosophers quite simply' and that criticism has other functions, and other pleasures to give.

There is another, quite different sense, in which Mr Eliot's work is of exceptional service to American letters. He is one of a small number of Americans who can be judged by the standards of the past—including therein the body of Occidental literature. It is a superficial indication of this that Mr. Eliot is almost the only young American critic who is neither ignorant of nor terrified by the classics, that he knows them (one includes Massinger as well as Euripides) and understands their relation to the work which went before and came after them. There are in his poems certain characters, certain scenes, and even certain attitudes of mind, which one recognizes as peculiarly American; yet there is nowhere in his work that 'localism' which at once takes so much of American writing out of the field of comparison with European letters and (it is often beneficial to their reputations) requires for American writers a special standard of judgement. We feel nothing aggressive and nothing apologetic in his writing; there is the assumption in it that the civilized American no less than the civilized German can count Shakespeare and even Poe as part of his inheritance.

When 'Prufrock' in paper covers first appeared, to become immediately one of the rarest of rare books (somebody stole ours as early as 1919) Mr. Eliot was already redoubtable. Since then, poet with true invention, whom lassitude has not led to repeat himself, critic again with invention and with enough metaphysics to draw the line at the metaphysical, his legend has increased. We do not fancy that we are putting a last touch to this climax; we express gratitude for pleasure received and assured. If pleasure is not sufficiently high-toned a word, you may, in the preceding paragraphs, take your pick.

Mr. Eliot's command of publicity is not exceptional, and we feel it necessary to put down, for those who care for information, these hardly gleaned facts of his biography. In 1888 he was born in St. Louis; in 1909 and 1910 he received, respectively, the degrees of Bachelor and of Master of Arts at Harvard; subsequently he studied at the Sorbonne, the Harvard Graduate School, and Merton College, Oxford. He has been a lecturer under both the

Oxford and the London University Extension Systems, and from 1917 to 1919 he was assistant editor of the 'Egoist.' We have heard it rumoured that he is still 'À Londres, un peu banquier'; those who can persuade themselves that facts are facts will find much more of importance in the 'Mélange Adultère de Tout,' from which the quotation comes; as that poem was written several years ago it omits the names of Mr. Eliot's books: 'The Sacred Wood,' 'Poems,' and 'The Waste Land' (not to speak of the several volumes later incorporated in 'Poems') and omits also the fact that Mr. Eliot is now editor of the 'Criterion,' a quarterly which we (as it were *en passant*) hereby make welcome. The most active and, we are told, the most influential editor-critic in London found nothing to say of one of the contributions to the first number except that it was 'an obscure, but amusing poem' by the editor. We should hate to feel that our readers can judge of the state of criticism in England by turning to the first page of our November issue and reading the same poem there.

86
The Poetry of Drouth*

EDMUND WILSON

Mr. T.S. Eliot's first meagre volume of twenty-four poems was dropped into the waters of contemporary verse without stirring more than a few ripples. But when two or three years had passed, it was found to stain the whole sea. Or, to change the metaphor a little, it became evident that Mr. Eliot had fished a murex up. His productions, which had originally been received as a sort of glorified *vers de société*, turned out to be unforgettable poems, which everyone was trying to rewrite. There might not be very much of him, but what there was had come somehow to seem precious and now the publication of his long poem, 'The Waste Land.' confirms the opinion which we had begun gradually to cherish, that Mr. Eliot, with all his limitations, is one of our only authentic poets. For this new poem—which presents itself as so far his most considerable claim to eminence—not only recapitulates all his earlier and already familiar motifs, but it sounds for the first time in all their intensity, untempered by irony or disguise, the hunger for beauty and the anguish at living which lie at the bottom of all his work.

Perhaps the best point of departure for a discussion of 'The Waste Land' is an explanation of its title. Mr. Eliot asserts that he derived this title, as well as the plan of the poem 'and much of the incidental symbolism,' from a book by Miss Jessie L. Weston called 'From Ritual to Romance.' 'The Waste Land' it appears, is one of the many mysterious elements which have made of the Holy Grail legend a perennial puzzle of folk-lore; it is a desolate and sterile country, ruled over by an impotent king, in which not only have the crops ceased to grow and the animals to reproduce their kind, but the very human inhabitants have become unable to bear children. The renewal of the Waste Land and the healing of the 'Fisher King's' wound depend somehow upon the success of the Knight who has come to find the Holy Grail.

Miss Weston, who has spent her whole life in the study of the Arthurian legends, has at last propounded a new solution for the problems presented by this strange tale. Stimulated by Frazer's 'Golden Bough'—of which this extraordinarily interesting book is a sort of offshoot— she has attempted to

Dial 73 (December 1922), pp. 611–16.

explain the Fisher King as a primitive vegetable god—one of those creatures who, like Attis and Adonis, is identified with Nature herself and in the temporary loss of whose virility the drouth or inclemency of the season is symbolized; and whose mock burial is a sort of earnest of his coming to life again. Such a cult, Miss Weston contends, became attached to the popular Persian religion of Mithraism and was brought north to Gaul and Britain by the Roman legionaries. When Christianity finally prevailed, Attis was driven underground and survived only as a secret cult, like the Venus of the Venusberg. The Grail legend, according to Miss Weston, had its origin in such a cult; the Lance and Grail are the sexual symbols appropriate to a fertility rite and the eerie adventure of the Chapel Perilous is the description of an initiation.

Now Mr. Eliot uses the Waste Land as the concrete image of a spiritual drouth. His poem takes place half in the real world—the world of contemporary London, and half in a haunted wilderness—the Waste Land of the mediæval legend; but the Waste Land is only the hero's arid soul and the intolerable world about him. The water which he longs for in the twilit desert is to quench the thirst which torments him in the London dusk.—And he exists not only upon these two planes, but as if throughout the whole of human history. Miss Weston's interpretation of the Grail legend lent itself with peculiar aptness to Mr. Eliot's extraordinarily complex mind (which always finds itself looking out upon the present with the prouder eyes of the past and which loves to make its oracles as deep as the experience of the race itself by piling up stratum upon stratum of reference, as the Italian painters used to paint over one another); because she took pains to trace the Buried God not only to Attis and Adonis, but further back to the recently revealed Tammuz of the Sumerian-Babylonian civilization and to the god invited to loosen the waters in the abysmally ancient Vedic Hymns. So Mr. Eliot hears in his own parched cry the voices of all the thirsty men of the past—of the author of Ecclesiastes in majestic bitterness at life's futility, of the Children of Israel weeping for Zion by the unrefreshing rivers of Babylon, of the disciples after the Crucifixion meeting the phantom of Christ on their journey; of Buddha's renunciation of life and Dante's astonishment at the weary hordes of Hell, and of the sinister dirge with which Webster blessed the 'friendless bodies of unburied men.' In the centre of his poem he places the weary figure of the blind immortal prophet Tiresias, who, having been woman as well as man, has exhausted all human experience and, having 'sat by Thebes below the wall and walked among the lowest of the dead,' knows exactly what will happen in the London flat between the typist and the house-agent's clerk; and at its beginning the almost identical figure of the Cumaean Sibyl mentioned in Petronius, who—gifted also with extreme longevity and preserved as a sort of living mummy—when asked by little boys what she wanted, replied only 'I want to die.' Not only is life sterile and futile, but men have tasted its sterility and futility a thousand times before. T.S. Eliot, walk-

The Waste Land (1922)

ing the desert of London, feels profoundly that the desert has always been there. Like Tiresias, he has sat below the wall of Thebes; like Buddha, he has seen the world as an arid conflagration; like the Sibyl, he has known everything and known everything vain.

Yet something else, too, reaches him from the past: as he wanders among the vulgarities which surround him, his soul is haunted by heroic strains of an unfading music. Sometimes it turns suddenly and shockingly into the jazz of the music-halls, sometimes it breaks in the middle of a bar and leaves its hearer with dry ears again, but still it sounds like the divine rumour of some high destiny from which he has fallen, like indestructible pride in the citizenship of some world which he never can reach. In a London boudoir, where the air is stifling with a dust of futility, he hears, as he approaches his hostess, an echo of Antony and Cleopatra and of Aeneas coming to the house of Dido—and a painted panel above the mantel gives his mind a moment's swift release by reminding him of Milton's Paradise and of the nightingale that sang there.—Yet though it is most often things from books which refresh him, he has also a slight spring of memory. He remembers someone who came to him with wet hair and with hyacinths in her arms, and before her he was stricken senseless and dumb—'looking into the heart of light, the silence.' There were rain and flowers growing then. Nothing ever grows during the action of the poem and no rain ever falls. The thunder of the final vision is 'dry sterile thunder without rain.' But as Gerontion in his dry rented house thinks wistfully of the young men who fought in the rain, as Prufrock longs to ride green waves and linger in the chambers of the sea, as Mr Apollinax is imagined drawing strength from the deep sea-caves of coral islands, so in this new poem Mr. Eliot identifies water with all freedom and illumination of the soul. He drinks the rain that once fell on his youth as—to use an analogy in Mr. Eliot's own manner—Dante drank at the river of Eunoë that the old joys he had known might be remembered. But—to note also the tragic discrepancy, as Mr. Eliot always does—the draught, so far from renewing his soul and leaving him pure to rise to the stars, is only a drop absorbed in the desert; to think of it is to register its death. The memory is the dead god whom—as Hyacinth—he buries at the beginning of the poem and which—unlike his ancient prototype—is never to come to life again. Hereafter, fertility will fail; we shall see women deliberately making themselves sterile; we shall find that love has lost its life-giving power and can bring nothing but an asceticism of disgust. He is travelling in a country cracked by drouth in which he can only dream feverishly of drowning or of hearing the song of the hermit-thrush which has at least the music of water. The only reappearance of the god is as a phantom which walks beside him, the delirious hallucination of a man who is dying of thirst. In the end the dry-rotted world is crumbling about him—his own soul is falling apart. There is nothing left to prop it up but some dry stoic Sanskrit maxims and the broken sighs from the past, of singers exiled or oppressed. Like de

Nerval, he is disinherited; like the poet of the 'Pervigilium Veneris,' he is dumb; like Arnaut Daniel in Purgatory, he begs the world to raise a prayer for his torment, as he disappears in the fire.

It will be seen from this brief description that the poem is complicated; and it is actually even more complicated than I have made it appear. It is sure to be objected that Mr. Eliot has written a puzzle rather than a poem and that his work can possess no higher interest than a full-rigged ship built in a bottle. It will be said that he depends too much upon books and borrows too much from other men and that there can be no room for original quality in a poem of little more than four hundred lines which contains allusions to, parodies of, or quotations from, the Vedic Hymns, Buddha, the Psalms, Ezekiel, Ecclesiastes, Luke, Sappho, Virgil, Ovid, Petronius, the 'Pervigilium Veneris,' St Augustine, Dante, the Grail Legends, early English poetry, Kyd, Spenser, Shakespeare, John Day, Webster, Middleton, Milton, Goldsmith, Gérard de Nerval, Froude, Baudelaire, Verlaine, Swinburne, Wagner, 'The Golden Bough,' Miss Weston's book, various popular ballads, and the author's own earlier poems. It has already been charged against Mr. Eliot that he does not feel enough to be a poet and that the emotions of longing and disgust which he does have belong essentially to a delayed adolescence. It has already been suggested that his distaste for the celebrated Sweeney shows a superficial mind and that if he only looked more closely into poor Sweeney he would find Eugene O'Neill's Hairy Ape; and I suppose it will be felt in connexion with this new poem that if his vulgar London girls had only been studied by Sherwood Anderson they would have presented a very different appearance. At bottom, it is sure to be said, Mr. Eliot is timid and prosaic like Mr. Prufrock; he has no capacity for life, and nothing which happens to Mr. Prufrock can be important.

Well: all these objections are founded on realities, but they are outweighed by one major fact—the fact that Mr. Eliot is a poet. It is true his poems seem the products of a constricted emotional experience and that he appears to have drawn rather heavily on books for the heat he could not derive from life. There is a certain grudging margin, to be sure, about all that Mr. Eliot writes—as if he were compensating himself for his limitations by a peevish assumption of superiority. But it is the very acuteness of his suffering from this starvation which gives such poignancy to his art. And, as I say, Mr. Eliot is a poet—that is, he feels intensely and with distinction and speaks naturally in beautiful verse—so that, no matter within what walls he lives, he belongs to the divine company. His verse is sometimes much too scrappy—he does not dwell long enough upon one idea to give it its proportionate value before passing on to the next—but these drops, though they be wrung from flint, are none the less authentic crystals. They are broken and sometimes infinitely tiny, but they are worth all the rhinestones on the market. I doubt whether there is a single other poem of equal length by a contemporary American which displays so high and so varied a mastery of English verse. The poem is—in spite of its lack of structural unity—simply one triumph after another—from the white April light of the opening and the sweet wistfulness of the nightingale passage—one of the only successful pieces of contemporary blank verse— to the shabby sadness of the Thames Maidens, the cruel irony of Tiresias' vision, and the dry grim stony style of the descriptions of the Waste Land itself.

That is why Mr. Eliot's trivialities are more valuable than other people's epics—why Mr. Eliot's detestation of Sweeney is more precious than Mr. Sandburg's sympathy for him, and Mr. Prufrock's tea-table tragedy more important than all the passions of the New Adam— sincere and carefully expressed as these latter emotions indubitably are. That is also why, for all its complicated correspondences and its recondite references and quotations, 'The Waste Land' is intelligible at first reading. It is not necessary to know anything about the Grail Legend or any but the most obvious of Mr. Eliot's allusions to feel the force of the intense emotion which the poem is intended to convey—as one cannot do, for example, with the extremely ill-focussed Eight Cantos of his imitator Mr. Ezra Pound, who presents only a bewildering mosaic with no central emotion to provide a key. In Eliot the very images and the sound of the words—even when we do not know precisely why he has chosen them—are charged with a strange poignancy which seems to bring us into the heart of the singer. And sometimes we feel that he is speaking not only for a personal distress, but for the starvation of a whole civilization—for people grinding at barren office-routine in the cells of gigantic cities, drying up their souls in eternal toil whose products never bring them profit, where their pleasures are so vulgar and so feeble that they are almost sadder than their pains. It is our whole world of strained nerves and shattered institutions, in which 'some infinitely gentle, infinitely suffering thing' is somehow being done to death—in which the maiden Philomel 'by the barbarous king so rudely forced' can no longer even fill the desert 'with inviolable voice.' It is the world in which the pursuit of grace and beauty is something which is felt to be obsolete—the reflections which reach us from the past cannot illumine so dingy a scene; that heroic prelude has ironic echoes among the streets and the drawing-rooms where we live. Yet the race of the poets—though grown rarer—is not yet quite dead: there is at least one who, as Mr. Pound says, has brought a new personal rhythm into the language and who has lent even to the words of his great predecessors a new music and a new meaning.

87
T.S. Eliot*

GILBERT SELDES

The poems and critical essays of T.S. Eliot have been known to a number of readers for six or seven years; small presses in England have issued one or two pamphlet-like books of poetry; in America the 'Little Review' and the 'Dial' have published both prose and verse. In 1920 he issued his collected 'Poems,' a volume of some sixty pages, through Knopf, and the following year the same publisher put forth 'The Sacred Wood,' a collection of fourteen essays devoted to two subjects, criticism and poetry. This year a volume no larger than the first, containing one long poem, is issued. The position, approaching eminence, which Mr. Eliot holds is obviously not to be explained in terms of bulk.

It is peculiarly difficult to write even the necessary journalism about Mr. Eliot. From its baser manifestation he is fortunately immune and his qualities do not lend themselves to trickery. The secret of his power (I will not say influence) as a critic is that he is interested in criticism and in the object of criticism, as a poet that he understands and practices the art of poetry. In the first of these he is exceptional, almost alone; in both, his work lies in the living tradition and outside the wilfulness of the moment. We are so far gone in the new movement that even to say that he practices aesthetic criticism and impersonal poetry will be confusing. I can only explain by distinguishing his work from others.

At the present moment criticism of literature is almost entirely criticism of the ideas expressed in literature; it is interested chiefly in morals, economics, sociology, or science. We can imagine a critic *circa* 1840 declaring that 'Othello' is a bad play because men should not kill their wives; and the progress is not very great to 1922 when we are as likely as not to hear that it is a bad play because Desdemona is an outmoded kind of woman. To be sure the economic, sociological, and psychoanalytical interest has largely displaced the moral one, and critics (whether they say a book is good or bad) are inclined to judge the importance of a writer of fiction by the accuracy of

*Nation 115 (6 December 1922), pp. 614–16.

his dream-interpretations or the soundness of his economic fundamentals. Their creative interest is in something apart from the art they are discussing; and what Mr. Eliot has done, with an attractive air of finality, is to indicate how irrelevant that interest is to the art of letters. He respects these imperfect critics in so far as they are good philosophers, moralists, or scientists, but he knows that in connection with letters they are the victims of impure desires (the poet *manqué* as critic) or of impure interests (the fanatical Single-taxer as critic). 'But Aristotle,' he says, 'had none of these impure desires to satisfy; in whatever sphere of interest, he looked solely and steadfastly at the object; in his short and broken treatise he provides an eternal example—not of laws, or even of method, for there is no method except to be very intelligent, but of intelligence itself swiftly operating the analysis of sensation to the point of principle and definition.' Again, more specifically, 'The important critic is the person who is absorbed in the present problems of art, and who wishes to bring the forces of the past to bear upon the solution of these problems. If the critic considers Congreve, for instance, he will always have at the back of his mind the question: What has Congreve got that is pertinent to our dramatic art? Even if he is solely engaged in trying to understand Congreve, this will make all the difference: inasmuch as to understand anything is to understand from a point of view.' Criticism, for Mr. Eliot, is the statement of the structures in which our perceptions, when we face a work of art, form themselves. He quotes Remy de Gourmont: 'To erect his personal impressions into laws is the great effort of man if he is sincere.'

The good critic, as I understand Mr. Eliot, will be concerned with the aesthetic problem of any given work of art; he will (I should add) not despise ideas, but if he is intelligent he will recognize their place in a work of art and he will certainly not dismiss as paradoxical nonsense Mr. Eliot's contention that his baffling escape from ideas made Henry James the most intelligent man of his time. It is not an easy task to discover in each case what the aesthetic problem is; but that is the task, precisely, which every good critic of painting, let us say, is always compelled to attempt and which no critic of letters need attempt because he can always talk (profoundly, with the appearance of relevance, endlessly) about ideas. Mr. Eliot has accomplished the task several times, notably in his essay on 'Hamlet,' about which essay a small literature has already been produced. I have not space here to condense the substance of that or of the other critical essays—they are remarkably concise as they are—nor to do more than say that they are written with an extraordinary distinction in which clarity, precision, and nobility almost always escaping magniloquence, are the elements.

In turning to Mr. Eliot as poet I do not leave the critic behind since it is from his critical utterances that we derive the clue to his poetry. He says that the historical sense is indispensable to anyone who would continue to be a poet after the age of twenty-five, and follows this with a statement which cannot be too closely pondered by those who misunderstand tradition and by those who imagine that American letters stand outside of European letters and are to be judged by other standards:

> The historical sense compels a man to write not merely with his own generation in his bones, but with a feeling that the whole of the literature of Europe from Homer and within it the whole of the literature of his own country has a simultaneous existence and composes a simultaneous order.

This is only the beginning of 'depersonalization.' It continues:

> What happens is a continual surrender of himself (the poet) as he is at the moment to something which is more valuable. The progress of an artist is a continual self-sacrifice, a continual extinction of personality . . . the more perfect the artist, the more completely separate in him will be the man who suffers and the mind which creates; the more perfectly will the mind digest and transmute the passions which are its material. . . . The intensity of the poetry is something quite different from whatever intensity in the supposed experience it may give the impression of. . . . Impressions and experiences which are important for the man may take no place in the poetry, and those which become important in the poetry may play quite a negligible part in the man, the personality. . . .

And finally:

> It is not in his personal emotions, the emotions provoked by particular events in his life, that the poet is in any way remarkable or interesting. His particular emotions may be simple, or crude, or flat. The emotion in his poetry will be a very complex thing, but not with the complexity of the emotions of people who have very complex or unusual emotions in life. . . . The business of the poet is not to find new emotions, but to use the ordinary ones and, in working them up into poetry, to express feelings which are not in actual emotions at all. . . . Poetry is not a turning loose of emotion, but an escape from emotion; it is not the expression of a personality, but an escape from personality. But, of course, only those who have personality and emotions know what it means to want to escape from these things.

The significant emotion has its life in the poem and not in the history of the poet; and recognition of this, Mr. Eliot indicates, is the true appreciation of poetry. Fortunately for the critic he has written one poem, 'The Waste Land,' to which one can apply his own standards. It develops, carries to conclusions, many things in his remarkable earlier work, in method and in thought. I have not that familiarity with the intricacies of French verse which could make it possible for me to affirm or deny the statement that technically he derives much from Jules Laforgue; if Remy de Gourmont's estimate of the latter be correct one can see definite points of similarity in the minds of the two poets:

> His natural genius was made up of sensibility, irony, imagination, and clairvoyance; he chose to nourish it with positive knowledge (*connaissances positives*), with all philosophies and all literatures, with all the images of nature and of art; even the latest views of science seem to have been known to him. . . . It is literature entirely made new and unforeseen, disconcerting and giving the curious and rare sensation that one has never read anything like it before.

The Waste Land (1922)

A series of sardonic portraits—of people, places, things—each the distillation of a refined emotion, make up Mr. Eliot's 'Poems.' The deceptive simplicity of these poems in form and in style is exactly at the opposite extreme from false naivete; they are unpretentiously sophisticated, wicked, malicious, humorous, and with the distillation of emotion has gone a condensation of expression. In 'The Waste Land' the seriousness of the theme is matched with an intensity of expression in which all the earlier qualities are sublimated.

In essence 'The Waste Land' says something which is not new: that life has become barren and sterile, that man is withering, impotent, and without assurance that the waters which made the land fruitful will ever rise again. (I need not say that 'thoughtful' as the poem is, it does not 'express an idea'; it deals with emotions, and ends precisely in that significant emotion, inherent in the poem, which Mr. Eliot has described.) The title, the plan, and much of the symbolism of the poem, the author tells us in his 'Notes,' were suggested by Miss Weston's remarkable book on the Grail legend, 'From Ritual to Romance'; it is only indispensable to know that there exists the legend of a king rendered impotent, and his country sterile, both awaiting deliverance by a knight on his way to seek the Grail; it is interesting to know further that this is part of the Life or Fertility mysteries; but the poem is self-contained. It seems at first sight remarkably disconnected, confused, the emotion seems to disengage itself in spite of the objects and events chosen by the poet as their vehicle. The poem begins with a memory of summer showers, gaiety, joyful and perilous escapades; a moment later someone else is saying 'I will show you fear in a handful of dust,' and this is followed by the first lines of 'Tristan und Isolde,' and then again by a fleeting recollection of loveliness. The symbolism of the poem is introduced by means of the Tarot pack of cards; quotations, precise or dislocated, occur; gradually one discovers a rhythm of alternation between the visionary (so to name the memories of the past) and the actual, between the spoken and the unspoken thought. There are scraps, fragments; then sustained episodes; the poem culminates with the juxtaposition of the highest types of Eastern and Western asceticism, by means of allusions to St. Augustine and Buddha; and ends with a sour commentary on the injunctions 'Give, sympathize, control' of the Upanishads, a commentary which reaches its conclusion in a pastiche recalling all that is despairing and disinherited in the memory of man.

A closer view of the poem does more than illuminate the difficulties; it reveals the hidden form of the work, indicates how each thing falls into place, and to the reader's surprise shows that the emotion which at first seemed to come in spite of the framework and the detail could not otherwise have been communicated. For the theme is not a distaste for life, nor is it a disillusion, a romantic pessimism of any kind. It is specifically concerned with the idea of the Waste Land—that the land was fruitful and now is not, that life had been rich, beautiful, assured, organized, lofty, and now is dragging itself out in a

Early Poems and *The Waste Land*

poverty-stricken, and disrupted and ugly tedium, without health, and with no consolation in morality; there may remain for the poet the labor of poetry, but in the poem there remain only 'these fragments I have shored against my ruins'—the broken glimpses of what was. The poem is not an argument and I can only add, to be fair, that it contains no romantic idealization of the past; one feels simply that even in the cruelty and madness which have left their record in history and in art, there was an intensity of life, a germination and fruitfulness, which are now gone, and that even the creative imagination, even hallucination and vision have atrophied, so that water shall never again be struck from a rock in the desert. Mr. Bertrand Russell has recently said that since the Renaissance the clock of Europe has been running down; without the feeling that it was once wound up, without the contrasting emotions as one looks at the past and at the present, 'The Waste Land' would be a different poem, and the problem of the poem would have been solved in another way.

The present solution is in part by juxtaposition of opposites. We have a passage seemingly spoken by a slut, ending

Goonight Bill. Goonight Lou. Goonight May. Goonight.
Ta ta. Goonight. Goonight.

and then the ineffable

Good night, ladies, good night, sweet ladies, good night, good night.

Conversely the turn is accomplished from nobility or beauty of utterance to

The sounds of horns and motors, which shall bring
Sweeney to Mrs. Porter in the spring.

And in the long passage where Tiresias, the central character of the poem, appears the method is at its height, for here is the coldest and unhappiest revelation of the assault of lust made in the terms of beauty:

[Quotes 'The Waste Land', 'At the violet hour' to 'the stairs unlit'.]

It will be interesting for those who have knowledge of another great work of our time, Mr. Joyce's 'Ulysses,' to think of the two together. That 'The Waste Land' is, in a sense, the inversion and the complement of 'Ulysses' is at least tenable. We have in 'Ulysses' the poet defeated, turning outward, savoring the ugliness which is no longer transmutable into beauty, and, in the end, homeless. We have in 'The Waste Land' some indication of the inner life of such a poet. The contrast between the forms of these two works is not expressed in the recognition that one is among the longest and one among the shortest of works in its genre; the important thing is that in each the theme, once it is comprehended, is seen to have dictated the form. More important still, I fancy, is that each has expressed something of supreme relevance to our present life in the everlasting terms of art.

88
Disillusion vs. Dogma*

♦

LOUIS UNTERMEYER

The 'Dial's' award to Mr. T.S. Eliot and the subsequent book-publication of his 'The Waste Land' have occasioned a display of some of the most enthusiastically naive superlatives that have ever issued from publicly sophisticated iconoclasts. A group, in attempting to do for Mr. Eliot what 'Ulysses' did for Mr. Joyce, has, through its emphatic reiterations, driven more than one reader to a study rather than a celebration of the qualities that characterize Mr. Eliot's work and endear him to the younger cerebralists. These qualities, apparent even in his earlier verses, are an elaborate irony, a twitching disillusion, a persistent though muffled hyperaesthesia. In 'The Love Song of J. Alfred Prufrock' and the extraordinarily sensitized 'Portrait of a Lady,' Mr. Eliot fused these qualities in a flexible music, in the shifting nuances of a speech that wavered dexterously between poetic colour and casual conversation. In the greater part of 'Poems,' however, Mr. Eliot employed a harder and more crackling tone of voice; he delighted in virtuosity for its own sake, in epigrammatic velleities, in an incongruously mordant and disillusioned *vers de société*.

In 'The Waste Land,' Mr. Eliot has attempted to combine these two contradictory idioms with a new complexity. The result—although, as I am aware, this conclusion is completely at variance with the judgment of its frenetic admirers—is a pompous parade of erudition, a lengthy extension of the earlier disillusion, a kaleidoscopic movement in which the bright-coloured pieces fail to atone for the absence of an integrated design. As an echo of contemporary despair, as a picture of dissolution of the breaking-down of the very structures on which life has modelled itself, 'The Waste Land' has a definite authenticity. But an artist is, by the very nature of creation, pledged to give form to formlessness; even the process of disintegration must be held within a pattern. This pattern is distorted and broken by Mr. Eliot's jumble of narratives, nursery-rhymes, criticism, jazz-rhythms, 'Dictionary of Favourite Phrases' and a few lyrical moments. Possibly the disruption of our ideals may be reduced through such a *mélange*,

* *Freeman* 6 (7 January 1923), p. 453.

Early Poems and *The Waste Land*

but it is doubtful whether it is crystallized or even clarified by a series of severed narratives—tales from which the connecting tissue has been carefully cut—and familiar quotations with their necks twisted, all imbedded in that formless plasma which Mr. Ezra Pound likes to call a Sordello-form. Some of the intrusions are more irritating than incomprehensible. The unseen sailor in the first act of 'Tristan und Isolde' is dragged in (without point or preparation) to repeat his 'Frisch weht der Wind'; in the midst of a metaphysical dialogue, we are assured.

> *O O O O that Shakespeherian Rag—*
> *It's so elegant*
> *So intelligent.*

Falling back on his earlier *métier*, a species of sardonic light verse, Mr. Eliot does not disdain to sink to doggerel that would be refused admission to the cheapest of daily columns:

> *When lovely woman stoops to folly and*
> *Paces about her room again, alone,*
> *She smoothes her hair with automatic hand,*
> *And puts a record on the gramophone.*

Elsewhere, the juxtaposition of Andrew Marvell, Paul Dresser and others equally incongruous is more cryptic in intention and even more dismal in effect:

> *But at my back from time to time I hear*
> *The sound of horns and motors, which shall bring*
> *Sweeney to Mrs. Porter in the spring.*
> *O the moon shone bright on Mrs. Porter*
> *And on her daughter*
> *They wash their feet in soda water*
> Et O ces voix d'enfants, chantant dans la coupole!

It is difficult to understand the presence of such cheap tricks in what Mr. Burton Rascoe has publicly informed us is 'the finest poem of his generation.' The mingling of wilful obscurity and weak vaudeville compels us to believe that the pleasure which many admirers derive from 'The Waste Land' is the same sort of gratification attained through having solved a puzzle, a form of self-congratulation. The absence of any verbal acrobatics from Mr. Eliot's prose, a prose that represents not the slightest departure from a sort of intensive academicism, makes one suspect that, were it not for the Laforgue mechanism, Mr. Eliot's poetic variations on the theme of a super-refined futility would be increasingly thin and incredibly second rate.

As an analyst of desiccated sensations, as a recorder of the nostalgia of this age, Mr. Eliot has created something whose value is, at least, documentary. Yet, granting even its occasional felicities, 'The Waste Land' is a misleading document. The world distrusts the illusions which the last few years have destroyed. One grants this latter-day truism. But it is groping among new ones: the power of the unconscious, an astringent scepticism, a mystical renaissance—these are some of the current illusions to which the Western World is turning for assurance of their, and its, reality. Man may be desperately insecure, but he has not yet lost the greatest of his emotional needs, the need to believe in something—even in his disbelief. For an ideal-demanding race there is always one more God—and Mr. Eliot is not his prophet.

89
Mr. Eliot's Slug Horn*

ELINOR WYLIE

The reviewer who must essay, within the limits of a few hundred temperate and well-chosen words, to lead even a willing reader into the ensorcelled mazes of Mr. T.S. Eliot's 'Waste Land' perceives, as the public prints have it, no easy task before him. He will appear to the mental traveller as dubious a guide as Childe Roland's hoary cripple with malicious eye; he lies in every word, unless by some stroke of luck, some lightning flash of revelation, he succeeds in showing forth the tragic sincerity and true power of that mysterious and moving spectacle, 'The Waste Land,' the mind of Mr. Eliot, the reflected and refracted mind of a good—or rather a bad—quarter of the present generation.

Amazing comparisons have been drawn between Mr. Eliot and certain celebrated poets; his admirers do not couple him with Pound nor his detractors with Dante, and both are justified in any annoyance which they may feel when others do so. His detractors say that he is obscure; his friends reply that he is no more cryptic than Donne and Yeats; his detractors shift their ground and point out with perfect truth that he has not the one's incomparable wit nor the other's incomparable magic; his friends, if they are wise, acquiesce. It is stated that he is not so universal a genius as Joyce; the proposition appears self-evident to any one who believes with the present reviewer, that Joyce is the sea from whose profundity Eliot has fished up that very Tyrian murex with which Mr. Wilson rightly credits him. Some comparisons, indeed, suggest the lunatic asylums where gentlemen imagine themselves to be the authors of Caesar's Commentaries and the Code Napoléon.

But when we begin to inquire what Mr. Eliot is, instead of what he is not—then if we fail to respond to his accusing cry of '*Mon semblable—mon frère!*' I am inclined to think that we are really either hypocrite readers or stubborn ones closing deliberate eyes against beauty and passion still pitifully alive in the midst of horror. I confess that once upon a time I believed Mr. Eliot to be a brutal person: this was when I first read the 'Portrait of a

*New York Evening Post Literary Review (20 January 1923), p. 396.

Lady.' I now recognize my error, but my sense of the hopeless sadness and humiliation of the poor lady was perfectly sound. I felt that Mr. Eliot had torn the shrinking creature's clothes from her back and pulled the drawing-room curtains aside with a click to admit a flood of shameful sunlight, and I hated him for his cruelty. Only now that I know he is Tiresias have I lost my desire to strike him blind as Peeping Tom.

This power of suggesting intolerable tragedy at the heart of the trivial or the sordid is used with a skill little less than miraculous in 'The Waste Land,' and the power is the more moving because of the attendant conviction, that this terrible resembling contrast between nobility and baseness is an agony in the mind of Mr. Eliot of which only a portion is transferred to that of the reader. He is a cadaver, dissecting himself in our sight; he is the god Atthis who was buried in Stetson's garden and who now arises to give us the benefit of an anatomy lesson. Of course it hurts him more than it does us, and yet it hurts some of us a great deal at that. If this is a trick, it is an inspired one. I do not believe that it is a trick; I think that Mr. Eliot conceived 'The Waste Land' out of an extremity of tragic emotion and expressed it in his own voice and in the voices of other unhappy men not carefully and elaborately trained in close harmony, but coming as a confused and frightening and beautiful murmur out of the bowels of the earth. 'I did not know death had undone so many.' If it were merely a piece of virtuosity it would remain astonishing; it would be a work of art like a fine choir of various singers or a rose window executed in bright fragments of glass. But is is far more than this; it is infused with spirit and passion and despair, and it shoots up into stars of brilliance or flows down dying falls of music which nothing can obscure or silence. These things, rather than other men's outcries, are shored against any ruin which may overtake Mr. Eliot at the hands of Fate or the critics. As for the frequently reiterated statement that Mr. Eliot is a dry intellectual, without depth or sincerity of feeling, it is difficult for me to refute an idea which I am totally at a loss to understand; to me he seems almost inexcusably sensitive and sympathetic and quite inexcusably poignant, since he forces me to employ this horrid word to describe certain qualities which perhaps deserve a nobler tag in mingling pity with terror. That he expresses the emotion of an intellectual is perfectly true, but of the intensity of that emotion there is, to my mind, no question, nor do I recognize any reason for such a question. A very simple mind expresses emotion by action: a kiss or a murder will not make a song until they have passed through the mind of a poet, and a subtile mind may make a simple song about a murder because the murder was a simple one. But the simplicity of the song will be most apparent to the subtlest minds; it will be like a queer masquerading as a dairy maid. But as for Mr. Eliot, he has discarded all disguises; nothing could be more personal and direct than his method of presenting his weariness and despair by means of a stream of memories and images the like of which, a little dulled and narrowed, runs through the brain of any educated and imaginative man whose thoughts are sharpened by suffering. I should perhaps have doubted the suitability of such a stream as material for poetry, just as I do now very much doubt the suitability of Sanskrit amens and abracadabras, but these dubieties are matters of personal taste and comparatively unimportant beside the fact that, though Mr. Eliot may speak with the seven tongues of men and of angels, he has not become as sounding brass and tinkling cymbal. His gifts, whatever they are, profit him much; his charity, like Tiresias, has suffered and foresuffered all. If he is intellectually arrogant and detached— and I cannot for the life of me believe that he is—he is not spiritually either the one or the other; I could sooner accuse him of being sentimental. Indeed, in his tortured pity for ugly and ignoble things he sometimes comes near to losing his hardness of outline along with his hardness of heart; his is not a kindly tolerance for weakness and misery, but an obsessed and agonized sense of kinship with it which occasionally leads him into excesses of speech, ejaculations whose flippancy is the expression of profound despair.

Were I unable to feel this passion shaking the dry bones of 'The Waste Land' like a great wind I would not give a penny for all the thoughts and riddles of the poem; the fact that Mr. Eliot has failed to convince many readers that he has a soul must be laid as a black mark against him. Either you see him as a parlor prestidigitator, a character in which I am personally unable to visualize him, or else you see him as a disenchanted wizard, a disinherited prince. When he says *Shantih* three times as he emerges from 'The Waste Land' you may not think he means it: my own impulse to write *Amen* at the end of a poem has been too often and too hardly curbed to leave any doubt in my mind as to Mr. Eliot's absorbed seriousness; he is fanatically in earnest. His 'Waste Land' is Childe Roland's evil ground, the names of all the lost adventurers his peers toll in his mind increasing like a bell. He has set the slug-horn to his lips and blown it once and twice: the squat, round tower, blind as the fool's heart, is watching him, but he will blow the horn again.

90
Notes for a Study of *The Waste Land*: an Imaginary Dialogue with T.S. Eliot*

HAROLD MONRO

1

An Imaginary Dialogue with T.S. Eliot
(*Mr. Eliot's answers are in Italics*)

I have just read your poem 'The Waste Land' five or six times. I don't suppose you consider me capable of understanding it?—*Well?*—I was much interested in your new periodical the 'Criterion,' in which it appeared, and I also saw it in the American 'Dial.'—*Well?*—I observed that in England it was treated chiefly with indignation or contempt, but that the 'Dial' awarded you its annual prize of two thousand dollars.—*Well?*

I suppose it is not very easy for those who have not read your book 'The Sacred Wood' to understand your poetry. Some insight into your mind is advisable.—*Possibly.*—An article appeared in a recent number of the 'Dial' purporting to elucidate your poem. Do you think that Mr. Edmund Wilson, Jr., the writer of that article, was justified in stating that (though it consists of little more than four hundred lines) it 'contains allusions to, parodies of, or quotations from' (here he enumerates thirty-three sources)?—*Possibly.*—I can only recognize a dozen or so. This may be because my reading is not sufficiently wide.—*Possibly.*—*Well?*

I have heard it suggested that you write for one hypothetical intelligent reader.—*Well?*—Do you think such a reader at present exists?—*I'm not sure.*—Do you think perhaps that he is yet to be born?—*That depends.*

I think you do your public an injustice. Presumably the Editors who

* *Chapbook* no. 34 (February 1923), pp. 20–4

awarded you that prize may be gifted with some intelligence?—*I am not prepared to judge.*—And Mr. Edmund Wilson, Jr., makes the assertion that your 'trivialities are more valuable than other people's epics.' He at any rate has an instinct for appreciation.—*I am not prepared to judge.*—Myself, I am inclined to think that some of your favourable critics, however unwillingly, do as much damage to your repu—*That doesn't matter anyway.*

Did you submit your poem to the 'London Mercury'?—*No.*—If you had, do you think the 'L.M.' would have accepted it?—*No.*—But if some friend of yours had submitted it for you, and if it had been accepted, would you have minded?—*Yes.*—Why?—*I don't know. It doesn't concern me.*

Let me see: where are we now? I was saying—*I haven't heard you say anything much yet.*—Very well: I was about to say that 'The Waste Land' seems to me as near to Poetry as our generation is at present capable of reaching. But, thinking about it the other evening, I suddenly remembered a sentence from 'The Sacred Wood': 'the moment an idea has been transferred from its pure state in order that it may become comprehensible to the inferior intelligence it has lost contact with art.' And then, another: 'It is not in his personal emotions, the emotions provoked by particular events in his life, that the poet is in any way remarkable or interesting.' These and other similar passages almost make one feel that one ought not to be appreciative, as if, indeed, it were low and vulgar to enjoy a work of literature for its own sake.—*That depends upon the condition of your mind, and the kind of enjoyment you feel.*—You, no doubt, felt nothing personal in writing 'The Waste Land'?—*No doubt.*—But, Mr. Eliot, surely your disgust for the society that constitutes the world of to-day may be described as a personal emotion?—*If you refer to 'The Sacred Wood' again you will find this sentence: 'Honest criticism and sensitive appreciation is directed not upon the poet but upon the poetry.'*

I am completely in agreement with it.

May I direct some criticism upon your poem? But first I should mention that I know it was not written for me. You never thought of me as among your potential appreciative audience. You thought of nobody, and you were true to yourself. Yet, in a sense, you did think of me. You wanted to irritate me, because I belong to the beastly age in which you are doomed to live. But, in another sense, your poem seems calculated more to annoy Mr. Gosse, or Mr. Squire, than me. I imagine them exclaiming: 'The fellow *can* write; but he *won't.*' That would be because just when you seem to be amusing yourself by composing what they might call *poetry*, at that moment you generally break off with a sneer. And, of course, they can't realise that your faults are as virtuous as their virtues are wicked, nor that your style is, as it were, a mirror that distorts the perfections they admire, which are in truth only imitations of perfections. Your truest passages seem to them like imitations of imperfections. I am not indulging in personalities, but only using those gentlemen as symbols.—*Well, direct your criticisms anywhere you like. You are becoming slightly amusing, but not yet worth answering. . . .*

The Waste Land (1922)

2

Most poems of any significance leave one definite impression on the mind. This poem makes a variety of impressions, many of them so contradictory that a large majority of minds will never be able to reconcile them, or conceive of it as an entity. Those minds will not go beyond wondering why it so often breaks itself up violently, changes its tone and apparently its subject. It will remain for them a *pot-pourri* of descriptions and episodes, and while deprecating the lack of *style*, those people will console themselves with soft laughter. That influential London Editor-critic who dismissed it as 'an obscure but amusing poem' is an instance.

Obscure it is, and amusing it can be too; but neither quite in the way he seems to have meant. They who have only one definition for the word poem may gnash their teeth, or smile. One definition will not be applicable to 'The Waste Land.' Of course, most poets write of *dreaming*, and use the expression that they *dream* in its conventional rhetorical sense, but this poem actually is a dream presented without any poetic boast, bluff or padding; and it lingers in the mind more like a dream than a poem, which is one of the reasons why it is both obscure and amusing. It is not possible to see it whole except in the manner that one may watch a cloud which, though remaining the same cloud, changes its form repeatedly as one looks. Or to others it may appear like a drawing that is so crowded with apparently unrelated details that the design or meaning (if there be one) cannot be grasped until those details have been absorbed into the mind, and assembled and related to each other.

3

A friend came to me with the discovery that he and I could not hope to understand Mr. Eliot's poems; we had not the necessary culture: impossible for us to recognise the allusions. I asked him whether the culture could be grown in a bottle or under a frame, or in the open. Mr. Edmund Wilson, Jr., tells us, on the other hand, that 'it is not necessary to know . . . any but the most obvious of Mr. Eliot's allusions to feel the force of the intense emotion which the poem is intended to convey.' I was inclined to side with Mr. Wilson, so we confined ourselves to discussing the permissibility of introducing, as Mr. Eliot does, into the body of a poem, wholly or partly, or in a distorted form, quotations from other poems. 'In the absence of inverted commas,' said my friend, 'the ignorant, when they are French quotations (seeing that Mr. Eliot has written several French poems) or German even, might mistake them for lines belonging to the poem itself. It is simple cribbing. The distortions are more serious still. For instance

> *When lovely woman stoops to folly and*
> *Paces about the room again, alone,*
> *She smooths her hair with automatic hand,*
> *And puts a record on the gramophone.*

is an outrage, and a joke worthier of 'Punch' than of a serious poet. Also I much prefer the Bible, Spenser, Shakespeare, Marvell and Byron to Eliot. Marvell wrote:

> *But at my back I always hear*
> *Time's wingèd chariot hurrying near.*

Eliot writes:

> *But at my back in a cold blast I hear*
> *The rattle of the bones, and chuckle spread from ear to ear.*

Well, that is simply a meretricious travesty of one of the most beautiful couplets in English poetry. It is wicked.'

I answered: 'It is only a natural jeer following upon an exposure of emotion. A schoolboy is hardly as nervous of showing his feelings. The matter cannot be judged in your manner. What we have to find out is whether T.S. Eliot is a sufficiently constructive or imaginative, or ingenious poet to justify this freedom that he exercises.'

He answered: 'Yes, but . . .

> *But at my back I always hear*
> *Eliot's intellectual sneer.*

—Now I'm doing it myself.'

4

This poem is at the same time a representation, a criticism, and the disgusted outcry of a heart turned cynical. It is calm, fierce, and horrible: the poetry of despair itself become desperate. Those poor little people who string their disjointed ejaculations into prosaic semblances of verse—they pale as one reads 'The Waste Land.' They have no relation to it: yet, through it, we realise that they were trying, but have failed, to represent. Our epoch sprawls, a desert, between an unrealised past and an unimaginable future. The Waste Land is one metaphor with a multiplicity of interpretations.

5

These are the opening lines:

> *April is the cruellest month, breeding*
> *Lilacs out of the dead land, mixing*
> *Memory and desire, stirring*
> *Dull roots with spring rain.*
> *Winter kept us warm, covering*
> *Earth in forgetful snow, feeding*
> *A little life with dried tubers.*

91
A Contrast*

♦

HARRIET MONROE

It happens that I have read these two books[1]—but neither for the first time—under the same lightly veiled sunshine of this mild winter afternoon; and the contrasts between them are so complete and so suggestive that I am tempted toward the incongruity of reviewing them together.

In the important title-poems of the two we have an adequate modern presentation of two immemorial human types. One might call these types briefly the indoor and the outdoor man, but that would be incomplete; they are also the man who affirms and the man who denies; the simple-hearted and the sophisticated man; the doer, the believer, and the observant and intellectual questioner. These two types have faced each other since time began and they will accuse each other till quarrels are no more. Both, in their highest development, are dreamers, men commanded by imagination; seers who are aware of their age, who know their world. Yet always they are led by separating paths to opposite instincts and conclusions.

Mr. Eliot's poem—kaleidoscopic, profuse, a rattle and rain of colors that fall somehow into place—gives us the malaise of our time, its agony, its conviction of futility, its wild dance on an ash-heap before a clouded and distorted mirror.

I will show you fear in a handful of dust,

he cries, and he shows us confusion and dismay and disintegration, the world crumbling to pieces before our eyes and patching itself with desperate gayety into new and strangely irregular forms. He gives us, with consummate distinction, what many an indoor thinker thinks about life today, what whole groups of impassioned intellectuals are saying to each other as the great ball spins.

Yet all the time there are large areas of mankind to whom this thinking does not apply; large groups of another kind of intellectuals whose faith is as vital and constructive as ever was the faith of their crusading forefathers. To the men of science, the inventors, the engineers, who are performing today's

*Poetry 21 (March 1923), pp. 325–30.

miracles, the miasma which afflicts Mr. Eliot is as remote a speculative conceit, as futile a fritter of mental confectionery, as Lyly's euphemism must have been to Elizabethan sailors. And these men are thinkers too, dreamers of larger dreams than any group of city-closeted artists may evoke out of the circling pipe-smoke of their scented talk. These men are creating that modern world which the half-aware and over-informed poets of London and Montmartre so darkly doom.

It is their spiritual attitude which Mr. Sarett's poem presents—not statedly and consciously, but by a larger and more absolute implication than he may be aware of. 'The Box of God' is an outdoor man's poem of faith—the creed of the pioneer, of the explorer, the discoverer, the inventor in whatever field; of the man who sees something beckoning ahead, and who must follow it, wherever it leads; of the hero who has the future in his keeping, who, though called by different names in different ages, is always the same type. Mr. Sarett makes an Indian guide his spokesman—an Indian guide who rebels against confinement in that ritualistic 'box of God', the little Catholic church in the mountains in which his 'conversion' has been registered.

> *Somebody's dere. . . . He's walk-um in dose cloud. . . .*
> *You see-um? Look! He's mak'-um for hees woman*
> *De w'ile she sleep, dose t'ing she want-um most—*
> *Blue dress for dancing. You see, my frien'? . . . ain't?*
> *He's t'rowing on de blanket of dose sky*
> *Dose plenty-plenty handfuls of white stars;*
> *He's sewing on dose plenty teet' of elk,*
> *Dose shiny looking-glass and plenty beads.*
> *Somebody's dere . . . somet'ing he's in dere . . .*
>
> *Sh-sh-sh-sh! Somet'ing's dere!. . . . You hear-um? ain't?*
> *Somebody—somebody's dere, calling . . . calling . . .*
> *I go . . . I go . . . me! . . . me . . . I go. . . .*

In primitive times the bard was aware of this man—he sang his deeds in heroic song. If the modern bard is not aware of him, the lack is due, not to superior intellectual subtlety, but to myopic vision, narrow experience and closely imprisoned thought. Mr. Eliot lives with specialists—poets of idle hands and legs and supersensitized brains; varied by a bank clerk routine with second-rate minds. One can not imagine him consorting with heroes or highwaymen, or getting on intimate terms with Thomas A. Edison if he were granted a confidential hour; and it is hopeless to expect an all-round great poem of our time from a man who could not thrill at such a contact.

Mr. Sarett's poem is not about Thomas A. Edison either; but the spirit of such men is in it, and something of the force of the world-builder, wherever he is found. We live in a period of swift and tremendous change: if Mr. Eliot feels it as chaos and disintegration, and a kind of wild impudent dance-of-death joy, Mr. Sarett feels it as a new and larger summons to faith in life and art. This poet has lived with guides and Indians; last summer, while taking his vacation as a forest ranger of the government, he chased a pair of bandits through Glacier Park for forty-eight hours alone, and single-handed brought them back to camp for trial. He could talk with Thomas A. Edison, or perhaps with a sequoia or a skyscraper. He has the experience and character-equipment to write poems expressive of the particular kind of heroic spirit which is building the future while nations are painfully digging their way out of the past. 'The Box of God' is one such poem; and in it his art, while less fluid and fluent and iridescent than Mr. Eliot's, is of a rich and nobly beautiful pattern and texture which suggests that he may prove adequate to the task. One feels that he is merely at the beginning, that he is just getting into his stride.

But I would not be understood as belittling the importance of Mr. Eliot's glistening, swiftly flowing poem of human and personal agony because it does not say the whole thing about the age we live in. Mr. Eliot would be the first to disclaim such an intention—he would probably say that 'The Waste Land' is the reaction of a suffering valetudinarian to the present after-the-war chaos in Europe, with its tumbling-down of old customs and sanctities. It is a condition, not a theory, which confronts him; and he meets the condition with an artist's invocation of beauty. One would expect a certain deliberateness in Mr. Eliot's art, but this poem surprises with an effect of unstudied spontaneity. While stating nothing, it suggests everything that is in his rapidly moving mind, in a series of shifting scenes which fade in and out of each other like the cinema. The form, with its play of many-colored lights on words that flash from everywhere in the poet's dream, is a perfect expression of the shifting scenes which fade in and out of each other like the cinema. The form, with its play of many-colored lights on words that flash from everywhere in the poet's dream, is a perfect expression of the shifting tortures in his soul. If one calls 'The Waste Land' a masterpiece of decadent art, the word must be taken as praise, for decadent art, while always incomplete, only half-interpretive, is pitifully beautiful and tragically sincere. The agony and bitter splendor of modern life are in this poem, of that part of it which dies of despair while the world is building its next age.

If Mr. Eliot's subject is essentially a phantasmagoric fade-out of God, Mr. Sarett's is the search for God, for a larger god than men have ever entrapped in the churchly boxes they have made for him. Both poems are, in a sense, the poet's meditations, interrupted by the intrusion of remembered words once uttered by others: in Sarett's case by the long-dead Indian guide, in Eliot's by Lil's husband, by Mrs. Porter, by Shakespeare, Spenser, Dante, Baudelaire, and many other poets of many languages. And both poems have a certain largeness and finality: they do excellent-well what they set out to do, and they suggest more than they say—they invite to thought and dreams.

The Waste Land (1922)

Note

1. 'The Waste Land' and 'The Box of God' by Lew Sarett.

92
Waste Lands*

———— ♦ ————

JOHN CROWE RANSOM

The imagination of a creative artist may play over the surface of things or it may go very deep, depending on the quality and the availability of the artist's mind. Here is fiction, for example, wherein the artist, its author, is going to recite a local body of fact; and this core of fact is not more definitely related to space and time by the illusions of his realism than it already has been related to the whole emotional and philosophical contexts of his life. The thing has been assimilated into his history. It is no longer pure datum, pure spectacle, like a visitation of the angels or like categorical disaster; it does not ravish nor appall him; for it has been thoroughly considered by the artist, through processes both conscious and unconscious, and has been allowed to sink infallibly into its connections.

An appalling thing to Hamlet evidently was death. But Claudius enjoyed the insuperable advantage of being elder to the Prince of Denmark, and therefore could invite him to consider the King's death in the light of authentic evidence of the common mortality of fathers; *sub specie omnium patrum obitorum*. And Horatio, a man of superior practical instincts, to him marvelling how the grave digger could sing at his trade, was enabled to return the inspired answer: 'Custom hath made it in him a property of easiness.'

A property of easiness is what the artist must come to, against even the terrible and the ecstatic moments of history. A great discrimination of nature against America is this requirement, in the field of the comparative literatures; in pioneering America a tribal ethic pronounces that life is real, life is earnest. The property of easiness in the mind is one of the blessings that compensate an old and perfected society for the loss of its youth. And likewise with the individual artist, it comes with experience, and it comes notably with age; though not entirely as reckoned by the Gregorian calendar. The young artist is not to think that his synthesis of experience is worth as much as the old one's. He is not to put an extravagant value on the freshness of his youthful passions, but to make sure that the work of art

***New York Evening Post Literary Review* 3 (14 July 1923), pp. 825–6. Reprinted in Christopher Morley (ed.), *Modern Essays, Second Series* (New York, 1924), pp. 345–59.

wants for its material the passion mellowed and toned and understood long after the event: 'recollected in tranquility,' to use the best of all the literary dogmas. A soul-shaking passion is very good if the artist will wait for it to age; the bigger the passion the deeper it will go in the integrating processes of the mind, and the wider will be the branching associations it will strike out. When it comes forth eventually it will have depth and context, too. It has been fertilized and romanticized. It has been made musical, or symphonic, where, before it gained its subsidiary pieces and was itself subdued to harmony, it was only monotone and meant nothing to delicate ears.

There is a subterranean chamber where the work of artistic gestation takes place. It has always been held that the artist draws for his sources from a depth beyond the fathom of the consciously reasoning mind. An immense literature to this effect—or at least the English fraction of it—has recently been minutely reported by Professor Prescott in 'The Poetic Mind'; and it is an application of the same principle, though quite spontaneous and fresh, which gives the English poet Robert Graves his doctrine of inspiration. We are not to dogmatize about this subliminal consciousness; the psychologists are terribly at sea in defining it; probably it is wrong to refer to it at all as a subconsciousness. Here we inevitably enter the province of pure theory; but critics have to have a revelation of first principles if they are going to speak with any authority about art.

Possibly the following statement of the case might be defended. At one moment we are conscious; but at the next moment we are self-conscious, or interested in the moment that is past, and we attempt to write it down. Science writes it down in one way, by abstracting a feature and trying to forget all the rest. Art writes it down in another way, by giving the feature well enough but by managing also to suggest the infinity of its original context. The excellence of science is its poverty, for it tries to carry only the abstractions into the record, but the excellence of art is its superfluity, since it accompanies these abstractions with much of that tissue of the concrete in which they were discovered. It is as if the thing will not live out of its own habitat, it is dead as soon as science hauls it up and handles it, but art tries to keep it alive by drawing up with it a good deal of its native element.

Today we are superbly in a position to consent to such a doctrine. Since James and Bradley and Bergson, since Kant if we have always had ears to hear, since the Carus Lectures of John Dewey if we only began to listen yesterday, it is borne in upon us that abstract science is incapable of placing the stream of consciousness—the source of all that is—upon the narrow tablets of the record. Art, too, in the last analysis is probably incapable, since at any moment it only complements the record of science and at no moment denies it, so that Coleridge, defining poetry as more than usual emotion, added the remarkable qualification, 'with more than usual order.' But art, if it is not destructive, is at least gently revolutionary. The specific of art which is enough to create its illusion and make it miraculous among the works of the mind is that it fishes out of the stream what would become the dead abstraction of science, but catches it still alive, and can exhibit to us not only its bones and structures but many of the free unaccountable motions of its life. These motions are the contributions that art makes to the record; these free and unpredictable associations discovered for the thing in its stream. They are impertinences to the scientific temper, but delightful to the soul that in the routine of scientific chores is oppressed with the sense of serving a godless and miserly master.

But returning to the level of practice, or the natural history of art. A man repeatedly must come to points where his science fails him, where his boasted intellect throws its little light and still leaves him in darkness; there is then nothing for him to do but to go off and sound the secret cavern for an oracle. That is to say, he abandons his problem to mysterious powers within him which are not the lean and labored processes of his self-conscious reason. And if this abandonment is complete the oracle will speak. After brief silence, after a sleep and a forgetting, but at all events with what must be considered an astonishing celerity, the answer comes out. It is a kind of revelation. He submitted facts, and he receives them related into truths. He deposited a raw realism; he receives it richly romanticized. Evidently the agency which worked for him simply referred his datum to a perfectly organized experience, where no item was missing, and returned it with a context of clinging natural affinities.

But the principle for the artist to proceed upon is that he must *release* his theme to the processes of imagination—a hard principle for the narrow-minded! He must wait like a non-partisan beside his theme, not caring whether it comes forth pro or con; and inevitably, of course, it will be neither. The truth that comes by inspiration is not simply the correct conclusion to premises already known; the Pythian never comes down to monosyllables and answers yes and no. The whole matter is worked over freshly by an agent more competent than reason and the conclusion is as unpredictable as the evidence was inaccessible. The man with a cause must abdicate before his genius will work for him. The history of inspiration does not offer cases where passions, even righteous passions, spasms of energy, rages and excitements, and even resolutions that seem likely to remove mountains have enabled artists to call the spirits from the vasty deep. History offers cases like Goethe's, who wrote, recalling certain moments in the composition of *Faust*: 'The difficulty was to obtain, by sheer force of will, what in reality is obtainable only by a spontaneous act of nature.' But this faculty of release is rare, and by the same token the artists are rare. Probably the history of most of the abortive efforts at art is the history of wilful men who could not abandon their cause, but continued to worry it as a dog worries a bone, expecting to perform by fingers and rules what can come by magic only. And release is peculiarly difficult for the hot blood of youth. The young artist stakes everything upon the heat of his passion and the purity of his fact. Very limited is the

The Waste Land (1922)

assistance which he is capable of receiving from his elders in speeding the tedious rites of time; he is convinced that *alla stoccata* will carry it away.

Other formulas would carry such first principles as well as these, and indeed, ideally, every critic could find them for himself. He needs them if he is to speak with a greater authority than we now hear him speaking. He needs to have a theory of inspiration in order that he may trace error back to its course, and show that the artist must always sin unless his heart is pure. The field of literature in our day—perhaps beyond all other days—is an unweeded garden, in which the flowers and weeds are allowed to grow side by side because the gardeners, who are the critics, do not know their botany. The commonest and fatallest error in the riot of our letters is the fundamental failure of the creative imagination, and it ought always to be exposed. Is it held that this sort of criticism would be too brutal? Is it equivalent to telling the artist that he is congenitally defective in the quality fundamental to art? It is not so bad as that; a part of the total error by which the artist misses his art may be due to the fact that his gift, which is genuine, is under the cloud of some inattention or poor policy, or, above all, immaturity, which is capable of treatment. But it does not matter; criticism should attend to its business anyway; criticism should be prepared to make an example of bad artists for the sake of the good artists and the future of art.

But what a congenial exercise is furnished the critic by that strange poem, 'The Waste Land.' In the first place, everybody agrees beforehand that its author is possessed of uncommon literary powers, and it is certain that, whatever credit the critic may try to take from him, a flattering residue will remain. And then his poem has won a spectacular triumph over a certain public and is entitled to an extra quantity of review. Best of all, Mr. Eliot's performance is the apotheosis of modernity, and seems to bring to a head all the specifically modern errors, and to cry for critic's ink of a volume quite disproportionate to its merits as a poem.

The most notable surface fact about 'The Waste Land' is of course its extreme disconnection. I do not know just how many parts the poem is supposed to have, but to me there are something like fifty parts which offer no bridges the one to the other and which are quite distinct in time, place, action, persons, tone, and nearly all the unities to which art is accustomed. This discreteness reaches also to the inside of the parts, where it is indicated by a frequent want of grammatical joints and marks of punctuation; as if it were the function of art to break down the usual singleness of the artistic image, and then to attack the integrity of the individual fragments. I presume that poetry has rarely gone further in this direction. It is a species of the same error which modern writers of fiction practice when they laboriously disconnect the stream of consciousness and present items which do not enter into wholes. Evidently they think with Hume that reality is facts and pluralism, not compounds and systems. But Mr. Eliot is more enterprising than they, because almost in so many words he assails the philosophical or cosmical principles under which we form the usual images of reality, naming the whole phantasmagoria Waste Land almost as plainly as if he were naming cosmos Chaos. His intention is evidently to present a wilderness in which both he and the reader may be bewildered, in which one is never to see the wood for the trees.

Against this philosophy—or negation of philosophy—the critic must stand fast. It is good for some purposes, but not for art. The mind of the artist is an integer, and the imaginative vision is a single act which fuses its elements. It is to be suspected that the author who holds his elements apart is not using his imagination, but using a formula, like a scientist anxious to make out a 'case'; at any rate, for art such a procedure suggests far too much strain and tension. For imagination things cohere; pluralism cannot exist when we relax our obsessions and allow such testimony as is in us to come out. Even the most refractory elements in experience, like the powerful opposing wills in a tragedy, arrive automatically at their 'higher synthesis' if the imagination is allowed to treat them.

There is a reason besides philosophical bias which makes the disconnection in the poem. The fragments could not be joined on any principle and remain what they are. And that is because they are at different stages of fertilization; they are not the children of a single act of birth. Among their disparities one notes that scraps from many tongues are juxtaposed; and yet one knows well that we are in different 'ages of intelligence' when we take the different languages on our lips; we do not quote Greek tragedy and modern cockney with the same breath or with the same kinds of mind. We cannot pass, in 'The Waste Land,' without a convulsion of the mind from 'O O O O that Shakespeherian Rag,' to 'Shantih shantih shantih.' And likewise, the fragments are in many metres, from the comparatively formal metre which we know as the medium of romantic experiences in the English thesaurus to an extremely free verse which we know as the medium of a half-hearted and disillusioned art. But, above all, some fragments are emotions recollected in tranquility and others are emotions kept raw and bleeding, like sores we continue to pick. In other words, the fragments vary through almost every stage, from pure realism to some point just short of complete fertilization by the romantic imagination, and this is a material which is incapable of synthesis.

A consequence of this inequality of material is a certain novelty of Mr. Eliot's which is not fundamentally different from parody. To parody is to borrow a phrase whose meaning lies on one plane of intelligence and to insert it into the context of a lower plane; an attempt to compound two incommensurable imaginative creations. Mr. Eliot inserts beautiful quotations into ugly contexts. For example:

> *When lovely woman stoops to folly, and*
> *Paces about her room again, alone,*
> *She smoothes her hair with automatic hand,*
> *And puts a record on the gramophone.*

The Waste Land (1922)

A considerable affront against aesthetic sensibilities. Using these lovely borrowed lines for his own peculiar purposes, Mr. Eliot debases them every time; there is not, I believe, a single occasion where his context is as mature as the quotation which he inserts into it; he does not invent such phrases for himself, nor, evidently, does his understanding quite appreciate them, for they require an organization of experience which is yet beyond him. The difficulty in which he finds himself is typically an American one. Our native poets are after novelty; they believe, as does Mr. Eliot in one of his prose chapters, that each age must have its own 'form.' The form in which our traditional poetry is cast is that of another generation and therefore Nothoroughfare. What the new form is to be they have not yet determined. Each of the new poets must experiment with a few usually, it appears, conceiving forms rather naïvely, as something which will give quick effects without the pains and delays of complete fertilization. Mr. Eliot has here tried out such a form and thereby reverted to the frailties of his nativity. The English poets, so far as they may be generalized, are still content to work under the old forms and, it must be said in their favor, it is purely an empirical question whether these are unfit for further use; the poets need not denounce them on principle. But it may be put to the credit of Mr. Eliot that he is a man of better parts generally than most of the new poets, as in the fact that he certainly bears no animus against the old poetry except as it is taken for a model by the new poets; he is sufficiently sensitive to its beauties at least to have held on with his memory to some of its ripest texts and to have introduced them rather wistfully into the forbidding context of his own poems, where they are thoroughly ill at ease.

The criticism does not complete itself till it has compared 'The Waste Land' with the earlier work of its author. The volume of 'Poems' which appeared a year previously hardly presaged the disordered work that was to follow. The discrepancy is astonishing. Sweeney and Prufrock, those heroes who bid so gayly for immortality in their own right, seem to come out of a fairly mature and at any rate an equal art. They are elegant and precious creations rather than substantial, with a very reduced emotional background, like the art of a man of the world rather than of a man of frankly poetic susceptibilities; but the putative author is at least responsible. He has 'arrived'; he has by self-discipline and the unconscious lessons of experience integrated his mind. The poem which comes a year later takes a number of years out of this author's history, restores him intellectually to his minority. I presume that 'The Waste Land,' with its burden of unregenerate fury, was disheartening to such critics as Mr. Aldington, who had found in the 'Poems' the voice of a completely articulate soul; I presume that for these critics the 'Poems' are automatically voided and recalled by the later testament; they were diabolically specious, and the true heart of the author was to be revealed by a very different gesture. But I prefer to think that they were merely precocious. They pretended to an intellectual synthesis of which the

Early Poems and *The Waste Land*

author was only intellectually aware, but which proved quite too fragile to contain the ferment of experience. One prefers 'The Waste Land' after all, for of the two kinds it bears the better witness to its own sincerity.

'The Waste Land' is one of the most insubordinate poems in the language, and perhaps it is the most unequal. But I do not mean in saying this to indicate that it is permanently a part of the language; I do not entertain that as a probability. The genius of our language is notoriously given to feats of hospitality: but it seems to me it will be hard pressed to find accommodations at the same time for two such incompatibles as Mr. Wordsworth and the present Mr. Eliot; and any realist must admit that what happens to be the prior tenure of the mansion in this case is likely to be stubbornly defended.

93
Waste Lands*

ALLEN TATE

Sir: John Crowe Ransom's article, Waste Lands, in the 'Literary Review' of July 14, violates so thoroughly the principle of free critical inquiry and at the same time does such scant justice to the school of so-called philosophic criticism, to which one supposes he belongs, that it may be of interest to your readers to consider the possible fallacy of his method and a few of the errors into which it leads him.

Mr. Ransom begins by building up a rather thorough-going schematism of the origin and process of artistic creation, and though he grants that 'other formulas would carry first principles just as well as these,' he urges that the critic, 'needs a theory of inspiration, in order that he may trace error back to its source.' The maker of these phrases evidently knows nothing of the genetic criticism since the day of Wundt or of the Freudian emphasis of later days on the psychological origins of art as a standard of aesthetics; at any rate, he is unaware of the ultimate futility of this kind of inquiry when its results are dragged in to serve as critical arbiters. Theories of inspiration are valuable, though less so than interesting, but Mr. Ransom, it seems to me, has offered only an abstract restatement of superannuate theories of consciousness, which do not constitute a theory of inspiration—whatever such a theory may be: all to the end that a philosophy of discontinuity is not only lamentable but entirely wrong. What this has to do with aesthetics it is hard to conceive. But Mr. Ransom rightly says that the critic 'should be prepared to make an example of the bad artists for the sake of the good artists'; but this example cannot be made by exorcising pluralism to the advantage of a gentler but equally irrelevant ghost: 'For the imagination things cohere; pluralism cannot exist when we relax our obsessions and allow such testimony as is in us to come out.' In other words, no honest man can be a pluralist—which is not only palpably untenable but quite outside the course of his argument. And if we *have* heeded too little the Carus lectures of John Dewey or failed to let the mire of Kantianism cling to our feet, what is Mr. Ransom going to do about the writings of Remy de

---

*New York Evening Post Literary Review 3 (4 August 1923), p. 886. A reply to Ransom.

Gourmont and, closer home, certain words uttered as far back as 1896 by Mr. George Santayana? And isn't it difficult to see how Professor Prescott and Robert Graves (!) can be heeded along with Kant and Bradley?

And coming to 'The Waste Land' itself, Mr. Ransom is quite consistent in so far as he condemns the poem for its anti-philosophical *mélouge*. He wonders why T.S. Eliot is chaotic in his verse and so rigidly coherent in his prose, and accounts for the discrepancy on the doubtful ground that T.S. Eliot is determined to exploit pluralism at all costs, even at the risk of being charged with insincerity. Doubtless Mr. Ransom knows the difference between the instrument, Logic, and the material, Reality; but I do not believe he shows it here. I take it that Keats wrote about as incoherent prose as we have, yet in certain odes he gives us Mr. Ransom's 'higher synthesis': how would Mr. Ransom explain this? I suppose Keats was insincere in his letters because he exposes a multiverse. Mr. Ransom asks whether this sort of criticism would be too brutal. Well not so brutal as irrelevant.

The real trouble with Mr. Ransom's article comes out when he proceeds to comment on specific aspects of 'The Waste Land.' Mr. Eliot is a pluralist; he has not 'achieved' a philosophy; *argal*, he is immature, and his poem is inconsiderable. I take it that Anatole France is immature. But Mr. Ransom's worry on this point really is his inability to discover the form of the poem, for, says he, it presents metres so varied and such lack of grammar and punctuation and such a bewildering array of discrete themes, that he is at loss to see the poem as one poem at all. Whatever form may be, it is not, I dare say, regularity of metre. Artistic forms are ultimately attitudes, and when Mr. Ransom fails to understand Mr. Eliot's purpose in using lines from other poets, like 'When lovely woman stoops to folly,' calling it parody, we are aware of a naivete somewhat grosser than that which he ascribes elsewhere in his essay to modern experimentation generally. He makes his point by a highly imaginative *petitio principii*: the fragments are at different stages of 'fertilization' and represent different levels of intelligence; and then, too, Eliot inserts these quotations into a context never so rich as their proper abode. Is it possible that Mr. Ransom thinks that these beautiful fragments were put into 'The Waste Land' simply to lend it a 'beauty' which its author could not achieve for himself? And is he confusing parody with irony? His definition of parody, without the dogmatic implication that one plane of consciousness is 'higher' than another, is really a definition of irony: the incongruous is not always the deformed or ludicrous. And it is probably true that metres are never more than an organic scaffolding upon which the poet hangs an attitude; the 'form' of 'The Waste Land' is this ironic attitude which Mr. Ransom relegates to the circus of Carolyn Wells. My remarks here are excessive; at this point in Mr. Ransom's argument we suspect that he should not be taken seriously.

It is to be regretted also that T.S. Eliot repudiates his first volume *ipso facto* by writing 'The Waste Land.' The only discoverable difference between

The Waste Land (1922)

'Poems' and 'The Waste Land' is certainly not one of central attitude. Mr. Eliot, an intellectual romanticist, need not commit himself to the same intuition of the world to-day as yesterday; he must shift all the time, for his motive is curiosity, not prepossession, even though he is driven always by the same thirst. The free intelligence cannot harbor a closed system.

And if tradition means sameness, then Mr. Eliot cannot survive with Wordsworth. But Mr. Ransom doesn't say just where it is that poems survive. However, it is likely that the value of 'The Waste Land' as art is historical rather than intrinsic, but the point of my objection to John Crowe Ransom's essay is that the method he employs is not likely to give T.S. Eliot much concern. And my excuse for this extended objection is that Mr. Ransom is not alone. He is a *genre*.

94
A Fragmentary Poem*

ANON (EDGELL RICKWORD)

Between the emotion from which a poem rises and the reader there is always a cultural layer of more or less density from which the images or characters in which it is expressed may be drawn. In the ballad 'I wish I were where Helen lies' this middle ground is but faintly indicated. The ballad, we say is *simpler* than the 'Ode to the Nightingale'; it evokes very directly an emotional response. In the ode the emotion gains resonance from the atmosphere of legendary association through which it passes before reaching us. It cannot be called better art, but it is certainly more sophisticated and to some minds less poignant. From time to time there appear poets and a poetic audience to whom this refractory haze of allusion must be very dense; without it the meanings of the words strike them so rapidly as to be inappreciable, just as, without the air, we could not detect the vibration of light. We may remember with what elaboration Addison, among others, was obliged to undertake the defence of the old ballads before it was recognized that their bare style might be admired by gentlemen familiar with the classics.

The poetic personality of Mr. Eliot is extremely sophisticated. His emotions hardly ever reach us without traversing a zig-zag of allusion. In the course of his four hundred lines he quotes from a score of authors and in three foreign languages, though his artistry has reached that point at which it knows the wisdom of sometimes concealing itself. There is in general in his work a disinclination to wake in us a direct emotional response. It is only, the reader feels, out of regard for some one else that he has been induced to mount the platform at all. From there he conducts a magic-lantern show; but being too reserved to expose in public the impressions stamped on his own soul by the journey through the Waste Land, he employs the slides made by others, indicating with a touch the difference between his reaction and theirs. So the familiar stanza of Goldsmith becomes

When lovely woman stoops to folly and
Paces about her room again, alone,

---

* *Times Literary Supplement* no. 1131 (20 September 1923), p. 616.

She smoothes her hair with automatic hand,
And puts a record on the gramophone.

To help us to elucidate the poem Mr. Eliot has provided some notes which will be of more interest to the pedantic than the poetic critic. Certainly they warn us to be prepared to recognize some references to vegetation ceremonies. This is the cultural or middle layer, which, whilst it helps us to perceive the underlying emotion, is of no poetic value in itself. We desire to touch the inspiration itself, and if the apparatus of reserve is too strongly constructed, it will defeat the poet's end. The theme is announced frankly enough in the title, 'The Waste Land'; and in the concluding confession,

These fragments I have shored against my ruins,

we receive a direct communication which throws light on much which had preceded it. From the opening part, 'The Burial of the Dead,' to the final one we seem to see a world, or a mind, in disaster and mocking its despair. We are aware of the toppling of aspirations, the swift disintegration of accepted stability, the crash of an ideal. Set at a distance by a poetic method which is reticence itself, we can only judge of the strength of the emotion by the visible violence of the reaction. Here is Mr. Eliot, a dandy of the choicest phrase, permitting himself blatancies like 'the young man carbuncular.' Here is a poet capable of a style more refined than that of any of his generation parodying without taste or skill—and of this the example from Goldsmith is not the most astonishing. Here is a writer to whom originality is almost an inspiration borrowing the greater number of his best lines, creating hardly any himself. It seems to us as if the 'The Waste Land' exists in the greater part in the state of notes. This quotation is a particularly obvious instance:—

London Bridge is falling down falling down falling down
Poi s'ascose nel foco che gli affina
Quando fiam uti chelidon—O swallow swallow
Le Prince d'Aquitaine à la tour abolie

The method has a number of theoretical justifications. Mr. Eliot has himself employed it discreetly with delicious effect. It suits well the disillusioned smile which he had in common with Laforgue; but we do sometimes wish to hear the poet's full voice. Perhaps if the reader were sufficiently sophisticated he would find these echoes suggestive hints, as rich in significance as the sonorous amplifications of the romantic poets. None the less, we do not derive from his poem as a whole the satisfaction we ask from poetry. Numerous passages are finely written; there is an amusing monologue in the vernacular, and the fifth part is nearly wholly admirable. The section beginning

What is that sound high in the air . . .

has a nervous strength which perfectly suits the theme; but he declines to a mere notation, the result of an indolence of the imagination.

Mr. Eliot, always evasive of the grand manner, has reached a stage at which he can no longer refuse to recognize the limitations of his medium; he is sometimes walking very near the limits of coherency. But it is the finest horses which have the most tender mouths, and some unsympathetic tug has sent Mr. Eliot's gift awry. When he recovers control we shall expect his poetry to have gained in variety and strength from this ambitious experiment.

95
T.S. Eliot*

CLIVE BELL

To be amongst the first to think, say, or do anything, is one of the silliest and most harmless of human ambitions: I was one of the first in England to sing the praises of Eliot. I shall not forget going down to a country house for the Easter of 1916—or was it '17?—with 'Prufrock' in my pocket, and hearing it read aloud to a circle of guests with whose names I am too modest to bribe your good opinion. Only this I will say, no poet could ask for a better send off. 'The Love Song of J. Alfred Prufrock' was read aloud two or three times and discussed at intervals; it was generally admired or, at any rate, allowed to be better than anything of the sort that had been published for some time: and it pleases me to remember that its two most ardent admirers were a distinguished mathematician (not Bertrand Russell) and an exquisite lady of fashion.

To me 'Prufrock' seemed a minor masterpiece which raised immense and permissible hopes: my opinion has not changed, but my hopes have dwindled slightly. For, as yet, Eliot has written nothing better than 'Prufrock,' which seems less surprising when we discover that, in a sense, he has written nothing else;—for the last seven years, I mean, he has been more or less repeating himself. He has lost none of the qualities which made me then describe him as 'about the best of our younger poets'; his intelligence and wit are as sharp as ever, and his phrasing is still superior to that of any of his contemporaries: but he has not improved.

Eliot, it seems to me, has written nothing wittier, more brilliantly evocative of a subtle impression, than 'Mr. Apollinax'; and that, I believe, he wrote before he came to England. It is proper to add that if in this style he has not improved upon himself, neither has anyone, in the interval, improved upon him. As for phrasing—a term which in this case I prefer to 'diction' (musicians will understand why)—it is his great accomplishment; and if you will open 'Prufrock' at the very first page you will come on the following passage:—

*Nation and Athenaeum 33 (22 September 1923), pp. 772–3.

Let us go, through certain half-deserted streets,
The muttering retreats
Of restless nights in one-night cheap hotels
And sawdust restaurants with oyster-shells:
Streets that follow like a tedious argument
Of insidious intent
To lead you to an overwhelming question . . .

than which, in my opinion, he has done nothing better. Before contradicting me let the reader count at least ten, and give his memory a jog. In Mr. Eliot's later poems he will find, to be sure, better phrases than any of these; but is he sure they are by Mr. Eliot? The poet has a disconcerting habit of omitting inverted commas. 'Defunctive music,' for instance, is from Shakespeare; and not only the Elizabethans are laid under contribution. The other day a rather intemperate admirer quoted at me the line,

'The army of unalterable law,'

and declared that no modern could match it. You know it is by Meredith.

If you will read carefully Eliot's three longer poems—'Prufrock,' 'Gerontion,' and 'The Waste Land'—I think you will see what I mean—even if you do not agree with me—in saying that he has been more or less repeating himself. And here we come at Eliot's essential defect. He lacks imagination; Dryden would have said 'invention,' and so will I if you think it would sweeten my discourse. Eliot belongs to that anything but contemptible class of artists whose mills are perfect engines in perpetual want of grist. He cannot write in the great manner out of the heart of his subject; his verse cannot gush as a stream from the rock: birdlike he must pile up wisps and straws of recollection round the tenuous twig of a central idea. And for these wisps and straws he must go generally to books. His invention, it would seem, cannot be eked out with experience, because his experience, too, is limited. His is not a receptive nature to experience greatly. Delicate and sensitive admirers have found, I know, the key to a lifelong internal tragedy in those lines with their choice Elizabethan tang:—

I that was near your heart was removed therefrom
To lose beauty in terror, terror in inquisition.
I have lost my passion: why should I need to keep it
Since what is kept must be adulterated?

But for my part, I cannot believe they are wrung from the heart of tragic experience. The despairing tone which pervades Eliot's poetry is not, it seems to me, so much the despair of disillusionment as the morbidity of 'The Yellow Book.'

But how the man can write! And the experience, if it be small, is perfectly digested and assimilated; it has gone into the blood and bones of his work.

The Waste Land (1922)

Admit that the butter is spread unconscionably thin; at least the poet may claim, with the mad hatter, that it was the best butter. By his choice of words, by his forging of phrases, by his twisting, stretching, and snapping of rhythms—manipulations possible only to an artist with an exact ear—Eliot can make out of his narrow vision and meagre reaction things of perpetual beauty.

> *At the violet hour, the evening hour that strives*
> *Homeward, and brings the sailor home from sea,*
> *The typist home at teatime, clears her breakfast, lights*
> *Her stove, and lays out food in tins.*

(Mark the transition—the technical one I mean—the stress and scarcely adumbrated stress—'HOMEward, and brings the sailor *home* from sea, the typist *home* at teatime,' so as to run on in a breath 'clears her breakfast.' A less dexterous artist would have had to break the flow with a full stop to show that he had changed the subject.) The line,

> *Her drying combinations touched by the sun's last rays,*

is a piece of obvious comic-weekly humour, unworthy of so fastidious a writer. But try a line or two lower down:

> *He, the young man carbuncular, arrives,*
> *A small house-agent's clerk, with one bold stare,*
> *One of the low on whom assurance sits*
> *As a silk hat on a Bradford millionaire.*

In its own modern way it is as neat as Pope, and one can almost see Mr. Arnold Bennett going to the races. I should be surprised if Eliot were ever to write a great poem; but he might easily write three or four which would take their place amongst the most perfect in our language.

Eliot reminds me of Landor: I believe he will not disdain the comparison. Landor wrote half-a-dozen of the most perfect poems in English, and reams of impeccable dullness. Like Eliot he had very little imagination or invention; a narrow vision and, as a rule, tepid reactions; unlike Eliot he was incontinent. Spiritually, he looked out of the window of a suburban villa on the furniture of a suburban garden: the classical statue he set up in the middle of the grass plot was more often than not a cast. No, it was something more spacious than a villa garden; but it bore a horrid likeness to a public park. Yet, on the rare occasions when Landor could apprehend the humdrum world he inhabited with something like passion, his art enabled him to create a masterpiece. There is not much more feeling or understanding of feeling in 'The Maid's Lament' than may be found in a prize copy of elegiacs by an accomplished sixth-form boy; most of the sentiments have grown smooth in circulation, and the images ('the shades of death,' 'this lorn bosom burns,' 'tears that had melted his soft heart,' 'more cold than daisies in the mould') have been the small change of minor poetry these three hundred years: yet 'The Maid's Lament' justly takes its place in 'The Oxford Book of Verse.'

Eliot is said to be obscure; and certainly 'The Waste Land' does not make easy reading. This I deplore, holding, with the best of English critics, that 'wit is most to be admired when a great thought comes dressed in words so commonly received that it is understood by the meanest apprehensions.' Only let us not forget that 'Prufrock' which at first seemed almost unintelligible, now seems almost plain sailing, and that 'Sweeney Erect,' which was described as 'gibberish,' turns out to be a simple and touching story; so when we cudgel our brains over his latest work let us hesitate to suppose that we cudgel in vain. It was decided, remember, that Gray's odes were quite incomprehensible; so were 'In Memoriam' and 'The Egoist'; and the instrumentalists—those practical experts—assured the conductor that no orchestra ever would play Beethoven's symphonies, for the very simple reason that they were unplayable. I respect the man who admits that he finds Eliot's poetry stiff; him who from its obscurity argues insincerity and mystification I take for an ass.

Turn to Eliot's criticism ('The Sacred Wood') if you want proof of his sincerity, and of one or two more qualities of his. Here he gives you some of the most interesting criticism and quite the silliest conclusions going. Here is a highly conscious artist, blessed with an unusually capable intellect and abnormal honesty, whose analysis of poetical methods is, therefore, bound to be masterly; who is never flabby, and who never uses well-sounding and little-meaning phrases to describe a quality in a work of art or a state of his own mind. Eliot is an exceptional critic. Unluckily, he is a cubist. Like the cubists, he is intent upon certain important and neglected qualities in art; these he detects unerringly, and he has no eyes for any others. His vision, you remember, was said to be narrow. He has an *a priori* theory, which is no sillier than any other *a priori* theory, and he applies it unmercifully. It leads him into telling us that 'Coriolanus' is better than 'Hamlet' and 'The Faithful Shepherdess' than 'Lycidas'—it leads him into absurdity. His conclusions are worthless; the argument and analysis by which he arrives at them are extraordinarily valuable. As in his poetry, in criticism his powerful but uncapacious mind can grasp but one thing at a time; that he grasps firmly. He disentangles with the utmost skill an important, hardly come at, and too often neglected quality in poetry; and if it were the only quality in poetry he would be almost the pontiff his disciples take him for. Not quite— for no aesthetic theory can explain his indiscreet boosting of the insignificant Miss Sinclair and the lamentable Ezra Pound. These predilections can be explained only by a less intelligent, though still perfectly honourable, misconception.

96
Poetry*

◆

J.C. SQUIRE

I read Mr. Eliot's poem several times when it first appeared; I have now read it several times more; I am still unable to make head or tail of it. Passages might easily be extracted from it which would make it look like one of those wantonly affected productions which are written by persons whose one hope of imposing on the credulous lies in the cultivation of a deliberate singularity. It is impossible to feel that when one reads the whole thing: it may bewilder and annoy, but it must leave the impression on any open-minded person that Mr. Eliot does mean something by it, has been at great pains to express himself, and believes himself to be exploring a new avenue (though we may think it a dark cul-de-sac) of poetic treatment. The work is now furnished with an extensive apparatus of notes. There are references to Ezekiel, Marvell, 'The Inferno,' Ovid, Wagner, St. Augustine, Sir James Frazer, and the Grail legend. But though these will tell those who do not know where Mr. Eliot got his quotations and symbolism from, they do not explain what these allusions are here for. The legend about the Cumæan Sibyl, which Rossetti paraphrased in verse, combined with the title and one casual reference, suggest that Mr. Eliot believes the poem to be about the decay of Western civilisation and his own utter sickness with life. But even with this knowledge I confess that I do not see where it comes in. There is a vagrant string of drab pictures which abruptly change, and these are interspersed with memories of literature, lines from old poets, and disconnected ejaculations.

[...]

Conceivably, what is attempted here is a faithful transcript, after Mr. Joyce's obscurer manner, of the poet's wandering thoughts when in a state of erudite depression. A grunt would serve equally well; what is language but communication, or art but selection and arrangement? I give it up; but it is a pity that a man who can write as well as Mr. Eliot writes in this poem should be so bored (not passionately disgusted) with existence that he doesn't mind what comes next, or who understands it. If I were to write a similar poem

London Mercury 8 (October 1923), pp. 655–6. From a longer review.

about this poem the first line from another work which would stray into the medley would be Mr. Chesterton's emphatic refrain 'Will someone take me to a pub?' The printing of the book is scarcely worthy of the Hogarth Press.

97
The Waste Land*

◆

F.L. LUCAS

'Solitudinem faciunt, poëma *appellant.'*

Among the maggots that breed in the corruption of poetry one of the commonest is the bookworm. When Athens had decayed and Alexandria sprawled, the new giant-city, across the Egyptian sands; when the Greek world was filling with libraries and emptying of poets, growing in erudition as its genius expired, then first appeared, as pompous as Herod and as worm-eaten, that *Professorenpoesie* which finds in literature the inspiration that life gives no more, which replaces depth by muddiness, beauty by echoes, passion by necrophily. The fashionable verse of Alexandria grew out of the polite leisure of its librarians, its Homeric scholars, its literary critics. Indeed, the learned of that age had solved the economic problem of living by taking in each other's dirty washing, and the 'Alexandra' of Lycophron, which its learned author made so obscure that other learned authors could make their fortunes by explaining what it meant, still survives for the curious as the first case of this disease and the first really bad poem in Greek. The malady reappears at Rome in the work of Catullus' friend Cinna (the same whom with a justice doubly poetic the crowd in 'Julius Caesar' 'tears for his bad verses'), and in the gloomy pedantry that mars so much of Propertius; it has recurred at intervals ever since. Disconnected and ill-knit, loaded with echo and allusion, fantastic and crude, obscure and obscurantist—such is the typical style of Alexandrianism.

Readers of 'The Waste Land' are referred at the outset, if they wish to understand the poem or even its title, to a work on the ritual origins of the legends of the Holy Grail by Miss J.L. Weston, a disciple of Frazer, and to the 'Golden Bough' itself. Those who conscientiously plunge into the two hundred pages of the former interesting, though credulous, work, will learn that the basis of the Grail story is the restoration of the virility of a Fisher King (who is an incarnation, like so many others in Frazer, of the Life-spirit), and thereby of the fertility of a Waste Land, the Lance and the Grail itself

---

**New Statesman 22 (3 November 1923), pp. 116–18.

being phallic symbols. While maintaining due caution and remembering how

> *Diodorus Siculus*
> *Made himself ridiculous,*
> *By thinking thimbles*
> *Were phallic symbols,*

one may admit that Miss Weston makes a very good case. With that, however, neither she nor Mr. Eliot can rest content, and they must needs discover an esoteric meaning under the rags of superstitious Adam. Miss Weston is clearly a theosophist, and Mr. Eliot's poem might be a theosophical tract. The sick king and the waste land symbolise, we gather, the sick soul and the desolation of this material life.

But even when thus instructed and with a feeling of virtuous research the reader returns to the attack, the difficulties are but begun. To attempt here an interpretation, even an intelligible summary of the poem, is to risk making oneself ridiculous; but those who lack the common modern gift of judging poetry without knowing what it means, must risk that. 'The Waste Land' is headed by an allusion from Petronius to the Sibyl at Cumae, shrunk so small by her incredible age that she was hung up in a bottle and could only squeak, 'I want to die.' She typifies, I suppose, the timeworn soul's desire to escape from the 'Wheel' of things. The first of the five sections opens in spring with one of the snatches of poetry that occur scattered about the poem:

> *April is the cruellest month, breeding*
> *Lilacs out of the dead land, mixing*
> *Memory and desire, stirring*
> *Dull roots with spring rain.*

The next moment comes a spasm of futile, society conversation from a Swiss resort, followed by a passionate outburst at the sterile barrenness of life, though not without hope of its redemption. This is far the best passage in the book:

> *What are the roots that clutch, what branches grow*
> *Out of this stony rubbish? Son of man,*
> *You cannot say, or guess, for you know only*
> *A heap of broken images where the sun beats,*
> *And the dead tree gives no shelter, the cricket no relief,*
> *And the dry stone no sound of water.*

Then, suddenly, a verse of 'Tristan und Isolde' and an echo of Sappho (the vanity of human love?). Next instant there appears a clairvoyante, and in the mystic 'Tarot' cards of her fortune-telling are revealed those mysterious figures that flit through the poem, melting into each other in a way that recalls Emerson's 'Brahma'—the Phoenician sailor, who 'is not wholly distinct from Prince Ferdinand of Naples' and seems to be reincarnate in the Smyrna currant-merchant; the Fisher King; and the Frazerite Hanged Man or sacrificed priest, who merges later into the Christ of the walk to Emmaus.

Then we are thrust into the squalid, 'unreal' Inferno of London Bridge.

The second section contains a dialogue between two jaded lovers in luxury, an interlude about the rape of Philomela the nightingale (spiritual beauty violated by the world?), and a pothouse story of a wrangle between two women about the husband of one of them. In the third part the Fisher King appears fishing in the first person behind the gashouse, and there recur the *motifs* of the nightingale and of unreal London, also:

> *Mr. Eugenides, the Smyrna merchant*
> *Unshaven, with a pocket full of currants*
> C.i.f. *London.*

But before the reader has time to breathe, 'I, Tiresias,' is watching the seduction of a tired typist after tea by a 'young man carbuncular'—a typical instance of that squalor which seems perpetually to obsess Mr. Eliot with mixed fascination and repulsion. A note explains that Tiresias, being a person of double sex, unites in some way all the other persons in the poem. There is more suburban sordidness, and the section ends gasping half a sentence from St. Augustine and another half from Buddha.

In 'IV.—Death by Water' (one of the stock ways, in Frazer, of killing the vegetation king and ensuring rain by sympathetic magic) the Phoenician sailor is duly drowned. Section V., which brings the rain of deliverance to the Waste Land, is, by the author's account, a mixture of the Walk to Emmaus, of the approach to the Chapel Perilous in Arthurian Legend (taken by Miss Weston to signify initiation into the mysteries of physical and spiritual union), and of the state of Eastern Europe! Deliverance comes with the magic formula; 'Datta, dayadhvam, damyata—give, sympathise, control', and the poem ends:

> *London Bridge is falling down falling down falling down*
> Poi s'ascose nel foco che gli affina
> Quando fiam uti chelidon—*O swallow, swallow*
> Le Prince d'Aquitaine à la tour abolie
> *These fragments I have shored against my ruins*
> *Why then Ile fit you. Hieronymo's mad againe.*
> *Datta. Dayadhvam. Damyata.*
>   *Shantih shantih shantih*

(The punctuation largely disappears in the latter part of the poem—whether this is subtlety or accident, it is impossible to say. 'Shantih' is equivalent to the 'Peace that passeth understanding'—which in this case it certainly does.)

All this is very difficult; as Dr. Johnson said under similar circumstances, 'I would it were impossible.' But the gist of the poem is apparently a wild revolt from the abomination of desolation which is human life, combined with a belief in salvation by the usual catchwords of renunciation—this salvation being also the esoteric significance of the savage fertility-rituals found in the 'Golden Bough,' a watering, as it were, of the desert of the suffering soul.

About the philosophy of the poem, if such it be, it would be vain to argue; but it is hard not to regret the way in which modern writers of real creative power abandon themselves to the fond illusion that they have philosophic gifts and a weighty message to deliver to the world, as well. In all periods creative artists have been apt to think they could think, though in all periods they have been frequently harebrained and sometimes mad; just as great rulers and warriors have cared only to be flattered for the way they fiddled or their flatulent tragedies. But now, in particular, we have the spectacle of Mr. Lawrence, Miss May Sinclair, and Mr. Eliot, all sacrificing their artistic powers on the altar of some fantastic Mumbo-Jumbo, all trying to get children on mandrake roots instead of bearing their natural offspring.

Perhaps this unhappy composition should have been left to sink itself: but it is not easy to dismiss in three lines what is being written about as a new masterpiece. For at present it is particularly easy to win the applause of the *blasé* and the young, of the coteries and the eccentricities. The Victorian 'Spasmodics' likewise had their day. But a poem that has to be explained in notes is not unlike a picture with 'This is a dog' inscribed beneath. Not, indeed, that Mr. Eliot's notes succeed in explaining anything, being as muddled as incomplete. What is the use of explaining 'laquearia' by quoting two lines of Latin containing the word, which will convey nothing to those who do not know that language, and nothing new to those who do? What is the use of giving a quotation from Ovid which begins in the middle of a sentence, without either subject or verb, and fails to add even the reference? And when one person hails another on London Bridge as having been with him 'at Mylae,' how is the non-classical reader to guess that this is the name of a Punic sea-fight in which as Phoenician sailor, presumably, the speaker had taken part? The main function of the notes is, indeed, to give the references to the innumerable authors whose lines the poet embodies, like a mediaeval writer making a life of Christ out of lines of Virgil. But the borrowed jewels he has set in its head do not make Mr. Eliot's toad the more prepossessing.

In brief, in 'The Waste Land' Mr. Eliot has shown that he can at moments write real blank verse; but that is all. For the rest he has quoted a great deal, he had parodied and imitated. But the parodies are cheap and the imitations inferior. Among so many other sources Mr. Eliot may have thought, as he wrote, of Rossetti's 'Card-Dealer,' of 'Childe Harold to the Dark Tower Came,' of the 'Vision of Sin' with its same question:

*To which an answer peal'd from that high land,
But in a tongue no man could understand.*

But the trouble is that for the reader who thinks of them the comparison is crushing. 'The Waste Land' adds nothing to a literature which contains things like these. And in our own day, though Professor Santayana be an inferior poet, no one has better reaffirmed the everlasting 'No' of criticism to this recurrent malady of tired ages, 'the fantastic and lacking in sanity':

*Never will they dig deep or build for time
Who of unreason weave a maze of rhyme,
Worship a weakness, nurse a whim, and bind
Wreaths about temples tenantless of mind,
Forsake the path the seeing Muses trod,
And shatter Nature to discover God.*

98
Waste Land and Waste Paper*

HUMBERT WOLFE

I begin by admitting that I do not understand Mr. Eliot's poem in the sense that I could not pass an examination upon it. If, for example, I were set the following three questions (two compulsory),

(1) What relation does the expressed desire of the Cumæan Sibyl to die bear to the poem that it prefaces?

(2) How far does each part of the poem carry on the meaning of its predecessor and point on to the conclusion?

(3) Is it really necessary, in order to understand the poem, to make a detailed study of the literature of anthropology? Illustrate your reply by reference to Miss Jessie L. Weston's book 'From Ritual to Romance,' 'Handbook of Birds of Eastern North America,' and Bradley's 'Appearance and Reality.'

I should be prepared to give answers, and I am certain that they would be quite unlike the answers that others who, equally with me, admire the poem, would give, and, like all the answers, would be unsatisfactory to Mr. Eliot. But that doesn't bother me in the least. Part of the truth about poetry is its beautiful and essential unintelligibility, just as obscurity is its most fatal defect. Unintelligibility, in my use of the word here, conveys that rushing sense of suggestion hiding behind the actual written word that almost stuns the receptive mind, as might a too bright light projected upon a sensitive eye. All poetry worthy of the name shakes just perceptibly beyond the ordinary power of the mind, but it shakes in brightness not in darkness. It is not that the poet can't make himself clear to us, but it is that true poetry is always reaching out beyond itself to the thoughts and feelings for which no words have yet been found. There is about it always an unprospected land, no-man's because it is trodden, in default of fools, by angels. From all of which it follows that everybody who cares for poetry must always fail in an examination of a strict kind. To confess, therefore, that I don't understand Mr.

* *Weekly Westminster* 1 n.s. (November 1923), p. 94.

The Waste Land (1922)

Eliot's poem seems to me to be no more a criticism of it than to say that (in the same sense) I don't understand Shakespeare's sonnets. Neither needs in that sense to be understood.

But that is not to say that I don't get from 'The Waste Land' just those thrills that I associate with what I believe to be poetry. I do emphatically, and if they come by unusual channels that after all is the best tribute that could be paid to any work of art. Let me first show how indisputably in the recognised fashion Mr. Eliot can produce his effect:

> . . . *yet there the nightingale*
> *Filled all the desert with inviolable voice*
> *And still she cried, and still the world pursues,*
> *'Jug Jug' to dirty ears.*
>
> *To Carthage then I came*
>
> *Burning burning burning burning*
> *O Lord thou pluckest me out*
> *O Lord thou pluckest*
>
> *burning*
>
>   *Gentile or Jew*
> *O you who turn the wheel and look to windward,*
> *Consider Phlebas, who was once handsome and tall as you.*

That is the old recognisable way of beauty, and having shown himself master of it, Mr. Eliot is at liberty to play any tricks that he chooses. Nobody can accuse him of writing queerly because he won't compete in the open. The queer stuff can now be approached with an easier mind. And what are we to suppose is hidden under these excursions from the Starnbergersee by way of a hyacinth garden and fortune-telling by cards to 'the brown fog of a winter dawn' in London? Is it the soul sprawling from mountains out of spring past a viscous summer into the drabbest of winters? I don't interpret, because even as I attempt interpretation Mr. Eliot assaults me with

> *You! hypocrite lecteur! mon semblable,—mon frère!*

Well, if I am his brother I shall proceed by saying that the next movement, 'The Game of Chess,' is the symbol of nightingale of beauty singing in the ears of all of us, choked with the dirt of the common burdens of mortality. Ending how? Why thus:

> *Good night, ladies, good night, sweet ladies, good night, good night.*

(That line hits me between the eyes. It is (to me) poetry's closing-time.)

As to the third movement, 'The Fire Sermon,' nightingale sings again:

> *Twit twit twit*
> *Jug jug jug jug jug jug*
> *So rudely forc'd.*
>
> *Tereu*

between the rats in the slime, the wanton typist in her sodden attic and

> *where the walls*
> *of Magnus Martyr hold*
> *Inexplicable splendour of Ionian white and gold.*

Rats, lust, inexplicable splendour all in one tumbled heap:

> *la la*

> *To Carthage then I came.*

So then the fourth movement, 'Death by Water,' and how things lovely endure by dying before loveliness decays, and here no nightingale need sing. Fifth movement and last, 'What the Thunder said.' Here are the 'falling towers,' the black end when:

> *A woman drew her long black hair out tight*
> *And fiddled whisper music on those strings*
> *And bats with baby faces in the violet light.*

Thus we have progressed through every form of ruin and despair over the Waste Land to where:

> *London Bridge is falling down falling down falling down.*

As I began by saying, I don't pretend to understand, but end with the sense that the five movements are knit together by some invulnerable strand. There remains in my mind a sound of high and desolate music. So poetry should end.

[. . .]

99
The Esotericism of T.S. Eliot*

◆

GORHAM B. MUNSON

Some expert—my choice would be Mr. Ezra Pound—should write a moderately long brochure on the versification of T.S. Eliot. Mr. Eliot wrote such a brochure on the metric of Pound and it sharpened considerably our insight into the construction and finesse of his poetry. We need much more of this precise service. Mr. Pound, for example, could show us very exactly the crossing of Mr. Eliot's style by French influences, he could discuss at length what he has already mentioned; 'Mr. Eliot's two sorts of metaphor: his wholly unrealizable, always apt, half ironic suggestion, and his precise realizable picture,' he could elaborate on Mr. Eliot's thematic invention.

Surely in reading the 'Poems' and 'The Waste Land' all serious students of poetry feel what Mr. Pound calls the sense of an unusual intelligence working behind the words. I shall make a trial at placing this intelligence in relation to the complicated and confused literary and cultural currents of our era. We can make a start toward such placement if we examine closely the peculiar esotericism of 'The Waste Land.' It is permissible to concentrate only on 'The Waste Land' because that poem is a summation of Mr. Eliot's intellectual and emotional attitudes: it recapitulates almost all the themes which were given shape in the collected 'Poems.'

The full purport of esoteric writing is concealed from the 'average reader.' It requires for comprehension a more or less stringent initiation in certain ways of feeling, thinking and expressing, which are not common. To the uninitiated such writing is simply obscure. But esotericism is not properly a term of reproach, for it may be inescapable.

One type, that arising from the nature of the subject-matter, Mr. Pound has admirably explained. 'Obscurities inherent in the thing occur when the author is piercing, or trying to pierce into, uncharted regions; when he is trying to express things not yet current, not yet worn into phrase; when he is ahead of the emotional, or philosophic sense (as a painter might be ahead of the color-sense) of his contemporaries.' I think this is true of certain modern

---

* *1924* no. 1 (1 July 1924), pp. 3–10.

Early Poems and *The Waste Land*

writers, whom I call the higher Romantics. If they have an intense desire to communicate experience, they suffer peculiarly, for their desire is constantly frustrated by the undeveloped emotional or philosophical sense of their readers.

Another type arises from obscurities inherent in the treatment. The author is an experimenter and tries to pierce into uncharted regions of technic and form. He tries to arrange the non-representative properties of literature *in vacuo*, to devise what Mr. Eliot in his essay on Jonson calls a 'creative fiction.' The subject-matter perhaps has little logic of its own, and the author's structural logic is ahead of the contemporary aesthetic sense.

Either type of esotericism is highly commendable. Each represents an advance and each if well done is complete in itself. The demand upon the reader is legitimate, for he has only to find the proper key in his own sensibility or in his own experience, and then turn it with his own intellect. If the reader fails, it is he who is deficient, not the work.

But the esotericism of 'The Waste Land' is different: it is deliberate mystification. For in structure the poem is loose: it is full of interstices. Episode does not inevitably follow episode: transitions do not carry us, willy-nilly, from theme to theme, from movement to movement. Its unity depends upon Mr. Eliot's personality, not upon the poem's functions and their adjustments and relations. The structural effect is very much like that given by a revolving light: a sequence of flashes and blanks without significance until referred to the purpose of the lighthouse and the controlling hand of the keeper. I say this in spite of certain formal achievements within the poem: the firm Virgilian outline of the seduction scene witnessed by Tiresias, the triumphant progression through most utterly banal chatter, speeded up by the bartender's cries, 'HURRY UP PLEASE IT'S TIME,' to the cool and lovely line from 'Hamlet,' 'Good night, ladies, good night, sweet ladies, good night, good night.' Themes are stated, caught up later, recur. There is a general cumulative movement, the poem has a half-visible crescendo. It dies nicely with 'shantih shantih shantih.' But the two planes on which 'The Waste Land' moves—the plane of myth and the plane of present day London—are not strictly related. Passages of fine poetry may be deleted without spoiling one's aesthetic pleasure of the whole, though diminishing the sum total derived from the detail. Symbols, characters, and associations appear quite arbitrarily.

I am compelled to reject the poem as a sustained harmoniously functioning structural unit.

On the other hand, it is amazing how simple is the state of mind which these broken forms convey. The poet is hurt, wistful, melancholy, frail: modern civilization is a waste land, a sterile desert, in which he wanders forlornly: there is no water to slake his spiritual drouth. Yet there was water once, there was beauty, and the poem shifts to the plane of the past, to the plane of great mythology.

The Waste Land (1922)

> *When lovely woman stoops to folly and*
> *Paces about her room again, alone,*
> *She smoothes her hair with automatic hand,*
> *And puts a record on the gramophone.*

The stanza is a minute simulacrum of the central process of the poem which is to take ancient beauty by the neck and twist it into modern ugliness. Mr. Eliot is very fatigued. There can be no question that he suffers, at moments his cry is as sharp as that of a man mangled by the speeding wheels of the subway express, it is bitter as a confession extorted by wheel and rack. We respect that cry.

But about the nature of this state of mind there is nothing occult. It is in fact a very familiar mood. We have had a great deal of the poetry of melancholy and drouth in the last half century, most of it inferior to Mr. Eliot's, but nevertheless it has worn into common currency its emotions.

Assuming that Mr. Eliot wished to convey such emotions to the reader, to make them still more deeply a part of our general experience, it should not have been difficult for him to escape opacity. Classical lucidity was entirely possible. How shall we account then for the obstacles he has placed to the reader's ready comprehension?

To win a complete understanding of 'The Waste Land,' the reader must scan eleven pages of notes, he must have a considerable learning in letters or be willing to look up references in Milton, Ovid, Middleton, Webster, Spenser, Verlaine, St. Augustine, etc., etc., in order to associate them with their first context, he must read Latin, Greek, French and German, he must know Frazer's 'Golden Bough' and steep himself in the legend of the Holy Grail, studying in particular Miss Weston's 'From Ritual to Romance.' The texture of 'The Waste Land' is excessively heavy with literary allusions which the reader of good will, knowing that it is not unjust to make severe requisitions upon his knowledge, will diligently track down. But our reader of good will is entitled, I think, to turn sour when he discovers that after all his research he has not penetrated into some strange uncharted region of experience but has only fathomed the cipher of a quite ordinary and easily understandable state of mind.

I know that more whole-hearted admirers of the poem than I are exclaiming at this point: 'But you are missing the point! Mr. Eliot wished to give a cumulative effect of his cries of hurt and barrenness. He wished to give a sense of one long cry of protest throughout history, a sense of dryness running through the ages, a yearning passed on from one individual to another until it reaches him in twentieth-century London.' To that my answer is that the sense of outcry reinforced by outcry is simply not created in the text. It is added to the text by deliberate processes of memory and learning by Mr. Eliot. It is added to the text by equally deliberate processes on the part of the reader. It is dependent on something too removed from the actual lines, and so I cannot feel it as integral.

The conclusion must be that the esotericism of 'The Waste Land' derives neither from abstruseness of subject nor from abstruseness of technic. It is artificially concocted by omissions, incompletions and unnecessary specialization in the assembling of those circumstances which ought to evoke in the reader the whole effect of the given emotion. Again the question rises, why does Mr. Eliot tamper with these circumstances so as to make them not explicable in themselves?

It is a reasonable conjecture to say that Mr. Eliot does not want to communicate his suffering to the general reader. To such he desires to be incomprehensible. His obfuscation of the circumstances which react together as a formula for his emotion is an example of dandyism. In his desire to make his suffering inscrutable to all but a chosen coterie of his similars, he is affecting what is commonly called a romantic mannerism, a mannerism that cannot be credited, however, to the great romantics. He constructs a mask for himself.

Our ideas of aristocracy have become sentimentalized. In its healthy state, the idea of aristocracy is a union of some idea of what is best in human nature with the idea of rule or control. For our purpose I suppose we can agree that the highest value is intelligence, so I can be more precise and say that the union of the ideas of intelligence and control constitutes the idea of aristocracy. In certain epochs the vortices of intelligence and social power have coincided, and the idea of aristocracy has been healthy. But in our epoch it is a truism that social power is vested in men of an inventive acquisitive narrow nature whose general intelligence is relatively low, whose care for humane values is slight, whose cunning is abnormally developed. The men of creative intelligence are thus forced to work against the grain of a society ruled by the acquisitive impulse. Many of them have become depressed at the odds against them and have pinned the insignia of an aloof defeat upon their work. Depression and even collapse in this state of affairs are certainly marks of a sensitive spirit. But it is a sentimentality of which I suspect Mr. Eliot guilty to believe that depression is a symptom of aristocracy. For the aristocrat cannot take pride in a dandyism of defeat, he cannot relinquish the effort to control. With the whole force of his being he seeks to understand: to understand the forces in himself, the forces of his age. With the whole force of his being he seeks to externalize his knowledge of these so lucidly and powerfully that it wins a place as leaven in the general cultural experience. He does not accept the crucifixion of his sensibility as a proof of superiority. He finds his proof in the transcendence of his crucifixions. Joy, serenity, the tokens of victory are his distinguishing marks. In the surrender to despair of its creative will the European mind loses its aristocracy.

Mr. Eliot, we know, has taken great pains to blend with the European mind. Who will dispute his thorough naturalization? But the mind into which he has been assimilated is in wretched case. Founded upon classicism, it has been shaken by the tremendous challenges issued to classical authorities from revolutionary science. It lacks the vitality to surrender the old and to make adjustment to the new. The upheavals of war and politics have agonized it to the last point. It has no hope, no vision. In 'Der Untergang des Abendlandes' Oswald Spengler crystallizes its resignation into an attitude. Herr Spengler is a fatalist. Cultures, he believes, obey definite biological laws. They are rigidly deterministic. They live out a birth, growth, brilliant maturity, decay, death, and these processes cannot be halted. Decay he calls 'civilization'; it is the stage of huge cities and their nomadic life, of great wars and dictators, of the advent of formless traditionless masses. We are in it: 'We must will the inevitable or nothing': the inevitable is fellahdom.

It is easy to see that in part 'The Waste Land' is a poetic equivalent to 'Der Untergang des Abendlandes.' Mr. Eliot recalls the brilliant apogee of culture, he portrays in contrast the sterile decay of contemporary 'civilization,' he makes his own positive assertion in the detestable apeneck guffawing Sweeney, symbol of the formless and the traditionless. Before the age, which he has characterized elsewhere as singularly dull, the poet is weary.

The reader has observed that I have been shifting the interest in 'The Waste Land' from the aesthetic to the moral and cultural, and that we are now wholly involved in the poem as a summary of the modern cultural situation. The possibility not allowed for by the mind of Mr. Eliot is this: the entrance into consciousness of some new factor. We can only say, the future will be so and thus, provided no indeterminable elements of human consciousness, now dormant, commence to function. The fallacy of rationalism of the determinist type is that it is not rational enough. It does not question its assumptions. Trace back far enough and its fundamental entities turn out to be matter and motion, both as a matter of fact unknowns, and defined in terms of each other. This type of rationalism is not a coordinating part of the complex vision of the whole human being: it is really uncontrolled and amok.

We may take heart in surveying 'The Waste Land' and the defunct state of the European mind if we turn again to science in the name of which some very leaden messages have been offered us in the past. I quote from that acute scientific observer, J.W.N. Sullivan.

> Once a crack has appeared in a closed universe, it goes on spreading. Since Maxwell's day the cracks have so multiplied and spread that already nothing remains of the old Newtonian inverse except a few fragments. It has not even the validity of a first sketch, for the main lines in a sketch are right. But the modern universe of physics is *essentially* different from the universe of the eighteenth century. All the primary entities are quite different. The directions in which explanations are sought are quite different. The relation of man to the universe is quite different. The universe of modern science has fundamentally nothing in common with the scientific universe on which rationalism was built. It is not merely that hypotheses have changed. The role of the hypothesis has changed. The universe, which was to be explained in terms of little billiard balls

and the law of the inverse square is now a universe where even mystics, to say nothing of poets and philosophers, have a right to exist. The present scientific picture of the universe, although incomparably more profound than that of the eighteenth century, allows much more room to possibilities. It allows them, and is not concerned to conflict with them.

So that we reach the conclusion that mysticism and science can quite well live together. Except on the basis of the rationalism whose foundations have long since crumbled there is no conflict whatever between mystical insight and science. And the man who prides himself on the complete absence of mystery in his view of the world is not only not representing the scientific outlook but will speedily become quite unable to understand it.

Let us not take too seriously the 'scientific' pretensions nor grant too much authority to those who tell us that in view of our future the arts are twaddle, for the future belongs to mechanics, technology, economics and especially politics.

How far the American mind reproduces the vision or rather the supine attitude of the European mind is a speculation. I say speculation, because in spite of the best will to discover it I cannot say that there exists, in the sense that the European mind exists, an American mind. There are in my estimation several American writers who contain the nucleus for a striking and vastly important American mind, but America is not yet an intelligent community. Europe is: it has a consensus of intelligent opinion which I have called its mind: I can find no such consensus in America to compare with it. But although we cannot make distinctions in thought, we can in those things that nourish thought. America has a fresh boundless energy which Europe has lost. Most of it is quantitative, but the possibility always exists of converting some of it to qualitative. Energy is the first requisite to meet the elastic situation of today. America has hope, whereas Europe moves toward hopelessness and resignation. Hope is the spur of energy. America has laxer traditions than Europe. Ordinarily, this is deplorable. But if we are called upon to put away old traditions and to formulate new, it is an advantage. There is less inertia to overcome. And from the laxness of traditions in America, it follows that we are by temperament probably romantics. In chaos, it is generally agreed, the romantic is better able to find footing than the less flexible classicist.

Consequently, it is not surprising that such a viewpoint as that published by Mr. Eliot does not initiate any movement in America, does not even secure a general passive acceptance, does not least of all awake anything in our experience which impulsively corroborates it. Nay, we are scarcely enough affected to make a serious contradiction. A decade ago, smarting with a sense of inferiority, blaspheming our environment on which we transferred our weaknesses, we looked to Europe as the determinator of values. It was the heyday of the exile and the cosmopolitan mind. Today, our painters, writers and intellectuals know that they are deeply implicated in the unformed and unpredictable American destiny. They hibernate in Europe

The Waste Land (1922)

and rush back as from a feast which has unexpectedly turned out to be a famine. They are conscious of a great though unarticulated difference between the activity of the American scene and that of Europe. They have even met Europeans who have calmly declared that Europe is dead and the future belongs to America. They realize that the power of initiative has crossed the Atlantic.

America has energy and hope. It has weak traditions and a romantic temperament. It is becoming conscious of a fundamental difference between it and Europe. In the words of the Cumaean Sibyl, inscribed at the top of 'The Waste Land,' Europe 'wants only to die.' America wants to live.

But America has not realized its responsibility in the present crisis. It has not realized that its national destiny is more than a matter of national self-respect. It has not recognized clearly that the leadership of the human spirit has been resigned and that it, if anyone, must assume it. It has the primary qualifications: untapped energetics and spiritual naivete. It has lately acquired self-reliance. It seems not fanciful to predict that it will next acquire a sense of international responsibility.

And then perhaps it will at last be ready to receive Whitman. It will be expectant and humble, waiting for the Word that will release it, for the Word that will spell a new slope of human consciousness. Whitman is not the Word, but he formed syllables of it, immense generative syllables. America will wait while these do their deep hidden work, arousing latent power. On the threshold of creative vision one must wait.

Mr. Eliot lacks those deeper dimensions that the new slope will utilize. He is almost purely a sensibility and an intellect: he seems a unified man: at least one gets no sense of a disastrous internecine conflict in him. He loves beauty, he is wounded by ugliness: the age is severe on 'beauty-lovers' who cannot go below the surface. It lacerates unmercifully those whose intellects work only at the tips of their sense, who make an ideal of the senses thinking, of sensuous thought. This formula Mr. Eliot believes accounts for much of the excellence of Elizabethan literature.

The formula for literary masterwork in our age will be more complex, more inclusive, much more difficult than that. It will involve the correlated functions of the whole human consciousness and it will demand the utmost purification of that consciousness. On a tremendous scale our age duplicates some of the features which introduced so much zest into Elizabethan life. Our vital source in antiquity will be, perhaps, the religious and philosophical cultures of the East instead of Graeco-Roman culture. Our New World will be Higher Space, and our explorers, our Columbuses and Magellans, will be such scientists as Einstein and Bohr. Our artists will have a wealth of new materials: our intellectual world expands and fills with possibilities: it is a time for curiosity and daring. 'The Waste Land' is a funeral keen for the nineteenth century. In the twentieth it is a subjective aberration from the facts.

Studies of *The Waste Land* and Other Poems

100
T.S. Eliot*

♦

EDMUND WILSON

I have noted the similarity between the English seventeenth-century poets and the French nineteenth-century Symbolists. The poetry of T.S. Eliot has, in our own time, brought together those two traditions, as it is Eliot who, so far as I know, has for the first time called attention to their resemblance. 'The form,' he says, 'in which I began to write, in 1908 or 1909, was directly drawn from the study of *Laforgue* together with the later Elizabethan drama; and I do not know anyone who started from exactly that point.'

I have so far, in discussing the early Symbolists, spoken chiefly of Mallarmé. But T.S. Eliot derived, as he indicates, from a different branch of the Symbolist tradition. In 1873 there had appeared in Paris a book of poems called 'Les Amours Jaunes,' by a writer who signed himself Tristan Corbière. 'Les Amours Jaunes' was received with complete indifference, and scarcely more than a year after it appeared, the author died of consumption. Only thirty at the time of his death, Tristan Corbière had been an eccentric and very maladjusted man: he was the son of a sea captain who had also written sea stories and he had had an excellent education, but he chose for himself the life of an outlaw. In Paris, he slept all day and spent the nights in the cafés or at his verses, greeting at dawn the Paris harlots as they emerged from the station house or the hotel with the same half-harsh, half-tender fellow-feeling for the exile from conventional society which, when he was at home in his native Brittany, caused him to flee the house of his family and seek the company of the customs-men and sailors—living skeleton and invalid as he was, performing, prodigies of courage and endurance in the navigation of a little cutter which he sailed by preference in the worst possible weather. He made a pose of his unsociability and of what he considered his physical ugliness, at the same time that he undoubtedly suffered over them. Melancholy, with a feverishly active mind, full of groanings and vulgar jokes, he used to amuse himself by going about in convict's clothes and by firing guns and revolvers out the window in protest against the singing of the village choir; and on one occasion, on a visit to

*From *Axel's Castle* (New York, 1931), pp. 93–131.

Rome, he appeared in the streets in evening dress, with a mitre on his head and two eyes painted on his forehead, leading a pig decorated with ribbons. And Corbière's poetry was a poetry of the outcast: often colloquial and homely, yet with a rhetoric of fantastic slang; often with the manner of slapdash doggerel, yet sure of its own morose artistic effects; full of the parade of romantic personality, yet incessantly humiliating itself with a self-mockery scurrilous and savage, out of which, as Huysmans said, would sometimes rise without warning 'a cry of sharp pain like the breaking of a 'cello string'—Corbière's verse brought back into French poetry qualities which had been alien to its spirit since François Villon's day.

So outlandish did Corbière appear even from the point of view of the Romantics that he was dismissed, when he was noticed at all, as not merely unseemly but insane—till Paul Verlaine, in 1883, did him honour in a series of articles, 'Les Poètes Maudits,' which was one of the important critical events in the development of Symbolism. Verlaine himself, a more accomplished artist, but a less original and interesting personality, had been strongly influenced by 'Les Amours Jaunes'—he seems, indeed, to have caught over from Corbière, not only certain artistic effects, but even something of his own poetic personality, his peculiar accent of wistful naïveté: compare Corbière's 'Rondels pour Après' with Verlaine's sonnet which begins, 'L'espoir luit comme un brin de paille dans l'étable'; or 'Paria' with 'Casper Hauser.'

But another French poet, Jules Laforgue, nineteen years younger than Corbière, had independently developed a tone and technique—poignant-ironic, grandiose-slangy, scurrilous-naïve—which had much in common with Corbière's. Laforgue was the son of a schoolmaster and, for all his nonchalance in handling rudely the conventions of French poetry, much more a professional man of letters than Corbière. Laforgue even errs through precosity in his fashion; what with Corbière seems a personal and inevitable, if eccentric, manner of speech, in Laforgue sounds self-conscious and deliberate, almost sometimes a literary exercise. He was tubercular, as Corbière was also, and dead at twenty-seven—and his gentleness and sadness are still those of a sick well-cared-for child; his asperities, his surprising images, his coquetries, his cynicism, and his impudence, are still those of a clever schoolboy. Laforgue's friends procured him a post as reader to the Empress Augusta of Germany; and, falling under the spell of German philosophy, he brought its jargon into his verse, contributing thereby to Symbolism perhaps the one element of obscurity which it had lacked.

Yet Laforgue is a very fine poet and one of the most remarkable of the Symbolists. He and Corbière had introduced a new variety of vocabulary and a new flexibility of feeling. With Mallarmé, it may be said that, on the whole, it is the imagery, not the feeling, which is variable: though sometimes playful, he is classical in the sense (as Yeats and Valéry are) that he sustains a certain grandeur of tone. But it is from the conversational-ironic, rather than from the serious-æsthetic, tradition of Symbolism that T.S. Eliot derives. Corbière and Laforgue are almost everywhere in his early work. The emphatic witty quatrains of Corbière, with their sudden lapses into tenderness or pathos, are heard again in the satiric verse of Eliot: a poem like 'Mr. Eliot's Sunday Morning Service' would hardly, one imagines, have been written without Corbière's 'Rapsodie Foraine.' And as 'Conversation Galante' derives clearly from certain poems in Laforgue's 'Complaintes' and 'Imitation de Notre-Dame la Lune,' so the more elaborate 'Portrait of a Lady' and 'The Love Song of J. Alfred Prufrock' follow closely the longer poems of Laforgue. Compare the conclusion of 'Mr. Prufrock' with the conclusion of the early version of Laforgue's poem 'Légende':

I grow old . . . I grow old . . .
I shall wear the bottoms of my trousers rolled.

Shall I part my hair behind? Do I dare to eat a peach?
I shall wear white flannel trousers, and walk upon the beach.
I have heard the mermaids singing, each to each.

I do not think that they will sing to me.

I have seen them riding seaward on the waves
Combing the white hair of the waves blown back
When the wind blows the water white and black.

We have lingered in the chambers of the sea
By sea-girls wreathed with seaweed red and brown
Till human voices wake us, and we drown.

Hier l'orchestre attaqua
Sa dernière polka

Oh! L'automne, l'automne!
   Les casinos
   Qu'on abandonne
Remisent leurs pianos! . . .

Phrases, verroteries,
Caillots de souvenirs.
Oh! comme elle est maigrie!
Que vais-je devenir? . . .

Adieu! Les filles d'ifs dans les grisailles
Ont l'air de pleureuses de funerailles
Sous l'autan noir qui veut que tout s'en aille.

   Assez, assez,
C'est toi qui as commencé.

Va, ce n'est plus l'odeur de tes fourrures.
Va, vos moindres clins d'yeux sont des parjures.
Tais-toi, avec vous autres rien ne dure.

   Tais-toi, tais-toi,
On n'aime qu'une fois . . .

Here it will be seen that Eliot has reproduced Laforgue's irregular metrical scheme almost line for line. Furthermore, the subject of Laforgue's poem—the hesitations and constraints of a man either too timid or too disillusioned to make love to a woman who provokes his ironic pity at the same time that she stirs gusts of stifled emotion—has a strong resemblance to the subjects of 'Mr. Prufrock' and the 'Portrait of a Lady.' And in another poem, 'La Figlia Che Piange,' Eliot has adapted a line of Laforgue's: 'Simple et sans foi comme un bonjour'—'Simple and faithless as a smile and shake of the hand.' He has even brought over into English some of the unstresed effect of French verse: how different, for example, is the alexandrine of Eliot's just quoted from the classical English alexandrine 'which like a wounded snake drags its slow length along' or 'with sparkless ashes loads an unlamented urn.' [In his exhaustive 'Influence du Symbolisme Français sur la Poésie Américaine de 1910 à 1920,' M. René Taupin has shown the influence of Gautier also in Eliot's satiric poems: 'The Hippopotamus,' it appears, is almost a transcript of a hippopotamus by Gautier, and the 'Grishkin is nice' passage in 'Whispers of Immortality' repeats a 'Carmen est maigre' of Gautier.]

It must not be supposed, however, that Eliot is not original or that he is not the equal of either of his masters. Those longer and more elaborate poems—'Derniers Vers' in the collected edition—which Laforgue was constructing at the time of his death out of more fragmentary and less mature work are certainly his most important performances: through his masterly flexibility of vocabulary and metric, he has here achieved one of the definitive expressions of the pathetic ironic, worldly-æsthetic moods of the *fin de siècle* temperament. Yet, though Eliot has, in certain obvious respects, applied Laforgue's formula so faithfully, he cannot properly be described as an imitator because he is in some ways a superior artist. He is more mature than Laforgue ever was, and his workmanship is perfect in a way that Corbière's and Laforgue's were rarely. T.S. Eliot's peculiar distinction lies, as Clive Bell has said, in his 'phrasing.' Laforgue's images are often far-fetched and inappropriately grotesque: his sins in this respect are really very closely akin to those of the English metaphysical poets; but Eliot's taste is absolutely sure—his images always precisely right. And the impression that Eliot leaves, even in these earliest poems, is clear, vivid and unforgettable: we do not subordinate him to his Symbolist predecessors any more than, when we find him, as in 'Gerontion,' writing in the rhythms of late Elizabethan blank-verse, we associate him with Middleton or Webster.

Studies of *The Waste Land* and poems

When we come to examine Eliot's themes, we recognise something which we have found already in Laforgue, but which appears in Eliot in a more intense form. One of the principal preoccupations of Flaubert—a great hero of Eliot's, as of Eliot's fellow-poet, Ezra Pound's—had been the inferiority of the present to the past: the Romantics had discovered the possibilities of the historical imagination; with their thirst for boldness, grandeur, and magnificence, they had located these qualities in past epochs—especially the Middle Ages and the Renaissance. And Flaubert, who shared with the Romantics this appetite for the gorgeous and the untamed, but who constrained himself, also, to confront the actual nineteenth-century world, pursued two parallel lines of fiction which lent significance and relief to each other. On the one hand, he reconstructed, in 'Salammbô' and in 'La Tentation de Saint Antoine,' the splendid barbarities of the pagan world and the heroic piety of the early Christian; and on the other, he caricatured, in 'Madame Bovary,' in 'L'Education Sentimentale' and in 'Bouvard et Pécuchet,' the pusillanimity and mediocrity of contemporary bourgeois France. This whole point of view of Flaubert's—summed up, as it were, in 'Trois Contes,' where the three periods are contrasted in one book—was profoundly to affect modern literature. We shall find it later on in Joyce; but in the meantime we must note its reappearance in the poetry of Eliot. Eliot, like Flaubert, feels at every turn that human life is now ignoble, sordid or tame, and he is haunted and tormented by intimations that it has once been otherwise. In 'Burbank with a Baedeker: Bleistein with a Cigar,' the young American tourist in Venice, superseded in his affair with the Princess Volupine by a vulgar Austrian Jew, meditates on the clipped wings and pared claws of the Lion of St. Mark's, the symbol of the old arrogant Venice and of the world where such a city was possible. In 'A Cooking Egg,' the poet demands, after a call upon a very mild, dull spinster: 'Where are the eagles and the trumpets?' and himself returns the saddened answer: 'Buried beneath some snow-deep Alps.' In 'Lune de Miel,' the Middle Western American travellers, stifled with the summer heat and devoured by the bedbugs of Ravenna, are contrasted with the noble crumbling beauty of the old Byzantine church less than a league away, of which they are totally unaware and to which they have apparently no relation; and in 'Mr. Eliot's Sunday Morning Service,' the combined grossness and aridity of the modern clergymen is contrasted with the pure and fresh religious feeling of a picture of the baptism of Christ by 'a painter of the Umbrian school.' In the best and most effective of these poems, 'Sweeney Among the Nightingales,' the poet, during a drowsy, idiotic and mildly sinister scene in some low dive, where two of the girls are supposed to be plotting against one of the men, remembers, at the sound of nightingales singing, the murder of Agamemnon in Æschylus:

The host with someone indistinct
Converses at the door apart,

> *The nightingales are singing near*
> *The Convent of the Sacred Heart,*
>
> *And sang within the bloody wood*
> *When Agamemnon cried aloud,*
> *And let their liquid siftings fall*
> *To stain the stiff dishonoured shroud.*

The present is more timid than the past: the bourgeois are afraid to let themselves go. The French had been preoccupied with this idea ever since the first days of Romanticism; but Eliot was to deal with the theme from a somewhat different point of view, a point of view characteristically American. For T.S. Eliot, though born in St. Louis, comes from a New England family and was educated at Harvard; and he is in some ways a typical product of our New England civilisation. He is distinguished by that combination of practical prudence with moral idealism which shows itself in its later developments as an excessive fastidiousness and scrupulousness. One of the principal subjects of Eliot's poetry is really that regret at situations unexplored, that dark rankling of passions inhibited, which has figured so conspicuously in the work of the American writers of New England and New York from Hawthorne to Edith Wharton. T.S. Eliot, in this respect, has much in common with Henry James. Mr. Prufrock and the poet of the 'Portrait of a Lady,' with their helpless consciousness of having dared too little, correspond exactly to the middle-aged heroes of 'The Ambassadors' and 'The Beast in the Jungle,' realising sadly too late in life that they have been living too cautiously and too poorly. The fear of life, in Henry James, is closely bound up with the fear of vulgarity. And Eliot, too, fears vulgarity—which he embodies in the symbolic figure of 'Apeneck Sweeney'—at the same time that he is fascinated by it. Yet he chafes at the limitations and pretences of the culture represented by Boston—a society 'quite uncivilised,' as he says, 'but refined beyond the point of civilisation.' He has some amusing satiric poems about old New England ladies—in one of which he reflects on his way to the house of his Cousin Harriet, how:

> *. . . evening quickens faintly in the street,*
> *Wakening the appetites of life in some*
> *And to others bringing the* Boston Evening Transcript.

And the 'Portrait of a Lady,' whether the scene be laid in Boston or in London, is essentially a poem of that New England Society 'refined beyond the point of civilisation': from the Lady, who serves tea among lighted candles—'an atmosphere of Juliet's tomb'—with her dampening efforts at flattery and flirtation through the medium of cultured conversation—her slightly stale and faded gush about Chopin and her memories of Paris in the spring—the poet is seized with an impulse to flee:

> *I take my hat: how can I make a cowardly amends*
> *For what she has said to me?*
> *You will see me any morning in the park*
> *Reading the comics and the sporting page.*
> *Particularly I remark*
> *An English countess goes upon the stage,*
> *A Greek was murdered at a Polish dance,*
> *Another bank defaulter has confessed.*
> *I keep my countenance,*
> *I remain self-possessed*
> *Except when a street piano, mechanical and tired,*
> *Reiterates some worn-out common song*
> *With the smell of hyacinths across the garden*
> *Recalling things that other people have desired.*

But he is always debating things with his conscience: his incurable moral solicitude makes him wonder:

> *Are these ideas right or wrong?*

So Mr. Prufrock in the room where:

> *. . . women come and go*
> *Talking of Michelangelo,*

wistfully asks himself:

> *Shall I say, I have gone at dusk through narrow streets*
> *And watched the smoke that rises from the pipes*
> *Of lonely men in shirt-sleeves, leaning out of windows? . . .*

And Mr. Prufrock wonders also whether he should not put a question to his lady—but he never gets to the point of putting it.

II

But Eliot's most complete expression of this theme of emotional starvation is to be found in the later and longer poem called 'The Waste Land' (1922). The Waste Land of the poem is a symbol borrowed from the myth of the Holy Grail: it is a desolate and sterile country ruled by an impotent king, in which not only have the crops ceased to grow and the animals to reproduce, but the very human inhabitants have become incapable of having children. But this sterility we soon identify as the sterility of the Puritan temperament. On the first pages we find again the theme of the girl with the hyacinths (themselves a symbol for the re-arisen god of the fertility rites who will save the rainless country from drought) which has already figured in 'La Figlia Che Piange' and 'Dans le Restaurant'—a memory which apparently represents for the poet some fulfilment foregone in youth and now agonisingly desired; and in the last pages it is repeated. We recognise throughout 'The Waste Land' the peculiar conflicts of the Puritan turned artist: the horror of vulgarity and the shy sympathy with the common life, the ascetic shrinking from sexual experience and the distress at the drying up of the springs of sexual emotion, with the straining after a religious emotion which may be made to take its place.

Yet though Eliot's spiritual and intellectual roots are still more firmly fixed in New England than is, I believe, ordinarily understood, there is in 'The Waste Land' a good deal more than the mere gloomy moods of a New Englander regretting an emotionally undernourished youth. The colonisation by the Puritans of New England was merely an incident in that rise of the middle-class which has brought a commercial industrial civilisation to the European cities as well as to the American ones. T.S. Eliot now lives in London and has become an English citizen; but the desolation, the æsthetic and spiritual drought, of Anglo-Saxon middle-class society oppresses London as well as Boston. The terrible dreariness of the great modern cities is the atmosphere in which 'The Waste Land' takes place—amidst this dreariness, brief, vivid images emerge, brief pure moments of feeling are distilled; but all about us we are aware of nameless millions performing barren office routines, wearing down their souls in interminable labours of which the products never bring them profit—people whose pleasures are so sordid and so feeble that they seem almost sadder than their pains. And this Waste Land has another aspect: it is a place not merely of desolation, but of anarchy and doubt. In our post-War world of shattered institutions, strained nerves and bankrupt ideals, life no longer seems serious or coherent—we have no belief in the things we do and consequently we have no heart for them.

The poet of 'The Waste Land' is living half the time in the real world of contemporary London and half the time in the haunted wilderness of the medieval legend. The water for which he longs in the twilight desert of his dream is to quench the spiritual thirst which torments him in the London dusk; and as Gerontion, 'an old man in a dry month,' thought of the young men who had fought in the rain, as Prufrock fancied riding the waves with mermaids and lingering in the chambers of the sea, as Mr. Apollinax has been imagined drawing strength from the deep sea-caves of coral islands—so the poet of 'The Waste Land,' making water the symbol of all freedom, all fecundity and flowering of the soul, invokes in desperate need the memory of an April shower of his youth, the song of the hermit thrush with its sound of water dripping and the vision of a drowned Phœnician sailor, sunk beyond 'the cry of gulls and the deep sea swell,' who has at least died by water, not thirst. The poet, who seems now to be travelling in a country cracked by drought, can only feverishly dream of these things. One's head may be well stored with literature, but the heroic prelude of the Elizabethans has ironic echoes in modern London streets and modern London drawing-rooms: lines remembered from Shakespeare turn to jazz or refer themselves to the sound of phonographs. And now it is one's personal regrets again—the girl in the hyacinth-garden—'the awful daring of a moment's surrender which an age of prudence can never retract'—the key which turned once, and once only, in the prison of inhibition and isolation. Now he stands on the arid plain again, and the dryrotted world of London seems to be crumbling about him—the poem ends in a medley of quotations from a medley of literatures—like Gérard de Nerval's 'Desdichado,' the poet is disinherited; like the author of the 'Pervigilium Veneris,' he laments that his song is mute and asks when the spring will come which will set it free like the swallow's; like Arnaut Daniel, in Dante, as he disappears in the refining fire, he begs the world to raise a prayer for his torment. 'These fragments I have shored against my ruins.'

'The Waste Land,' in method as well as in mood, has left Laforgue far behind. Eliot has developed a new technique, at once laconic, quick, and precise, for representing the transmutations of thought, the interplay of perception and reflection. Dealing with subjects complex in the same way as those of Yeats's poem 'Among School Children' and Valéry's 'Cimetière Marin,' Eliot has found for them a different language. As May Sinclair has said of Eliot, his 'trick of cutting his corners and his curves makes him seem obscure when he is clear as daylight. His thoughts move very rapidly and by astounding cuts. They move not by logical stages and majestic roundings of the full literary curve, but as live thoughts move in live brains.' Let us examine, as an illustration, the lovely nightingale passage from 'The Waste Land.' Eliot is describing a room in London:

> *Above the antique mantel was displayed*
> *As though a window gave upon the sylvan scene*
> *The change of Philomel, by the barbarous king*
> *So rudely forced; yet there the nightingale*
> *Filled all the desert with inviolable voice*
> *And still she cried, and still the world pursues,*
> *'Jug Jug' to dirty ears.*

That is, the poet sees, above the mantel, a picture of Philomela changed to a nightingale, and it gives his mind a moment's swift release. The picture is like a window opening upon Milton's earthly paradise—the 'sylvan scene,' as Eliot explains in a note, is a phrase from 'Paradise Lost'—and the poet associates his own plight in the modern city, in which some 'infinitely gentle, infinitely suffering thing,' to quote one of Eliot's earlier poems, is somehow being done to death, with Philomela, raped and mutilated by Tereus. But in the earthly paradise, there had been a nightingale singing: Philomela had wept her woes in song, though the barbarous king had cut out her tongue— her sweet voice had remained inviolable. And with a sudden change of tense, the poet flashes back from the myth to his present situation:

Early Poems and *The Waste Land*

And still she cried, and still the world pursues,
'Jug Jug' to dirty ears.

The song of birds was represented in old English popular poetry by such outlandish syllables as 'Jug Jug'—so Philomela's cry sounds to the vulgar. Eliot has here, in seven lines of extraordinary liquidity and beauty, fused the picture, the passage from Milton and the legend from Ovid, into a single moment of vague poignant longing.

'The Waste Land' is dedicated to Ezra Pound, to whom Eliot elsewhere acknowledges a debt; and he has here evidently been influenced by Pound's 'Cantos.' 'The Waste Land,' like the 'Cantos,' is fragmentary in form and packed with literary quotation and allusion. In fact, the passage just discussed above has a resemblance to a passage on the same subject—the Philomela-Procne myth—at the beginning of Pound's Fourth Canto. Eliot and Pound have, in fact, founded a school of poetry which depends on literary quotation and reference to an unprecedented degree. Jules Laforgue had sometimes parodied, in his poems, the great lines of other poets:

O Nature, donne-moi la force et le courage
De me croire en âge . . .

And Eliot had, in his early poetry, introduced phrases from Shakespeare and Blake for purposes of ironic effect. He has always, furthermore, been addicted to prefacing his poems with quotations and echoing passages from other poets. But now, in 'The Waste Land,' he carries this tendency to what one must suppose its extreme possible limit: here, in a poem of only four hundred and three lines (to which are added, however, seven pages of notes), he manages to include quotations from, allusions to, or imitations of, at least thirty-five different writers (some of them, such as Shakespeare and Dante, laid under contribution several times)—as well as several popular songs; and to introduce passages in six foreign languages, including Sanskrit. And we must also take into consideration that the idea of the literary medley itself seems to have been borrowed from still another writer, Pound. We are always being dismayed, in our general reading, to discover that lines among those which we had believed to represent Eliot's residuum of original invention had been taken over or adapted from other writers (sometimes very unexpected ones: thus, it appears now, from Eliot's essay on Bishop Andrewes, that the first five lines of 'The Journey of the Magi,' as well as the 'word within a word, unable to speak a word' of 'Gerontion,' had been salvaged from Andrewes's sermons; and the 'stiff dishonoured shroud' of 'Sweeney Among the Nightingales' seems to be an echo of the 'dim dishonoured brow' of Whittier's poem about Daniel Webster). One would be inclined *a priori* to assume that all this load of erudition and literature would be enough to sink any writer, and that such a production as 'The Waste Land' must be a work of second-hand inspiration. And it is true that, in reading Eliot and Pound, we are sometimes visited by uneasy recollections of Ausonius, in the fourth century, composing Greek-and-Latin macaronics and piecing together poetic mosaics out of verses from Virgil. Yet Eliot manages to be most effective precisely—in 'The Waste Land'— where he might be expected to be least original—he succeeds in conveying his meaning, in communicating his emotion, in spite of all his learned or mysterious allusions, and whether we understand them or not.

In this respect, there is a curious contrast between Eliot and Ezra Pound. Pound's work *has* been partially sunk by its cargo of erudition, whereas Eliot, in ten years' time, has left upon English poetry a mark more unmistakable than that of any other poet writing in English. It is, in fact, probably true at the present time that Eliot is being praised too extravagantly and Pound, though he has deeply influenced a few, on the whole unfairly neglected. I should explain Eliot's greater popularity by the fact that, for all his fragmentary method, he possesses a complete literary personality in a way that Pound, for all his integrity, does not. Ezra Pound, fine poet though he is, does not dominate us like a master imagination—he rather delights us like a miscellaneous collection of admirably chosen works of art. It is true that Pound, in spite of his inveterate translating, is a man of genuine originality— but his heterogeneous shorter poems, and the heterogeneous passages which go to make his longer ones, never seem to come together in a whole—as his general prose writing gives scrappy expression to a variety of ideas, a variety of enthusiasms and prejudices, some ridiculous and some valid, some learned and some half-baked, which, though valuable to his generation as polemic, as propaganda and as illuminating casual criticism, do not establish and develop a distinct reasoned point of view as Eliot's prose-writings do. T.S. Eliot has thought persistently and coherently about the relations between the different phases of human experience, and his passion for proportion and order is reflected in his poems. He is, in his way, a complete man, and if it is true, as I believe, that he has accomplished what he has credited Ezra Pound with accomplishing— if he has brought a new personal rhythm into the language—so that he has been able to lend even to the borrowed rhythms, the quoted words, of his great predecessors a new music and a new meaning—it is the intellectual completeness and soundness which has given his rhythm its special prestige.

Another factor which has probably contributed to Eliot's extraordinary success is the essentially dramatic character of his imagination. We may be puzzled by his continual preoccupation with the possibilities of a modern poetic drama—that is to say, of modern drama in verse. Why, we wonder, should he worry about drama in verse—why, after Ibsen, Hauptmann, Shaw and Chekov, should he be dissatisfied with plays in prose? We may put it down to an academic assumption that English drama ended when the blank verse of the Elizabethans ran into the sands, until it occurs to us that Eliot himself is really a dramatic poet. Mr. Prufrock and Sweeney are characters as none of the personages of Pound, Valéry or Yeats is—they have become a part of our modern mythology. And most of the best of Eliot's poems are based on unexpected dramatic contrasts: 'The Waste Land' especially, I am sure, owes a large part of its power to its dramatic quality, which makes it peculiarly effective read aloud. Eliot has even tried his hand at writing a play, and the two episodes from 'Wanna Go Home, Baby' which he has published in *The Criterion* seem rather promising. They are written in a sort of jazz dramatic metre which suggests certain scenes of John Howard Lawson's 'Processional'; and there can be no question that the future of drama in verse, if it has any future, lies in some such direction. 'We cannot reinstate,' Eliot has written, 'either blank verse or the heroic couplet. The next form of drama will have to be a verse drama, but in new verse forms. Perhaps the conditions of modern life (think how large a part is now played in our sensory life by the internal combustion engine!) have altered our perception of rhythms. At any rate, the recognised forms of speech-verse are not as efficient as they should be; probably a new form will be devised out of colloquial speech.'

In any case, that first handful of Eliot's poems, brought out in the middle of the War (1917) and generally read, if at all, at the time, as some sort of modern *vers de société*, was soon found, as Wyndham Lewis has said, to have had the effect of a little musk that scents up a whole room. And as for 'The Waste Land,' it enchanted and devastated a whole generation. Attempts have been made to reproduce it—by Aldington, Nancy Cunard, etc.—at least a dozen times. And as Eliot, lately out of Harvard, assumed the rôle of the middle-aged Prufrock and to-day, at forty, in one of his latest poems, 'The Song of Simeon,' speaks in the character of an old man 'with eighty years and no to-morrow'—so 'Gerontion' and 'The Waste Land' have made the young poets old before their time. In London, as in New York, and in the universities both here and in England, they for a time took to inhabiting exclusively barren beaches, cactus-grown deserts, and dusty attics overrun with rats—the only properties they allowed themselves to work with were a few fragments of old shattered glass or a sparse sprinkling of broken bones. They had purged themselves of Masefield as of Shelley for dry tongues and rheumatic joints. The dry breath of the Waste Land now blighted the most amiable country landscapes; and the sound of jazz, which had formerly seemed jolly, now inspired only horror and despair. But in this case, we may forgive the young for growing prematurely decrepit: where some of even the finest intelligences of the elder generation read 'The Waste Land' with blankness or laughter, the young had recognised a poet.

III

As a critic, Eliot occupies to-day a position of distinction and influence equal in importance to his position as a poet. His writings have been comparatively brief and rare—he has published only four small books of criticism—yet he has probably affected literary opinion, during the period since the War, more profoundly than any other critic writing English. Eliot's prose style has a kind of felicity different from that of his poetic style; it is almost primly precise and sober, yet with a sort of sensitive charm in its austerity—closely reasoned and making its points with the fewest possible words, yet always even, effortless and lucid. In a reaction against the impressionistic criticism which flourished at the end of the century and which has survived into our own time—the sort of criticism which, in dealing with poetry, attempts to reproduce its effect by having recourse to poetic prose—T.S. Eliot has undertaken a kind of scientific study of æsthetic values: avoiding impressionistic rhetoric and *a priori* æsthetic theories alike, he compares works of literature coolly and tries to distinguish between different orders of artistic effects and the different degrees of satisfaction to be derived from them.

And by this method, Eliot has done more than perhaps any other modern critic to effect a revaluation of English literature. We sometimes follow his literary criticism with the same sort of eagerness and excitement with which we follow a philosophical inquiry. Professor Saintsbury has played in literature much the same sort of rôle that he has played as a connoisseur of wines, that of an agreeable and entertaining guide of excellent taste and enormous experience; Edmund Gosse, often intelligent and courageous in dealing with French or Scandinavian writers, could never quite, when it came to English literature, bring himself to drop his official character of Librarian of the House of Lords—his attitude was always a little that of the Beefeater in the Tower of London, who assumes the transcendent value of the Crown Jewels which he has been set to guard and does not presume to form a personal opinion as to their taste or their respective merits; and the moral passion of Paul Elmer More has ended by paralysing his æsthetic appreciation. But T.S. Eliot, with an infinitely sensitive apparatus for æsthetic appreciation, approaching English literature as an American, with an American's peculiar combination of avidity and detachment and with more than the ordinary English critic's reading in the literatures, ancient and modern, of the Continent, has been able to succeed as few writers have done in the excessively delicate task of estimating English, Irish and American writers in relation to one another, and writers in English in relation to writers on the Continent. The extent of Eliot's influence is amazing: these short essays sent out without publicity as mere scattered notes on literature, yet sped with so intense a seriousness and weighted with so wide a learning, have not only had the effect of discrediting the academic clichés of the textbooks, but are even by way of establishing in the minds of the generation now in college a new set of literary clichés. With the ascendancy of T.S. Eliot, the Elizabethan dramatists have come back into fashion, and the nineteenth-century poets gone out. Milton's poetic reputation has sunk, and Dryden's and Pope's have risen. It is as much as one's life is worth nowadays, among young people, to say an approving word for Shelley or a dubious one about Donne. And as for the enthusiasm for Dante—to paraphrase the man in Hemingway's novel, there's been nothing like it since the Fratellinis!

Eliot's rôle as a literary critic has been very similar to Valéry's in France: indeed, the ideas of the two men and their ways of stating them have corresponded so closely that one guesses they must influence each other a good deal. Like Valéry, Eliot believes that a work of art is not an oracular outpouring, but an object which has been constructed deliberately with the aim of producing a certain effect. He has brought back to English criticism something of that trenchant rationalism which he admires in the eighteenth century, but with a much more catholic appreciation of different styles and points of view than the eighteenth century allowed. The Romantics, of course, fare badly before this criticism. Vague sentiment vaguely expressed, rhetorical effusion disguising bad art—these Eliot's laconic scorn has nipped. For him, Byron is 'a disorderly mind, and an uninteresting one': Keats and Shelley 'not nearly such great poets as they are supposed to be', whereas the powers of Dryden are 'wider, but no greater than those of Milton.' Just as Valéry lately protested in a lecture that he was unable to understand the well-known lines of Alfred de Musset:

Les plus désespérés sont les chants les plus beaux,
Et j'en sais d'immortels qui sont de purs sanglots.

so Eliot, in an essay on Crashaw, has confessed, with a certain superciliousness, his inability to understand the following stanza from Shelley's 'Skylark':

Keen as are the arrows
   Of that silver sphere
Whose intense lamp narrows
   In the white dawn clear,
Until we hardly see, who feel that it is there.

'For the first time, perhaps,' says Eliot, 'in verse of such eminence, sound exists without sense.'

It will be seen that Eliot differs from Valéry in believing that poetry should make 'sense.' And he elsewhere, in his essay on Dante in 'The Sacred Wood,' remonstrates with Valéry for asserting that philosophy has no place in poetry. Yet Eliot's point of view, though more intelligently reasoned and expressed, comes down finally to the same sort of thing as Valéry's and seems to me open to the same sort of objection. Eliot's conclusion in respect to the relation of philosophy to poetry is that, though philosophy *has* its place in poetry, it is only as something which we 'see' among the other things with which the poet presents us, a set of ideas which penetrate his world, as in the case of the 'Divina Commedia': in the case of such a poet as Lucretius, the philosophy sometimes seems antagonistic to the poetry only because it happens to be a philosophy 'not rich enough in feeling . . . incapable of complete expansion into pure vision.' Furthermore, 'the original form of philosophy cannot be poetic': the poet must use a philosophy already invented by somebody else. Now, though we may admire the justice of Eliot's judgments on the various degrees of artistic success achieved by Dante, Lucretius and others, it becomes plainer and plainer, as time goes on, that the real effect of Eliot's, as of Valéry's literary criticism, is to impose upon us a conception of poetry as some sort of pure and rare æsthetic essence with no relation to any of the practical human uses for which, for some reason never explained, only the technique of prose is appropriate.

Now this point of view, as I have already suggested in writing about Paul Valéry, seems to me absolutely unhistorical—an impossible attempt to make æsthetic values independent of all the other values. Who will agree with Eliot, for example, that a poet cannot be an original thinker and that it is not possible for a poet to be a completely successful artist and yet persuade us to accept this idea at the same time? There is a good deal in Dante's morality which he never got out of the Scholastics, as, for all we know, there may be a good deal in Lucretius which he never got out of Epicurus. When we read Lucretius and Dante, we are affected by them just as we are by prose writers of eloquence and imagination—we are compelled to take their opinions seriously. And as soon as we admit that prose writing may be considered on the same basis with verse, it becomes evident that we cannot, in the case of Plato, discriminate so finely as to the capacity of his philosophy for being 'expanded into pure vision' that we are able to put our finger on the point where the novelist or poet stops and the scientist or metaphysician begins; nor, with Blake any more than with Nietzsche and Emerson, distinguish the poet from the aphorist. The truth is, of course, that, in Lucretius' time, verse was used for all sorts of didactic purposes for which we no longer consider it appropriate—they had agricultural poems, astronomical poems, poems of literary criticism. How can the 'Georgics,' the 'Ars Poetica' and Manilius be dealt with from the point of view of the capacity of their material for being 'expanded into pure vision'? To modern readers, the subjects of the 'Georgics—bee-keeping, stock-raising, and so forth—seem unsuitable and sometimes annoying in verse; yet for Virgil's contemporaries, the poem must have been completely successful—as, indeed, granted the subject, it is. Nor does it follow that, because we are coming to use poetry for fewer and fewer literary purposes, our critical taste is becoming more and more refined, so that we are beginning to perceive for the first time the true, pure and exalted function of poetry: that is, simply, as Valéry says, to produce a 'state'—as

Eliot says, to afford a 'superior amusement.' It is much more likely that for some reason or other, verse as a technique of literary expression is being abandoned by humanity altogether—perhaps because it is a more primitive, and hence a more barbarous technique than prose. Is it possible to believe, for example, that Eliot's hope of having verse reinstated on the stage—even verse of the new kind which he proposes—is likely ever to be realised?

The tendency to keep verse isolated from prose and to confine it to certain highly specialised functions dates in English at least from the time of Coleridge, when, in spite of the long narrative poems which were fashionable, verse was already beginning to fall into disuse. Coleridge defined a poem as 'that species of composition which is opposed to works of science by proposing for its *immediate* object pleasure, not truth; and from all other species (having *this* object in common with it), it is discriminated by proposing to itself such delight from the *whole*, as is compatible with a distinct gratification from each component part.' Poe, who had doubtless read Coleridge on the subject, wrote thirty years later that there was no such thing as a long poem, that 'no very long poem would ever be popular again,' etc. Eliot and Valéry follow Coleridge and Poe in their theory as well as in their verse, and they seem to me to confuse certain questions by talking as if the whole of literature existed simultaneously in a vacuum, as if Homer's and Shakespeare's situations had been the same as Mallarmé's and Laforgue's, as if the latter had been attempting to play the same sort of rôles as the former and could be judged on the same basis. It is inevitable, of course, that we should try to arrive at absolute values through the comparison of the work of different periods—I have just praised Eliot for his success at this—but it seems to me that in this particular matter a good many difficulties would be cleared up if certain literary discussions could be removed from the artifically restricted field of verse—in which it is assumed that nothing is possible or desirable but a quintessential distillation called 'poetry,' and that that distillation has nothing in common with anything possible to obtain through prose—to the field of literature in general. Has not such a great modern novel as 'Madame Bovary,' for example, at least as much in common with Virgil and Dante as with Balzac and Dickens? Is it not comparable from the point of view of intensity, music and perfection of the parts, with the best verse of any period? And we shall consider Joyce in this connection later.

With all gratitude, therefore, for the salutary effect of Eliot's earlier criticism in curbing the carelessness and gush of the aftermath of Romanticism, it seems plain that the anti-Romantic reaction is leading finally into pedantry and into a futile æstheticism. 'Poetry,' Eliot wrote in 'The Sacred Wood,' 'is not a turning loose of emotion, but an escape from emotion; it is not the expression of personality, but an escape from personality. But, of course, only those who have personality and emotion know what it means to want to escape from them.' This was valid, and even noble, in 1920 when 'The

Sacred Wood' was published; but to-day, after ten years of depersonalised and over-intellectualised verse, so much of it written in imitation of Eliot, the same sort of thing in the mouths of Eliot's disciples sounds like an excuse for *not* possessing emotion and personality.

Yet, in spite of the weaknesses of Eliot's position as he has sometimes been driven to state it dogmatically, he has himself largely succeeded in escaping the vices which it seems to encourage. The old nineteenth-century criticism of Ruskin, Renan, Taine, Sainte-Beuve, was closely allied to history and novel writing, and was also the vehicle for all sorts of ideas about the purpose and destiny of human life in general. The criticism of our own day examines literature, art, ideas and specimens of human society in the past with a detached scientific interest or a detached æsthetic appreciation which seems in either case to lead nowhere. A critic like Herbert Read makes dull discriminations between different kinds of literature; a critic like Albert Thibaudet discovers dull resemblances between the ideas of philosophers and poets; a critic like I.A. Richards writes about poetry from the point of view of a scientist studying the psychological reactions of readers; and such a critic as Clive Bell writes about painting so exclusively and cloyingly from the point of view of the varying degrees of pleasure to be derived from the pictures of different painters that we would willingly have Ruskin and all his sermonising back. And even Virginia Woolf and Lytton Strachey have this in common with Clive Bell that they seem to feel they have done enough when they have distinguished the kind of pleasure to be derived from one kind of book, the kind of interest to be felt in one kind of personality, from the kind to be found in another. One is supposed to have read everything and enjoyed everything and to understand exactly the reasons for one's enjoyment, but not to enjoy anything excessively nor to raise an issue of one kind of thing against another. Each of the essays of Strachey or Mrs. Woolf, so compact yet so beautifully rounded out, is completely self-contained and does not lead to anything beyond itself; and finally, for all their brilliance, we begin to find them tiresome.

Now there is a good deal in T.S. Eliot of this pedantry and sterility of his age. He is very much given, for example, to becoming involved in literary Houses-that-Jack-Built: 'We find this quality occasionally in Wordsworth,' he will write, 'but it is a quality which Wordsworth shares with Shenstone rather than with Collins and Gray. And for the right sort of enjoyment of Shenstone, we must read his prose as well as his verse. The "Essays on Men and Manners" are in the tradition of the great French aphorists of the seventeenth century, and should be read with the full sense of their relation to Vauvenargues, La Rochefoucauld and (with his wider range) La Bruyère. We shall do well to read enough of Theophrastus to understand the kind of effect at which La Bruyère aimed. (Professor Somebody-or-other's book on "Theophrastus and the Peripatetics" gives us the clue to the intellectual atmosphere in which Theophrastus wrote and enables us to gauge the influences on his work—very different from each other—of Plato and Aristotle.)' At this rate (though I have parodied Eliot), we should have to read the whole of literature in order to appreciate a single book, and Eliot fails to supply us with a reason why we should go to the trouble of doing so. Yet against the background of the criticism of his time, Eliot has stood out unmistakably as a man passionately interested in literature. The real intensity of his enthusiasm makes us forget the primness of his tone; and his occasional dogmatism is redeemed by his ability to see beyond his own ideas, his willingness to admit the relative character of his own conclusions.

IV

But if Eliot, in spite of the meagreness of his production, has become for his generation a leader, it is also because his career has been a progress, because he has evidently been on his way somewhere, when many of his contemporaries, more prolific and equally gifted, have been fixed in their hedonism or despair. The poet of 'The Waste Land' was too serious to continue with the same complacence as some of his contemporaries inhabiting that godforsaken desert. It was certain he would not stick at that point, and one watched him to see what he would do.

This destination has now, however, become plain. In the preface to the new 1928 edition of 'The Sacred Wood,' poetry is still regarded as a 'superior amusement,' but Eliot reports on his part 'an expansion or development of interests.' Poetry is now perceived to have 'something to do with morals, and with religion, and even with politics perhaps, though we cannot say what.' In 'For Lancelot Andrewes,' published in the same year, Eliot declares himself a classicist in literature, an Anglo-Catholic in religion and a royalist in politics, and announces that he has in preparation 'three small books' treating of these subjects and to be called respectively 'The School of Donne,' 'The Principles of Modern Heresy,' and 'The Outline of Royalism.' There follows a slender selection of essays, which hint quietly at what may be expected.

We must await the further exposition of Eliot's new body of doctrine before it will be possible to discuss it properly. In the meantime, we can only applaud his desire to formulate a consistent central position, at the same time that we may regret the unpromising character of the ideals and institutions which he invokes. One cannot but recognise in Eliot's recent writings a kind of reactionary point of view which had already been becoming fashionable among certain sorts of literary people—a point of view which has much in common with that of the neo-Thomists in France and that of the Humanists in America. 'Unless by civilisation,' writes Eliot, 'you mean material progress, cleanliness, etc. . . . if you mean a spiritual co-ordination on a high level, then it is doubtful whether civilisation can endure without religion, and religion without a church.' Yet you can hardly have an effective church without a cult of Christ as the son of God; and you cannot have such a cult without more willingness to accept the supernatural than most of us to-day are able to muster. We feel in contemporary writers like Eliot a desire to believe in religious revelation, a belief that it would be a good thing to believe, rather than a genuine belief. The faith of the modern convert seems to burn only with a low blue flame. 'Our literature,' Eliot has himself recently made a character in a dialogue say, 'is a substitute for religion, and so is our religion.' From such a faith, uninspired by hope, unequipped with zeal or force, what guidance for the future can we expect?

One cannot, however, doubt the reality of the experience to which Eliot testifies in his recent writings—though it seems to us less an Anglo-Catholic conversion than a reawakening of the New Englander's conscience, of the never quite exorcised conviction of the ineradicable sinfulness of man. Eliot admires Machiavelli because Machiavelli assumes the baseness of human nature as an unalterable fact; and he looks for light to the theologians who offer salvation, not through economic readjustment, political reform, education or biological and psychological study, but solely through 'grace.' Eliot apparently to-day regards 'Evil' as some sort of ultimate reality, which it is impossible either to correct or to analyse. His moral principles seem to me stronger and more authentic than his religious mysticism—and his relation to the Anglo-Catholic Church appears largely artificial. The English seventeenth century divines whose poetry and sermons he admires so much, upon whom he seems so much to depend for nourishment, exist in a richer, a more mysterious, a more heavily saturated atmosphere, in which even monumental outlines are blurred; Eliot himself is stiffer and cooler, more intent, more relentless, more clear. He has his own sort of graciousness, but he seems, as the phrase is, a little thin-lipped. His religious tradition has reached him by way of Boston.

In any case, Eliot's new phase of piety has brought with it a new humility. He apologises in his 1928 preface for the 'assumption of pontifical solemnity' which he now detects in 'The Sacred Wood,' and his recent little book on Dante (a most admirable introduction) not merely surprises but almost embarrasses us by the modesty with which Eliot professes to desire nothing but to be of use to beginners and to tell us of a few of the beautiful things which he has found in the great poet. I will not say that this humility has enfeebled his poetry. The three devout little poems which he has published as Christmas cards since 'The Hollow Men' announced the nadir of the phase of sterility and despair given such effective expression in 'The Waste Land,' seem comparatively uninspired; but the long poem or group of poems, 'Ash-Wednesday' (1930), which follows a scheme somewhat similar to that of 'The Waste Land,' is a not unworthy successor to it.

The poet begins with the confession of his bankruptcy:

Early Poems and *The Waste Land*

> *Because I do not hope to turn again*
> *Because I do not hope*
> *Because I do not hope to turn*
> *Desiring this man's gift and that man's scope*
> *I no longer strive to strive towards such things*
> *(Why should the agèd eagle stretch its wings?)*
> *Why should I mourn*
> *The vanished power of the usual reign? . . .*
>
> *Because these wings are no longer wings to fly*
> *But merely vans to beat the air*
> *The air which is now thoroughly small and dry*
> *Smaller and dryer than the will*
> *Teach us to care and not to care*
> *Teach us to sit still.*
>
> *Pray for us sinners now and at the hour of our death*
> *Pray for us now and at the hour of our death.*

There follow passages in which the prayer is apparently answered: the poet's contrition and pious resignation are rewarded by a series of visions which first console then lighten his heart. We find an imagery new for Eliot, a symbolism semi-ecclesiastical and not without a Pre-Raphaelite flavour: white leopards, a Lady gowned in white, junipers and yews, 'The Rose' and 'The Garden,' and jewelled unicorns drawing a gilded hearse: these are varied by an interlude which returns to the imagery and mood of 'The Waste Land,' and a swirling churning anguished passage which suggests certain things of Gertrude Stein's. At last the themes of the first section recur: the impotent wings of the agèd eagle seem to revive as,

> *From the wide window toward the granite shore*
> *The white sails still fly seaward, seaward flying*
> *Unbroken wings.*
>
> *And the lost heart stiffens and rejoices*
> *In the lost lilac and the lost sea voices*
> *And the weak spirit quickens to rebel*
> *For the bent golden-rod and the lost sea smell*
> *Quickens to recover*
> *The cry of quail and the whirling plover*
> *And the blind eye creates*
> *The empty forms between the ivory gates*
> *And smell renews the salt savour of the sandy earth . . .*

The broken prayer, at once childlike and mystically subtle, with which the poem ends seems to imply that the poet has come closer to the strength and revelation he craves: grace is about to descend.

Blessèd sister, holy mother, spirit of the fountain, spirit of the garden,
Suffer us not to mock ourselves with falsehood
Teach us to care and not to care
Teach us to sit still
Even among these rocks,
Our peace in His will
And even among these rocks
Sister, mother
And spirit of the river, spirit of the sea,
Suffer me not to be separated

And let my cry come unto Thee.

The literary and conventional imagery upon which 'Ash-Wednesday' so largely relies and which is less vivid because more artificial than that of Eliot's earlier poems, seems to me a definite feature of inferiority; the 'devil of the stairs' and the 'shape twisted on the banister,' which are in Eliot's familiar and unmistakable personal vein, somehow come off better than the jewelled unicorn, which incongruously suggests Yeats. And I am made a little tired at hearing Eliot, only in his early forties, present himself as an 'agèd eagle' who asks why he should make the effort to stretch his wings. Yet 'Ash-Wednesday,' though less brilliant and intense than Eliot at his very best, is distinguished by most of the qualities which made his other poems remarkable: the exquisite phrasing in which we feel that every word is in its place and that there is not a word too much; the metrical mastery which catches so naturally, yet with so true a modulation, the faltering accents of the supplicant, blending the cadences of the liturgy with those of perplexed brooding thought; and, above all, that 'peculiar honesty' in 'exhibiting the essential sickness or strength of the human soul 'of which Eliot has written in connection with Blake and which, in his own case, even at the moment when his psychological plight seems most depressing and his ways of rescuing himself from it least sympathetic, still gives him a place among those upon whose words we reflect with most interest and whose tones we remember longest.

101
From *The Coming Struggle for Power*[*]

◆

JOHN STRACHEY

And if an Englishman ventures to call in question any of the claims of poetry, he does so with trepidation. For poetry, for 'pure' literature in its widest sense, has been by far the greatest æsthetic achievement of the English. Laggards and dunces at the plastic arts, heirs to a tradition of native music which somehow died before it had had the opportunity to come to maturity, the English have century after century poured their fancy into a golden stream of poetry, which is without rival in the world. For the English nature, like that, indeed, of all the major peoples of the world has contained, as well as its predominantly extrovert strain, an element of profound, subtle and dreaming contemplation. Keats was as typical an Englishman as Wellington—D.H. as T.E. Lawrence. From Chaucer to Shelley the stream flows unbroken. Then it begins to trickle. The nineteenth century produced its great poets; men as gifted as their ancestors. Yet somehow they all, Tennyson and Browning, Arnold and Swinburne, failed to establish their place in the essential tradition. And as the old century closed and as the new one began, a new and strange thing happened. It was not that poets failed to appear: it was not, principally, that their quality deteriorated. It was rather that they began to shrink in size. The poets were there all right, but they became smaller and smaller—till now most of them are hardly visible to the naked eye. Beautiful and satisfying individual poems are occasionally still written: but they appear at longer and longer intervals, and with, it seems, greater and greater difficulty: more and more tortured efforts are necessary to write them, and one or two short books are the most that any individual poet achieves.

Mr. A.E. Housman is the very last of the English classical poets: and one of the most typical. But what a little one! Two tiny volumes are all that he has written. And the second is called, conclusively, *Last Poems*. The lovely and sombre verses which it contains are indeed ultimate in a larger sense than that they are all that we can expect from Mr. Housman. They are the

[*] New York, 1933, pp. 218–21.

last streamlet of that glorious river of verse, in which the joy of man in nature, a simple and yet satisfying philosophy, and an abounding, untamed fantasy have mingled to refresh the lives of successive generations of Englishmen.[1] And if we are apt to prize Mr. Housman above his real worth, it is because:

No spring, nor summer beauty hath such grace
As I have seen in one autumnal face.

True, a new school of poets has arisen in the last decades. They are, however, in spite of their deep appreciation of, and erudition in, the English classics, a new species, sharply different from any which have ever appeared in England before. They admit to the impossibility of the old tradition of poetry. This is a place totally inappropriate for a discussion of their work.[2] The most considerable product, however, of this school, Mr. T.S. Eliot's poem *The Waste Land*, is such an extraordinarily vivid example of the reactions of a sensitive man to the decay of the whole system of society into which he has been born, that it cannot be overlooked. It was published in 1922, and was, therefore, written at the most acute point of the post-war crisis of capitalism. *The Waste Land* is the most considerable poem produced in English in our day. It expresses the whole agonizing disintegration of an old and once strong social system with the greatest poignancy. The sad purpose of the poet is perfectly served by the poem's very form. It has a lack of formal eloquence; it has queer, haunting, broken, almost furtive, numbers which are for ever rising towards a passage of classic eloquence and are for ever falling back before they have achieved it; which are scattered into fragments, dismembered into snatches of song, as if they were themselves disenchanted of the possibility of all achievement and completion anywhere, any more, on the whole earth. Naturally, there is a more personal side to the poem. In many earlier, and far inferior poems, Mr. Eliot had shown himself not much more than a typical New England Puritan, lamenting delicately over lost opportunities.[3] Mr. Prufrock [prudent frock?], his favourite impersonation of himself, is little more than this. And it is, of course, quite legitimate to identify *The Waste Land* with this side of Mr. Eliot's character instead of with contemporary society. And yet, as a matter of fact, what the poem itself tells us is quite simply that the Waste Land is London. (And the poem will always remain supremely moving to Londoners on that account.) London, and the life being led to-day by different classes of people in London is quite straightforwardly and directly the subject of almost every one of the five sections of the poem. Even towards the end of the first introductory section, after a little comment on the 'stony rubbish' of contemporary European life, we come to the first invocation of the city—

Unreal City,
Under the brown fog of a winter dawn,
A crowd flowed over London Bridge, so many,
I had not thought death had undone so many.

155

Early Poems and *The Waste Land*

The second part is the simplest and most direct of all. It consists entirely of two sections contrasting the lives of the rich and the poor, and finding them both hideous. It begins with a passage of sustained eloquence describing an exquisite setting for the life of a rich woman, and then breaks up sharply into dismembered futility.

> '*My nerves are bad to-night. Yes, bad. Stay with me.*
> *Speak to me. Why do you never speak. Speak.*
> *What are you thinking of? What thinking? What?*
> *I never know what you are thinking. Think.*'
>
> *I think we are in rats' alley.*
> *Where the dead men lost their bones.*
>
> '*What is that noise?*'
>   *The wind under the door.*
> '*What is that noise now? What is the wind doing?*'
>   *Nothing again nothing.*
>   '*Do*
> *You know nothing? Do you see nothing? Do you remember*
> *Nothing?*'
>
>   . . .
>
> '*What shall I do now? What shall I do?*'
> '*I shall rush out as I am, and walk the street*
> *With my hair down, so. What shall we do to-morrow?*
> *What shall we ever do?*'
>   *The hot water at ten.*
> *And if it rains, a closed car at four.*

Then comes the life of the poor—the conversation between the women as the pub is closing.

> *When Lil's husband got demobbed, I said—*
> *I didn't mince my words, I said to her myself,*
> *HURRY UP PLEASE ITS TIME*
> *Now Albert's coming back, make yourself a bit smart.*
> *He'll want to know what you done with that money he gave you*
> *To get yourself some teeth. He did, I was there.*
> *You have them all out, Lil, and get a nice set,*
> *He said, I swear, I can't bear to look at you.*
> *And no more can't I, I said, and think of poor Albert.*

There follows a long, terrible catalogue of the premature ageing of the women of the working class, enforced by poverty, ignorance, clumsy abortions and the like. The section ends with a half ironic, half tragic use of Ophelia's farewell.

> HURRY UP PLEASE ITS TIME
> Goonight Bill. Goonight Lou. Goonight May. Goonight.
> Ta Ta. Goonight. Goonight.
> Good night, ladies, good night, sweet ladies, good night, good night.

Part III. is all London again. The Thames in Autumn gradually clearing itself of the debris of the river parties—

> *The nymphs are departed.*
> *And their friends, the loitering heirs of City directors* . . .

And then the invocation again.

> *Unreal City*
> *Under the brown fog of a winter noon*
> *Mr. Eugenides, the Smyrna merchant*
> *Unshaven, with a pocket full of currants*
> *C.i.f. London: documents at sight* . . .

There follows the famous scene of lower middle-class life, in which the bored, tired, typist is, meaninglessly, futilely and therefore horribly, possessed after tea in her bed-sitting-room by the 'small house-agent's clerk,' 'carbuncular.'

At this point appears the poet's romantic longing for a less arid and intolerable past. We get the memory of London as it had been when Elizabeth and Leicester sailed the Thames, and, with Part IV., of the days when tragedy was at any rate beautiful and fertile, the exquisite short lyric of the 'Death by Water' of Phlebas the Phœnician.

Finally, in Part V., we have repeatedly expressed the falling apart and dying of everything that the poet knows.

> *He who was living is now dead*
> *We who were living are now dying*
> *With a little patience.*

> *Falling towers*
> *Jerusalem Athens Alexandria*
> *Vienna London*
> *Unreal.*

> *London Bridge is falling down falling down falling down.*

There are, of course, other elements in the poem. There is the theme, as we have suggested already, of Mr. Eliot's personal predicament, and there is the theme which foreshadows the mystical solution which he has since found for both his own problems and society's. But perhaps such quotations as have been given are sufficient to demonstrate beyond argument the overruling influence of current social decay on the first poet of the day.

Since writing *The Waste Land* Mr. Eliot, encouraged no doubt by the 1922–1929 period of capitalist recovery, has left the despair of the Waste Land behind him and taken up the typical position of a highly intellectual reactionary. He has become, he tells us, 'a classicist in literature, a royalist in politics, and an Anglo-Catholic in religion. (Why cannot he be, at any rate, a real Catholic? Becoming an Anglo-Catholic must surely be a sad business—rather like becoming an amateur conjurer.)

Notes

1. Thomas Hardy, and even Bridges, have a few lines in the great tradition. So has Mr. Davies and Mr. De La Mare. These are but lingering drops.

2. Mr. Max Eastman has written a sensible study of what the modern poets are and why they write as oddly as they do. He comes to the conclusion that when a mountain of pretentious nonsense has been stripped off them, some of their work does really represent an attempt to create the only kind of literature which will, in the immediate future be possible. His account of the literary man's reactions both to the growth of science and to the ever-increasing crisis in capitalism is valuable. See his book, *The Literary Mind*.

3. Mr. Eliot's feverish erudition is characteristically American. In *The Waste Land*, for example, he does not so much use the accumulated culture of the old world, as ransack it. Yet perhaps it is just because he is an American that he has had the courage and energy to write the epitaph of the culture of the old world.

102
T.S. Eliot

F.R. LEAVIS

The title poem, *The Love Song of J. Alfred Prufrock*, which is printed at the beginning of *Poems 1909–1925*, represents a complete break with the nineteenth-century tradition, and a new start. It must indeed have been difficult to take seriously in 1917, for it defies the traditional canon of seriousness:

> *I grow old . . . I grow old . . .*
> *I shall wear the bottoms of my trousers rolled.*

Can this be poetry? And yet there are passages that, for all their oddness of imagery and tone, do not immediately condemn themselves as 'unpoetical' even by anthological standards:

> *The yellow fog that rubs its back upon the window-panes,*
> *The yellow smoke that rubs its muzzle on the window-panes*
> *Licked its tongue into the corners of the evening,*
> *Lingered upon the pools that stand in drains,*
> *Let fall upon its back the soot that falls from chimneys,*
> *Slipped by the terrace, made a sudden leap,*
> *And seeing that it was a soft October night,*
> *Curled once about the house, and fell asleep.*

—Indeed, it is as necessary to revise the traditional idea of the distinction between seriousness and levity in approaching this poetry as in approaching the Metaphysical poetry of the seventeenth century. And as striking as this subtlety and flexibility of tone, this complexity of attitude, is the nature (exemplified in the passage just quoted) of the imagery. The canons of the poetical are forgotten; the poet assumes the right to make use of any materials that seem to him significant. We have here, in short, poetry that expresses freely a modern sensibility, the ways of feeling, the modes of experience, of one fully alive in his own age. Already the technical achievement is such as to be rich in promise of development and application.

Yet it must be admitted that if *The Love Song of J. Alfred Prufrock* stood

---

*From *New Bearings in English Poetry* (London, 1932), pp. 75–132.

alone there would be some excuse for unreadiness to recognize in it this kind of significance. A certain heaviness about the gestures ('heavy' in the sense of caricature)—

*Do I dare
Disturb the universe?*

and

Though I have seen my head (grown slightly bald) brought in upon a platter

—emphasizes the touch of conscious elegance in the disillusion, and makes 'clever' seem a more adequate description than it ought:

*I have seen the moment of my greatness flicker,
And I have seen the eternal Footman hold my coat, and snicker,
And in short, I was afraid.*

But in *Portrait of a Lady* the poise is more subtle, and it is maintained with sure and exquisite delicacy. The poet's command both of his experience and of his technique (if we can distinguish) is perfect. Without any limiting suggestion of caricature he can write:

*And I must borrow every changing shape
To find expression . . . dance, dance
Like a dancing bear,
Cry like a parrot, chatter like an ape.
Let us take the air, in a tobacco trance—*

*Well! and what if she should die some afternoon,
Afternoon grey and smoky, evening yellow and rose;
Should die and leave me sitting pen in hand
With the smoke coming down above the house-tops . . .*

The flexibility and the control of this are maintained throughout the poem. The utterances of the lady are in the idiom and cadence of modern speech, and they go perfectly with the movement of the verse, which, for all its freedom and variety, is nevertheless very strict and precise. The poet is as close to the contemporary world as any novelist could be, and his formal verse medium makes possible a concentration and a directness, audacities of transition and psychological notation, such as are forbidden to the novelist. Only a very strong originality could so have triumphed over traditional habits, and only very strong preconceptions could hinder the poem's being recognized as the work of a major poet.

Portrait of a Lady is the most remarkable thing in the *Prufrock* section. *Preludes* and *Rhapsody on a Windy Night* develop that imagery of urban disillusion which has since done so much service in the verse of adolescent romantic pessimists. The use of this imagery relates him to Baudelaire, and the occasion now arises to note his debt to certain later French poets. To a young practitioner faced with Mr Eliot's problems, Tristan Corbière and Jules Laforgue offered starting points such as were not to be found in English poetry of the nineteenth century. How closely he studied French verse may be gathered from the verse, retained in *Poems 1909–1925*, that he himself wrote in French. He learnt, by his own account, from Jules Laforgue in particular, and the evidence is apparent in his early work. The evidence lies not so much in a Laforguian exercise like *Conversation Galante* as in *The Love Song of J. Alfred Prufrock* and *Portrait of a Lady*. It is difficult to distinguish between attitude and technique: he was able to derive means of expression from Laforgue because of a certain community with him in situation and sensibility. The self-ironical, self-distrustful attitudes of *Prufrock* owe their definition largely to Laforgue, and there the technical debt shows itself; it shows itself in the ironical transitions, and also in the handling of the verse. But this last head has been made too much of by some critics: French moves so differently from English that to learn from French verse an English poet must be strongly original. And to learn as Mr Eliot learnt in general from Laforgue is to be original to the point of genius. Already in the collection of 1917 he is himself as only a major poet can be.

The other derivation he assigns to his verse—'the form in which I began to write, in 1908 or 1909, was directly drawn from the study of Laforgue together with the later Elizabethan drama'[1]—manifests itself plainly in the first poem of the section following *Prufrock*, that dated 1920. It is not for nothing that in *Gerontion* he alludes to one of the finest passages of Middleton:

> *I that was near your heart was removed therefrom*
> *To lose beauty in terror, terror in inquisition.*
> *I have lost my passion: why should I need to keep it*
> *Since what is kept must be adulterated?*
>
> Gerontion

> *I that am of your blood was taken from you*
> *For your better health; look no more upon it,*
> *But cast it to the ground regardlessly.*
> *Let the common sewer take it from distinction.*
>
> The Changeling, V, iii

The comparison would be worth making at greater length in order to bring out, not only the likeness in movement of Mr Eliot's verse to mature Elizabethan dramatic verse, but also Mr Eliot's astonishing power. Nowhere in Middleton, or, for that matter, Webster, Tourneur, or anywhere outside Shakespeare, can we find a passage so sustained in quality as *Gerontion*. In his essay on Massinger[2] he says: 'with the end of Chapman, Middleton, Webster, Tourneur, Donne, we end a period when the intellect was immediately at the tips of the senses. Sensation became word and word sensation.' *Gerontion* answers to this description as well as anything by any of the authors

Early Poems and *The Waste Land*

enumerated: it expresses psychological subtleties and complexities in imagery of varied richness and marvellously sure realization. The whole body of the words seems to be used. Qualities that (if we ignore Hopkins as he was ignored) have been absent from English poetry since the period that Mr Eliot describes (his critical preoccupation with it is significant) reappear with him.

The effect of his few and brief critical references to Milton is notorious. The effect upon Miltonic influence of his practice is likely to be even more radical. If we look at the first *Hyperion* of Keats we see that it points forward to Tennyson and backward to Milton. This simple reminder (a safe generalization would call for more qualifying than is in place here) serves to bring home the prevalence of certain limitations in the way in which English has been used in poetry since Milton. Milton and Tennyson are very different, but when Tennyson, or any other poet of the nineteenth century (which saw a rough first draft in the revised *Hyperion*), wrote blank verse, even when he intended it to be dramatic, it followed Milton rather than Shakespeare—a Milton who could be associated with Spenser. Even when Shakespeare was consciously the model, it was a Shakespeare felt through Milton. Language was used in a generally Miltonic way even in un-Miltonic verse. To justify the phrase, 'a generally Miltonic way', a difficult and varying analysis would be necessary; but I have in mind Milton's habit of exploiting language as a kind of musical medium outside himself, as it were. There is no pressure in his verse of any complex and varying current of feeling and sensation; the words have little substance or muscular quality: Milton is using only a small part of the resources of the English language. The remoteness of his poetic idiom from his own speech is to be considered here. ('English must be kept up,' said Keats, explaining his abandonment of the Miltonic first *Hyperion*.) A man's most vivid emotional and sensuous experience is inevitably bound up with the language that he actually speaks.

The brief account given above of the relation of *Gerontion* to Middleton and his contemporaries must not be allowed to suggest that Mr Eliot's verse has anything in it of pastiche. For all its richness and variety and power of assimilating odds and ends from Lancelot Andrewes [for instance], its staple idiom and movement derive immediately from modern speech.

These considerations have been put too briefly to be critically impregnable: no simple formula will cover poetic practice in the nineteenth century. That they can be put so briefly and yet serve their purpose, that one can take so much for understood, is due to Mr Eliot. That young practitioners are now using words very differently from the poets of the last age is also due mainly to him.

The dramatic derivation of the verse is not all that there is dramatic about *Gerontion*: it has a really dramatic detachment. In this respect it represents a great advance upon anything printed earlier in *Poems 1909–1925*. *Prufrock* and *Portrait of a Lady* are concerned with the directly personal embarrassments,

Studies of *The Waste Land* and poems

disillusions, and distresses of a sophisticated young man. It is not a superficial difference that *Gerontion* has for *persona* an old man, embodying a situation remote from that of the poet. From a position far above his immediate concerns as a particular individual, projecting himself, as it were, into a comprehensive and representative human consciousness, the poet contemplates human life and asks what it all comes to. The introductory quotation gives the hint:

> *Thou hast nor youth nor age*
> *But as it were an after dinner sleep*
> *Dreaming of both.*

—*Gerontion* has the impersonality of great poetry.

In method, too, *Gerontion* represents a development. Since the method is that, or a large part of that, of *The Waste Land*, it seems better to risk some elementary observations upon it, for *The Waste Land* has been found difficult. Instructions how to read the poem (should anything more than the title and the epigraph be necessary) are given in the last line:

> *Tenants of the house,*
> *Thoughts of a dry brain in a dry season.*

It has neither narrative nor logical continuity, and the only theatre in which the characters mentioned come together, or could, is the mind of the old man. The Jew who squats on the window-sill could not hear the old man even if he spoke his thoughts aloud, and the field overhead in which the goat coughs has no geographical relation to the house. All the persons, incidents, and images are there to evoke the immediate consciousness of the old man as he broods over a life lived through and asks what is the outcome, what the meaning, what the residue. This seems simple enough, and the transitions and associations are not obscure.

The poem opens with what is to be a recurrent theme of Mr Eliot's: the mixing of 'memory and desire' in present barrenness. The old man in his 'dry month', waiting for the life-giving 'rain' that he knows will never come, is stirred to envy, then to poignant recollection, by the story of hot-blooded vitality, which contrasts with the squalor of his actual surroundings. Youthful desire mingles in memory with the most exalted emotions, those associated with the mysteries of religion:

> *The word within a word, unable to speak a word,*
> *Swaddled with darkness. In the juvescence of the year*
> *Came Christ the tiger.*
>
> *In depraved May . . .*

Here, in the last two phrases, Mr Eliot does in concentration what he does by his notorious transitions from theme to theme: widely different emotions and

Early Poems and *The Waste Land*

feelings are contrasted and fused. It is the kind of effect that Shakespeare gets in such a line as

Lilies that fester smell far worse than weeds,[3]

where the associations that cluster round 'lilies'—fragrant flowers and emblems of purity—are contrasted and fused with those attaching to 'fester', which applies to rotting flesh.

In *Gerontion* the contrast is developed: the emotional intensities evoked by the reference to the Sacrament are contrasted with the stale cosmopolitan depravity evoked by the names and by the suggested incidents and associations:

To be eaten, to be divided, to be drunk
Among whispers; by Mr Silvero
With caressing hands, at Limoges
Who walked all night in the next room;

By Hakagawa, bowing among the Titians;
By Madame de Tornquist, in the dark room
Shifting the candles; Fräulein von Kulp
Who turned in the hall, one hand on the door.

'Among whispers' may be pointed to as a characteristic transition. They are first the whispers of religious awe; then, in the new context, they become clandestine and sinister, the whispers of intrigue. The reference to 'the Titians' brings in art: art and religion, the two refuges from time and the sordid actuality, suffer the same staling depravation. Fräulein von Kulp is seen vividly, a precise particular figure in a precise particular posture, but far in the past; she serves only to emphasize the present vacancy:

Vacant shuttles
Weave the wind. I have no ghosts,
An old man in a draughty house
Under a windy knob.

But this kind of elucidation is perhaps insulting. At any rate, no more can be needed: more than enough has been done to illustrate the method. And only an analysis on Mr Empson's lines[4] could be anything like fair to the subtleties of the poem; for Mr Eliot's effects depend a great deal upon ambiguity. One of the most obvious instances occur near the end:

. . . De Bailhache, Fresca, Mrs Cammel, whirled
Beyond the circuit of the shuddering Bear
In fractured atoms. Gull against the wind, in the windy straits
Of Belle Isle, or running on the Horn,
White feathers in the snow, the Gulf claims,

And an old man driven by the Trades
To a sleepy corner.

The gulf following upon those names that evoke the *News of the World* enforces partly to the inevitable end, the common reduction to 'fractured atoms'. A bunch of feathers blown in the gale, it brings home poignantly the puny helplessness of the individual life. But also, in its clean, swift vitality, it contrasts with the frowsy squalor of finance, crime, and divorce. Similarly with respect to the old man: it stands to him for inevitable death and dissolution; but it also stands for the strength and ardour that he has lost.

There would seem to be little to impede the recognition of *Gerontion* as great poetry. But *Burbank with a Baedeker: Bleistein with a Cigar* and certain other of the poems that follow develop (giving definition at the same time to a characteristic preoccupation of the poet) a technical device that seems to have been responsible for some of the recalcitrance shown towards *The Waste Land*. They use as essential means quotation and allusion. The references in *Burbank* to *Antony and Cleopatra* are obvious, and their purpose is plainly a kind of ironical contrast: heroic love, lust in the grand style, and the pitiful modern instance. The characteristic preoccupation which I have mentioned some critics see as a tendency to condemn the present by the standards of an ideal past. This is too simple an account. In *Sweeney Among the Nightingales*, for example, the contrast is clearly something more than that between the sordid incident in a modern brothel and the murder of Agamemnon:

The circles of the stormy moon
Slide westward towards the River Plate,
Death and the Raven drift above
And Sweeney guards the hornèd gate.

Gloomy Orion and the Dog
Are veiled; and hushed the shrunken seas;
The person in the Spanish cape
Tries to sit on Sweeney's knees,

Slips and pulls the table cloth
Overturns a coffee-cup

Moreover, the number of allusions in *Burbank* has not yet been taken account of. There is no need to enumerate them: they refer to half a dozen or more authors. The best commentary on them, perhaps, is *A Cooking Egg*, which does not represent Mr Eliot at his best, but exhibits his *procédé* with especial plainness. It is not merely as foils to the mean actuality that these varied references are there. The wide culture, the familiarity with various cultures, that they represent has a closer bearing upon the sense of stale disillusion. This point will be made clear when we come to *The Waste Land*.

I have been a good deal embarrassed by the fear of dwelling on the

Early Poems and *The Waste Land*

obvious to the extent of insulting the reader. But where Mr Eliot's poetry is concerned it still seems necessary to say elementary things. It is still possible for a critic belonging to a younger generation than Mr Eliot's to remark of one of those ironical contrasts that we have been considering:

> In regard to the pretty-pretty element, it seems evident that the names Nausicaa and Polypheme, while not to be regarded merely as pretty-pretty (because the poem contains sordid phrases too), are, to a certain extent, conversely, to be looked on as jam to help us take the bitter sordid powder.[5]

The essay to which this is a footnote appears in the second volume of *Scrutinies*, and itself deserves a brief scrutiny, since that volume makes some pretension to represent the young advance-guard of criticism, and the essayist is in intelligent company. The misgiving aroused by the title—*The Lyric Impulse in the Poetry of T.S. Eliot*—finds unexpectedly thorough confirmation. Mr Eliot's 'lyric impulse,' we discover, is 'his poetic, Shelleyan impulse'. When, in spite of his resistant sophistication, he yields to it he breaks into 'pure English lyric style'. The third part of *The Waste Land* is judged to be more unified than the rest 'perhaps because the subject, sensual love, is naturally more close to Mr Eliot's heart (as to the heart of a lyric poet) than the most abstract considerations with which the other parts of the poem wish to deal. . . .' We find propounded as a theme for critical treatment 'the poetization of the unpoetical'. In short, what the critic, in the latest idiom and accent, is applying to the diagnosis of Mr Eliot is the familiar idea of the intrinsically poetical.

Some elementary observation, then, is not unwarranted. And, immediately, it may be noted that this testimony to the strength of the 'poetical' tradition brings out the greatness of Mr Eliot's achievement: in his work by 1920 English poetry had made a new start.

It was *The Waste Land* that compelled recognition for the achievement. The poem appeared first in the opening numbers of the *Criterion* (October 1922 and January 1923). The title, we know, comes from Miss J.L. Weston's book, *From Ritual to Romance*, the theme of which is anthropological: the Waste Land there has a significance in terms of Fertility Ritual. What is the significance of the modern Waste Land? The answer may be read in what appears as the rich disorganization of the poem. The seeming disjointedness is intimately related to the erudition that has annoyed so many readers[6] and to the wealth of literary borrowings and allusions. These characteristics reflect the present state of civilization. The traditions and cultures have mingled, and the historical imagination makes the past contemporary; no one tradition can digest so great a variety of materials, and the result is a break-down of forms and the irrevocable loss of that sense of absoluteness which seems necessary to a robust culture. The bearing of this on the technique developed in *Burbank* and *A Cooking Egg* does not need enlarging upon.

Studies of *The Waste Land* and poems

In considering our present plight we have also to take account of the incessant rapid change that characterizes the Machine Age. The result is breach of continuity and the uprooting of life. This last metaphor has a peculiar aptness, for what we are witnessing today is the final uprooting of the immemorial ways of life, of life rooted in the soil. The urban imagery that affiliates Mr Eliot to Baudelaire and Laforgue has its significance; a significance that we touched on in glancing at the extreme contrast between Mr Eliot and Hardy. We may take Mr T.F. Powys today as the successor of Hardy: he is probably the last considerable artist of the old order (he seems to me a great one). It does not seem likely that it will ever again be possible for a distinguished mind to be formed, as Mr Powys has been, on the rhythms, sanctioned by nature and time, of rural culture. The spirt of *Mr Weston's Good Wine* could not be described as one of traditional faith; all the more striking, then, is the contrast in effect between Mr Powys's and Mr Eliot's preoccupation with 'birth, copulation, and death'.[7] Mr Powys's disillusion belongs to the old world, and the structure and organization of his art are according. There is no need to elaborate the comparison.

The remoteness of the civilization celebrated in *The Waste Land* from the natural rhythms is brought out, in ironical contrast, by the anthropological theme. Vegetation cults, fertility ritual, with their sympathetic magic, represent a harmony of human culture with the natural environment, and express an extreme sense of the unity of life. In the modern Waste Land

> *April is the cruellest month, breeding*
> *Lilacs out of the dead land,*

but bringing no quickening to the human spirit. Sex here is sterile, breeding not life and fulfilment but disgust, accidia, and unanswerable questions. It is not easy today to accept the perpetuation and multiplication of life as ultimate ends.

But the anthropological background has positive functions. It plays an obvious part in evoking that particular sense of the unity of life which is essential to the poem. It helps to establish the level of experience at which the poem works, the mode of consciousness to which it belongs. In *The Waste Land* the development of impersonality that *Gerontion* shows in comparison with *Prufrock* reaches an extreme limit: it would be difficult to imagine a completer transcendence of the individual self, a completer projection of awareness. We have, in the introductory chapter, considered the poet as being at the conscious point of his age. There are ways in which it is possible to be too conscious; and to be so is, as a result of the break-up of forms and the loss of axioms noted above, one of the troubles of the present age (if the abstraction may be permitted, consciousness being in any case a minority affair). We recognize in modern literature the accompanying sense of futility.

The part that science in general has played in the process of disintegration is matter of commonplace: anthropology is, in the present context, a pecu-

Early Poems and *The Waste Land*

liarly significant expression of the scientific spirit. To the anthropological eye beliefs, religions, and moralities are human habits—in their odd variety too human. Where the anthropological outlook prevails, sanctions wither. In a contemporary consciousness there is inevitably a great deal of the anthropological, and the background of *The Waste Land* is thus seen to have a further significance.

To be, then, too much conscious and conscious of too much—that is the plight:

> *After such knowledge, what forgiveness?*

At this point Mr Eliot's note[8] on Tiresias deserves attention:

> Tiresias, although a mere spectator and not indeed a 'character', is yet the most important personage in the poem, uniting all the rest. Just as the one-eyed merchant, seller of currants, melts into the Phoenician Sailor, and the latter is not wholly distinct from Ferdinand Prince of Naples, so all the women are one woman, and the two sexes meet in Tiresias. What Tiresias *sees*, in fact, is the substance of the poem.

If Mr Eliot's readers have a right to a grievance, it is that he has not given this note more salience; for it provides the clue to *The Waste Land*. It indicates plainly enough what the poem is: an effort to focus an inclusive human consciousness. The effort, in ways suggested above, is characteristic of the age; and in an age of psycho-analysis, an age that has produced the last section of *Ulysses*, Tiresias—'*venus huic erat utraque nota*'—presents himself as the appropriate impersonation. A cultivated modern is (or feels himself to be) intimately aware of the experience of the opposite sex.

Such an undertaking offers a difficult problem of organization, a distinguishing character of the mode of consciousness that promotes it being a lack of organizing principle, the absence of any inherent direction. A poem that is to contain all myths cannot construct itself upon one. It is here that *From Ritual to Romance* comes in. It provides a background of reference that makes possible something in the nature of a musical[9] organization. Let us start by considering the use of the Tarot pack. Introduced in the first section, suggesting, as it does, destiny, chance, and the eternal mysteries, it at once intimates the scope of the poem, the mode of its contemplation of life. It informs us as to the nature of the characters: we know that they are such as could not have relations with one another in any narrative scheme, and could not be brought together on any stage, no matter what liberties were taken with the Unities. The immediate function of the passage introducing the pack, moreover, is to evoke, in contrast with what has preceded, cosmopolitan 'high life', and the charlatanism that battens upon it:

> *Madame Sosostris, famous clairvoyante,*
> *Had a bad cold, nevertheless*
> *Is known to be the wisest woman in Europe,*
> *With a wicked pack of cards.*

Mr Eliot can achieve the banality appropriate here, and achieve at the same time, when he wants it, a deep undertone, a resonance, as it were, of fate:

> ... *and this card,*
> *Which is blank, is something he carries on his back,*
> *Which I am forbidden to see. I do not find*
> *The Hanged Man. Fear death by water.*
> *I see crowds of people, walking round in a ring.*

The peculiar menacing undertone of this associates it with a passage in the fifth section:

> *Who is the third who walks always beside you?*
> *When I count, there are only you and I together*
> *But when I look ahead up the white road*
> *There is always another one walking beside you*
> *Gliding wrapt in a brown mantle, hooded*
> *I do not know whether a man or a woman*
> *—But who is that on the other side of you?*

The association establishes itself without any help from Mr Eliot's note; it is there in any case, as any fit reader of poetry can report; but the note helps us to recognize its significance:

> The Hanged Man, a member of the traditional pack, fits my purpose in two ways: because he is associated in my mind with the Hanged God of Frazer, and because I associate him with the hooded figure in the passage of the disciples to Emmaus in Part v.

The Tarot pack, Miss Weston has established, has affiliations with fertility ritual, and so lends itself peculiarly to Mr Eliot's purpose: the instance before us illustrates admirably how he has used its possibilities. The hooded figure in the passage just quoted is Jesus. Perhaps our being able to say so depends rather too much upon Mr Eliot's note; but the effect of the passage does not depend so much upon the note as might appear. For Christ has figured already in the opening of the section (see *What the Thunder Said*):

> *After the torchlight red on sweaty faces*
> *After the frosty silence in the gardens*
> *After the agony in stony places*
> *The shouting and the crying*
> *Prison and palace and reverberation*
> *Of thunder of spring over distant mountains*
> *He who was living is now dead*
> *We who were living are now dying*
> *With a little patience*

The reference is unmistakable. Yet it is not only Christ; it is also the Hanged God and all the sacrificed gods: with the 'thunder of spring' 'Adonis, Attis,

Osiris' and all the others of *The Golden Bough* come in. And the 'agony in stony places' is not merely the agony in the Garden; it is also the agony of the Waste Land, introduced in the first section (*The Burial of the Dead*, ll.19ff.):

> *What are the roots that clutch, what branches grow*
> *Out of this stony rubbish? Son of man,*
> *You cannot say, or guess, for you know only*
> *A heap of broken images, where the sun beats,*
> *And the dead tree gives no shelter, the cricket no relief,*
> *And the dry stone no sound of water.*

In *What the Thunder Said* the drouth becomes (among other things) a thirst for the waters of faith and healing, and the specifically religious enters into the orchestration of the poem. But the thunder is 'dry sterile thunder without rain'; there is no resurrection or renewal; and after the opening passage the verse loses all buoyancy, and takes on a dragging, persistent movement as of hopeless exhaustion—

> *Here is no water but only rock*
> *Rock and no water and the sandy road*
> *The road winding above among the mountains*
> *Which are mountains of rock without water*

—the imagined sound of water coming in as a torment. There is a suggestion of fever here, a sultry ominousness—

> *There is not even solitude in the mountains*

—and it is this which provides the transition to the passage about the hooded figure quoted above. The ominous tone of this last passage associates it, as we have seen, with the reference [ll.55–6] to the Hanged Man in the Tarot passage of *The Burial of the Dead*. So Christ becomes the Hanged Man, the Vegetation God; and at the same time the journey through the Waste Land along 'the sandy road' becomes the Journey to Emmaus. Mr Eliot gives us a note on the 'third who walks always beside you':

> The following lines were stimulated by the account of one of the Antarctic expeditions (I forget which, but I think one of Shackleton's): it was related that the party of explorers, at the extremity of their strength, had the constant delusion that there was *one more member* than could actually be counted.

This might be taken to be, from our point of view, merely an interesting irrelevance, and it certainly is not necessary. But it nevertheless serves to intimate the degree of generality that Mr Eliot intends to accompany his concrete precision: he is both definite and vague at once. 'Just as the one-eyed merchant, seller of currants, melts into the Phoenician Sailor, and the latter is not wholly distinct from Ferdinand Prince of Naples'—so one experience is not wholly distinct from another experience of the same general

Studies of *The Waste Land* and poems

order; and just as all experiences 'meet in Tiresias', so a multitude of experiences meet in each passage of the poem. Thus the passage immediately in question has still further associations. That same hallucinatory quality which relates it to what goes before recalls also the neurasthenic episode [ll.111 ff.] in *A Game of Chess* (the second section):

> *'What is that noise?'*
>   *The wind under the door.*
> *'What is that noise now?* . . . '

All this illustrates the method of the poem, and the concentration, the depth of orchestration, that Mr Eliot achieves; the way in which the themes move in and out of one another and the predominance shifts from level to level. The transition from this passage is again by way of the general ominousness, which passes into hallucinated vision and then into nightmare:

> *—But who is that on the other side of you?*
>
> *What is that sound high in the air*
> *Murmur of maternal lamentation*
> *Who are those hooded hordes swarming*
> *Over endless plains, stumbling in cracked earth*
> *Ringed by the flat horizon only*
> *What is the city over the mountains*
> *Cracks and reforms and bursts in the violet air*
> *Falling towers*
> *Jerusalem Athens Alexandria*
> *Vienna London*
> *Unreal.*

The focus of attention shifts here to the outer disintegration in its large, obvious aspects, and the references to Russia and to post-war Europe in general are plain. The link between the hooded figure of the road to Emmaus and the 'hooded hordes swarming' is not much more than verbal (though appropriate to a fevered consciousness), but this phrase has an essential association with a line (56) in the passage that introduces the Tarot pack:

> *I see crowds of people, walking round in a ring.*

These 'hooded hordes', 'ringed' by the flat horizon only, are not merely Russians, suggestively related to the barbarian invaders of civilization; they are also humanity walking endlessly round in a ring, a further illustration of the eternal futility. 'Unreal' picks up the 'Unreal city' of *The Burial of the Dead* (1.60), where 'Saint Mary Woolnoth kept the hours', and the unreality gets further development in the nightmare passage that follows:

> *And upside down in air were towers*

> *Tolling reminiscent bells, that kept the hours*
> *And voices singing out of empty cisterns and exhausted wells.*

Then, with a transitional reference (which will be commented on later) to the theme of the Chapel Perilous, the focus shifts inwards again. 'Datta', 'dayadhvam', and 'damyata', the admonitions of the thunder, are explained in a note, and in this case, at any rate, the reliance upon the note justifies itself. We need only be told once that they mean 'give, sympathize, control', and the context preserves the meaning. The Sanscrit lends an appropriate portentousness, intimating that this is the sum of wisdom according to a great tradition, and that what we have here is a radical scrutiny into the profit of life. The irony, too, is radical:

> Datta: *what have we given?*
> *My friend, blood shaking my heart*
> *The awful daring of a moment's surrender*
> *Which an age of prudence can never retract*
> *By this, and this only, we have existed*

—it is an equivocal comment. And for comment on 'sympathize' we have a reminder of the irremediable isolation of the individual. After all the agony of sympathetic transcendence, it is to the individual, the focus of consciousness, that we return:

> *Shall I at least set my lands in order?*

The answer comes in the bundle of fragments that ends the poem, and, in a sense, sums it up.

Not that the *poem* lacks organization and unity. The frequent judgements that it does betray a wrong approach. The author of *The Lyric Impulse in the Poetry of T.S. Eliot*, for instance, speaks of 'a definitely willed attempt to weld various fine fragments into a metaphysical whole'. But the unity of *The Waste Land* is no more 'metaphysical' than it is narrative or dramatic, and to try to elucidate it metaphysically reveals complete misunderstanding. The unity the poem aims at is that of an inclusive consciousness: the organization it achieves as a work of art is of the kind that has been illustrated, an organization that may, by analogy, be called musical. It exhibits no progression:

> *I sat upon the shore*
> *Fishing, with the arid plain behind me*

—the thunder brings no rain to revive the Waste Land, and the poem ends where it began.

At this point the criticism has to be met that, while all this may be so, the poem in any case exists, and can exist, only for an extremely limited public equipped with special knowledge. The criticism must be admitted. But that the public for it is limited is one of the symptoms of the state of culture that

Studies of *The Waste Land* and poems

produced the poem. Works expressing the finest consciousness of the age in which the word 'high-brow' has become current are almost inevitably such as to appeal only to a tiny minority.[10] It is still more serious that this minority should be more and more cut off from the world around it—should, indeed, be aware of a hostile and overwhelming environment. This amounts to an admission that there must be something limited about the kind of artistic achievement possible in our time: even Shakespeare in such conditions could hardly have been the 'universal' genius. And *The Waste Land*, clearly, is not of the order of *The Divine Comedy* or of *Lear*. The important admission, then, is not that *The Waste Land* can be appreciated only by a very small minority (how large in any age has the minority been that has really comprehended the masterpieces?), but that this limitation carries with it limitations in self-sufficiency.

These limitations, however, are easily over-stressed. Most of the 'special knowledge', dependence upon which is urged against *The Waste Land*, can fairly be held to be common to the public that would in any case read modern poetry. The poem does, indeed, to some extent lean frankly upon *From Ritual to Romance*. And sometimes it depends upon external support in ways that can hardly be justified. Let us take, for instance, the end of the third section, *The Fire Sermon*:

> *la la*
>
> *To Carthage then I came*
>
> *Burning, burning, burning, burning*
> *O Lord Thou pluckest me out*
> *O Lord Thou pluckest*
>
> *burning*

It is plain from Mr Eliot's note on this passage—'The collocation of these two representatives of eastern and western asceticism, as the culmination of this part of the poem, is not an accident'—that he intends St Augustine and the Buddha to be actively present here. But whereas one cursory reading of *From Ritual to Romance* does all (practically) that is assigned as function to that book, no amount of reading of the *Confessions* or *Buddhism in Translation* will give these few words power to evoke the kind of presence of 'eastern and western asceticism' that seems necessary to the poem: they remain, these words, mere pointers to something outside. We can only conclude that Mr Eliot here has not done as much as he supposes. And so with the passage (ll.385 ff.) in *What the Thunder Said* bringing in the theme of the Chapel Perilous: it leaves too much to Miss Weston; repeated recourse to *From Ritual to Romance* will not invest it with the virtue it would assume. The irony, too of the

> *Shantih shantih shantih*

Early Poems and *The Waste Land*

that ends the poem is largely ineffective, for Mr Eliot's note that '"The Peace which passeth understanding" is a feeble translation of the content of this word' can impart to the word only a feeble ghost of that content for the Western reader.

Yet the weaknesses of this kind are not nearly as frequent or as damaging as critics of *The Waste Land* seem commonly to suppose. It is a self-subsistent poem, and should be obviously such. The allusions, references, and quotations usually carry their own power with them as well as being justified in the appeal they make to special knowledge. 'Unreal City' (1.60), to take an extreme instance from one end of the scale, owes nothing to Baudelaire (whatever Mr Eliot may have owed); the note is merely interesting—though, of course, it is probable that a reader unacquainted with Baudelaire will be otherwise unqualified. The reference to Dante that follows—

> *A crowd flowed over London Bridge, so many,*
> *I had not thought death had undone so many*

—has an independent force, but much is lost to the reader who does not catch the implied comparison between London and Dante's Hell. Yet the requisite knowledge of Dante is a fair demand. The knowledge of *Antony and Cleopatra* assumed in the opening of *A Game of Chess*, or of *The Tempest* in various places elsewhere, no one will boggle at. The main references in *The Waste Land* come within the classes represented by these to Dante and Shakespeare; while of the many others most of the essential carry enough of their power with them. By means of such references and quotations Mr Eliot attains a compression, otherwise unattainable, that is essential to his aim; a compression approaching simultaneity—the co-presence in the mind of a number of different orientations, fundamental attitudes, orders of experience.

This compression and the method it entails do make the poem difficult reading at first, and a full response comes only with familiarity. Yet the complete rout so often reported, or inadvertently revealed—as, for instance, by the critic who assumes that *The Waste Land* is meant to be a 'metaphysical whole'—can be accounted for only by a wrong approach, an approach with inappropriate expectations. For the general nature and method of the poem should be obvious at first reading. Yet so commonly does the obvious seem to be missed that perhaps a little more elucidation (this time of the opening section) will not be found offensively superfluous. What follows is a brief analysis of *The Burial of the Dead*, the avowed intention being to point out the obvious themes and transitions: anything like a full analysis would occupy many times the space.

The first seven lines introduce the vegetation theme, associating it with the stirring of 'memory and desire'. The transition is simple: 'April', 'spring', 'winter',—then

> *Summer surprised us, coming over the Starnbergersee*
> *With a shower of rain . . .*

We seem to be going straight forward, but (as the change of movement intimates) we have modulated into another plane. We are now given a particular 'memory', and a representative one. It introduces the cosmopolitan note, a note of empty sophistication:

> *In the mountains, there you feel free.*
> *I read, much of the night, and go south in the winter.*

[Cf. '*Winter kept us warm*']

The next transition is a contrast and a comment, bringing this last passage into relation with the first. April may stir dull roots with spring rain, but

> *What are the roots that clutch, what branches grow*
> *Out of this stony rubbish?*

And there follows an evocation of the Waste Land, with references to Ezekiel and Ecclesiastes, confirming the tone that intimates that this is an agony of the soul ('Son of man' relates with the Hanged Man and the Hanged God: with him 'who was living' and 'is now dead' at the opening of *What the Thunder Said*). The 'fear'—

> *I will show you fear in a handful of dust*

—recurs, in different modes, in the neurasthenic passage (ll.111 ff.) of *A Game of Chess*, and in the episode of the hooded figure in *What the Thunder Said*. The fear is partly the fear of death, but still more a nameless, ultimate fear, a horror of the completely negative.

Then comes the verse from *Tristan und Isolde*, offering a positive in contrast—the romantic absolute, love. The 'hyacinth girl', we may say, represents 'memory and desire' (the hyacinth, directly evocative like the lilacs bred out of the Waste Land, was also one of the flowers associated with the slain vegetation god), and the 'nothing' of the Waste Land changes into the ecstasy of passion—a contrast, and something more:

> *—Yet when we came back, late, from the hyacinth garden,*
> *Your arms full, and your hair wet, I could not*
> *Speak, and my eyes failed, I was neither*
> *Living nor dead, and I knew nothing,*
> *Looking into the heart of light, the silence.*

In the Waste Land one is neither living nor dead. Moreover, the neurasthenic passage referred to above recalls these lines unmistakably, giving them a sinister modulation:

> '*Speak to me. Why do you never speak. Speak.*

Early Poems and *The Waste Land*

> '*What are you thinking of? What thinking? What?*
> '*I never know what you are thinking. Think.*'
>
> . . .
>
>   '*Do*
> '*You know nothing? Do you see nothing? Do you remember*
> '*Nothing?*'

The further line from *Tristan und Isolde* ends the passage of romantic love with romantic desolation. Madam Sosostris, famous clairvoyante, follows; she brings in the demi-monde, so offering a further contrast—

> *Here is Belladonna, the Lady of the Rocks,*
> *The lady of situations*

—and introduces the Tarot pack. This passage has already received some comment, and it invites a great deal more. The 'lady of situations', to make an obvious point, appears in the *Game of Chess*. The admonition, 'Fear death by water', gets its response in the fourth section, *Death by Water*: death is inevitable, and the life-giving water thirsted for (and the water out of which all life comes) cannot save. But enough has been said to indicate the function of the Tarot pack, the way in which it serves in the organization of the poem.

With the 'Unreal City' the background of urban—of 'megalopolitan'—civilization becomes explicit. The allusion to Dante has already been remarked upon, and so has the way in which Saint Mary Woolnoth is echoed by the 'reminiscent bells' of *What the Thunder Said*. The portentousness of the 'dead sound on the final stroke of nine' serves as a transition, and the unreality of the City turns into the intense but meaningless horror, the absurd inconsequence, of a nightmare:

> *There I saw one I knew, and stopped him, crying: 'Stetson!*
> '*You who were with me in the ships at Mylae!*
> '*That corpse you planted last year in your garden,*
> '*Has it begun to sprout? Will it bloom this year? . . .*'

These last two lines pick up again the opening theme. The corpse acquires a kind of nightmare association with the slain god of *The Golden Bough*, and is at the same time a buried memory. Then, after a reference to Webster (Webster's sepulchral horrors are robust), *The Burial of the Dead* ends with the line in which Baudelaire, having developed the themes of

> *La sottise, l'erreur, le péché, la lésine*

and finally *L'Ennui*, suddenly turns upon the reader to remind him that he is something more.

The way in which *The Waste Land* is organized, then, should be obvious even without the aid of notes. And the poet's mastery should be as apparent in the organization as in the parts (where it has been freely acclaimed). The

Studies of *The Waste Land* and poems

touch with which he manages his difficult transitions, his delicate collocations, is exquisitely sure. His tone, in all its subtle variations, exhibits a perfect control. If there is any instance where this last judgement must be qualified, it is perhaps here (from the first passage of *The Fire Sermon*):

> *Sweet Thames, run softly till I end my song,*
> *Sweet Thames, run softly, for I speak not loud or long.*
> *But at my back in a cold blast I hear*
> *The rattle of the bones, and chuckle spread from ear to ear.*

These last two lines seem to have too much of the caricature quality of *Prufrock* to be in keeping—for a certain keeping is necessary (and Mr Eliot commonly maintains it) even in contrats. But even if the comment is just, the occasion for it is a very rare exception.

The Waste Land, then, whatever its difficulty, is, or should be, obviously a poem.[11] It is a self-subsistent poem. Indeed, though it would lose if the notes could be suppressed and forgotten, yet the more important criticism might be said to be, not that it depends upon them too much, but rather that without them, and without the support of *From Ritual to Romance*, it would not lose more. It has, that is, certain limitations in any case; limitations inherent in the conditions that produced it. Comprehensiveness, in the very nature of the undertaking, must be in some sense at the cost of structure: absence of direction, of organizing principle, in life could hardly be made to subserve the highest kind of organization in art.

But when all qualifications have been urged, *The Waste Land* remains a great positive achievement, and one of the first importance for English poetry. In it a mind fully alive in the age compels a poetic triumph out of the peculiar difficulties facing a poet in the age. And in solving his own problems as a poet Mr Eliot did more than solve the problem for himself. Even if *The Waste Land* had been, as used to be said, a 'dead end' for him, it would still have been a new start for English poetry.

But, of course, to judge it a 'dead end' was shallow. It was to ignore the implications of the effort that alone could have availed to express formlessness itself as form. So complete and vigorous a statement of the Waste Land could hardly (to risk being both crude and impertinent) forecast an exhausted, hopeless sojourn there. As for the nature of the effort, the intimacy with Dante that the poem betrays has its significance. There is no great distance in time and no gulf of any kind between the poet of *The Waste Land* and the critic who associates[12] himself later with 'a tendency—discernible even in art—towards a higher and clearer conception of Reason, and a more severe and serene control of the emotions by Reason'; and who writes[13] of Proust 'as a point of demarcation between a generation for whom the dissolution of value had in itself a positive value, and the generation which is beginning to turn its attention to an athleticism, a *training*, of the soul as severe and ascetic as the training of the body of a runner'.

Nevertheless, the poem succeeding *The Waste Land* in *Poems 1909–1925*, and bringing that collection to a close, gave some plausibility to the superficial verdict. The epigraph of *The Hollow Men*—'*Mistah Kurtz—he dead*'—coming from *The Heart of Darkness*, suggests a dissolution of all the sanctions of life; and the tailing off of the poem into

> *This is the way the world ends*
> *Not with a bang but a whimper*

so completely justifies itself that it does not appear the audacity it is: 'audacity' suggests too much vigour. The poem develops certain elements of *The Waste Land* in a kind of neurasthenic agony. Yet this evocation of

> *Shape without form, shade without colour,*
> *Paralysed force, gesture without motion*

is a marvellous positive achievement, and if we should be tempted to relate too crudely the 'mind that created' with 'the man who suffered'[14] we have the various drafts[15] to remind us that it is after all a poem that we are dealing with. The terrible closing section, with its nightmare poise over the grotesque, is a triumph of aplomb. The three middle sections begin that exploration of 'the dreamcrossed twilight'[16] which (in a different spirit) is to be pursued in *Ash-Wednesday*.

Between *The Hollow Men* and *Ash-Wednesday* come three poems published separately in the *Ariel* series. These show a curious change. We find in them, instead of the fevered torment of *The Hollow Man*, a kind of inert resignation. The movements are tired and nerveless; they suggest marvellously the failure of rhythm. If the extreme agony of consciousness has passed, so has the extraordinary vitality that went with it. But the change has another aspect. These three poems reveal a significant preoccupation; they have a direction and they all point the same way. *Journey of the Magi* and *A Song for Simeon* deal dramatically with their religious theme, the promise of salvation, but the dramatic form amounts to little more than delicacy in the presentment of intimate personal issues:

> *. . . were we led all that way for*
> *Birth or Death? There was a Birth, certainly,*
> *We had evidence and no doubt. I had seen birth and death,*
> *But had thought they were different; this Birth was*
> *Hard and bitter agony for us, like Death, our death.*
> *We returned to our places, these Kingdoms,*
> *But no longer at ease here, in the old dispensation,*
> *With an alien people clutching their gods.*
> *I should be glad of another death.*

The queer, essential equivocalness of this is the poet's, and the dramatic theme, it becomes clear, is a means to the expression of it. The ambivalence

Studies of *The Waste Land* and poems

comes out still more strikingly in the end of *A Song for Simeon*:

> *I am tired with my own life and the lives of those after me,*
> *I am dying in my own death and the deaths of those after me.*
> *Let thy servant depart,*
> *Having seen thy salvation.*

It is something very different from an affirmation that so transforms the original theme: the air is 'thoroughly small and dry'.[17] And yet there is something positive present, if only a direction of feeling and contemplation—something specifically religious. At the end of *Animula*, the third *Ariel* poem, the liturgical note characteristic of *Ash-Wednesday* appears.

What seemed most to distinguish the first poem of *Ash-Wednesday*, when, as *Perch' io non spero*, it appeared in *Commerce*,[18] from the *Ariel* poems was the rhythm. The rhythm varies within the sequence from part to part, but it is in general very much more nerved and positive than that of the *Ariel* poems. In the comparison it is not extravagant to speak of it as having certain qualities of ritual; it produces in a high degree the frame-effect, establishing apart from the world a special order of experience, dedicated to spiritual exercises. To discuss *Ash-Wednesday*, then, is a delicate business, incurring danger both of crudity and impertinence. We remind ourselves of Mr Eliot's precept and practice in criticism: the sequence is poetry, and highly formal poetry. Yet it is impossible not to see in it a process of self-scrutiny, of self-exploration; or not to feel that the poetical problem at any point was a spiritual problem, a problem in the attainment of a difficult sincerity. The poetry belongs to

> *... the time of tension between dying and birth*
> *The place of solitude where three dreams cross*

and is a striving after a spiritual state based upon a reality elusive and yet ultimate.

We cannot help recalling Mr Eliot's various observations about the problem of belief. This,[19] for instance, seems germane:

> I cannot see that poetry can ever be separated from something which I should call belief, and to which I cannot see any reason for refusing the name of belief, unless we are to reshuffle names together. It should hardly be needful to say that it will not inevitably be orthodox Christian belief, although that possibility can be entertained, since Christianity will probably continue to modify itself, as in the past, into something that can be believed in (I do not mean *conscious* modifications like modernism, etc., which always have the opposite effect). The majority of people live far below the level of belief or doubt. It takes application, and a kind of genius, to believe anything, and to believe *anything* (I do *not* mean merely to believe in some 'religion') will probably become more and more difficult as time goes on.

Mr Eliot's concern is specifically religious. Certain qualities of genius he indubitably has, and *Ash-Wednesday* is a disciplined application of them to the realizing of a spiritual state conceived as depending upon belief—belief

Early Poems and *The Waste Land*

in something outside himself. The result is a most subtle poetry of great technical interest; and it is on the technical aspect that critical attention must in any case focus.

For the poet 'technique' was the problem of sincerity.[20] He had to achieve a paradoxical precision-in-vagueness; to persuade the elusive intuition to define itself, without any forcing, among the equivocations of 'the dream-crossed twilight'. The warning against crude interpretation, against trying to elicit anything in the nature of prose statement, is there in the unexpected absences of punctuation; and in the repetitive effects, which suggest a kind of delicate tentativeness. The poetry itself is an effort at resolving diverse impulsions, recognitions, and needs.

Ash-Wednesday is a whole. Faced with *Perch' io non spero* as a separate poem, one might pardonably, perhaps, see an odd affectation in

> *Why should the agèd eagle stretch its wings?*

But (though the criticism is still made[21]) in a reading of the whole sequence the ironical function of this self-dramatization becomes obvious. It is an insurance against the pride of humility; a self-admonition against the subtle treasons, the refinements, of egotism that beset the quest of sincerity in these regions. Again,

> *And I pray that I may forget*
> *These matters that with myself I too much discuss*
> *Too much explain*

intimates a capacity for a critical attitude towards the 'discussing' that the poetry is.

To take fragments separately at their face value is to misunderstand this poetry, which works by compensations, resolutions, residuums, and convergences. What, we ask, does the poet resign and renounce in the first poem, and what is the nature of his renunciation? The line from the Shakespeare sonnet suggests that it is worldly ambition, personal glory, that he renounces. This becomes

> *The infirm glory of the positive hour;*

and

> *The one veritable transitory power*

together with the next lines—

> *Because I cannot drink*
> *There, where trees flower, and springs flow, for there is nothing again*

—seems to identify it with the vital illusion of youth. But, it next appears, what we have here is the sensory evocation of a spiritual state:

Studies of *The Waste Land* and poems

> *Because I know that time is always time*
> *And place is always and only place*
> *And what is actual is actual only for one time*
> *And only for one place*
> *I rejoice that things are as they are and*
> *I renounce the blessèd face*
> *And renounce the voice*

—This, with its bare prose statement, has the effect of a complete renunciation of supernatural assurance. And the general effect of the poem is negative. Yet the formula of renunciation—

> *Teach us to care and not to care*
> *Teach us to sit still*

—registers a positive religious impulse, which is confirmed by the liturgical close. And the positive element comes out more significantly in

> *Consequently I rejoice, having to construct something*
> *Upon which to rejoice*

—if the air is 'throughly small and dry' it is 'smaller and dryer than the will'. Not for nothing have the rhythms of *Ash-Wednesday* so much more life than those of the *Ariel* poems. After this introduction, then, we know what are to be the themes of the following poetry, and what the mode of debate.

It is common to ask of the second poem, 'Who is the Lady, and what do the three white leopards stand for?' As for the first question, Mr Eliot in his *Dante*[22] writes: 'In the Earthly Paradise Dante encounters a lady named Matilda, whose identity need not at first bother us'; the identity of the Lady in this poem need not bother us at all. She reminds us not only of Matilda but of Beatrice and Piccarda too, and helps to define a mode of religious contemplation that characterizes the poem. The theme of the poem is death, and death is evoked as complete extinction:

> *End of the endless*
> *Journey to no end*
> *Conclusion of all that*
> *Is inconclusible . . .*

—But the effect has extraordinarily little in common with that of the same theme in *The Hollow Men* or *Journey of the Magi* or *A Song for Simeon*. The desire for extinction (ἀτοθανεῖν θέλω)[23]—

> *I should be glad of another death*

and

> *I am tired with my own life and the lives of those after me*

Early Poems and *The Waste Land*

—becomes curiously transmuted by association with something positive:

> *As I am forgotten*
> *And would be forgotten, so I would forget*
> *Thus devoted, concentrated in purpose.*

The devotion and the concentration are represented by the Lady, who serves to intimate the poet's recourse, in his effort 'to construct something upon which to rejoice', to a specific religious tradition, and they manifest themselves throughout in rhythm and tone. The 'burden of the grasshopper' (a fine instance, this, of Mr Eliot's genius in borrowing), through a burden, potently evoked, of annihilation, has nevertheless its share of the religious emotion that pervades the poem. The 'garden where all love ends' is associated with the garden in which God walked 'in the cool of the day'. A religious sense of awe, an apprehension of the supernatural, seems to inform the desert where the bones are scattered.

As for the 'three white leopards', they are not symbols needing interpretation; they act directly, reinforcing the effect of ritual that we have noted in the verse and suggesting the mode of experience, the kind of spiritual exercise, to which *Ash-Wednesday* is devoted. They belong with the 'jewelled unicorns' that have bothered some critics in the fourth poem:

> *Redeem*
> *The unread vision in the higher dream*
> *While jewelled unicorns draw by the gilded hearse.*

Perhaps in this last passage Mr Eliot has been too helpful and 'the higher dream' is too like explicit elucidation. But it at any rate reminds us conveniently of certain things that he says in his *Dante*. He remarks[24] of the 'pageantry' of the *Paradise*:

> It belongs to the world of what I call the *high dream* and the modern world seems capable only of the low dream.

And he says elsewhere:[25]

> Dante's is a *visual* imagination. It is a visual imagination in a different sense from that of a modern painter of still life: it is visual in the sense that he lived in an age in which men still saw visions. It was a psychological habit, the trick of which we have forgotten, but as good as any of our own. We have nothing but dreams, and we have forgotten that seeing visions—a practice now relegated to the aberrant and the uneducated—was once a more significant, interesting, and disciplined kind of dreaming.

When Mr Eliot says that we have forgotten the trick he means it. He no more supposes that Dante's mode of vision can be recaptured than that Dante's belief can.[26] But his frequentation of Dante has its place in that effort 'to construct something' and that 'training of the soul' which he speaks of. And his leopards and unicorns seem to insist on the peculiar kind of 'disciplined dreaming' that he strives to attain in 'the dream-crossed twilight' of *Ash-Wednesday*. They go with the formal quality of the verse, in which we have already noted a suggestion of ritual, and with the liturgical element, to define the plane at which this poetry works. The spiritual discipline is one with the poetical.

The third poem of the sequence offers an admirable example of the way in which Mr Eliot blends the reminiscent (literary or conventional) in imagery with the immediately evocative. The 'stairs' of this poem (they have a 'banister') have their effect for a reader who recognizes no reminiscence. They concentrate the suggestion of directed effort that distinguishes this poetry from the earlier, and they define the nature of the effort. The poem epitomizes, as it were, a spiritual history, and records a sense of an advance and a hardly-dared hope of attainment (qualified by the humility that becomes explicit at the end). But the stairs also recall the stairs of the *Purgatorio*—a reminiscence that is picked up again in the next poem, in a further quotation from that Provençal passage of Canto xxvi which Mr Eliot has used so much:

> *Ara vos prec, per aquella valor*
> *que vos guida al som de l'escalina*
> *sovegna vos a temps de ma dolor.*[27]

This, in a new spirit, is the art that he practised in *The Waste Land*.

The opening of the fourth poem recalls a passage of the third, that giving the view through the 'slotted window':

> *. . . beyond the hawthorn blossom and a pasture scene*
> *The broadbacked figure drest in blue and green*
> *Enchanted the maytime with an antique flute.*
> *Blown hair is sweet, brown hair over the mouth blown,*
> *Lilac and brown hair . . .*

This backward glimpse of youth 'where trees flower and springs flow' seems to be dismissed here as 'distraction'. But the sense of refreshment that distinguishes the fourth poem seems to owe something to the same source. The 'violet', the 'larkspur', and the 'varied green' have an effect like that of 'lilac', and she 'who walked' may well have had brown hair. But this imagery, which is directly evocative, also lends itself to symbolic associations—

> *Going in white and blue, in Mary's colour*

and

> *In blue of larkspur, blue of Mary's colour*

—and she who 'made strong the fountains and made fresh the springs' takes on a specifically religious significance. Is the poet remembering an actual religious experience, or is he using the memory of the time when the springs were fresh as a symbol? The case is subtler. The unspecified 'who' and the indeterminate syntax, together with the element of 'higher dream' that we have already discussed, and the

White light folded, sheathed about her, folded,

intimate that the process here is analogous to that represented by Dante's Beatrice.[28] The 'yews' again are directly evocative: they have current values; beneath them

> *ghostly shapes*
> *May meet at noontide; Fear and trembling Hope,*
> *Silence and Foresight; Death the Skeleton*
> *And Time the Shadow*

—though these yews, owing to the context, suggest a particular religious tradition.

A process analogous to Dante's; but the modern poet can make no pretence to Dante's certitude—to his firm possession of his vision. The ambiguity that constructs a precarious base for rejoicing in the fourth poem brings doubt and fear of inner treachery in the fifth. The breathless, circling, desperately pursuing movement of the opening, with its repetitions and its play upon 'word', 'Word', 'world', and 'whirled', suggests both the agonized effort to seize the unseizable, and the elusive equivocations of the thing grasped. The doubts and self-questionings are developed, and the poem ends with a despairing recognition of the equivocal that recalls, in a significant way, the second poem:

> *In the last desert between the last blue rocks*
> *The desert in the garden the garden in the desert*
> *Of drouth, spitting from the mouth the withered apple-seed.*
>
> *O my people.*

In the earlier poem the desert that the bones inherit—the 'garden where all love ends'—is associated with the garden in which God walked 'in the cool of the day'. The ambiguity is the condition of a poise between widely divergent impulses and emotions that produces a strange serenity. But here, in the fifth poem, we have instead an equivocation of experience that produces agonizing doubt: which is garden and which is desert?

In the last poem of the sequence the doubt becomes an adjuvant of spiritual discipline, ministering to humility. But an essential ambiguity remains an ambiguity inescapable

> *In this brief transit where the dreams cross.*

To symbolize, to conceive for himself, the spiritual order that he aspires towards, the poet inevitably has recourse to his most vital mundane experience. But the memories of this present themselves also as temptation, as incitement to subtle treacheries:

> . . . *though I do not wish to wish these things*
> *From the wide window towards the granite shore*
> *The white sails still fly seaward, seaward flying*
> *Unbroken wings*
>
> *And the lost heart stiffens and rejoices*
> *In the lost lilac and the lost sea voices*
> *And the weak spirit quickens to rebel*
> *For the bent golden-rod and the lost sea smell.* . . .

—The 'lost heart' is itself ambiguous: the heart is 'lost' because it succumbs to temptation and 'rebels'; but 'lost' also records a pang of regret, a rebellious questioning of the renunciation: the heart is 'lost' because it has lost the lilac and the sea voices. With 'merely vans to beat the air' the poet looks enviously at the unbroken wings that fly seaward, and prays:

> *Suffer us not to mock ourselves with falsehood.*

In the *Ariel* poem that appeared after *Ash-Wednesday* it is Marina, who was lost and found again, who becomes the symbol for the new realization striven after. But this is to simplify too much. *Marina* belongs, like *Ash-Wednesday*, to 'the time of tension between dying and birth', and exhibits an even more subtle ambiguity than anything in the sequence. The liturgical note is absent, and one may indicate the change in rhythm by saying that it has about it nothing of ritual; yet the poem expresses something approaching nearer to assurance than anything in *Ash-Wednesday*. Images like the things that the poet 'did not wish to wish' now 'return', bringing with them a sense of ineffable peace.

The coming of 'this grace' by which the various forms of death

> *Are become unsubstantial, reduced by a wind,*
> *A breath of pine, and the woodsong fog*

is associated with the approach of a ship to 'granite islands'. The 'white sails' and the 'granite shore' of *Ash-Wednesday* have taken another value here. The ship—'I made this'—represents the effort 'to construct something upon which to rejoice'. Marina, the daughter lost and recovered, evokes the peculiar sense of victory over death that attends upon 'this grace':

> *This form, this face, this life*
> *Living to live in a world of time beyond me; let me*
> *Resign my life for this life, my speech for that unspoken,*
> *The awakened, lips parted, the hope, the new ships.*

Just what is the nature of the new life we cannot say. It is an elusive apprehension, conveyed poignantly, but in essential ambiguities. The poem is the resultant of diverse suggestions and orientations. The imagery belongs to the 'higher dream':

> *What is this face, less clear and clearer*
> *The pulse in the arm, less strong and stronger—*
> *Given or lent? more distant than stars and nearer than the eye . . .*

The indeterminate syntax intimates the kind of relation that exists between the various elements of the poem: one would not, to put it crudely, think of trying to relate Marina, her father, the ship, and the islands in a story. And the elusiveness of the relations suggests at the same time the felt transcendence of the vision and its precariousness.

The poetry of the last phase may lack the changed richness and the range of *Gerontion* and *The Waste Land*. But it is, perhaps, still more remarkable by reason of the strange and difficult regions of experience that it explores. Its association with Mr Eliot's explicit Anglo-Catholicism has encouraged, in the guise of criticism, an extraordinarily crude and superficial approach. Critics speak of 'Pre-Raphaelite imagery' and a 'Pre-Raphaelite flavour' and deplore [or applaud] the return to the fold. But this poetry is more disconcertingly modern than *The Waste Land*: the preoccupation with traditional Christianity, the use of the Prayer Book, and the devotion to spiritual discipline should not hinder the reader from seeing that the modes of feeling, apprehension, and expression are such as we can find nowhere earlier. If it is likely to be significant for young poets, that is not because of the intellectual fashions that attribute so much importance to T.E. Hulme, but because contemporary poets are likely to find that the kind of consciousness represented by *Ash-Wednesday* and *Marina* has a close bearing upon certain problems of their own. It is not for nothing that in the field of critical thought—in the consideration of those general problems that literary criticism nowadays cannot ignore—Mr Eliot remains a directing influence.[29]

Notes

1. *Selected Poems of Ezra Pound*: Introduction, p. viii.
2. *The Sacred Wood*, p. 117.
3. Sonnet 94.
4. See Empson, W., *Seven Types of Ambiguity* [Chatto and Windus].
5. *Scrutinies*, ii. Collected by Edgell Rickword, p. 16.
6. 'I don't like his erudition-traps,' said a very distinguished author to me once. And this, from *Gallion's Reach* (pp. 35–6), by H.M. Tomlinson, is representative:

'His grin broadened. "All I can say is, my dear, give me the old songs, though I can't sing them, if they're the new. What does poetry want with footnotes about psycho-analysis and negro mythology?"

'"Suppose," someone asked him, "that you don't know anything about them?"

'"Well, I couldn't get them out of footnotes and the poetry all at one stride, could I? But

Doris, they were very clever and insulting poems, I think. Sing a song of mockery. Is that the latest? But it was a surprising little book, though it smelt like the dissection of bad innards."'

The novelist, with a certain subtle *naïveté*, clearly identifies himself with the attitude, and he clearly means the reader to do the same. And there is every reason to suppose that he would not object to the reader's supposing that he had Mr Eliot in mind. The First Edition of *Gallion's Reach* is valuable.

7.   '. . . .
         Nothing at all but three things
DORIS: What things?
SWEENEY: Birth, copulation, and death.
         That's all, that's all, that's all, that's all.
         Birth, copulation, and death.
DORIS: I'd be bored.
SWEENEY: You'd be bored.
         Birth, copulation, and death.'
                                    Fragment of an Agon. Criterion, January 1927

8. Note to line 218 of *The Waste Land* (*Poems 1909–1925*, p. 88).

9. Mr I.A. Richards uses the analogy from music in some valuable notes on Mr Eliot that are printed in an appendix to the later editions of *The Principles of Literary Criticism*.

10. This matter is discussed at length by the present author in *Mass Civilization and Minority Culture* (see *For Continuity*).

11. 'It is a test [a positive test, I do not assert that it is always valid negatively], that genuine poetry can communicate before it is understood.'—T.S. Eliot, *Dante*, p. 16.

12. *Criterion*, January 1926, vol. iv, p. 5.

13. *Criterion*, October 1926, vol. iv, pp. 752–3.

14. '. . . . the more perfect the artist, the more completely separate in him will be the man who suffers and the mind which creates. . . .'—*The Sacred Wood*, p. 48.

15. See *The Chapbook*, 1924 (No. 39), and *Criterion*, vol. x, p. 170.

16. See *Ash-Wednesday*, p. 20.

17. *Ash-Wednesday*, p. 10.

18. XV (Printemps, MCMXXVIII).

19. *The Enemy*, January 1927.

20. Cf. 'And this honesty never exists without great technical accomplishment.'—T.S. Eliot on Blake (*The Sacred Wood*, p. 137).

21. 'And I am made a little tired at hearing Eliot, only in his early forties, present himself as an "agèd eagle" who asks why he should make the effort to stretch his wings.'—Edmund Wilson, *Axel's Castle*, p. 130.

22. p. 47.

23. See the epigraph of *The Waste Land*.

24. *Dante*, p. 48.

25. ibid., p. 23.

26. See 'A Note on Poetry and Belief' (*The Enemy*, January 1927), p. 10.

27. 'Now I pray you, by that goodness which guideth you to the summit of the stairway, be mindful in due time of my pain.'—*Poi s'ascose nel foco che gli affina*.

28. See Santayana's *Poetry and Religion*, pp. 128-9:

'Neither the conscious spell of the senses nor the affinities of taste and character can then be powerful, but the sense of loneliness and the vague need of loving may easily conspire with the innocence of the eyes to fix upon a single image and to make it the imaginary goal of all those instincts which as yet do not know themselves.

'When with time these instincts become explicit and select their respective objects, if the inmost heart still remains unsatisfied, as it must in all profound or imaginative natures, the name and memory of that vague early love may well subsist as a symbol for the perfect good yet unattained. . . . Having recognized that she was to his childish fancy what the ideals of religion were to his mature imagination, Dante intentionally fuses the two, as every poet intentionally fuses the general and the particular, the universal and the personal.'

29. See Review of *Science and Poetry* (I.A. Richards) in *The Dial*, March 1927. *The Enemy*, January 1927: 'Note on Poetry and Belief.' *Dante*, T.S. Eliot: Note to Chap. 2.

103
The Bloody Wood*

♦

T.H. THOMPSON

A chance remark of a friend of mine sent me back recently to a re-reading of Mr. Eliot's poems. And the re-reading in the light of that remark furnished me with a new interpretation of a certain aspect of his poetic labyrinth—an interpretation, I hope, sufficiently interesting to be included in the corpus of Eliotic criticism.

While out for a walk I had been quoting *Sweeney Among the Nightingales*, and when I came to the line:

And sang within the bloody wood,

my friend interrupted me. He pointed out that the man who wrote the *Sacred Wood* could not possibly have written 'bloody wood' in this poem. 'Bloody' was the wrong word. It had no meaning here, even as a transferred epithet. I at once started to doubt my memory, but later on looking up the poem I found I had been right. It was 'bloody wood.' Eliot had written it, and must have done so purposely. I re-read all the poems, and in doing so made one vital discovery. I think I have solved the Sweeney problem.

Sweeney is a baffling person. He runs in and out poems like a naughty boy; scarcely offers an explanation of his conduct; and generally confounds critics by his bad manners and rude behaviour. Ah, say the critics, he is a symbol, and pass on. That is an easy way of getting over a difficulty, but it is untrue. Sweeney is anything but a symbol, very far from it, as I shall show in a moment.

The reason for the usual misinterpretation is largely due to Mr. Eliot's peculiar methods. He tries to write in three centuries at the same time. That is, he adopts the mind of a seventeenth century metaphysical poet to write twentieth century detective fiction with a romantic nineteenth century pen. The result is confusing. And that is precisely Mr. Eliot's object. By a brilliant piece of literary obfuscation, by skilfully ringing the changes with metaphysical and romantic, he has managed to embody in his poems a gruesome murder story without anyone being any wiser.

London Mercury 29 (January 1934), pp. 233–9.

Sweeney of course is the central figure of the story, and the reader is the detective. From scattered hints and clues, from dark sayings and mysterious exclamations, we are left to unfold for ourselves the sordid little tale. What a search it is. It demands the greatest patience. Mr. Eliot plays a subtle game; drawing red herrings across our path; confronting us with quotations in many tongues; and adding notes to lead us astray. He does not try to make it easy for us. His object seems to be to produce a work more intricate and ingenious than the best Crime Club novel.

Let us look at the story: Sweeney, the hero of this murder drama, appears in five poems. Three times in the 1920 volume; in *The Waste Land*; and in the more recently published *Sweeney Agonistes*. These poems must be read as a sequence. He makes his bow in a poem called *Sweeney Erect*. The poem opens with all the Miltonic stops out; a grand piece of rhetoric, rich in subtle allusions so beloved by the Alexandrians. The raging seas of the Aegean are before us, and Ariadne deserted by her lover stands in the gales on her lonely island. This is the text of the poem—woman forsaken. Then follows a fragmentary allusion to Homer: (Nausicaa and Polypheme).

This flickering reference at once suggests to the reader the voyage of Odysseus, man the wanderer. As Theseus' perjured sails hasten from Ariadne, so Odysseus is torn from Nausicaa. Nausicaa and Polypheme, Beauty and the Beast. Man the wanderer encounters both. Every word of the two opening stanzas is overcharged with meaning. But we must not delay. The next line introduces us to Sweeney. It is morning and he is getting out of bed:

> *Gesture of orang-outang*
> *Rises from the sheets in steam*

Sweeney, the modern Polyphemus, shakes off sleep in Mrs. Turner's brothel. He is not a beautiful specimen. We see him a gross featured creature, stretching and clawing at the pillow slip. His movements are bestial and his knowledge is circumscribed by sex, for we learn:

> *He knows the female temperament.*

He appears to be a man for the ladies. (O Ariadne! O Nausicaa!) And this is later confirmed by the dramatically enigmatic conclusion of the poem. The razor; the hysterical woman in bed; the chatter of the ladies in the corridor; Mrs. Turner fussily righteous; and finally Doris, as *dea ex machina*, entering from the bath-room with a glass of brandy. At the end we are left dizzy and bewildered. What exactly did happen? What is it all about? I think we can safely say from the data at our disposal that the Ariadne theme, that of the injured or forsaken woman, has been played in Mrs. Turner's house, and that Sweeney has been responsible. He has brought tragedy to this little world of women, and as Mrs. Turner says, it does the house no sort of good. But the full nature of the tragedy we have yet to discover. And who is Ariadne?

The next reference to Sweeney is surprising. In a poem entitled *Mr. Eliot's Sunday Morning Service* he is introduced in an abrupt and unexpected fashion. While Mr. Eliot is pursuing his devotions, but not, as he himself admits, with absorbed attention, we are told that:

> *Sweeney shifts from ham to ham*
> *Stirring the water in his bath.*

Now what can we make of this inappropriate snapshot produced in the middle of a Church Service? The reader blinks, perplexed, and unless he remembers he is reading a detective story, he dismisses the lines as pointless. But notice two things: we are definitely told that Sweeney has a bath on Sunday morning—probably in the very room Doris has just vacated: but more important, we gather that while having his bath he debated some difficult problem with himself. He was in meditative mood. He 'shifts from ham to ham'; he 'stirs the water.' The actions of a man in serious thought. If it were an ordinary bath he would splash the water, not stir it; he would sing, not shift from ham to ham. Yes, he has something on his mind. But the whole sinister significance of the incident is not yet apparent. We shall hear more of that Sunday morning bath.

The last poem in the 1920 volume is devoted to Sweeney, Mr. Eliot does his best to confuse us here. He draws all kinds of red herrings across our path; he disguises Sweeney till he resembles a character from *Alice in Wonderland*—(his ape neck swells into a giraffe)—he talks Greek to us; he introduces Hebrews who wear Spanish capes; he also puts us off the scent by saying that Sweeney is among the nightingales, which of course is fantastically untrue. Our hero is drinking with the cosmopolitan crowd in the inn, and does not worry about nightingales. He is no little St. Francis as the title of the poem would suggest, though Mr. Eliot would have us believe so. No, Sweeney's visit to the Inn near the Convent of the Sacred Heart has nothing to do with nightingales. They are red herrings and are used to throw dust in our eyes. The motive for his visit will be revealed in time.

Mention of the nightingales, however, brings us to our initial problem, the problem of the 'bloody wood' in which they sang. What was Mr. Eliot's meaning? The adjective is so precise that it stamps the wood with a distinct identity. To casual readers it may suggest little, but actually it has a deep significance. The 'bloody wood' stands on the threshold of that grim poetic vault 'The Waste Land.' It is a suburb. That is, a place of horror. A suburb of the Waste Land. In this wood, life is found in its rawest, lowest, most lustful state. Here was the home of our primitive ancestors, some of whose fierce blood passions can cut through the trappings of civilization and visit us even today. Here was Agamemnon murdered, and beasts of prey like Sweeney hunt in its thickets and tear their victims with their claws. The 'bloody wood' therefore is the dwelling of atavistic recollections, where man the animal prowls, from which man the angel shrinks. Yet while the ape-man hunts,

Studies of *The Waste Land* and poems

nightingales sing in the branches for those who have ears to hear.

From the 'bloody wood' it is a short step into *The Waste Land*, Mr. Eliot's most important poem. Quite unexpectedly Sweeney makes a sudden intrusion as he did on an earlier occasion during a Sunday morning service. In Part 3, *The Fire Sermon* we read:

> *But at my back from time to time I hear*
> *The sound of horns and motors, which shall bring*
> *Sweeney to Mrs. Porter in the spring.*
> *O the moon shone bright on Mrs. Porter*
> *And on her daughter*
> *They wash their feet in soda water*
> *Et O ces voix d'enfants, chantant dans la coupole!*

And the next lines are startling:

> *Twit twit twit*
> *Jug jug jug jug jug jug*
> *So rudely forc'd.*
> *Tereu*

It is the chant of the nightingales singing in the 'bloody wood' while the children sing in French in the Convent of the Sacred Heart near by. It is a complete echo from the previous poem. Sweeney meanwhile, oblivious of the singing around him, accompanied by the sound of motor horns, hurries on his way to visit a new love, a Mrs. Porter, whose amazing ablutions appear to have won his regard. This is an important development in the Sweeney story. Observe that Mrs. Turner's brothel no longer attracts him. He is a fickle ape. Observe also that Mrs. Porter must be a woman of means if she can afford to use soda water for washing purposes. Lastly observe that Mrs. Porter has a daughter.

The scene for the tragedy is laid. Sweeney arrives in a motor car on a moonlight night in spring at the home of these unsuspecting women. He plays the role of the wealthy lover. The ladies wash their feet. Sweeney prepares his plan. All the most evil passions of 'the bloody wood' are aroused. The nightingales wail plaintively. Then:

> *So rudely forced.*
> *Tereu*

That is all. If Mr. Eliot had said no more about it the whole thing would have remained wrapped in mystery for ever, and we should never have known what happened at Mrs. Porter's, or who was rudely forced. But in *Sweeney Agonistes*, a publication which appeared ten years after *The Waste Land*, the details of the crime are revealed to us, and it is Sweeney himself who makes a personal confession. For the first time we hear the genuine accents of a beast

Early Poems and *The Waste Land*

of the 'bloody wood,' and his words are like his physical form, gross, revolting, bestial.

Once more we find ourselves back in Mrs. Turner's brothel. Doris and Dusty, two of the ladies, are entertaining some Americans. Then Sweeney enters. He is apparently very drunk. His first remark to Doris, the woman who had been so helpful with her brandy on his last visit there, is cruel but characteristic:

> *I'll carry you off*
> *To a cannibal isle.*

The latent ferocity of the 'bloody wood' is in these words, they denote the primitive, the barbaric, the uncivilised. Evidently Doris has annoyed him and he retaliates by showing his claws. He will eat her, he says. A little later he defines life as:

> *Birth, and copulation, and death.*

This is the orang-outang speaking, the apenecked giraffe, as he shuffles in the stench of the 'bloody wood.'

Meanwhile the other guests in Maison Turner, inspired by, or resenting Sweeney's morbid talk, strike up a song of an aphrodisiac nature to excite the girls, but Doris remains unmoved. Sweeney breaks in once more. He has altered his definition of life, perhaps the singing of the Americans has upset him. He now asserts, 'Life is death,' After which profound statement he embarks upon a gloomy recitation of a murder story, shocking the reader and spoiling the merry evening at Mrs. Turner's:

> *I knew a man once did a girl in*
> *Any man might do a girl in*
> *Any man has to, needs to, wants to*
> *Once in a lifetime, do a girl in.*
> *Well he kept her there in a bath.*
> *With a gallon of lysol in a bath.*

At once the attentive reader becomes alert. His memory switches back to a scene at Mrs. Turner's months before: the flashing razor; the shrieking woman in bed; Doris rushing in with the brandy. And also that sinister bathroom incident inserted in the poem on Mr. Eliot's Sunday Morning Service: Sweeney stirring the water in his bath while the poet prayed. And also that visit to Mrs. Porter on a spring night while she and her daughter were washing their feet, probably in their bathroom. This wild story has the appearance of a confession. A chain of clues rises before us.

But to continue: apparently the man having drowned the girl in a bath lived in the same house with the corpse for two months and eventually hounded by the furies of conscience went mad. As Sweeney recites this sorry tale he grows more and more excited and incoherent, and finally drifts into drunken madness:

We're gona sit here and drink this booze
We're gona sit here and have a tune
We're gona stay and we're gona go
And somebody's gotta pay the rent.

At this point Doris interrupts with three simple but pregnant words:

I know who.

Now obviously this is not the answer to the wild drunken effusions that Sweeney has just belched into the air. No, she conveys very clearly, and Sweeney realises it, that she knows who is the man that did the girl in. He quickly silences her by saying:

That's nothing to me and nothing to you.

He does not wish her to give away any secrets in public. But it is too late. Even if the American guests don't know, we do. We see Sweeney in his true proportions, a self-confessed murderer. Having collected the evidence we are now at liberty to trace the whole story which Mr. Eliot has so cunningly concealed in his poems.

Sweeney, a licentious libertine of Irish-American extraction domiciled in London, had a lady friend, a Miss Ariadne Porter, who was employed at the time of their liaison in a house of ill fame under Mrs. Turner's efficient management. Miss Porter must have acquired an absorbing affection for her lover, which at length became irksome to him; for he threatened to desert her. Hysterics followed, and Sweeney, influenced by the morbid idea that every man in his time should kill a woman, proceeded to threaten his pretty mistress with a razor. Her screams roused the house, and Doris opportunely intervened and prevented his murderous intention, thereby earning his ingratitude. In his bath on Sunday morning Sweeney meditated on possibilities of ridding himself of the tiresome Ariadne, and the bath suggested a solution—he would drown her. Ariadne meanwhile frightened of his rough usage had fled to the home of her mother, Mrs. Porter, where she lay in hiding for awhile. Sweeney in dudgeon withdrew his allegiance from Mrs. Turner and took to frequenting the Inn near the Convent. It was here he met Ariadne again. One gloomy night he saw her conversing indistinctly with the inn-keeper at the door. He made inquiries, found out where she lived, and pursued her in his motor car (the whole passage is associated with ideas of pursuit). He found Ariadne and her mother washing themselves with soda water. Note the significance of this episode: the poor girl who washed in soda water by moonlight was soon to have a bath with a gallon of lysol. The moonlight innocence of the soda water is contrasted with the horror of the lysol to follow.

As the nightingales tell us Sweeney 'rudely forced' his way in and committed the act he had premeditated. The 'rudely forced' passage may refer to the actual immersion of Miss Porter, and the line which immediately precedes it:

Jug jug jug jug jug jug

would then represent onomatopoetically the sound of the lysol being poured into the bath from a jug.

Of Mrs. Porter's reactions to all this we are told nothing. She may have fled for refuge to the Convent of the Sacred Heart, or again she may be that mad woman who appears later in *The Waste Land* using her fair hair for fiddle strings. There is no direct evidence for either theory, but both are conceivable. We trust the first mentioned is the true one.

After the crime Sweeney established himself in the house. Mrs. Porter, as we have mentioned before, was a woman of comfortable income. Sweeney at once appropriated her money which he used for paying the rent collector and the milkman; milk appears to have been his staple diet during the two months he lived there. But he was unable to dispose of the body in the bath, and this got on his nerves. Probably the first irritation was caused by finding the bath occupied on Sunday morning, his usual time for practising the ritual of cleanliness. But as the weeks passed he grew worse and worse, he began to brood and conscience played havoc with him.

At last overwhelmed by the torment in his mind and lacerated by the whips and scourges of the Furies he crept back, half mad, half drunk, to Mrs. Turner's brothel. The wheel has come full circle. The pink broad-bottomed ape who rose from bed here lustily one morning over two months before, has returned a drivelling lunatic at night to die. We know the rest. How he insulted Doris; how prompted by bravado or despair he gave details of the murder; how Doris at once guessed his meaning, and how in the words 'I know who' she passed on the secret to the world at large. Amid the noise of laughter from the brothel and an imperative knocking at the door Sweeney passes out of the poem.

Such is his history. A story which will intrigue all readers of detective fiction by its subtlety, finesse, and cunning air of mystification. Yet the last word may not have been spoken. Sweeney is a wily person and sufficiently elusive to dodge an English hangman. Who knows, he may have returned to New York with Mr. Klipstein and Mr. Krumpacker; he may still live to trouble and delight us with a few more graceful antics, perhaps on Broadway this time or among the whippoorwills.

104
From *Archetypal Patterns in Poetry**

MAUD BODKIN

To one whose early delight in verse took the bias of the nineteenth century, the poetry of to-day presents an alien air. Jarred by incongruity in the sequence of images and phrases, one is disposed to judge—in the words of Mrs. Woolf's *Letter to a Young Poet*—'instead of acquiring a whole object, rounded and entire, I am left with broken parts in my hands'.

Writing from the psychological standpoint, I intend this statement less as criticism than as recognition of the limitations of the vital perspective present in these essays. In commenting on certain aspects of T.S. Eliot's poem, *The Waste Land*, I am conscious of this bias and limitation. Though the poem is now to me one of the most satisfying of distinctively modern poems, and parts of it were found beautiful from the first, yet I imagine that a sense of the poem's contemporary importance may have served as 'the wire'[1] sustaining the uncertain growth of my response to the whole, until I could begin to feel value in parts loved less through their relation to those loved more.

The aspect of the poem which I wish to consider here is its character as exemplifying the pattern I have termed Rebirth. Notably the poem accomplishes—in Jung's phrase—'a translation of the primordial image into the language of the present,' through its gathering into simultaneity of impression images from the remote past with incidents and phrases of the everyday present.

It has been observed[2] that the re-entrance into myth and legend achieved through phantasmagoria—the shifting play of figures, as in dream, delirium, or the half-discerned undercurrents of consciousness—is an art-form characteristic both of Eliot's poetry, and of the present day; and this form has been criticized as unsatisfying, shapeless, in comparison with the clear definite outline that current belief and story made possible in the art of other ages. One might test one's own attitude to this criticism by bringing the total impression of *The Waste Land* into relation with that of Dante's *Comedy*. As a slighter illustration of the same kind of contrast, let us consider the way in

*London, 1934, pp. 307–14.

Early Poems and *The Waste Land*

which the agony of drought is conveyed and used in Eliot's poem, as compared with the communication of the experience in Coleridge's straightforward vivid tale of the Ancient Mariner.

In analysing *The Ancient Mariner*, we commented on the relation, within the communicated experience, of the imagined sequence of outer events—the calm, drought, the mariner's prayer, storm, rain, renewed motion—and the inner sequence of pent-up energy, discharge, and relief. We saw how the compelling story of outer events, with its vivid detail, could carry the reader's attention from point to point, while, below the level of conscious attention, emotional forces combined in modes ancient and satisfying.

> *The silly buckets on the deck,*
> *That had so long remained,*
> *I dreamt that they were filled with dew;*
> *And when I awoke, it rained.*

The single realistic detail of the buckets long unused can carry the whole impression, of the sufferings of the frustrated voyage, on with the rhythm of the simple verse-form into the moment of poignantly experienced relief, physical and spiritual. Compare the lines from *The Waste Land*:

> *Here is no water but only rock*
> *Rock and no water and the sandy road*
> *The road winding above among the mountains*
> *Which are mountains of rock without water*
> *If there were water we should stop and drink*
> *Amongst the rock one cannot stop or think*
> *Sweat is dry and feet are in the sand*
> *If there were only water amongst the rock*
> *Dead mountain mouth of carious teeth that cannot spit*
> *Here one can neither stand nor lie nor sit*
> *There is not even silence in the mountains*
> *But dry sterile thunder without rain*
> *There is not even solitude in the mountains*
> *But red sullen faces sneer and snarl*
> *From doors of mudcracked houses . . .*

One ceases to quote with reluctance; since the cumulative effect of the rhythm and repeated word-sounds is needed before one has a nucleus of experience with which to fuse the wide-ranging associations of the words. Since there is no story, no concrete dramatic situation, to bind associations together, the words within the haunting rhythm must play their part unaided, holding attention while the forces of feeling and attendant imagery negotiate in the antechambers of the mind.

The few powerfully evocative words played upon in the lines quoted create for us the bare form of an emotional situation realizable in any period of history, or pre-history, and multiplied, beyond actual occasions, infinitely, in dream and delirium. The horrible image of the dead mountain mouth— echoed later in 'the decayed hole among the mountains'—the craving for ease, for true silence and solitude, instead of faces that sneer and snarl— echoed, again, by the hooded hordes stumbling in cracked earth—all these are potent elements serving, as in the delirious dream, to express together memories and forces both of the individual and of the collective life.

In the lines that follow the nightmare atmosphere is exchanged for the clear beauty of the image that focuses desire:

> *If there were the sound of water only*
> *Not the cicada*
> *And dry grass singing*
> *But sound of water over a rock*
> *Where the hermit thrush sings in the pine trees*
> *Drip drop drip drop drop drop drop*
> *But there is no water*

The question concerning the poetic effectiveness of the modern vision, as compared with the medieval, might be illustrated from these lines, set beside those from the *Inferno* where Master Adam of Brescia, in the torment of thirst, recalls the streams he knew on earth:

> . . . when alive I had enough of what I wished: and now, alas! I crave one little drop of water. The rivulets that from the verdant hills of Casantino descend into the Arno, making their channels cool and moist, stand ever before me. . . .

In each poem the lovely image gains poignancy from its imagined background of frustration and pain. How far do we feel it a loss that the modern poem has no edifice of accepted tradition within whose ordered structure a distinct incident may hold, like a little darkened separate shrine, the fair image shining with the inner light of desire and hope? Hope, I would say, is present in Dante's image, though shown in Hell; because it is only as a transient episode in Dante's journey, or element deep at the foundation of his heavenly vision, that we find beauty in his descriptions of torment.[3] For our poetic experience to-day, I have argued, the traditional edifice of imagery that Dante uses can serve to sustain imaginative intuition, only in so far as it has the form of those archetypal patterns that changes of experience and outlook cannot render obsolete.

When I ask myself the question how far in Eliot's poem I miss 'the formal beauty of the medieval vision' of heaven and hell, I find that I care for it very little, when I realize in its stead such nexus of relations as Eliot weaves round the lyric image, within the sustaining pattern present through the whole poem. Let us consider farther this nexus of relations.

The hostile crowds that, in this section, are recalled from the agony in the garden, and seen sneering from mud-cracked houses or stumbling over endless plains, link this passage with that in the earlier division of the poem, where in the fog of winter dawn a crowd flowed over London Bridge. The line there quoted from Dante, 'I had not thought death had undone so many,' draws to the surface the underlying relation to the *Inferno*, and hints at the extinction of human fellowship in these self-absorbed figures—recalling the *Inferno*'s terrible note of malice in misery, that is repeated in the snarling faces that break the mountain solitude. The murmur of lamentation that sounds in the air above the stumbling hordes, and, fused with the central experience of drought, recalls those wailings in Eanna, for plants that grow not and perishing children, serves to reinforce the impression of that other ancient memory abruptly introduced in the wintry dawn on London Bridge:

> *There I saw one I knew, and stopped him, crying: 'Stetson!*
> *You who were with me in the ships at Mylae!*
> *That corpse you planted last year in your garden,*
> *Has it begun to sprout? Will it bloom this year?*
> *Or has the sudden frost disturbed its bed?'*

A hazardous stroke, yet to me it seems a triumphant one—to choose that glimpse of unreal crowds in city fog, for the stirring of associations of Osiris and his mysteries: the grain, or corpse, under the huddled earth, with its uncertain hope of resurrection, that frost or rifling beast may destroy.

One could cite many such links and associations. The reader who knows the poem will have found them for himself, and, reconstructing the interwoven tissue, will have realized some degree of unity in what appeared perhaps at first mere juxtaposition of fragments. Within my own experience of growing familiarity with the poem, I have found the reading over of certain of the lines come to seem like a ritual entrancing the mind with ancient memories.

When, following the guidance of Eliot's note, we turn to Miss Weston's research into the Grail romances, we meet testimony to the presence in these tales of the same atmosphere. The various forms of the Grail legend, Miss Weston believes, preserve traces of an ancient ritual of initiation: 'the sense of mystery, of a real danger to be faced, of an overwhelming spiritual gain to be won, were of the essential nature of the tale.'[4]

It is the initiation, or rebirth, pattern present in Eliot's poem that seems to me to mould and dominate the emotional response to the whole, when the various internal links and associations have worked their effect upon the mind. After the haunted perilous wanderings, the agony of drought and night and delirium, after we have experienced with almost physical relief the cock's dawn cry and the 'damp gust bringing rain', we await the poem's closing message even as a candidate for initiation, after laborious wanderings without issue, journeyings through the dark, full of misgivings and terror and anguish, might await the final redeeming vision.[5]

The words of ancient wisdom spoken in the thunder receive significance both from their place in the entire emotional pattern and from their special relations to earlier passages:

> Datta: *what have we given?*
> *My friend, blood shaking my heart*
> *The awful daring of a moment's surrender*
> *Which an age of prudence can never retract*
> *By this, and this only, we have existed*
> *Which is not to be found in our obituaries*
> *Or in memories draped by the beneficent spider*
> *Or under seals broken by the lean solicitor*
> *In our empty rooms.*

The vision of self-surrender—related, in subsequent interpretations of the thunder-word, to the angelic power of sympathy, and the divine power of control—occurring in the poem's pattern at the moment of energy-release and revulsion, recalls in contrast the earlier pictures of arid human relations: the joyless embraces, for instance, of the typist and her lover on the squalid divan which Tiresias' vision finds indistinguishable from marriage-beds of royal splendour—while their transactions belong to that realm in which the solicitor and the obituary notice have the final word. It is to a world other and more real than this that we are called by the challenge of the thunder.

> Damyata: *the boat responded*
> *Gaily, to the hand expert with sail and oar*
> *The sea was calm, your heart would have responded*
> *Gaily, when invited, beating obedient*
> *To controlling hands.*

These lines that interpret the divine task of control are of a subtlety, in their relation to an earlier passage, that may well communicate diversity of meanings. Mr. H.R. Williamson suggests[6] that the implied renunciation—*would have responded*—is related, through the imagery of the boat, to the 'selfish passion' of Tristian and Isolde. But the lines placed between the quotations that recall the story of those lovers seem to me to convey not so much the selfishness of their passion as its fatality, their helplessness beneath its stroke.

> *. . .I could not*
> *Speak, and my eyes failed, I was neither*
> *Living nor dead, and I knew nothing,*
> *Looking into the heart of light, the silence.*

The deep-stricken love suggested in these lines, and in the legend of Tristan and Isolde—whether, within love's fatality, its consummation be accepted or renounced—seems associated positively with the Grail symbol, as the less to the greater mystery.

Here, as in other poems we have studied, the lines of the pattern present the Paradisal love of earth, and urge the imagination beyond it; though it is for each reader to interpret as he may that indication of a Beyond.

Notes

1. *Supra*, p. 28 of the original edition.
2. By G.W. Stonier, *Gog Magog* (Dent, 1933), pp. 5–6.
3. I find within my own memory-impression of the *Comedy* this poignant image, of the streams that bring to the sufferer in Hell additional torment, becomes, through the poem's pattern of a narrated pilgrimage, an image of hope, pointing forward to the thought of the pilgrim's emerging from the dead air, rejoicing to cleanse his afflicted eyes with dew and to recognize the trembling of the sea.
4. *From Ritual to Romance*, by J.L. Weston (Camb. Univ. Press, 1920), p. 177.
5. Cf. the description of the initiation experience referred to *supra*, p. 125 of the original edition.
6. *The Poetry of T.S. Eliot* (Hodder and Staughton, 1932), p. 146.

105
Herbert Read; D.H. Lawrence; T.S. Eliot*

GEOFFREY BULLOUGH

While both Mr Read and Lawrence found some resolution of their spiritual difficulties in the exercise of individuality rebellious against external impulsion, Mr T.S. Eliot became the leader of a movement back to authority. The heir of Matthew Arnold and T.E. Hulme in criticism, he turned away, almost at the beginning of his career, from romantic self-exploitation in poetry. 'Poetry is not a turning loose of emotion but an escape from emotion; it is not the expression of personality, but an escape from personality.' 'No poet, no artist or any art, has his complete meaning alone. His significance, his appreciation, is the appreciation of his relation to the dead poets and artists.' The poet must be a scholar, obedient to the pressure of the past; but tradition as he thought of it was not insular. 'The historical sense compels a man to write not merely with his own generation in his bones, but with a feeling that the whole literature of Europe from Homer and within it the whole of the literature of his own country has a simultaneous existence and composes a simultaneous order. This historical sense ... is at the same time what makes a writer most acutely conscious of his place in time, of his own contemporaneity.'

Among the permanent influences on Mr Eliot we may note that of the post-Shakespearian dramatists; but many of his first poems, in *Prufrock* (1917), owe much to Corbière and Laforgue. Mr Eliot indeed carried on the symbolist influence when many other poets were turning to a more unmitigated realism. Something of Laforgue's shamefaced romanticism remained for a long time with him. The flippant irony which is a refuge for the imaginative idealist in an uncomprehending world shows itself in *Conversation Galante*. Self-deprecation, sentimentality at one remove, delicate analysis of mood, evocation of atmosphere by casual conversation, irrelevant verisimilitude, a loosening of iambic rhythms analogous to Laforgue's experiments with French verse (as well as to Jacobean practice), the use of contemporary material everyday urban life, salons, dismal streets; all are

---

* *The Trend of Modern Poetry* (Edinburgh, 1934), pp. 133–54.

introduced to suggest ironies of feeling and situation. Laforgue lacked the hardness and assurance of satiric portraiture in Mr Eliot's *Portrait* and his *Love Song of J. Alfred Prufrock*. The method is epitomised in the lines:

> *It is impossible to say just what I mean!*
> *But as if a magic lantern threw the nerves in patterns on a screen.*

He suggests an emotional impasse by veiled hints corresponding to a 'hundred indecisions' of mood. A mastery of phrase is already apparent:

> *I have measured out my life with coffee spoons . . .*
>
> *I grow old . . . I grow old . . .*
> *I shall wear the bottoms of my trousers rolled—*

each image mingling concreteness with spiritual deflation. No poet had so cleverly captured the atmosphere of mean streets and mean rooms (*Preludes*). What to Henley or the Georgians seemed a daring invasion was for Mr Eliot a natural entry into the age's imaginative heritage. In *Rhapsody on a Windy Night* impressionism unites with memory in ennui and horror. Its success depends on the fact that the 'crowd of twisted things' thrown up by the memory in free association, are really transfused by the dominant mood, and although Mr Sparrow would deny it, the mood becomes intelligible through this association. Mr Eliot's development brought an increased economy and a more varied use of such an organisation of images.

His love of word-patterns gives to his work a certain slowness of evolution, at times a preciosity. He repeats images and words like phrases in music, makes use of refrains and word-play:

> *There will be time, there will be time*
> *To prepare a face to meet the faces that you meet . . .*

His cadences owe something to the Imagists; he acknowledges a debt to Mr Pound. Like the latter he turned to social satire in such American studies as *Cousin Nancy* and *Mr Apollinax*. But free verse was not congenial. Like Mr Pound again he returned to traditional forms and helped in the revival of the four-stressed quatrain. To this he added, in *Poems* 1920, experiment in the blank verse of Webster and Middleton.

This volume is especially valuable as showing Mr Eliot's preparation for the greater achievement of *The Waste Land* (1922). He was developing his skill in hitting off representative types, but now left the peccadilloes of refined society for the vices of cosmopolitan Europe. Satiric detachment replaced dramatic self-analysis. His imagery became more and more heterogeneous; moods were evoked by the clash of wit and an increased indirection.

Another important factor now entered. Haunted by the contrast in Europe between present and past, he beheld the latter chiefly through its art. So when he wished, in *Burbank with a Baedeker, Bleistein with a Cigar*, to summon up the lost glory of Venice, he did so by referring to some half-dozen literary sources, including *The Merchant of Venice, Othello, A Toccata of Galuppi's,* and Ruskin. Mordant irony was obtained by sudden juxtapositions of ornate description and sordid realism. Thus he compressed into two or three stanzas a whole history of decline and fall; and his poem, far from seeming a mere mosaic of quotations, became a light of incredible intensity showing past and present in perspective.

The *Sweeney* poems, with their satire on sexual vulgarity, conveyed in dry objective statement his growing disgust with modern manners. *Whispers of Immortality* showed that his dissatisfaction was more than the revulsion of a fastidious scholar against vice. 'Webster was much possessed by death,' and Mr Eliot set not only modern self-indulgence but modern religion against a background of ultimate values. 'Our literature is a substitute for religion, and so is our religion.' If *A Cooking Egg* satirises modern ideals, *The Hippopotamus* satirises the Church in the world, as can best be seen by reading Gautier's *L'Hippopotame*, on which it is based.

Gerontion expounds most clearly Mr Eliot's criticism of life. Here a man, old in spirit, spinning disconnected 'Thoughts of a dry brain in a dry season,' inhabits 'a decayed house' in a composite squalor, and looks back on the changes and futility of life. He remembers how, in the spring, when a sign was demanded of God, 'Came Christ the Tiger.' But the coming of the Word was unavailing; the reverence due to His Body was given to 'flowering Judas'; and he remembers the postures of various types who carried on the betrayal. He remarks on the wasteful operations of life, the imbroglio of vice and virtue due to the 'wrath-bearing tree' of original sin. His own life has failed; he sees the emptiness of all sensual acts; at the last, mundane selfseekers are brought to nothing, like gulls in a storm; and he himself is driven to a sleepy corner.

The poem is incoherent, and criticism cannot be disarmed by Gerontion's senility. But it contains some fine lines, and shows Mr Eliot's growing insistence on religion. He came to agree more and more with T.E. Hulme that 'dogmas like that of Original Sin are the closest expression of the categories of the religious attitude. That man is in no sense perfect, but a wretched creature, who can yet apprehend perfection.' *The Waste Land* was a demand for such a realisation.

Before considering this poem, something more must be said of Mr Eliot's method. Abandoning Laforgue's adolescent nostalgia, he had developed a satiric dryness of witty statement in which 'facts' were left to evoke emotion with a minimum of explicit correlation. The technique was difficult. In such poetry the mood is too complex for initial statement, but is the implied resultant of the whole poem and is often (as in *Sweeney among the Nightingales*) not formulated until the close. Hence the final emergence of harmony out of heterogeneity is entirely dependent upon a clear concatenation of imagery. Now it is precisely in the concatenation of imagery that the poetry of Mr Eliot (and his followers) sets up obstacles. When the poet asks

> *But where is the penny world I bought*
> *To eat with Pipit behind the screen?*

and immediately continues

> *The red-eyed scavengers are creeping*
> *From Kentish Town and Golder's Green . . .*

(A Cooking Egg.)

the clash of symbols—the contrast of childish idealism and aged hopelessness—is harmonised into a profound sense of loss. But when in *Mr Eliot's Sunday Morning Service*, after describing the progress of theology to Origen, the *Baptism* of an Umbrian painter, the formalism of ecclesiastical penance, the bees at work in the garden, he shows us Sweeney in his bath, the reader of some education may be forgiven for having merely a vague suspicion that the poem deals with the forgiveness of sins. The first word of the poem, 'Polyphiloprogenitive,' initiates an obscurity that seems wilfully to mock. Among the many gifts received by Mr Eliot from the Metaphysicals is a poetry involved with far-fetched erudition. The fashion is a salutary reaction against contemporary mindlessness; it is pursued with something of the naive enthusiasm of the Renaissance, a love of new words, strange instances, subtle allusions. But for all its idiomatic rhythm and urban references, modern Metaphysical verse is more out of touch with the habits and expression of ordinary men than was the poetry of Donne and Carew. And the work of many of Mr Eliot's imitators is farther from poetical imagination than are the Georgian fantasies against which they rebel.

The success of quotations is contingent on two factors: the intrinsic value of the quotation in its new context quite apart from any recognition of its original source; and the density of colour resulting from the recognition of the original source, and its relation to the new context. Given the intrinsic value, the average reader will find an adequate (though not the full) significance in the most recondite allusions; and many of Mr Eliot's quotations make this possible. Where it is lacking, success depends entirely upon a community of literary background between writer and reader. Obviously this community is impossible to assess; but equally obviously the frequent use of unattributed allusions demanding a close knowledge of even the accepted 'classics' puts a strain on the relationship between poet and audience. In *The Waste Land*, Mr Eliot did not conquer this tendency of *Poems*, 1920; yet it comes near to being a great poem.

> *I that was near your heart was removed therefrom*
> *To lose beauty in terror, terror in inquisition,*

said *Gerontion*, aptly describing Mr Eliot's attitude during what may be called his second period. *The Waste Land* goes beyond a mere diagnosis of the spiritual distempers of the age; it is a lament over man's fallen nature, a prophecy, and a promise.

Formally the poem has been described as 'a music of ideas' and as 'a poetic cryptogram'; the second phrase suggests some weaknesses of the structure by which the poet sought the scope of the long poem without the relaxations of tension decried by Poe. Apart from the dominant mood, connecting links between the several parts may be found in a book of anthropology, Miss Jessie M. Weston's *From Ritual to Romance*. There Miss Weston showed that the legend of the Holy Grail originated in a fertility cult related to those of Thammuz and Adonis. It tells how a questing Knight saved the Waste Land from drought occasioned by the old age of the ruler, known as the Fisher King. The Knight must restore the latter's youth by riding to the Chapel Perilous and there questioning the Lance and the Grail, symbols of the male and female principles. Mr Eliot's poem is an allegorical application of this story to modern society and religion. Our civilisation is the Waste Land; we can obtain youth and life-giving rain only by journeying far, questioning our condition, and learning a hard lesson. To enforce this, Mr Eliot makes use of symbols drawn from kindred myths and religions. The relationship between these must be known before the poem can be understood. And the difficulties of this anthropological background are increased by the methods of thought which we have seen are natural to him. There are five parts, each containing sections bound variously, by superficial association of ideas, by contrast, or by no link save the underlying message. To the uninitiated reader the poem may seem chaotic. Only those with some knowledge of Dante, Jacobean drama, Buddhism, mythology, and the works of Sir James Frazer, as well as of *From Ritual to Romance*, can appreciate its structure, even with help from the poet's notes. Yet no one could fail to be struck by the vigour and beauty of much of the detail. What ironic pictures of modern manners, what a superb mingling of satiric vulgarity and sensuous delicacy, what prophetic earnestness, what variety of imagery and rhythm!

The best way to begin reading the poem is to regard it as a phantasmagoria of futility, a series of trains of thought in the mind of a social observer. Mr Eliot indeed introduces such an observer (in a not very effective attempt at suggesting comprehensiveness and impersonality) in the person of Tiresias, the seer, who, having been both man and woman, suggests the characteristics of all humanity.

Part 1, called *The Burial of the Dead*, to emphasise the inevitable dissolution which must precede new life, begins with a lament over the loss of fertility in what should be a spring-season, and illustrates this by reproducing typical chatter of cosmopolitan idlers, passing thence to symbols of our barrenness:

> *A heap of broken images, where the sun beats,*
> *And the dead tree gives no shelter, the cricket no relief,*
> *And the dry stone no sound of water . . .*

The decay of love in the modern world is then suggested by a quotation from

Wagner's *Tristan and Isolde* (romantic idolatry), with which he compares an instance of amorous sentimentality. That secret wisdom, too, has fallen on evil days is shown by the introduction of the Tarot pack of cards, used formerly for divination, now for fortune-telling. He ends with a vision of London as an Unreal City, in a nightmare of memories:

> *That corpse you planted last year in your garden,*
> *Has it begun to sprout? Will it bloom this year?*

The connection with the fertility cult is thus emphasised.

In Part 2, called *A Game of Chess*, to suggest purposeless activity and to recall the dramatic irony of Middleton's Bianca and the fatal power of woman, he gives a glimpse of two types of modern woman in contrasted literary styles. After a picture of a luxurious boudoir which rivals Keats, he gives the petulant conversation of its tenant, and the eternal question:

> *What shall we do to-morrow?*
> *What shall we ever do? . . .*

The man replies:

> *The hot water at ten.*
> *And if it rains, a closed car at four.*
> *And we shall play a game of chess,*
> *Pressing lidless eyes and waiting for a knock upon the door.*

Then answering the word *knock*, the scene changes to a public-house at closing time, and the garrulous mean talk of another woman.

In Part 3 the tone of disgust deepens. It is called *The Fire Sermon*, to suggest to the initiated the sermon of the Buddha, in which he spoke of mankind as burning in the flames of lust, hatred, and infatuation. Here we are shown the sordidness of urban pleasures. Just as he introduced into the boudoir touches of Cleopatra and Dido, so now he recalls the river of Spenser's *Prothalamion*, and with equally devastating irony goes on to parody Goldsmith's 'When lovely woman,' in order to contrast the cynicism of the modern girl with the eighteenth-century sentimental ideal. Similarly he uses Wagner's *Rheingold* melodies, and a picture of Queen Elizabeth flirting with Leicester in her barge, to emphasise the permanence of human sensuality and the degradation to which it has now fallen. With agony of soul he finally alludes to the repentance of Saint Augustine and to the teaching of the Buddha.

After a short fourth part, translated from one of his earlier experiments in French and emphasising the brevity of sensual life, the several themes are recapitulated in Part 5, and the way of escape suggested. Our sterility is again asserted:

> *Here is no water but only rock,*
> *Rock and no water and the sandy road,*

> *The road winding above among the mountains*
> *Which are mountains of rock without water. . . .*

In this desert we suffer illusions; where two walk there goes a shadowy third. There are murmurs and lamentations. When we reach the Chapel Perilous it seems empty; but as we doubt (betraying Christ) and the cock crows twice, God gives a sign, by thunder bringing rain. And the message of the thunder is threefold: Da, Dayadhvam, Damyata—Self-surrender, sympathy, self-control. These three are the way to salvation.

In a coda the poet speaks of setting his own house in order though London Bridge is falling down. He must pass through the fire of purification, as Dante has shown. He is haunted by images of desolation, and a shower of literary allusions shows him slipping into frenzy. But like a charm of healing rain he repeats the message of the thunder and ends with the Sanskrit blessing: 'Shantih, shantih, shantih': (The peace of God which passeth all understanding. . . .)

This crude sketch of the general outline of *The Waste Land* obscures the peculiar technique as well as many subtleties of the poem. The repetition of images is the means of carrying on the symbolism from section to section. That is what is meant by 'music of ideas.' The image of the rocky desert, for instance, is brought in again and again; 'crowds of people walking,' in Part 1, is repeated almost immediately, as 'A crowd flowed over London Bridge,' is associated with the frequent mention of footsteps, and becomes in Part 5 the 'hooded hordes swarming'; allusions to bells, thunder, rain, spring, bones, rats, recur with varying emotional tones. The whole poem gains its unity from the interweaving of such thematic material. This is the literary counterpart of the symphony to which the Symbolists aspired.

'Genuine poetry can communicate before it is understood,' wrote Mr Eliot in his important essay on Dante. That must be true within limits, otherwise the success of Miss Sitwell's *Façade*, and of great patches of Swinburne, which rely entirely on the music and colour of words without anything to understand, would be inexplicable. But communication of this elementary sort is only preparatory to the true work of poetry; beyond this, communication is contingent on 'understanding,' on the linking of associations, of ideas.

The Waste Land is a perfectly intelligible poem, the most notable poem of our time. But it has serious defects inherent in its origin and its method. Mr Eliot's attempt at rectifying the old divorce between intelligence and sensibility fails by the remoteness of much of his material. In a word, *The Waste Land* does not carry within itself all that is necessary for understanding. Its structural basis lies in a specialised branch of learning, and it involves continual reference to other branches of knowledge with which few readers can be acquainted. The poem is not a self-contained entity. Despite its great influence, therefore, it is not Mr Eliot's most successful work. That title I should give to his *Ash Wednesday*.

Early Poems and *The Waste Land*

In *The Waste Land* Mr Eliot's attitude was more negative than positive, analytic rather than synthetic. He was more aware of the facts of disintegration than of the universal system in which the disintegration took place. Poetically it was a cry in the dark, a longing for imaginative stability, for participation in an unknown ultimate order.

The poems immediately succeeding *The Waste Land* enforce this conclusion. In *Journey of the Magi* the wise men return home having seen God, but unrefreshed, dissatisfied with 'the old dispensation,' while the *Nunc Dimittis* of *A Song for Simeon* is a melancholy burden of oppression. *Ash Wednesday* makes clear that Mr Eliot's poetry is now occupied with personal salvation, with experiences closely akin to those undergone by the 'twice-born' in their progress towards a state of Grace. It is not purely fanciful to regard *The Waste Land* as corresponding to the phase in which (according to *Theologica Germanica*) the soul perceives 'how and what our own life is, what God is and is doing in us'; and to see the 'hard and bitter agony' of the *Magi* as introducing the phase of suffering and self-mortification. *Ash Wednesday*, while not a mystical poem, inasmuch as it describes no experience of mystical union, deals faithfully with certain common aspects of the Mystic Way, with the putting off of self, the passivity, the spiritual darkness, the fluctuations following on conversion. Its title suggests the beginning of contrition and the distant hope of Easter.

In the first section the soul turns away from human emulation, 'The infirm glory of the positive hour,' and finds some little joy in extreme renunciation. But this is a remnant of selfishness; all thought, even the desire to soar above abasement, must be abandoned. 'Teach us to sit still.' Patience and prayer alone dwell in the 'dark night of the soul.' The second section describes the acceptance of spiritual death. Its powers consumed, the soul is like the dry bones in Ezekiel. When God tells them to prophesy they do so with the burden of the grasshopper, for desire has failed, and, invoking the 'Lady of Silences,' give thanks for their death in the desert.

The third section is perhaps the finest of all. The soul is climbing the stairs from earthly to heavenly things; it is on the second stair, for it has turned from the world, and on the first flight has left behind its struggle with hope and despair. At the second turning of the second stair nothing is seen but darkness, an aged maw, the wreck of life, utter abandonment and negation. Beyond this, at the first turning of the third stair, comes temptation, memories of the life of the senses: 'Distraction, music of the flute, stops and steps of the mind over the third stair.' But the soul presses on, climbing, and prays: 'Lord, I am not worthy,' for God is up there under his roof, and the end of ascent is healing and peace. As he wrote in his essay on Dante, which illuminates the problems of this poem: 'The souls in purgatory suffer because they wish to suffer.'

The fourth part deals with the transmutation of earthly experience into heavenly. Remembering one who 'Going in white and blue, in Mary's colour,' once gave him strength and joy, he wishes to 'Redeem the time,' to regain the lost innocence, not by returning, but by sublimating what was of the world into a higher dream. So Dante's Beatrice was transfigured in the life of vision; the process of religious 'illumination' is assisted by symbols, 'The token of the word unheard, unspoken.'

This reference to the word leads on to the fifth section which tells how the Logos, the inexpressible Word of God immanent in the world, is rejected by men. The poet asks a 'Veiled Sister' to pray for the divided souls, the renegades, the cowards, for all who sit where the garden of God has been made desert.

The last section returns to the main theme of the first, incidentally recalling elements from the others, in a summary of the soul's position. It has not yet achieved peace, but still fluctuates between the old and the new, still wavers between 'the profit and the loss.' Self is not dead; temptation recurs:

> *And the weak spirit quickens to rebel*
> *For the spent golden rod and the lost sea-smell.*

He is at 'the time of tension between dying and birth,' in 'the place of solitude where three dreams cross.' His only trust is that the veiled lady, who suggests Mary herself, will bring truth and unity of spirit. He ends, repeating the idea of the first section, but more hopefully, though Easter is not yet:

> *Teach us to sit still . . .*
> *Our peace in His will . . .*
> *Suffer me not to be separated.*

Once again such a brief account misses the subtleties of this remarkable sequence, which is linked by many repetitions of idea and similarities of symbol. Allusiveness is here more restrained, the literary references are less recondite, largely owing to the use made of the Bible and the Liturgy, which also assist in the attainment of a grave, ceremonious style fitted to the dignity of the subject. The greater simplicity of imagery is fostered by the influence of Dante, considerable throughout. But the superiority of *Ash Wednesday* over *The Waste Land* is due to the intimacy of the whole conception, and above all to the universality of its intellectual background. 'That is the advantage of a coherent traditional system of dogma and morals like the Catholic; it stands apart, for understanding and assent even without belief, from the single individual who propounds it' (*Essay on Dante*). The poem derives its power from its participation in such a coherent religious tradition.

After this poem, *Sweeney Agonistes* (1932) must seem a somewhat trivial return to an earlier mood. But it portrays inanity, the inarticulate converse of empty vulgarians in bold jazz rhythms. Similar rhythms had been used before by Miss Sitwell, but at the expense of meaning. Here, however, rhythm and idiom combine in a perfect suggestion of futility:

> *I gotta use words when I talk to you*
> *But if you understand or if you don't*
> *That's nothing to me and nothing to you*
> *We all gotta do what we gotta do . . .*

The Rock (1934), a pageant play on behalf of a London church building fund—for which Mr Eliot contributed the libretto to someone else's scenario—is closer to *Ash Wednesday* in spirit. Though institutional in theme and purpose and dramatically stiff with the conventional movement of historical pageantry, it reveals the poet's personal apprehension of the Anglican faith, and has many fine passages on 'the perpetual struggle of Good and Evil,' and man's 'knowledge of words, and ignorance of the Word.' A minor work, *The Rock* is, nevertheless, remarkable for its variety of rhythmical experiment. Biblical prose, loose accentual passages with and without rhyme, antiphonal movements, popular-song measures, irregular strophes reminiscent of *Samson Agonistes*, choral odes recalling those of Paul Claudel, long rolling breakers of free verse, prove the poet's mastery of a new fullness of rhetoric, 'the beauty of incantation.' The old power of succinct suggestion appears in the songs and speeches of social types, such as the Unemployed:

> *In this land*
> *There shall be one cigarette to two men. . . .*

and the Communist poets, 'young, with fairly intelligent faces,' whose 'turbines all turning, our sparrows all chirping—all denounce you, deceivers of the people.'

'There is no hope from those who march in step,' a chorus chants, and this might well be Mr Eliot's own comment on modern extremes of authoritarianism. It is even truer as a reflection of his poetic practice than are his other dicta on tradition. At times his individuality has been free to the point of eccentricity. Now that he has attained the metaphysical synthesis to which he aspired, there is no reason to suppose (as some critics have done) that his poetic talent will be any the less vital. But a new discipline, the simplicity of universality, is apparent in his later poems.

It is dangerous to generalise, but perhaps we may say that, on the whole, Mr Eliot's influence on the present generation has been more one of tone and attitude, Mr Pound's one of technique. Mr Eliot crystallised post-war dissatisfaction with the decaying standards of individualism, however much some might quarrel with his remedies. Mr Pound on the other hand offered in *Mauberley* a clear-cut procedure of self-analysis and social criticism which appealed by its simplicity to minds impatient of romantic veils, nebulous words, confused thought. Their common plea for a literature of scholarly intelligence deified both poets at a time when the largely factitious opposition of art and science was bridged in the search for a new synthesis of knowledge and faith. But the cerebral poetry that resulted had little in common with the plain manner advocated by Thomas Spray in his *History of the Royal Society* (1667) as the product of a scientific mind, and concrete symbolism *after* Mr Eliot consorted ill with theoretic statement *after* Mr Pound in the work of their followers. Such poems as Miss Nancy Cunard's *Parallax* proved the ineffectuality of direct imitations of Mr Eliot's manner.

106
The Waste Land:
Critique of the Myth*

CLEANTH BROOKS

Though much has been written on *The Waste Land*, it will not be difficult to show that most of its critics misconceive entirely the theme and the structure of the poem. There has been little or no attempt to deal with it as a unified whole. F.R. Leavis and F.O. Matthiessen have treated large sections of the poem in detail, and I am obviously indebted to both of them. I believe, however, that Leavis makes some positive errors of interpretation. I find myself in almost complete agreement with Matthiessen in his commentary on the sections which he deals with in his *Achievement of T.S. Eliot*, but the plan of his book does not allow for a complete consecutive examination of the poem.

In view of the state of criticism with regard to the poem, it is best for us to approach it frankly on the basis of its theme. I prefer, however, not to raise just here the question of how important it is for the reader to have an explicit intellectual account of the various symbols and a logical account of their relationships. It may well be that such rationalization is no more than a scaffolding to be got out of the way before we contemplate the poem itself as poem. But many readers (including myself) find the erection of such a scaffolding valuable—if not absolutely necessary—and if some readers will be tempted to lay more stress upon the scaffolding than they should, there are perhaps still more readers who, without the help of such a scaffolding, will be prevented from getting at the poem at all.

The basic symbol used, that of the waste land, is taken of course, from Miss Jessie Weston's *From Ritual to Romance*. In the legends which she treats there, the land has been blighted by a curse. The crops do not grow and the animals cannot reproduce. The plight of the land is summed up by, and connected with, the plight of the lord of the land, the Fisher King, who has been rendered impotent by maiming or sickness. The curse can be removed only by the appearance of a knight who will ask the meanings of the various symbols which are displayed to him in the castle. The shift in meaning from

---

*From *Modern Poetry and the Tradition* (Chapel Hill, 1939), pp. 136–72.

physical to spiritual sterility is easily made, and was, as a matter of fact, made in certain of the legends. As Eliot has pointed out, a knowledge of this symbolism is essential for an understanding of the poem.

Of hardly less importance to the reader, however, is a knowledge of Eliot's basic method. *The Waste Land* is built on a major contrast—a device which is a favorite of Eliot's and is to be found in many of his poems, particularly his later poems. The contrast is between two kinds of life and two kinds of death. Life devoid of meaning is death; sacrifice, even the sacrificial death, may be life-giving, an awakening to life. The poem occupies itself to a great extent with this paradox, and with a number of variations upon it.

Eliot has stated the matter quite explicitly himself in one of his essays. In his 'Baudelaire' he says: 'One aphorism which has been especially noticed is the following: *la volupté unique et suprême de l'amour gît dans la certitude de faire le mal.* This means, I think, that Baudelaire has perceived that what distinguishes the relations of man and woman from the copulation of beasts is the knowledge of Good and Evil (*of moral* Good and Evil which are not natural Good and Bad or puritan Right and Wrong.) Having an imperfect, vague romantic conception of Good, he was at least able to understand that the sexual act as evil is more dignified, less boring, than as the natural, "life-giving," cheery automatism of the modern world. . . . So far as we are human, what we do must be either evil or good; so far as we do evil or good, we are human; and it is better, in a paradoxical way, to do evil than to do nothing: at least, *we exist* [italics mine].' The last statement is highly important for an understanding of *The Waste Land.* The fact that men have lost the knowledge of good and evil, keeps them from being alive, and is the justification for viewing the modern waste land as a realm in which the inhabitants do not even exist.

This theme is stated in the quotation which prefaces the poem. The Sybil says: 'I wish to die.' Her statement has several possible interpretations. For one thing, she is saying what the people who inhabit the waste land are saying. But she may also be saying what the speaker of 'The Journey of the Magi' says '. . . this Birth was/Hard and bitter agony for us, like Death, our death/. . . I should be glad of another death.'

I

The first section of 'The Burial of the Dead' develops the theme of the attractiveness of death, or of the difficulty in rousing oneself from the death in life in which the people of the waste land live. Men are afraid to live in reality. April, the month of rebirth, is not the most joyful season but the cruelest. Winter at least kept us warm in forgetful snow. The idea is one which Eliot has stressed elsewhere. Earlier in 'Gerontion' he had written

Early Poems and *The Waste Land*

> *In the juvescence of the year*
> *Came Christ the tiger*
>
> *The tiger springs in the new year. Us he devours.*

More lately, in *Murder in the Cathedral*, he has the chorus say

> *We do not wish anything to happen.*
> *Seven years we have lived quietly,*
> *Succeeded in avoiding notice,*
> *Living and partly living.*

And in another passage: 'Now I fear disturbance of the quiet seasons.' Men dislike to be roused from their death-in-life.

The first part of 'The Burial of the Dead' introduces this theme through a sort of reverie on the part of the protagonist—a reverie in which speculation on life glides off into memory of an actual conversation in the Hofgarten and back into speculation again. The function of the conversation is to establish the class and character of the protagonist. The reverie is resumed with line 19.

> *What are the roots that clutch, what branches grow*
> *Out of this stony rubbish?*

The protagonist answers for himself:

> *Son of man,*
> *You cannot say, or guess, for you know only*
> *A heap of broken images, where the sun beats,*
> *And the dead tree gives no shelter, the cricket no relief,*
> *And the dry stone no sound of water.*

In this passage there are references to Ezekiel and to Ecclesiastes, and these references indicate what it is that men no longer know: The passage referred to in Ezekiel 2, pictures a world thoroughly secularized:

> 1. And he said unto me, Son of man, stand upon thy feet, and I will speak unto thee.
> 2. And the spirit entered into me when he spake unto me, and set me upon my feet, that I heard him that spake unto me.
> 3. And he said unto me, Son of man, I send thee to the children of Israel, to a rebellious nation that hath rebelled against me: they and their fathers have transgressed against me, even unto this very day.

Other passages from Ezekiel are relevant to the poem, Chapter 37 in particular, which describes Ezekiel's waste land, where the prophet, in his vision of the valley of dry bones, contemplates the 'burial of the dead' and is asked: 'Son of man, can these bones live? And I answered, O Lord God, thou knowest. 4. Again he said unto me, Prophesy over these bones, and say unto them, O ye dry bones, hear the word of the Lord.'

One of Ezekiel's prophecies was that Jerusalem would be conquered and the people led away into the Babylonian captivity. That captivity is alluded to in Section III of *The Waste Land*, line 182, where the Thames becomes the 'waters of Leman.'

The passage from Ecclesiastes 12, alluded to in Eliot's notes, describes the same sort of waste land:

> 1. Remember now thy Creator in the days of thy youth, while the evil days come not, nor the years draw nigh, when thou shalt say, I have no pleasure in them;
> 2. While the sun, or the light, or the moon, or the stars, be not darkened, nor the clouds return after the rain;
> 3. In the day when the keepers of the house shall tremble, and the strong men shall bow themselves, and the grinders cease because they are few, and those that look out of the windows be darkened;
> 4. And the doors shall be shut in the streets, when the sound of the grinding is low, and he shall rise up at the voice of the bird, and all the daughters of musick shall be brought low;
> 5. Also when they shall be afraid of that which is high, and fears shall be in the way, and the almond tree shall flourish, and the grasshopper shall be a burden, *and desire shall fail* [italics mine]: because man goeth to his long home, and the mourners go about the streets;
> 6. Or ever the silver cord be loosed, or the golden bowl be broken, or the pitcher be broken at the fountain, or the wheel broken at the cistern.
> 7. Then shall the dust return to the earth as it was: and the spirit shall return unto God who gave it.
> 8. Vanity of vanities, saith the preacher; all is vanity.

A reference to this passage is also evidently made in the nightmare vision of Section V of the poem.

The next section of 'The Burial of the Dead' which begins with the scrap of song quoted from Wagner (perhaps another item in the reverie of the protagonist), states the opposite half of the paradox which underlies the poem: namely, that life at its highest moments of meaning and intensity resembles death. The song from Act I of Wagner's *Tristan und Isolde*, '*Frisch weht der Wind*,' is sung in the opera by a young sailor aboard the ship which is bringing Isolde to Cornwall. The '*Irisch Kind*' of the song does not properly apply to Isolde at all. The song is merely one of happy and naïve love. It brings to the mind of the protagonist an experience of love—the vision of the hyacinth girl as she came back from the hyacinth garden. The poet says

> ... *my eyes failed, I was neither*
> *Living nor dead, and I knew nothing.*
> *Looking into the heart of light, the silence.*

The line which immediately follows this passage, '*Oed' und leer das Meer*,' seems at first to be simply an extension of the last figure: that is, 'Empty and wide the sea [of silence].' But the line, as a matter of fact, makes an ironic

Early Poems and *The Waste Land*

contrast; for the line, as it occurs in Act III of the opera, is the reply of the watcher who reports to the wounded Tristan that Isolde's ship is nowhere in sight; the sea is empty. And, though the '*Irisch Kind*' of the first quotation is not Isolde, the reader familiar with the opera will apply it to Isolde when he comes to the line '*Oed' und leer das Meer.*' For the question in the song is in essence Tristan's question in Act III: 'My Irish child, where dwellest thou?' The two quotations from the opera which frame the ecstasy-of-love passage thus take on a new meaning in the altered context. In the first, love is happy; the boat rushes on with a fair wind behind it. In the second, love is absent; the sea is wide and empty. And the last quotation reminds us that even love cannot exist in the waste land.

The next passage, that in which Madame Sosostris figures, calls for further reference to Miss Weston's book. As Miss Weston has shown, the Tarot cards were originally used to determine the event of highest importance to the people, the rising of the waters. Madame Sosostris has fallen a long way from the high function of her predecessors. She is engaged merely in vulgar fortune-telling—is merely one item in a generally vulgar civilization. But the symbols of the Tarot pack are still unchanged. The various characters are still inscribed on the cards, and she is reading in reality (though she does not know it) the fortune of the protagonist. She finds that his card is that of the drowned Phoenician Sailor, and so she warns him against death by water, not realizing any more than do the other inhabitants of the modern waste land that the way into life may be by death itself. The drowned Phoenician sailor is a type of the fertility god whose image was thrown into the sea annually as a symbol of the death of summer. As for the other figures in the pack: Belladonna, the Lady of the Rocks, is woman in the waste land. The man with three staves, Eliot says he associates rather arbitrarily with the Fisher King. The term 'arbitrarily' indicates that we are not to attempt to find a logical connection here. (It may be interesting to point out, however, that Eliot seems to have given, in a later poem, his reason for making the association. In 'The Hollow Men' he writes, speaking as one of the Hollow Men:

> *Let me also wear*
> *Such deliberate disguises*
> *Rat's coat, crowskin, crossed staves*
> *In a field*
> *Behaving as the wind behaves.*

The figure is that of a scarecrow, fit symbol of the man who possesses no reality, and fit type of the Fisher King, the maimed, impotent king who ruled over the waste land of the legend. The man with three staves in the deck of cards may thus have appealed to the poet as an appropriate figure to which to assign the function of the Fisher King, although the process of identification was too difficult to expect the reader to follow and although knowledge of the process was not necessary to an understanding of the poem.)

The Hanged Man, who represents the hanged god of Frazer (including the Christ), Eliot states in a note, is associated with the hooded figure who appears in 'What the Thunder Said.' That he is hooded accounts for Madame Sosostris' inability to see him; or rather, here again the palaver of the modern fortune-teller is turned to new and important account by the poet's shifting the reference into a new and serious context. The Wheel and the one-eyed merchant will be discussed later.

After the Madame Sosostris passage, Eliot proceeds to complicate his symbols for the sterility and unreality of the modern waste land by associating it with Baudelaire's '*fourmillante cité*' and with Dante's Limbo. The passages already quoted from Eliot's essay on Baudelaire will indicate one of the reasons why Baudelaire's lines are evoked here. In Baudelaire's city, dream and reality seem to mix, and it is interesting that Eliot in 'The Hollow Men' refers to the same realm of death-in-life as 'death's dream kingdom' in contradistinction to 'death's other kingdom.'

The references to Dante are most important. The line, 'I had not thought death had undone so many,' is taken from the Third Canto of the *Inferno*; the line, 'Sighs, short and infrequent, were exhaled,' from the Fourth Canto. Mr. Matthiessen has already pointed out that the Third Canto deals with Dante's Limbo which is occupied by those who on earth had 'lived without praise or blame.' They share this abode with the angels 'who were not rebels, nor were faithful to God, but were for themselves.' They exemplify almost perfectly the secular attitude which dominates the modern world. Their grief, according to Dante, arises from the fact that they 'have no hope of death; and their blind life is so debased, that they are envious of every other lot.' But though they may not hope for death, Dante calls them 'these wretches who never were alive.' The people described in the Fourth Canto are those who lived virtuously but who died before the proclamation of the Gospel—they are the unbaptized. They form the second of the two classes of people who inhabit the modern waste land: those who are secularized and those who have no knowledge of the faith. Without a faith their life is in reality a death. To repeat the sentence from Eliot previously quoted: 'So far as we do evil or good, we are human; and it is better, in a paradoxical way, to do evil than to do nothing: at least, we exist.'

The Dante and Baudelaire references, then, come to the same thing as the allusion to the waste land of the medieval legends; and these various allusions, drawn from widely differing sources, enrich the comment on the modern city so that it becomes 'unreal' on a number of levels: as seen through 'the brown fog of a winter dawn'; as the medieval waste land and Dante's Limbo and Baudelaire's Paris are unreal.

The reference to Stetson stresses again the connection between the modern London of the poem and Dante's hell. After the statement, 'I could never have believed death had undone so many,' follow the words, 'After I had distinguished some among them, I saw and knew the shade of him who made, through cowardice, the great refusal.' The protagonist, like Dante, sees among the inhabitants of the contemporary waste land one whom he recognizes. (The name 'Stetson' I take to have no ulterior significance. It is merely an ordinary name such as might be borne by the friend one might see in a crowd in a great city.) Mylae, as Mr. Matthiessen has pointed out, is the name of a battle between the Romans and the Carthaginians in the Punic War. The Punic War was a trade war—might be considered a rather close parallel to our late war. At any rate, it is plain that Eliot in having the protagonist address the friend in a London street as one who was with him in the Punic War rather than as one who was with him in the World War is making the point that all the wars are one war; all experience, one experience. As Eliot put the idea in *Murder in the Cathedral*:

> *We do not know very much of the future*
> *Except that from generation to generation*
> *The same things happen again and again*

I am not sure that Leavis and Matthiessen are correct in inferring that the line, 'That corpse you planted last year in your garden,' refers to the attempt to bury a memory. But whether or not this is true, the line certainly refers also to the buried god of the old fertility rites. It also is to be linked with the earlier passage—'What are the roots that clutch, what branches grow,' etc. This allusion to the buried god will account for the ironical, almost taunting tone of the passage. The burial of the dead is now a sterile planting—without hope. But the advice to 'keep the Dog far hence,' in spite of the tone, is, I believe, well taken and serious. The passage in Webster goes as follows

> *But keep the wolf far thence, that's foe to men,*
> *For with his nails he'll dig them up again.*

Why does Eliot turn the wolf into a dog? And why does he reverse the point of importance from the animal's normal hostility to men to its friendliness? If, as some critics have suggested, he is merely interested in making a reference to Webster's darkest play, why alter the line? I am inclined to take the Dog (the capital letter is Eliot's) as Humanitarianism[1] and the related philosophies which, in their concern for man, extirpate the supernatural—dig up the corpse of the buried god and thus prevent the rebirth of life. For the general idea, see Eliot's essay, 'The Humanism of Irving Babbitt.'

The last line of 'The Burial of the Dead'—'You! hypocrite lecteur!—mon semblable,—mon frère!' the quotation from Baudelaire, completes the universalization of Stetson begun by the reference to Mylae. Stetson is every man including the reader and Mr. Eliot himself.

II

If 'The Burial of the Dead' gives the general abstract statement of the situation, the second part of *The Waste Land*, 'A Game of Chess,' gives a more concrete illustration. The easiest contrast in this section—and one which may easily blind the casual reader to a continued emphasis on the contrast between the two kinds of life, or the two kinds of death, already commented on—is the contrast between life in a rich and magnificent setting, and life in the low and vulgar setting of a London pub. But both scenes, however antithetical they may appear superficially, are scenes taken from the contemporary waste land. In both of them life has lost its meaning.

I am particularly indebted to Mr. Allen Tate's comment on the first part of this section. To quote from him, 'The woman . . . is, I believe, the symbol of man at the present time. He is surrounded by the grandeurs of the past, but he does not participate in them; they don't sustain him.' And to quote from another section of his commentary: 'The rich experience of the great tradition depicted in the room receives a violent shock in contrast with a game that symbolizes the inhuman abstraction of the modern mind.' Life has no meaning; history has no meaning; there is no answer to the question: 'What shall we ever do?' The only thing that has meaning is the abstract game which they are to play, a game in which the meaning is assigned and arbitrary, meaning by convention only—in short, a game of chess.

This interpretation will account in part for the pointed reference to Cleopatra in the first lines of the section. But there is, I believe, a further reason for the poet's having compared the lady to Cleopatra. The queen in Shakespeare's drama—'Age cannot wither her, nor custom stale/Her infinite variety'—is perhaps the extreme exponent of love for love's sake, the feminine member of the pair of lovers who threw away an empire for love. But the infinite variety of the life of the woman in 'A Game of Chess' *has* been staled. There is indeed no variety at all, and love simply does not exist. The function of the sudden change in the description of the carvings and paintings in the room from the heroic and magnificent to 'and other withered stumps of time' is obvious. But the reference to Philomela is particularly important, for Philomela, it seems to me, is one of the major symbols of the poem.

Miss Weston points out (in *The Quest of the Holy Grail*) that a section of one of the Grail manuscripts, which is apparently intended to be a gloss on the Grail story, tells how the court of the rich Fisher King was withdrawn from the knowledge of men when certain of the maidens who frequented the shrine were raped and had their golden cups taken from them. The curse on the land follows from this act. Miss Weston conjectures that this may be a statement, in the form of a parable, of the violation of the older mysteries which were probably once celebrated openly, but were later forced under-

Early Poems and *The Waste Land*

ground. Whether or not Mr. Eliot noticed this passage or intends a reference, the violation of a woman makes a very good symbol of the process of secularization. John Crowe Ransom makes the point very neatly for us in *God Without Thunder*. Love is the aesthetic of sex; lust is the science. Love implies a deferring of the satisfaction of the desire; it implies a certain asceticism and a ritual. Lust drives forward urgently and scientifically to the immediate extirpation of the desire. Our contemporary waste land is in large part the result of our scientific attitude—of our complete secularization. Needless to say, lust defeats its own ends. The portrayal of 'the change of Philomel, by the barbarous king' is a fitting commentary on the scene which it ornaments. The waste land of the legend came in this way; the modern waste land has come in this way.

This view is corroborated by the change of tense to which Edmund Wilson has called attention: 'And still she *cried*, and still the world *pursues* [italics mine].' Apparently the 'world' partakes in the barbarous king's action, and still partakes in that action.

To 'dirty ears' the nightingale's song is not that which filled all the desert with inviolable voice—it is 'jug, jug.' Edmund Wilson has pointed out that the rendition of the bird's song here represents not merely the Elizabethans' neutral notation of the bird's song, but carries associations of the ugly and coarse. The passage is one, therefore, of many instances of Eliot's device of using something which in one context is innocent but in another context becomes loaded with a special meaning.

The Philomela passage has another importance, however. If it is a commentary on how the waste land became waste, it also repeats the theme of the death which is the door to life, the theme of the dying god. The raped woman becomes transformed through suffering into the nightingale; through the violation comes the 'inviolable voice.' The thesis that suffering is action, and that out of suffering comes poetry is a favorite one of Eliot's. For example, 'Shakespeare, too, was occupied with the struggle—which alone constitutes life for a poet—to transmute his personal and private agonies into something rich and strange, something universal and impersonal.' Consider also his statement with reference to Baudelaire: 'Indeed, in his way of suffering is already a kind of presence of the supernatural and of the superhuman. He rejects always the purely natural and the purely human; in other words, he is neither "naturalist" nor "humanist."' The theme of the life which is death is stated specifically in the conversation between the man and the woman. She asks the question, 'Are you alive, or not?' Compare the Dante references in 'The Burial of the Dead.' (She also asks, 'Is there nothing in your head?' He is one of the Hollow Men—'Headpiece filled with straw.') These people, as people living in the waste land, know nothing, see nothing, do not even live.

But the protagonist, after this reflection that in the waste land of modern life even death is sterile—'I think we are in rats' alley/Where the dead men lost their bones'—remembers a death that was transformed into something rich and strange, the death described in the song from *The Tempest*—'Those are pearls that were his eyes.'

The reference to this section of *The Tempest* is, like the Philomela reference, one of Eliot's major symbols. A general comment on it is therefore appropriate here, for we are to meet with it twice more in later sections of the poem. The song, one remembers, was sung by Ariel in luring Ferdinand, Prince of Naples, on to meet Miranda, and thus to find love, and through this love, to effect the regeneration and deliverance of all the people on the island. Ferdinand, hearing the song, says:

The ditty does remember my drowned father.
This is no mortal business, nor no sound
That the earth owes . . .

The allusion is an extremely interesting example of the device of Eliot's already commented upon, that of taking an item from one context and shifting it into another in which it assumes a new and powerful meaning. The description of a death which is a portal into a realm of the rich and strange—a death which becomes a sort of birth—assumes in the mind of the protagonist an association with that of the drowned god whose effigy was thrown into the water as a symbol of the death of the fruitful powers of nature but which was taken out of the water as a symbol of the revivified god. (See *From Ritual to Romance*.) The passage therefore represents the perfect antithesis to the passage in 'The Burial of the Dead': 'That corpse you planted last year in your garden,' etc. It also, as we have already pointed out, finds its antithesis in the sterile and unfruitful death 'in rats' alley' just commented upon. (We shall find that this contrast between the death in rats' alley and the death in *The Tempest* is made again in 'The Fire Sermon.')

We have yet to treat the relation of the title of the second section, 'A Game of Chess,' to Middleton's play, *Women Beware Women*, from which the game of chess is taken. In the play, the game is used as a device to keep the widow occupied while her daughter-in-law is being seduced. The seduction amounts almost to a rape, and in a *double entendre*, the rape is actually described in terms of the game. We have one more connection with the Philomela symbol, therefore. The abstract game is being used in the contemporary waste land, as in the play, to cover up a rape and is a description of the rape itself.

In the latter part of 'A Game of Chess' we are given a picture of spiritual emptiness, but this time, at the other end of the social scale, as reflected in the talk between two cockney women in a London pub. (It is perhaps unnecessary to comment on the relation of their talk about abortion to the theme of sterility and the waste land.)

The account here is straightforward enough, and the only matter which calls for comment is the line spoken by Ophelia in *Hamlet*, which ends the passage. Ophelia, too, was very much concerned about love, the theme of conversation between the women in the pub. As a matter of fact, she was in very much the same position as that of the woman who has been the topic of conversation between the two ladies whom we have just heard. And her poetry, like Philomela's, had come out of suffering. We are probably to look for the relevance of the allusion to her here rather than in an easy satiric contrast between Elizabethan glories and modern sordidness. After all, Eliot's criticism of the present world is not merely the sentimental one that this happens to be the twentieth century after Christ and not the seventeenth.

III

'The Fire Sermon' makes much use of several of the symbols already developed. The fire is the sterile burning of lust, and the section is a sermon, although a sermon by example only. This section of the poem also contains some of the most easily apprehended uses of literary allusion. The poem opens on a vision of the modern river. In Spenser's 'Prothalamion' the scene described is also a river scene at London, and it is dominated by nymphs and their paramours, and the nymphs are preparing for a wedding. The contrast between Spenser's scene and its twentieth century equivalent is jarring. The paramours are now 'the loitering heirs of city directors,' and, as for the nuptials of Spenser's Elizabethan maidens, in the stanzas which follow we learn a great deal about those. At the end of the section the speech of the third of the Thames-nymphs summarizes the whole matter for us.

The waters of the Thames are also associated with those of Leman—the poet in the contemporary waste land is in a sort of Babylonian Captivity.

The castle of the Fisher King was always located on the banks of a river or on the sea shore. The title 'Fisher King,' Miss Weston shows, originates from the use of the fish as a fertility or life symbol. This meaning, however, was often forgotten, and so his title in many of the later Grail romances is accounted for by describing the king as fishing. Eliot uses the reference to fishing for reverse effect. The reference to fishing is part of the realistic detail of the scene—'While I was fishing in the dull canal.' But to the reader who knows the Weston references, the reference is to that of the Fisher King of the Grail legends. The protagonist is the maimed and impotent king of the legends.

Eliot proceeds now to tie the waste-land symbol to that of *The Tempest*, by quoting one of the lines spoken by Ferdinand, Prince of Naples, which occurs just before Ariel's song, 'Full Fathom Five,' is heard. But he alters *The Tempest* passage somewhat, writing not, 'Weeping again the king my father's wreck,' but

*Musing upon the king my brother's wreck
And on the king my father's death before him.*

It is possible that the alteration has been made to bring the account taken from *The Tempest* into accord with the situation in the Percival stories. In Wolfram von Eschenbach's *Parzival*, for instance, Trevrezent, the hermit, is the brother of the Fisher King, Anfortas. He tells Parzival, 'His name all men know as Anfortas, and I weep for him evermore.' Their father, Frimutel, is dead.

The protagonist in the poem, then, imagines himself not only in the situation of Ferdinand in *The Tempest* but also in that of one of the characters in the Grail legend; and the wreck, to be applied literally in the first instance, applies metaphorically in the second.

After the lines from *The Tempest*, appears again the image of a sterile death from which no life comes, the bones, 'rattled by the rat's foot only, year to year,' (The collocation of this figure with the vision of the death by water in Ariel's song has already been commented on. The lines quoted from *The Tempest* come just before the song.)

The allusion to Marvell's 'To His Coy Mistress' is of course one of the easiest allusions in the poem. Instead of 'Time's winged chariot' the poet hears 'the sound of horns and motors' of contemporary London. But the passage has been further complicated. The reference has been combined with an allusion to Day's 'Parliament of Bees.' 'Time's winged chariot' of Marvell has not only been changed to the modern automobile; Day's 'sound of horns and hunting' has changed to the horns of the motors. And Actaeon will not be brought face to face with Diana, goddess of chastity; Sweeney, type of the vulgar bourgeois, is to be brought to Mrs. Porter, hardly a type of chastity. The reference in the ballad to the feet 'washed in soda water' reminds the poet ironically of another sort of foot-washing, the sound of the children singing in the dome heard at the ceremony of the foot-washing which precedes the restoration of the wounded Anfortas (the Fisher King) by Parzival and the taking away of the curse from the waste land. The quotation thus completes the allusion to the Fisher King commenced in line 189— 'While I was fishing in the dull canal.'

The pure song of the children also reminds the poet of the song of the nightingale which we have heard in 'The Game of Chess.' The recapitulation of symbols is continued with a repetition of 'Unreal city' and with the reference to the one-eyed merchant.

Mr. Eugenides, the Smyrna merchant, is the one-eyed merchant mentioned by Madame Sosostris. The fact that the merchant is one-eyed apparently means, in Madame Sosostris' speech, no more than that the merchant's face on the card is shown in profile. But Eliot applies the term to Mr. Eugenides for a totally different effect. The defect corresponds somewhat to Madame Sosostris' bad cold. He is a rather battered representative of the fertility cults: the prophet, the *seer*, with only one eye.

The Syrian merchants, we learn from Miss Weston's book, were, along with slaves and soldiers, the principal carriers of the mysteries which lie at the core of the Grail legends. But in the modern world we find both the representatives of the Tarot divining and the mystery cults in decay. What he carries on his back and what the fortune-teller is forbidden to see is evidently the knowledge of the mysteries (although Mr. Eugenides himself is hardly likely to be more aware of it than Madame Sosostris is aware of the importance of her function). Mr. Eugenides, in terms of his former function, ought to be inviting the protagonist into the esoteric cult which holds the secret of life, but on the realistic surface of the poem, in his invitation to 'a weekend at the Metropole' he is really inviting him to a homosexual debauch. The homosexuality is 'secret' and now a 'cult' but a very different cult from that which Mr. Eugenides ought to represent. The end of the new cult is not life but, ironically, sterility.

In the modern waste land, however, even the relation between man and woman is also sterile. The incident between the typist and the carbuncular young man is a picture of 'love' so exclusively and practically pursued that it is not love at all. The tragic chorus to the scene is Tiresias, into whom perhaps Mr. Eugenides may be said to modulate, Tiresias, the historical 'expert' on the relation between the sexes.

The fact that Tiresias is made the commentator serves a further irony. In *Oedipus Rex*, it is Tiresias who recognizes that the curse which has come upon the Theban land has been caused by the sinful sexual relationship of Oedipus and Jocasta. But Oedipus' sin has been committed in ignorance, and knowledge of it brings horror and remorse. The essential horror of the act which Tiresias witnesses in the poem is that it is not regarded as a sin at all—is perfectly casual, is merely the copulation of beasts.

The reminiscence of the lines from Goldsmith's song in the description of the young woman's actions after the departure of her lover, gives concretely and ironically the utter break-down of traditional standards.

It is the music of her gramophone which the protagonist hears 'creep by' him 'on the waters.' Far from the music which Ferdinand heard bringing him to Miranda and love, it is, one is tempted to think, the music of 'O O O O that Shakespeherian Rag.'

But the protagonist says that he can *sometimes* hear 'the pleasant whining of a mandoline.' Significantly enough, it is the music of the fishmen (the fish again as a life symbol) and it comes from beside a church (though—if this is not to rely too much on Eliot's note—the church has been marked for destruction). Life on Lower Thames Street, if not on the Strand, still has meaning as it cannot have meaning for either the typist or the rich woman of 'A Game of Chess.'

The song of the Thames-daughters brings us back to the opening section of 'The Fire Sermon' again, and once more we have to do with the river and the river-nymphs. Indeed, the typist incident is framed by the two river-nymph scenes.

The connection of the river-nymphs with the Rhine-daughters of Wagner's *Götterdämmerung* is easily made. In the passage in Wagner's opera (to which Eliot refers in his note), the opening of Act III, the Rhine-daughters bewail the loss of the beauty of the Rhine occasioned by the theft of the gold, and then beg Siegfried to give them back the Ring made from this gold, finally threatening him with death if he does not give it up. Like the Thames-daughters they too have been violated; and like the maidens mentioned in the Grail legend, the violation has brought a curse on gods and men. The first of the songs depicts the modern river, soiled with oil and tar. (Compare also with the description of the river in the first part of 'The Fire Sermon.') The second song depicts the Elizabethan river, also evoked in the first part of 'The Fire Sermon.' (Leicester and Elizabeth ride upon it in a barge of state. Incidentally, Spenser's 'Prothalamion' from which quotation is made in the first part of 'The Fire Sermon' mentions Leicester as having formerly lived in the house which forms the setting of the poem.)

In this second song there is also a definite allusion to the passage in *Antony and Cleopatra* already referred to in the opening line of 'A Game of Chess.'

> *Beating oars*
> *The stern was formed*
> *A gilded shell*

And if we still have any doubt of the allusion, Eliot's note on the passage with its reference to the 'barge' and 'poop' should settle the matter. We have already commented on the earlier allusion to Cleopatra as the prime example of love for love's sake. The symbol bears something of the same meaning here, and the note which Eliot supplies does something to reinforce the 'Cleopatra' aspect of Elizabeth. Elizabeth in the presence of the Spaniard De Quadra, though negotiations were going on for a Spanish marriage, 'went so far that Lord Robert at last said, as I [De Quadra was a bishop] was on the spot there was no reason why they should not be married if the queen pleased.' The passage has a sort of double function. It reinforces the general contrast between Elizabethan magnificence and modern sordidness: in the Elizabethan age love for love's sake has some meaning and therefore some magnificence. But the passage gives something of an opposed effect too: the same sterile love, emptiness of love, obtained in this period too: Elizabeth and the typist are alike as well as different. (One of the reasons for the frequent allusion to Elizabethan poetry in this and the preceding section of the poem may be the fact that with the English Renaissance the old set of supernatural sanctions had begun to break up. See Eliot's various essays on Shakespeare and the Elizabethan dramatists.)

The third Thames-daughter's song depicts another sordid 'love' affair, and unites the themes of the first two songs. It begins 'Trams and *dusty* trees.'

Early Poems and *The Waste Land*

With it we are definitely in the waste land again. Pia, whose words she echoes in saying 'Highbury bore me. Richmond and Kew/Undid me' was in Purgatory and had hope. The woman speaking here has no hope—she too is in the Inferno: 'I can connect/Nothing with nothing.' She has just completed, floating down the river in the canoe, what Eliot has described in *Murder in the Cathedral* as

> . . . *the effortless journey, to the empty land*
>
> *Where those who were men can no longer turn the mind*
> *Where the soul is no longer deceived, for there are no objects, no tones,*
> *To distraction, delusion, escape into dream, pretence,*
> *No colours, no forms to distract, to divert the soul*
> *From seeing itself, foully united forever, nothing with nothing,*
> *Not what we call death, but what beyond death is not death* . . .

Now, 'on Margate Sands,' like the Hollow Men, she stands 'on this beach of the tumid river.'

The sons of the three Thames-daughters, as a matter of fact, epitomize this whole section of the poem. With reference to the quotations from St. Augustine and Buddha at the end of 'The Fire Sermon' Eliot states that 'the collocation of these two representatives of eastern and western asceticism, as the culmination of this part of the poem, is not an accident.'

It is certainly not an accident. The moral of all the incidents which we have been witnessing is that there must be an asceticism—something to check the drive of desire. The wisdom of the East and the West comes to the same thing on this point. Moreover, the imagery which both St. Augustine and Buddha use for lust is fire. What we have witnessed in the various scenes of 'The Fire Sermon' is the sterile burning of lust. Modern man, freed from all restraints, in his cultivation of experience for experience's sake burns, but not with a 'hard and gemlike flame.' One ought not to pound the point home in this fashion, but to see that the imagery of this section of the poem furnishes illustrations leading up to the Fire Sermon is the necessary requirement for feeling the force of the brief allusions here at the end to Buddha and St. Augustine.

IV

Whatever the specific meaning of the symbols, the general function of the section, 'Death by Water,' is readily apparent. The section forms a contrast with 'The Fire Sermon' which precedes it—a contrast between the symbolism of fire and that of water. Also rapidly apparent is its force as a symbol of surrender and relief through surrender.

Some specific connections can be made, however. The drowned Phoenician Sailor recalls the drowned god of the fertility cults. Miss Weston tells that each year at Alexandria an effigy of the head of the god was thrown into the water as a symbol of the death of the powers of nature, and that this head was carried by the current to Byblos where it was taken out of the water and exhibited as a symbol of the reborn god.

Moreover, the Phoenician Sailor is a merchant—'Forgot . . . the profit and loss.' The vision of the drowned sailor gives a statement of the message which the Syrian merchants originally brought to Britain and which the Smyrna merchant, unconsciously and by ironical negatives, has brought. One of Eliot's notes states that the 'merchant . . . melts into the Phoenician Sailor, and the latter is not wholly distinct from Ferdinand Prince of Naples.' The death by water would seem to be equated with the death described in Ariel's song in *The Tempest.* There is a definite difference in the tone of the description of this death—'A current under sea/Picked his bones in whispers,' as compared with the 'other' death—'bones cast in a little low dry garret,/Rattled by the rat's foot only, year to year.'

Further than this it would not be safe to go, but one may point out that whirling (the whirlpool here, the Wheel of Madame Sosostris' palaver) is one of Eliot's symbols frequently used in other poems (*Ash Wednesday*, 'Gerontion,' *Murder in the Cathedral*, and 'Burnt Norton') to denote the temporal world. And I may point out, supplying the italics myself, the following passage from *Ash Wednesday*:

Although I do not hope to turn *again*

Wavering between the profit and the loss
In this brief transit where the dreams cross
The dreamcrossed twilight between birth and dying.

At least, with a kind of hindsight, one may suggest that 'Death by Water' gives an instance of the conquest of death and time, the 'perpetual recurrence of determined seasons,' the 'world of spring and autumn, birth and dying' through death itself.

V

The reference to the 'torchlight red on sweaty faces' and to the 'frosty silence in the gardens' obviously associates Christ in Gethsemane with the other hanged gods. The god has now died, and in referring to this, the basic theme finds another strong restatement:

He who was living is now dead

We who were living are now dying
With a little patience

The poet does not say 'We who *are* living.' It is 'We who *were* living.' It is the death-in-life of Dante's Limbo. Life in the full sense has been lost.

The passage on the sterility of the waste land and the lack of water provides for the introduction later of two highly important passages:

There is not even silence in the mountains
But dry sterile thunder without rain—

lines which look forward to the introduction later of 'what the thunder said' when the thunder, no longer sterile, but bringing rain, speaks.

The second of these passages is, 'There is not even solitude in the mountains,' which looks forward to the reference to the Journey to Emmaus theme a few lines later: 'Who is the third who walks always beside you?' The god has returned, has risen, but the travelers cannot tell whether it is really he, or mere illusion induced by their delirium.

The parallelism between the 'hooded figure' who 'walks always beside you,' and the 'hooded hordes' is another instance of the sort of parallelism that is really a contrast. In the first case, the figure is indistinct because spiritual; in the second, the hooded hordes are indistinct because completely *unspiritual*—they are the people of the waste land—

Shape without form, shade without colour,
Paralysed force, gesture without motion—

to take two lines from 'The Hollow Men,' where the people of the waste land once more appear. Or to take another line from the same poem, perhaps their hoods are the 'deliberate disguises' which the Hollow Men, the people of the waste land, wear.

Eliot, as his notes tell us, has particularly connected the description here with the 'decay of eastern Europe.' The hordes represent, then, the general waste land of the modern world with a special application to the breakup of Eastern Europe, the region with which the fertility cults were especially connected and in which today the traditional values are thoroughly discredited. The cities, Jerusalem, Athens, Alexandria, Vienna, like the London of the first section of the poem are 'unreal,' and for the same reason.

The passage which immediately follows develops the unreality into nightmare, but it is a nightmare vision which is something more than an extension of the passage beginning, 'What is the city over the mountains'—in it appear other figures from earlier in the poem: the lady of 'A Game of Chess,' who, surrounded by the glory of history and art, sees no meaning in either and threatens to rush out into the street 'With my hair down, so,' has here let down her hair and fiddles 'whisper music on those strings.' One remembers in 'A Game of Chess' that it was the woman's hair that spoke:

> ... *her hair*
> *Spread out in fiery points*
> *Glowed into words, then would be savagely still.*

The hair has been immemorially a symbol of fertility, and Miss Weston and Frazer mention sacrifices of hair in order to aid the fertility god.

As we have pointed out earlier, this passage is also to be connected with the twelfth chapter of Ecclesiastes. The doors 'of mudcracked houses,' and the cisterns in this passage are to be found in Ecclesiastes, and the woman fiddling music from her hair is one of 'the daughters of musick' brought low. The towers and bells from the Elizabeth and Leicester passage of 'The Fire Sermon' also appear here, but the towers are upside down, and the bells, far from pealing for an actual occasion or ringing the hours, are 'reminiscent.' The civilization is breaking up.

The 'violet light' also deserves comment. In 'The Fire Sermon' it is twice mentioned as the 'violet hour,' and there it has little more than a physical meaning. It is a description of the hour of twilight. Here it indicates the twilight of the civilization, but it is perhaps something more. Violet is one of the liturgical colors of the Church. It symbolizes repentance and it is the color of baptism. The visit to the Perilous Chapel, according to Miss Weston, was an initiation—that is, a baptism. In the nightmare vision, the bats wear baby faces.

The horror built up in this passage is a proper preparation for the passage on the Perilous Chapel which follows it. The journey has not been merely an agonized walk in the desert, though it is that; nor is it merely the journey after the god has died and hope has been lost; it is also the journey to the Perilous Chapel of the Grail story. In Miss Weston's account, the Chapel was part of the ritual, and was filled with horrors to test the candidate's courage. In some stories the perilous cemetery is also mentioned. Eliot has used both: 'Over the tumbled graves, about the chapel.' In many of the Grail stories the Chapel was haunted by demons.

The cock in the folk-lore of many people is regarded as the bird whose voice chases away the powers of evil. It is significant that it is after his crow that the flash of lightning comes and the 'damp gust/Bringing rain.' It is just possible that the cock has a connection also with *The Tempest* symbols. The first song which Ariel sings to Ferdinand as he sits 'Weeping again the king my father's wreck' ends

> *The strain of strutting chanticleer,*
> *Cry, cock-a-doodle-doo.*

The next stanza is the 'Full Fathom Five' song which Eliot has used as a vision of life gained through death. If this relation holds, here we have an extreme instance of an allusion, in itself innocent, forced into serious meaning through transference to a new context.

Early Poems and *The Waste Land*

As Miss Weston has shown, the fertility cults go back to a very early period and are recorded in Sanscrit legends. Eliot has been continually, in the poem, linking up the Christian doctrine with the beliefs of as many peoples as he can. Here he goes back to the very beginnings of Aryan culture, and tells the rest of the story of the rain's coming, not in terms of the setting already developed but in its earliest form. The passage is thus a perfect parallel in method to the passage in 'The Burial of the Dead':

> *You who were with me in the ships at Mylae!*
> *That corpse you planted last year in your garden . . .*

The use of Sanscrit in what the thunder says is thus accounted for. In addition, there is of course a more obvious reason for casting what the thunder said into Sanscrit here: onomatopoeia.

The comments on the three statements of the thunder imply an acceptance of them. The protagonist answers the first question, 'What have we given?' with the statement:

> *The awful daring of a moment's surrender*
> *Which an age of prudence can never retract*
> *By this, and this only, we have existed.*

Here the larger meaning is stated in terms which imply the sexual meaning. Man cannot be absolutely self-regarding. Even the propagation of the race—even mere 'existence'—calls for such a surrender. Living calls for—see the passage already quoted from Eliot's essay on Baudelaire—belief in something more than 'life.'

The comment on *dayadhvam* (sympathize) is obviously connected with the foregoing passage. The surrender to something outside the self is an attempt (whether on the sexual level or some other) to transcend one's essential isolation. The passage gathers up the symbols previously developed in the poem just as the foregoing passage reflects, though with a different implication, the numerous references to sex made earlier in the poem. For example, the woman in the first part of 'A Game of Chess' has also heard the key turn in the door, and confirms her prison by thinking of the key:

> *Speak to me. Why do you never speak? Speak.*
> *What are you thinking of? What thinking? What?*
> *I never know what you are thinking. Think.*

The third statement made by the thunder, *damyata* (control), follows the condition necessary for control, sympathy. The figure of the boat catches up the figure of control already given in 'Death by water'—'O you who turn the wheel and look to windward'—and from 'The Burial of the Dead' the figure of happy love in which the ship rushes on with a fair wind behind it: '*Frisch weht der Wind . . .*'

I cannot accept Mr. Leavis' interpretation of the passage, 'I sat upon the shore/Fishing, with the arid plain behind me,' as meaning that the poem 'exhibits no progression.' The comment upon what the thunder says would indicate, if other passages did not, that the poem does 'not end where it began.' It is true that the protagonist does not witness a revival of the waste land; but there are two important relationships involved in his case: a personal one as well as a general one. If secularization has destroyed, or is likely to destroy, modern civilization, the protagonist still has a private obligation to fulfill. Even if the civilization is breaking up—'London Bridge is falling down falling down falling down'—there remains the personal obligation: 'Shall I at least set my lands in order?' Consider in this connection the last sentences of Eliot's 'Thoughts After Lambeth': 'The World is trying the experiment of attempting to form a civilized but non-Christian mentality. The experiment will fail; but we must be very patient in awaiting its collapse; meanwhile redeeming the time: so that the Faith may be preserved alive through the dark ages before us; to renew and rebuild civilization, and save the World from suicide.'

The bundle of quotations with which the poem ends has a very definite relation to the general theme of the poem and to several of the major symbols used in the poem. Before Arnaut leaps back into the refining fire of Purgatory with joy he says: 'I am Arnaut who weep and go singing; contrite I see my past folly, and joyful I see before me the day I hope for. Now I pray you by that virtue which guides you to the summit of the stair, at times be mindful of my pain.' This theme is carried forward by the quotation from *Pervigilium Veneris*: 'When shall I be like the swallow.' The allusion is also connected with the Philomela symbol. (Eliot's note on the passage indicates this clearly.) The sister of Philomela was changed into a swallow as Philomela was changed into a nightingale. The protagonist is asking therefore when shall the spring, the time of love, return, but also when will he be reborn out of his sufferings, and—with the special meaning which the symbol takes on from the preceding Dante quotation and from the earlier contexts already discussed—he is asking what is asked at the end of one of the minor poems: 'When will Time flow away.'

The quotation from 'El Desdichado,' as Edmund Wilson has pointed out, indicates that the protagonist of the poem has been disinherited, robbed of his tradition. The ruined tower is perhaps also the Perilous Chapel, 'only the wind's home,' and it is also the whole tradition in decay. The protagonist resolves to claim his tradition and rehabilitate it.

The quotation from *The Spanish Tragedy*—'Why then Ile fit you. Hieronymo's mad againe'—is perhaps the most puzzling of all these quotations. It means, I believe, this: The protagonist's acceptance of what is in reality the deepest truth will seem to the present world mere madness. ('And still she cried . . . "Jug Jug" to dirty ears.') Hieronymo in the play, like Hamlet, was 'mad' for a purpose. The protagonist is conscious of the interpretation which will be placed on the words which follow—words which will seem to many apparently meaningless babble, but which contain the oldest and most permanent truth of the race:

Datta. Dayadhvam. Damyata.

Quotation of the whole context from which the line is taken confirms this interpretation. Hieronymo, asked to write a play for the court's entertainment, replies:

Why then, I'll fit you; say no more.
When I was young, I gave my mind
And plied myself to fruitless poetry;
Which though it profit the professor naught,
Yet it is passing pleasing to the world.

He sees that the play will give him the opportunity he has been seeking to avenge his son's murder. Like Hieronymo, the protagonist in the poem has found his theme; what he is about to perform is not 'fruitless.'

After this repetition of what the thunder said comes the benediction:

Shantih shantih shantih

The foregoing account of *The Waste Land* is, of course, not to be substituted for the poem itself. Moreover, it certainly is not to be considered as representing *the method by which the poem was composed*. Much which the prose expositor must represent as though it had been consciously contrived obviously was arrived at unconsciously and concretely.

The account given above is a statement merely of the 'prose meaning,' and bears the same relation to the poem as does the 'prose meaning' of any other poem. But one need not perhaps apologize for setting forth such a statement explicitly, for *The Waste Land* has been almost consistently misinterpreted since its first publication. Even a critic so acute as Edmund Wilson has seen the poem as essentially a statement of despair and disillusionment, and his account sums up the stock interpretation of the poem. Indeed, the phrase, 'the poetry of drouth,' has become a cliché of left-wing criticism. It is such a misrepresentation of *The Waste Land* as this which allows Eda Lou Walton to entitle an essay on contemporary poetry, 'Death in the Desert'; or which causes Waldo Frank to misconceive of Eliot's whole position and personality. But more than the meaning of one poem is at stake. If *The Waste Land* is not a world-weary cry of despair or a sighing after the vanished glories of the past, then not only the popular interpretation of the poem will have to be altered but also the general interpretations of post-War poetry which begin with such a misinterpretation as a premise.

Such misinterpretations involve also misconceptions of Eliot's technique. Eliot's basic method may be said to have passed relatively unnoticed. The popular view of the method used in *The Waste Land* may be described as follows: Eliot makes use of ironic contrasts between the glorious past and the sordid present—the crashing irony of

> But at my back from time to time I hear
> The sound of horns and motors, which shall bring
> Sweeney to Mrs. Porter in the spring.

But this is to take the irony of the poem at the most superficial level, and to neglect the other dimensions in which it operates. And it is to neglect what are essentially more important aspects of his method. Moreover, it is to over-emphasize the difference between the method employed by Eliot in this poem and that employed by him in later poems.

The basic method used in *The Waste Land* may be described as the application of the principle of complexity. The poet works in terms of surface parallelisms which in reality make ironical contrasts, and in terms of surface contrasts which in reality constitute parallelisms. (The second group sets up effects which may be described as the obverse of irony.) The two aspects taken together give the effect of chaotic experience ordered into a new whole, though the realistic surface of experience is faithfully retained. The complexity of the experience is not violated by the apparent forcing upon it of a predetermined scheme.

The fortune-telling of 'The Burial of the Dead' will illustrate the general method very satisfactorily. On the surface of the poem the poet reproduces the patter of the charlatan, Madame Sosostris, and there is the surface irony: the contrast between the original use of the Tarot cards and the use made by Madame Sosostris. But each of the details (justified realistically in the palaver of the fortune-teller) assumes a new meaning in the general context of the poem. There is then, in addition to the surface irony, something of a Sophoclean irony too, and the 'fortune-telling,' which is taken ironically by a twentieth-century audience, becomes *true* as the poem develops—true in a sense in which Madame Sosostris herself does not think it true. The surface irony is thus reversed and becomes an irony on a deeper level. The items of her speech have only one reference in terms of the context of her speech: the 'man with three staves,' the 'one-eyed merchant,' the 'crowds of people, walking round in a ring,' etc. But transferred to other contexts they become loaded with special meanings. To sum up, all the central symbols of the poem head up here; but here, in the only section in which they are explicitly bound together, the binding is slight and accidental. The deeper lines of association only emerge in terms of the total context as the poem develops—and this is, of course, exactly the effect which the poet intends.

This transference of items from an 'innocent' context into a context in which they become charged and transformed in meaning will account for many of the literary allusions in the poem. For example, the 'change of Philomel' is merely one of the items in the decorative detail in the room in the opening of 'A Game of Chess.' But the violent change of tense—'And still she cried, and still the world pursues'—makes it a comment upon, and a symbol of, the modern world. And further allusions to it through the course of the poem gradually equate it with the general theme of the poem. The allusions to *The Tempest* display the same method. The parallelism between Dante's Hell and the waste land of the Grail legends is fairly close; even the equation of Baudelaire's Paris to the waste land is fairly obvious. But the parallelism between the death by drowning in *The Tempest* and the death of the fertility god is, on the surface, merely accidental, and the first allusion to Ariel's song is merely an irrelevant and random association of the stream-of-consciousness:

Is your card, the drowned Phoenician Sailor,
(Those are pearls that were his eyes. Look!)

And on its second appearance in 'A Game of Chess' it is still only an item in the protagonist's abstracted reverie. Even the association of *The Tempest* symbol with the Grail legends in the lines

While I was fishing in the dull canal

Musing upon the king my brother's wreck

and in the passage which follows, is ironical merely. But the associations have been established, even though they may seem to be made in ironic mockery, and when we come to the passage, 'Death by Water,' with its change of tone, they assert themselves positively. We have a sense of revelation out of material apparently accidentally thrown together. I have called the effect the obverse of irony, for the method, like that of irony, is indirect, though the effect is positive rather than negative.

The melting of the characters into each other is, of course, an aspect of this general process. Elizabeth and the girl born at Highbury both ride on the Thames, one in the barge of state, the other supine in a narrow canoe, and they are both Thames-nymphs, who are violated and thus are like the Rhine-nymphs who have also been violated, etc. With the characters as with the other symbols, the surface relationships may be accidental and apparently trivial and they may be made either ironically or through random association or in hallucination, but in the total context of the poem the deeper relationships are revealed. The effect is a sense of the oneness of experience, and of the unity of all periods, and with this, a sense that the general theme of the poem is true. But the theme has not been imposed—it has been revealed.

This complication of parallelisms and contrasts makes, of course, for ambiguity, but the ambiguity, in part, resides in the poet's fidelity to the complexity of experience. The symbols resist complete equation with a simple meaning. To take an example, 'rock' throughout the poem seems to be one of the 'desert' symbols. For example, the 'dry stone' gives 'no sound of water'; woman in the waste land is 'the Lady of the Rocks,' and most pointed of all, there is the long delirium passage in 'What the Thunder Said': 'Here is no water but only rock,' etc. So much for its general meaning, but in 'The Burial of the Dead' occur the lines

> *Only*
> *There is shadow under this red rock,*
> *(Come in under the shadow of this red rock).*

Rock here is a place of refuge. (Moreover, there may also be a reference to the Grail symbolism. In *Parzival*, the Grail is a stone: 'And this stone all men call the grail . . . As children the Grail doth call them, 'neath its shadow they wax and grow.') The paradox, life through death, penetrates the symbol itself.

To take an even clearer case of this paradoxical use of symbols, consider the lines which occur in the hyacinth girl passage. The vision gives obviously a sense of the richness and beauty of life. It is a moment of ecstasy (the basic imagery is obviously sexual); but the moment in its intensity is like death. The protagonist looks in that moment into the 'heart of light, the silence,' and so looks into—not richness—but blankness: he is neither 'living nor dead.' The symbol of life stands also for a kind of death. This duality of function may, of course, extend to a whole passage. For example, consider:

> *Where fishmen lounge at noon: where the walls*
> *Of Magnus Martyr hold*
> *Inexplicable splendour of Ionian white and gold.*

The function of the passage is to indicate the poverty into which religion has fallen: the splendid church now surrounded by the poorer districts. But the passage has an opposed effect also: the fishmen in the 'public bar in Lower Thames Street' next to the church have a meaningful life which has been largely lost to the secularized upper and middle classes.

The poem would undoubtedly be 'clearer' if every symbol had a single unequivocal meaning; but the poem would be thinner, and less honest. For the poet has not been content to develop a didactic allegory in which the symbols are two-dimensional items adding up directly to the sum of the general scheme. They represent dramatized instances of the theme, embodying in their own nature the fundamental paradox of the theme.

We shall better understand why the form of the poem is right and inevitable if we compare Eliot's theme to Dante's and to Spenser's. Eliot's theme is not the statement of a faith held and agreed upon (Dante's *Divine Comedy*) nor is it the projection of a 'new' system of beliefs (Spenser's *Faerie Queene*). Eliot's theme is the rehabilitation of a system of beliefs, known but now discredited. Dante did not have to 'prove' his statement; he could assume it and move within it about a poet's business. Eliot does not care, like Spenser, to force the didacticism. He prefers to stick to the poet's business. But, unlike

Dante, he cannot assume acceptance of the statement. A direct approach is calculated to elicit powerful 'stock responses' which will prevent the poem's being *read* at all. Consequently, the only method is to work by indirection. The Christian material is at the center, but the poet never deals with it directly. The theme of resurrection is made on the surface in terms of the fertility rites; the words which the thunder speaks are Sanscrit words.

We have been speaking as if the poet were a strategist trying to win acceptance from a hostile audience. But of course this is true only in a sense. The poet himself is audience as well as speaker; we state the problem more exactly if we state it in terms of the poet's integrity rather than in terms of his strategy. He is so much a man of his own age that he can indicate his attitude toward the Christian tradition without falsity only in terms of the difficulties of a rehabilitation; and he is so much a poet and so little a propagandist that he can be sincere only as he presents his theme concretely and dramatically.

To put the matter in still other terms; the Christian terminology is for the poet a mass of clichés. However 'true' he may feel the terms to be, he is still sensitive to the fact that they operate superficially as clichés, and his method of necessity must be a process of bringing them to life again. The method adopted in *The Waste Land* is thus violent and radical, but thoroughly necessary. For the renewing and vitalizing of symbols which have been crusted over with a distorting familiarity demands the type of organization which we have already commented on in discussing particular passages: the statement of surface similarities which are ironically revealed to be dissimilarities, and the association of apparently obvious dissimilarities which culminates in a later realization that the dissimilarities are only superficial—that the chains of likeness are in reality fundamental. In this way the statement of beliefs emerges *through* confusion and cynicism—not in spite of them.

Note

[1]. The reference is perhaps more general still: it may include Naturalism, and Science in the popular conception as the new magic which will enable man to conquer his environment completely.

107
T.S. Eliot as the International Hero*

DELMORE SCHWARTZ

A culture hero is one who brings new arts and skills to mankind. Prometheus was a culture hero and the inventors of the radio may also be said to be culture heroes, although this is hardly to be confounded with the culture made available by radio.

The inventors of the radio made possible a new range of experience. This is true of certain authors; for example, it is true of Wordsworth in regard to nature, and Proust in regard to time. It is not true of Shakespeare, but by contrast it is true of Surrey and the early Elizabethan playwrights who invented blank verse. Thus the most important authors are not always culture heroes, and thus no rank, stature, or scope is of necessity implicit in speaking of the author as a culture hero.

When we speak of nature and of a new range of experience, we may think of a mountain range: some may make the vehicles by means of which a mountain is climbed, some may climb the mountain, and some apprehend the new view of the surrounding countryside which becomes possible from the heights of the mountain. T.S. Eliot is a culture hero in each of these three ways. This becomes clear when we study the relationship of his work to the possible experiences of modern life. The term, possible, should be kept in mind, for many human beings obviously disregard and turn their backs upon much of modern life, although modern life does not in the least cease to circumscribe and penetrate their existence.

The reader of T.S. Eliot by turning the dials of his radio can hear the capitals of the world, London, Vienna, Athens, Alexandria, Jerusalem. What he hears will be news of the agony of war. Both the agony and the width of this experience are vivid examples of how the poetry of T.S. Eliot has a direct relationship to modern life. The width and the height and the depth of modern life are exhibited in his poetry; the agony and the horror of modern life are represented as inevitable to any human being who does not wish to deceive himself with systematic lies. Thus it is truly significant that E.M.

*Partisan Review 12, no. 2 (Spring 1945), pp. 199–206.

Forster, in writing of Eliot, should recall August 1914 and the beginning of the First World War; it is just as significant that he should speak of first reading Eliot's poems in Alexandria, Egypt, during that war, and that he should conclude by saying that Eliot was one who had looked into the abyss and refused henceforward to deny or forget the fact.

We are given an early view of the international hero in the quasi-autobiographical poem which Eliot entitles: '*Mélange Adultère de Tout.*' The title, borrowed from a poem by Corbière, is ironic, but the adulterous mixture of practically everything, every time and every place, is not ironic in the least: a teacher in America, the poem goes, a journalist in England, a lecturer in Yorkshire, a literary nihilist in Paris, overexcited by philosophy in Germany, a wanderer from Omaha to Damascus, he has celebrated, he says, his birthday at an African oasis, dressed in a giraffe's skin. Let us place next to this array another list of names and events as heterogeneous as a circus or America itself: St. Louis, New England, Boston, Harvard, England, Paris, the First World War, Oxford, London, the Russian Revolution, the Church of England, the postwar period, the world crisis and depression, the Munich Pact, and the Second World War. If this list seems farfetched or forced, if it seems that such a list might be made for any author, the answer is that these names and events are *presences* in Eliot's work in a way which is not true of many authors, good and bad, who have lived through the same years.

Philip Rahv has shown how the heroine of Henry James is best understood as the heiress of all the ages. So, in a further sense, the true protagonist of Eliot's poems is the heir of all the ages. He is the descendant of the essential characters of James in that he is the American who visits Europe with a Baedeker in his hand, just like Isabel Archer. But the further sense in which he is the heir of all the ages is illustrated when Eliot describes the seduction of a typist in a London flat from the point of view of Tiresias, a character in a play by Sophocles. To suppose that this is the mere exhibition of learning or reading is banal misunderstanding. The important point is that the presence of Tiresias illuminates the seduction of the typist just as much as a description of her room. Hence Eliot writes in his notes to *The Waste Land* 'what Tiresias *sees* is the substance of the poem.' The illumination of the ages is available at any moment, and when the typist's indifference and boredom in the act of love must be represented, it is possible for Eliot to invoke and paraphrase a lyric from a play by Oliver Goldsmith. Literary allusion has become not merely a Miltonic reference to Greek gods and Old Testament geography, not merely the citation of parallels, but a powerful and inevitable habit of mind, a habit which issues in judgment and the representation of different levels of experience, past and present.

James supposed that his theme was the international theme: would it not be more precise to speak of it as the transatlantic theme? This effort at a greater exactness defines what is involved in Eliot's work. Henry James was concerned with the American in Europe. Eliot cannot help but be concerned with the whole world and all history. Tiresias sees the nature of love in all times and all places and when Sweeney outwits a scheming whore, the fate of Agamemnon becomes relevant. So too, in the same way exactly, Eliot must recognize and use a correspondence between St. Augustine and Buddha in speaking of sensuality. And thus, as he writes again in his notes to *The Waste Land*, 'The collocation of these two representatives of eastern and western asceticism as the culmination of this part of the poem is not an accident.' And it is not an accident that the international hero should have come from St. Louis, Missouri, or at any rate from America. Only an American with a mind and sensibility which is cosmopolitan and expatriated could have seen Europe as it is seen in *The Waste Land*.

A literary work may be important in many ways, but surely one of the ways in which it is important is in its relationship to some important human interest or need, or in its relationship to some new aspect of human existence. Eliot's work is important in relationship to the fact that experience has become international. We have become an international people, and hence an international hero is possible. Just as the war is international, so the true causes of many of the things in our lives are world-wide, and we are able to understand the character of our lives only when we are aware of all history, of the philosophy of history, of primitive peoples and the Russian Revolution, of ancient Egypt and the unconscious mind. Thus again it is no accident that in *The Waste Land* use is made of *The Golden Bough*, and a book on the quest of the Grail; and the way in which images and associations appear in the poem illustrates a new view of consciousness, the depths of consciousness and the unconscious mind.

The protagonist of *The Waste Land* stands on the banks of the Thames and quotes the Upanishads, and this very quotation, the command to 'give, sympathize, and control,' makes possible a comprehensive insight into the difficulty of his life in the present. But this emphasis upon one poem of Eliot's may be misleading. What is true of much of his poetry is also true of his criticism. When the critic writes of tradition and the individual talent, when he declares the necessity for the author of a consciousness of the past as far back as Homer, when he brings the reader back to Dante, the Elizabethans and Andrew Marvell, he is also speaking as the heir of all the ages.

The emphasis on a consciousness of literature may also be misleading, for nowhere better than in Eliot can we see the difference between being merely literary and making the knowledge of literature an element in vision, that is to say, an essential part of the process of seeing anything and everything. Thus, to cite the advent of Tiresias again, the literary character of his appearance is matched by the unliterary actuality by means of which he refers to himself as being 'like a taxi throbbing waiting.' In one way, the subject of *The Waste Land* is the sensibility of the protagonist, a sensibility which is literary, philosophical, cosmopolitan and expatriated. But this sensibility is concerned not with itself as such, but with the common things of modern life, with two such important aspects of existence as religious belief and making love. To summon to mind such profound witnesses as Freud and D.H. Lawrence is to remember how often, in modern life, love has been the worst sickness of human beings.

The extent to which Eliot's poetry is directly concerned with love is matched only by the extent to which it is concerned with religious belief and the crisis of moral values. J. Alfred Prufrock is unable to make love to women of his own class and kind because of shyness, self-consciousness, and fear of rejection. The protagonists of other poems in Eliot's first book are men or women laughed at or rejected in love, and a girl deserted by her lover seems like a body deserted by the soul.

In Eliot's second volume of poems, an old man's despair issues in part from his inability to make love, while Sweeney, an antithetical character, is able to make love, but is unable to satisfy the woman with whom he copulates. In *The Waste Land*, the theme of love as a failure is again uppermost. Two lovers return from a garden after a moment of love, and the woman is overcome by despair or pathological despondency. A lady, perhaps the same woman who has returned from the garden in despair, becomes hysterical in her boudoir because her lover or her husband has nothing to say to her and cannot give her life any meaning or interest: 'What shall I do now?' she says, 'what shall I ever do?' The neurasthenic lady is succeeded in the poem by cockney women who gossip about another cockney woman who has been made ill by contraceptive pills taken to avoid the consequences of love; which is to say that the sickness of love has struck down every class in society: 'What you get married for, if you don't want children?' And then we witness the seduction of the typist; and then other aspects of the sickness of love appear when, on the Thames bank, three girls ruined by love rehearse the sins of the young men with whom they have been having affairs. In the last part of the poem, the impossibility of love, the gulf between one human being and another, is the answer to the command to give, that is to say, to give oneself or surrender oneself to another human being in the act of making love.

Elsewhere love either results in impotence, or it is merely copulation. In 'The Hollow Men,' the hollow men are incapable of making love because there is a shadow which falls between the desire and the spasm. The kinship of love and belief is affirmed when the difficulties of love and of religious belief are expressed in the same way and as parallels, by means of a paraphrase and parody of the Lord's Prayer. In 'Sweeney Agonistes,' Sweeney returns to say that there is nothing in love but copulation, which, like birth and death, is boring. Sweeney's boredom should be placed in contrast with the experience of Burbank, who encountered the Princess Volupine in Venice, and found himself impotent with her. A comparison ought also to be made between Sweeney and the protagonist of one of Eliot's poems in French who harks back to a childhood experience of love: 'I tickled her to make her laugh. I experienced a moment of power and delirium.' Eliot's characters when they make love either suffer from what the psychoanalysts term 'psychic impotence,' or they make love so inadequately that the lady is left either hysterical or indifferent when the episode is over. The characters who are potent and insensitive are placed in contrast with the characters who are impotent and sensitive. Grishkin has a bust which promises pneumatic bliss, while Burbank's kind, the kind of a man who goes to Europe with a Baedeker, has to crawl between the dry ribs of metaphysics because no contact possible to flesh is satisfactory. The potent and the insensitive, such as Sweeney, are not taken in by the ladies, the nightingales and the whores; but Burbank, like Agamemnon, is betrayed and undone.

This synoptic recitation might be increased by many more examples. Its essence is expressed perfectly in 'Little Gidding': 'Love is the unfamiliar name.' But we ought to remember that the difficulty of making love, that is to say, of entering into the most intimate of relationships, is not the beginning but the consequence of the whole character of modern life. That is why the apparatus of reference which the poet brings to bear upon failure in love involves all history ('And I Tiresias have foresuffered all') and is international. So too the old man who is the protagonist of 'Gerontion' must refer to human beings of many nationalities, to Mr. Silvero at Limoges, Hakagawa, Madame de Tornquist, Fräulein von Kulp and Christ [the tiger] and he finds it necessary to speak of all history as well as his failure in love. History is made to illuminate love and love is made to illuminate history. In modern life, human beings are whirled beyond the circuit of the constellations: their intimate plight is seen in connection or relation with the anguish of the Apostles after Calvary, the murder of Agamemnon, the insanity of Ophelia and children who chant that London bridge is falling down. In the same way, the plight of Prufrock is illuminated by means of a rich, passing reference to Michelangelo, the sculptor of the strong and heroic man. Only when the poet is the heir of all the ages can he make significant use of so many different and distant kinds of experience. But conversely, only when experience becomes international, only when many different and distant kinds of experience are encountered by the poet, does he find it necessary to become the heir of all the ages.

Difficulty in love is inseparable from the deracination and the alienation from which the international man suffers. When the traditional beliefs, sanctions and bonds of the community and of the family decay or disappear in the distance like a receding harbor, then love ceases to be an act which is in relation to the life of community, and in immediate relation to the family and other human beings. Love becomes purely personal. It is isolated from the past and the future, and since it is isolated from all other relationships, since it is no longer celebrated, evaluated and given a status by the community, love does become merely copulation. The protagonist of 'Gerontion' uses one of the most significant phrases in Eliot's work when he speaks of himself as living in a *rented* house; which is to say, not in the house where his forebears lived. He lives in a rented house, he is unable to make love, and he knows that history has many cunning, deceptive, and empty corridors. The nature of the house, of love and history are interdependent aspects of modern life.

When we compare Eliot's poetry to the poetry of Valéry, Yeats and Rilke, Eliot's direct and comprehensive concern with the essential nature of modern life gains an external definition. Yeats writes of Leda and he writes of the nature of history; Valéry writes of Narcissus and the serpent in the Garden of Eden; Rilke is inspired by great works of art, by Christ's mother and by Orpheus. Yet in each of these authors the subject is transformed into a timeless essence. The heritage of Western culture is available to these authors and they use it in many beautiful ways; but the fate of Western culture and the historical sense as such does not become an important part of their poetry. And then if we compare Eliot with Auden and with Pound, a further definition becomes clear. In his early work, Auden is inspired by an international crisis in a social and political sense; in his new work, he writes as a teacher and preacher and secular theologian. In neither period is all history and all culture a necessary part of the subject or the sensibility which is dealing with the subject. With Pound, we come closer to Eliot and the closeness sharpens the difference. Pound is an American in Europe too, and Pound, not Eliot, was the first to grasp the historical and international dimension of experience, as we can see in an early effort of his to explain the method of the *Cantos* and the internal structure of each Canto: 'All times are contemporaneous,' he wrote, and in the *Cantos*, he attempts to deal with all history as if it were part of the present. But he fails; he remains for the most part an American in Europe, and the *Cantos* are never more than a book of souvenirs of a tour of the world and a tour of culture.

To be international is to be a citizen of the world and thus a citizen of no particular city. The world as such is not a community and it has no constitution or government: it is the turning world in which the human being, surrounded by the consequences of all times and all places, must live his life as a human being and not as the citizen of any nation. Hence, to be the heir of all the ages is to inherit nothing but a consciousness of how all heirlooms are rooted in the past. Dominated by the historical consciousness, the international hero finds that all beliefs affect the holding of any belief (he cannot think of Christianity without remembering Adonis); he finds that many languages affect each use of speech (*The Waste Land* concludes with a passage in four languages).

When nationalism attempts to renew itself, it can do so only through the throes of war. And when nationalism in America attempts to become articulate, when a poet like Carl Sandburg writes that 'The past is a bucket of ashes,' or when Henry Ford makes the purely American remark that

'History is bunk,' we have only to remember such a pilgrimage as that of Ford in the Peace Ship in which he attempted to bring the First World War to an end in order to see that anyone can say whatever he likes: no matter what anyone says, existence has become international for everyone.

Eliot's political and religious affirmations are at another extreme, and they do not resemble Ford's quixotic pilgrimage except as illustrating the starting point of the modern American, and his inevitable journey to Europe. What should be made explicit here is that only one who has known fully the deracination and alienation inherent in modern life can be moved to make so extreme an effort at returning to the traditional community as Eliot makes in attaching himself to Anglo-Catholicism and Royalism. Coming back may well be the same thing as going away; or at any rate, the effort to return home may exhibit the same predicament and the same topography as the fact of departure. Only by going to Europe, by crossing the Atlantic and living thousands of miles from home, does the international hero conceive of the complex nature of going home.

Modern life may be compared to a foreign country in which a foreign language is spoken. Eliot is the international hero because he has made the journey to the foreign country and described the nature of the new life in the foreign country. Since the future is bound to be international, if it is anything at all, we are all the bankrupt heirs of the ages, and the moments of the crisis expressed in Eliot's work are a prophecy of the crises of our own future in regard to love, religious belief, good and evil, the good life and the nature of the just society. *The Waste Land* will soon be as good as new.

108
A New Interpretation of *The Waste Land*[*]

JOHN PETER

It is easy to concede to *The Waste Land* the title of the most discussed poem of our age. I suspect, however, there are still many readers who feel, as I do, that the discussion has done little to make it more immediately intelligible and coherent to an unsophisticated audience. One might even say that in their eagerness to tease out the allusions and cross-references in it the published interpretations have rendered it rather less accessible than it already is. Any teacher who has had to introduce the poem to students unfamiliar with its sort of idiom, and honest enough to admit their bewilderment, is likely to feel that the critics and commentators, even the best of them, afford him little assistance in the preliminary stages of its elucidation. What he would like to be able to give his students is some comprehensive but relatively simple formula, in terms of which its apparent diffuseness and seemingly wanton diversity would begin to disapppear, some single thread by means of which they might be guided, Theseus-like, through its labyrinths: an interpretation, in short, which would allow them to see the wood as well as the trees. Once the formula had served its turn like this it would, I suppose, be necessary to use it with more discretion, and at this more advanced stage the subtler commentaries of critics like F.R. Leavis, F.O. Matthiessen and Cleanth Brooks would no doubt yield their true value. But it seems that until some simpler and more palpable epitome of the poem's meaning is allowed to intervene, subtlety is likely only to perplex and confuse. In what follows I shall try to rough out an epitome of this kind, one that has for a long time seemed to me to provide a useful entry into the poem. My epitome being what it is and my space being limited I shall not attempt a complete exposition of *The Waste Land*, nor shall I dilate upon the significance of the interpretation in clearing up some of the poem's obscurity. Again, I shall necessarily neglect the bearing which it has on certain other of Mr. Eliot's compositions (*The Family Reunion*, for example), and the way in which one or two hints elsewhere in his writings (a Commentary in *The Cri-*

[*] *Essays in Criticism* 2 (July 1952), pp. 242–66.

terion, a sentence in an essay, a dedication and so on) may be felt to sustain it. My purpose here being simply to offer a straightforward reading of a poem by now well enough established in the canon of literary studies to justify such a reading, I feel it is best to ignore these broader issues. The reader who finds the interpretation persuasive will, I hope, be stimulated to read the poem again, in order to test its cogency at first hand, and he may also be led to canvass its bearing on the other poems and plays for himself. I hope at some future date to be able to go into these questions, to show that the interpretation I offer is not as eccentric as at first sight, to those familiar only with the readings of other critics, it may appear to be. But for the present it seems best to limit the discussion to *The Waste Land*, and to state my case as tersely as possible.

A friend seemed to me to put the case for a simple elucidation of this poem very neatly when he described it as 'variations on a theme, the theme being omitted'. I am inclined to feel that until a plain and even bald statement of that theme has been volunteered to the reader he may well find, even where he can claim some familiarity with the techniques of modern verse, that the poem as a whole evades and perplexes him almost as persistently as isolated passages in it compel his interest and respect. What the commentator accordingly finds himself doing is, I think, to search for an hypothesis in terms of which the poem shall become sufficiently coherent and unified to present some sort of meaning—incomplete, of course, but not negligible—even after a single reading. And here perhaps the rule of the sciences, that the simplest hypothesis is to be preferred, can be allowed to have some weight. I do not of course deny the value of an exegesis in which the poem's links with *The Golden Bough* and Miss Weston's *From Ritual to Romance* are investigated. The mere fact that Eliot has cited these books at the beginning of his notes shows that he wished his reader to be conscious of the anthropological references. At the same time it seems to me that if we begin by concentrating too exclusively upon these references we shall be tempted to neglect the poem's less cerebral elements and to miss the tragedy of the situation in which the dramatic protagonist—the 'I' in it—is placed. Does any poet, even a learned one, embark upon a poem of over four hundred lines because he is interested primarily in anthropology? Such a question oversimplifies, no doubt, but I think it points to the right sort of answer too. For the more generalized symbols and connotations in *The Waste Land* are there, not because they themselves constitute its theme but in order to confer on that theme, already implicit in the first section (*The Burial of the Dead*), a wider validity than it could otherwise have claimed. To take one's start from the symbolism in the poem is thus, on the whole, to place oneself at its periphery; to begin with the theme, if that could be determined, would be to penetrate at once to the centre. Students, in my experience, are quick to detect the fallacy in a too circuitous approach. They feel, and I think justly, that a poem in which such strong emotion is stored up—stored up in some-

Early Poems and *The Waste Land*

thing like the way in which a condenser retains an electric charge, to flow as soon as the circuit is completed—should have a more vital and moving subject than any perusal of Miss Weston's book can suggest. Where their difficulty arises is in not being able to locate that subject with any confidence or precision; and it is surely here that the commentator should offer what assistance he can, by advancing an hypothesis which will cover the situation with which the poem presupposes its protagonist to have been faced. In general the commentators seem to have been reluctant to do this, and some have even felt it to be impossible. 'There is', wrote Charles Williams in his entertaining, perfectly honest and in all other respects useless essay on Eliot's poems,[1] 'a clue to this maze, but we shall never know it'. But that was in 1930, and today even a flippant critic would hesitate before expressing such an insouciant despair. To me at least there seems to be no occasion for it.

I am inclined to think that the situation of the poem's protagonist is not as recondite as it has generally appeared to be, and that we need only to fill in for ourselves some of the 'story' leading up to his meditations and reminiscences for its outline to become apparent. Philip Henderson's synoptic account of the theme of the poem ('the inability to love') is useful here, but I do not myself feel that it is specific enough to give the reader much real assistance, nor that his commentary is as pertinent as such a thing needs to be.[2] What the poem seems to require is some preliminary statement, rather like those prefixed to magazine serials, to explain what has gone before. Of course, it is true that the protagonist's monologue implies its own history and that it is from the monologue itself that any sketch of this history must be deduced. But the implications are not always as clear as they might be and it is perhaps permissible to do temporary violence to the poem in order to set them out more explicitly. If we try to do this I believe that we shall find ourselves gravitating towards an account in some such terms as these:

> At some previous time the speaker has fallen completely—perhaps the right word is 'irretrievably'—in love.
> The object of this love was a young man who soon afterwards met his death, it would seem by drowning.
> Enough time has now elapsed since his death for the speaker to have realized that the focus for affection that he once provided is irreplaceable.
> The monologue which, in effect, the poem presents is a meditation upon this deprivation, upon the speaker's stunned and horrified reactions to it, and on the picture which, as seen through its all but insupportable bleakness, the world presents.

Such an introduction is obviously inadequate and may, I fear, even seem brutally insensitive; but if we take it simply as a rather clumsy stage-direction, to be inserted at the beginning of the monologue, it may go some way to justify itself on the grounds of usefulness, if not subtlety.

There is, however, one point which perhaps needs to be noticed before we proceed to examine the poem itself. It will be seen that in phrasing my stage-direction I have, while making the sex of the deceased youth male, allowed the sex of the protagonist to remain ambiguous. There is, I need hardly point, out some warrant for this: one of the author's most helpful notes tells us that 'Tiresias ... is ... the most important personage in the poem, uniting all the rest' and that 'What Tiresias *sees*, in fact, is the substance of the poem', and the poem itself twice stresses his hermaphroditism (ll.219 and 228). A certain fluidity, if one may so describe it, in the sex of the two main 'characters', the speaker and the dead beloved, is indeed a feature of the presentation, and it is to be noted that even the latter is allowed to modify his sex, appearing (in his own words at least) once as 'keine Russin' and once as 'the hyacinth girl'. That this vagueness is deliberate we cannot doubt and any comprehensive analysis of the poem would have, I suppose, to include some discussion of its probable purpose. I do not intend to be comprehensive, however, and here perhaps it will be enough merely to raise the question. Leavis attributes the introduction of the hermaphrodite Tiresias to 'an effort to focus an inclusive human consciousness'[3] and if we extend this interpretation we could simply say that the bipolarity of the love-relationship has been carefully doubled so as to make that relationship as inclusive as possible. On the other hand, the poem certainly reads more lucidly if we suppose both the main characters to be male rather than epicene.

Let us now consider the meaning of the poem more closely. I have pointed out that it is not my intention to make an exhaustive analysis of it, and I should warn the reader again that I am here simply concerned to sketch of it the sort of abstract that might with advantage be offered to a student approaching it for the first time. I have no doubt that there will be some points and cross-references which I shall not discuss and which it will seem to others I should have discussed; but I shall try not to exclude anything of any real importance, lest it be said that only by omitting or glossing over certain passages can my interpretation be vindicated.

The first section, *The Burial of the Dead*, opens simply enough with the speaker's reaction to spring. Tillyard has suggested[4] that we are to be reminded of *The Canterbury Tales* here, but I doubt very much whether so specific a reference is intended. Everyone knows well enough that spring is the amorous season, and if Eliot's erudition obliges us to be bookish about it there is a whole tradition of lyric verse to remind us that sweet lovers love the spring. The point here is simply that these stirrings, disturbing the torpor of winter, are poignant and remind the speaker of a loss to which he had thought himself reconciled and to which, he now realizes, he can never be. Springtime violates the defences he has built up for with its onset the buried dead rise up to walk the earth again in memories. By an easy shift from spring to summer he is led into reminiscences of a conversation with the dead man (we should note, I think, that Marie is on the Continent a name given to both sexes), and remembering his companion's enthusiasm for the mountains and the sense of relief they brought him, he is driven back upon the emptiness of his present existence, the nights spent reading and the winters avoided in a sunnier climate. Even if, as is perhaps more likely, this last line is not disjoined from the rest, and is merely another fragment of the dead man's conversation, the next paragraph certainly returns us to the speaker's predicament. Its emotional aridity is symbolized in images of desiccation and the reader, invited to enter it, is warned that there are elements of terror in its sterility:

> *I will show you fear in a handful of dust.*

There follows the first *Tristan* passage, suggesting at once the ardour with which the young sailor sings it in the opera, an ardour once shared by the speaker, and also, its question taking on a new force in this context, the desolation which he now endures. The former suggestion predominates for a moment and we are given a beautifully evocative passage (it is here of course that the dead man becomes 'the hyacinth girl') to recreate a tremulous moment of bliss which the speaker himself once experienced. And immediately and brutally the second fragment from the opera intrudes: the sea is empty, the sailor (now Phoenician) drowned.

Much has been written concerning the meaning of Madame Sosostris, who appears next, and it is true that her Tarot pack, used to predict the rise of the waters of the Nile, is a significant item in a poem so much concerned with fertility. In what she says, however, I can find nothing very obscure. Like a modern fortune-teller she indicates to the speaker 'your card, the drowned Phoenician Sailor' ('your card' meaning 'the card which has been or is fatal to you'), and her quotation from *The Tempest* is the first link in a chain of images that stretches to Part IV of the poem. Other cards, similarly, inaugurate symbols which are to reappear later. Eliot has commented that 'all the women are one woman', and Belladonna, 'The lady of situations', is clearly no more than a type-symbol for amorous Woman, whose overtures must necessarily seem designing to one in the speaker's position and whose mere presence can be expected to cause him pain. She appears again later. The one-eyed merchant, Mr. Eugenides, is also to reappear, and in a later phase of the poem so are the crowds of godless people 'walking round in a ring'. It is only when they reappear that their significance becomes more than enigmatic and I accordingly defer my remarks about them until these reappearances. Madame Sosostris's 'Fear death by water' makes explicit the warning already symbolized by the card depicting the drowned Phoenician Sailor, and her dialogue ends as we should expect it to do, with confidences designed to recommend her discretion and reliability.

The treatment here, it will be observed, is rather freer than heretofore. To interpret the paragraph as a description of an actual consultation with a fortune-teller, whether before or after the drowning, would be naïve and I suppose its purpose is really to give a subtle emphasis to the protagonist's bereavement and, by means of the cards mentioned (not all of which are apparently authentic members of the Tarot pack), to introduce the several symbols, which are to recur later, in a natural way. In the next paragraph, the last in this section, the treatment is still less realistic and it is as though the speaker, while in effect admitting the sense of guilt which oppresses him, had been driven into an elliptical fantasy to safeguard his privacy. The title of the whole section is of some use when we try to disentangle the meaning of these concluding lines. Their opening, paraphrasing two passages from the *Inferno* and with a further gloss from Baudelaire, warns us that the London which they present is a city of ghosts rather than men, a subjective rather than a geographic reality, and with the 'dead sound on the final stroke of nine' one such spectre or emanation from the speaker's own mind manifests itself. The ghost has some substance conferred upon it by the name ('Stetson') with which the speaker salutes it and for a moment we are tempted to think it a flesh and blood compatriot; but when the speaker claims that this Stetson was with him 'in the ships at Mylae' we realize that the encounter, like the city in which it takes place, is 'Unreal'. Cleanth Brooks has said that 'Eliot in having the protagonist address the friend in a London street as one who was with him in the Punic War rather than as one who was with him in the World War is making the point that all the wars are one war; all experience, one experience'.[5] It is a useful comment but perhaps we may add that, as the last line of this section suggests, the poet's intention was also to imply that all guilt is one guilt, from whatever source it may arise. The references that follow to a corpse which Stetson has buried in his garden may have some connection with the buried god of the fertility rites but, as Matthiessen and Leavis have noted, they also seem to allude to the mental process by which guilty memories are repressed, to lie smouldering in the subconscious. We might say that the speaker, having his own memories to bury, presumes that the other must have his also and may note how this presumption itself keeps up the idea of a guilt that is all-pervading and ineluctable. Since the speaker passionately desires to free himself from the consciousness of his own memories even if this is only to be accomplished by a process ('Burial') which the onset of spring has already shown to be ineffectual, he is naturally reluctant to expose himself to the probes of others, even of those whose motives are sympathy and compassion; and, typifying this class of inquirer as 'the Dog . . . that's friend to men', he warns Stetson to keep his guilty secrets secure against even the most benevolent of investigators. The dead must be buried and those who inter them must see to it that they are not dug up again. And, with one more quotation from Baudelaire, the speaker rounds upon the reader and demands whether he too has not his guilty secrets which he is anxious to keep private from the eyes of others. So, with a plea for that understanding or charity which the second of the thunder's imperatives is to enjoin upon the main character himself, the first section ends.

A Game of Chess is probably the simplest of the longer sections, though there is at least one rather obscure passage in it. Any careful reader of the poem will have observed that the section is composed of two 'scenes', and he will probably also have noticed that though they are in some ways contrasted the two scenes also reinforce each other. I do not wish to make extravagant claims for my interpretation of the poem, but I think it might be a fair defence of it to claim that it allows us to integrate this section into the rest of the poem more smoothly and completely than do those of other critics. On my reading what we have here is a new slant on the misery which the speaker endures, and an opportunity to observe the rationalizations by which he seeks to extenuate or justify the love which he still feels and which, as we have seen, a part of his mind at least still regards as depraved. What the section gives us is, in fact, two scenes involving women and it is his rejection of the first woman and his shrinking from the situation of the second which helps us to understand the speaker's wretchedness and the guilt which exacerbates it. It is not mere arbitrary custom which decrees that Woman is Man's natural mate and, where a man or a woman has in effect to maintain that it is, an invidious picture of the opposite sex, such as the first scene here suggests, is often enough the result. That picture may be true enough, of course, at least in the sense that the person who sees it may believe that it is an accurate and honest abridgement of their own experience. The fact that in so believing they are likely to forget how their own prepossession determines their experience, by its influence on the opposite sex's attitude towards them and by the emphases that it projects into their experience (rather than finds there), does not mean that they are dishonest. It means only that their unhappiness is not so complete that it cannot be given a last ironic twist. Here we have the speaker selecting from his experiences with women, and the men who desire women, two that are for him representative. Comparatively few readers will find the first of these representative of their own experience, and certainly one cannot imagine many women doing so. In another context it might seem venomous, and even here we may be inclined to call it pitiless when we remember the woman's probable frustration and bewilderment. Yet we are invited to enter into the speaker's consciousness and to see that if there is venom in his presentation of Belladonna it is also in his veins, that it is his torment that makes him see as he sees. In some ways it is a challenge to our ability to comprehend his situation, and we ought not, I think, to decline it.

The section opens with a description of Belladonna the opulence of which is so unusual in Eliot's poetry that it should warn us that he had some intention other than that of mere description in writing it. The opulence is in fact sardonic, deliberately exaggerated so as to emphasize the flatness of the conversation that follows. Here is the fatal Cleopatra, Love's Martyr, discovered among surroundings quite as appropriately romantic as the barge in which she floated down the Cydnus. We await the accents of passion and are given those of neurasthenia instead.

Perhaps we might notice that it is 'sea-wood' which burns in the lady's fireplace, and certainly I do not think it is an accident that there is 'a carvèd dolphin' glimmering in the firelight. It was the dolphins that rescued the Greek poet Arion when he was cast overboard to drown and the introduction of such an emblem here, even casually, reminds us that it is with the speaker's eclectic gaze that we are viewing the room. We see, in fact, only those objects which are significant to him and we see them with his eyes. At least I feel that some such assumption is necessary if we are to disentangle the passage immediately following (this is the one I find obscure) in which the picture depicting 'The change of Philomel' is described. The passage is very condensed and it is not quite clear why the contrast between the nightingale's 'inviolable voice' and the crude 'Jug Jug' by which literary convention represents it should seem to be insisted upon. As I say, I think we have to remember that we are seeing the picture through the speaker's eyes and I think these lines are more a comment on his sensibility than on the rape itself. To him the rape is purged of all unpleasantness: not only is it stylized (a mere 'change'), frozen first into a decorative myth and then into a picture, but also the metamorphosis of the woman into a bird allows him to project his sympathies into her story more readily than he probably could have done had she remained a woman. Thus he is conscious of the forlorn magic of the nightingale's plaint, but when that magic is translated from the sphere of mythology to that of everyday life, and his own life especially, it fades into the brute pursuit of female by male. He notes with distaste that this pursuit is still the habit of the world and, as it were, consoles himself with the reflection that 'dirty ears' can give to the song little more attention than they would give to a bawdy joke. The sublimate to which lust gave rise, the 'inviolable voice', is itself profaned and dragged down to a level of unlovely onomatopoeia. There seems also to be the suggestion that his own lament, which make take its origin from a type of desire less often condoned even than that of King Tereus, will be vulgarized and debased in the same way by those who read it unsympathetically. At any rate it is this picture alone, with its emphasis on the least attractive side of intersexual passion, that the speaker notices. The other scenes on the walls he dismisses as 'other withered stumps of time'. We are thus prepared to find that the relationship between Belladonna and himself is a strained one.

In Belladonna's speeches which follow the strain is obvious. Most critics have commented on their neurasthenic intensity and I have myself just used the same word. But perhaps in the light of what has been said we can see that her frustration is tragic too, and that it is only because the speaker's own image of her is sharp with the sharpness of repugnance that her remarks seem so querulous. She in her incomprehension is trying to strike some sparks of 'normal' affection or solicitude from him; he for his part remains flinty, aware of his own incapacity to respond and of the impasse in which they are locked:

> *I think we are in rats' alley*
> *Where the dead men lost their bones.*

Asked what he is thinking, what he remembers, he can only recall Madame Sosostris's quotation from *The Tempest* and his own private memories associated with it. This beats in his head with the maddening insistence of a cheap tune, a 'Shakespeherian Rag', as he calls it, sealing him off from all Belladonna's advances and questions, and she is reduced to making fantastic proposals ('I shall rush out as I am . . .') in order to claim some of his attention. Even if not actually engaged in playing a game of chess they sit opposite each other as if they were, locked in a circle of behaviour where the moves are unspontaneous and cold-blooded, 'Pressing lidless eyes' and waiting for the arrival of a third party to disturb the stalemate of their personal Hell.

The relationship between these two having been vividly sketched the poem cuts at once into a Cockney woman's monologue in a pub. Here we have again a record of the immoderate desire symbolized in the picture of Philomela, but now there is no remoteness or artistry to soften it and it is accordingly realistic and harsh. The scene is not perhaps as devoid of compassion as the previous one (these men and women are sufficiently removed from the speaker's own world for him to feel secure against them, and thus more sympathetic), but the general effect is nevertheless to stress the selfishness and brute carnality into which domestic love can degenerate. Albert, the husband of whom the woman is speaking, 'can't bear to look at' his ailing wife. He 'wants a good time' and is not unwilling to seek it elsewhere if his wife cannot provide it. The wife, worn out after repeated pregnancies, has resorted to an abortion upon herself and admits that since doing so she has 'never been the same'. It is a sordid and pitiful glimpse of a marriage where the parties are too poor to afford contraceptives, but this is not quite how the speaker seems to regard it. As the pub closes for the night and as the Cockneys are exchanging their flat valedictions he remembers Ophelia's 'Good night, ladies, good night, sweet ladies, good night, good night', and it is as though he were persuading himself that even Ophelia's gentle devotion, like Cleopatra's impetuous desire, comes down to this in the end: the shabby pursuit of man by woman, or of woman by man, for the pursuer's own selfish satisfaction. Cleopatra, with whom the section began, is the predatory woman and Ophelia, with whom it ends, the type of the preyed upon. The speaker cannot see beyond this sordidness and cries out in effect, with Hamlet, 'Go to, I'll no more on't; it hath made me mad'.

The Fire Sermon is just as much a repudiation of sex as *A Game of Chess*, but it carries the speaker's meditations a stage further and forms a sort of pivotal centre in the poem. I shall accordingly allot it a little more space in my discussion. What is presented here is the speaker's complete dissatisfaction with human relationships and his first tentative attempts to withdraw from them into the life of the spirit. I do not say 'Christianity', because both here and in the final section the poem is deliberately vague as to the particular religion which he is to embrace.

Some time has passed and now the leaves are falling. It is important to remember that with the passage of time the speaker's attitude itself is developing. Most of the action now takes place on or beside the Thames and the opening lines indicate his attitude to the river. It is as the resort of the untidy, giggling lovers that he sees it—the canoes at Richmond on a Sunday afternoon or evening—but now the colder air has driven the lovers indoors and he is left alone to brood over his own isolation from their carefree promiscuity. Emphasizing the fact that it is still a revulsion against marriage and the courtship preceding it that he feels he quotes more than once from Spenser's *Prothalamion*, and when he repeats a snatch from the Psalms to symbolize the feeling of bondage which oppresses him he alters 'Babylon' to 'Leman' as if to suggest that it is the sweethearts on the river who are his captors. Suddenly horror rises up in him again and he is back 'in rats' alley' where small slimy creatures move close to him while, like the Fisher King of the myths, he sits 'fishing in the dark canal . . . behind the gashouse' for the fertility, that is the desire, which he has lost. The reference to a king allows him to observe that his predicament is in some sense a dynastic affair, a matter of heredity (I find myself thinking of Harry in *The Family Reunion* here), but the horror remains. Naked bodies writhe on the bank of the canal and the rats' feet patter among the bones 'in a little low dry garret'. His thoughts return with tormented insistence to the sort of love-affair that he cannot participate in, and once again he feels that it is not so much because of a personal aversion but because of the inanity of the affair itself that he despises it. The spring no longer brings Actaeon to the naked Diana, but Sweeney to Mrs. Porter on an errand of trivial and vulgar lust. He compares the vanity of these petty intrigues with the dedicated purpose of Parsifal, hero in a myth in which sterility is redeemed, and once again the contrast between the actual and the symbol—Mrs. Porter assuaging Sweeney's desires on the one hand and Parsifal retrieving the emblems of fertility on the other—comes shockingly home to him. And again he hears the nightingale, the voice that is so lavish with its sweetness and which, as the myth would have it, owes its very existence to the brutality of lust.

But the nightingale's song is really in the nature of an interpolation. It is the line from Verlaine that is the cue for Mr. Eugenides to make his second, and last, appearance in the poem. Verlaine's own private life, his tempestuous relations with Rimbaud and so on, is familiar enough today and here he is writing of choristers—obvious enough symbols of boyish innocence. It is into this sort of context that the merchant, the type of the seedy pederast, intrudes. I used to think that this character had been introduced merely to show the speaker's awareness of the sordid level to which his own sort of love could sink, but I am now inclined to believe that there is more to his appearance than this. Eliot's own notes tell us that 'the one-eyed merchant, seller of currants, melts into the Phoenician Sailor' and if there is as close an identification as this between the two I think that what we have here must be meant to suggest that the speaker is now beginning to feel almost as disgusted with his own emotions as with those of the 'nymphs' and their beaux on the Thames. The Phoenician Sailor, the drowned man, is not I suppose *personally* identified with Mr. Eugenides. It would surely be a gross error to suppose that the speaker is here repudiating the memory of the man upon whom all his affection was centred. What he does seem to have realized is that even that affection comes down in the end to the level of the brutes. The disenchanted gaze with which he regarded the motives and behaviour of the husband, Albert, is now turned upon his own feelings and he has to admit (with what pain we are to imagine) that even they, the basis upon which his whole view of life had rested, are rooted in selfishness and appetite. Mr. Eugenides is in fact one of the most ghastly apparitions in the poem for he is a caricature, and thus a destroyer, of those very emotions and attitudes by which until now the speaker has been sustained. Where in the field of human relationships is he now to turn? There is, surely, nowhere.

What stage have the speaker's introspections now reached? To call it detachment would be, I think, to exaggerate its stability and completeness. It is rather a state of dislocation where the honesty he has achieved is liable at any moment to decompose. He is not so much limp from exhaustion as tense from it and, like some kinds of fever, his inward perturbation gives him a sort of clairvoyance. In order to symbolize this condition he now becomes Tiresias, a being helplessly suspended between the poles of male and female yet one to whom was also entrusted the gift of prevision; and because the whole subject of the poem is the transcending of physical love, normal or otherwise, the notes declare that 'What Tiresias *sees*, in fact, is the substance of the poem'. There is, of course, an ambiguity here since it might be argued that, strictly speaking, all that Tiresias sees is the seduction of the typist by the house agent's clerk which follows. But Eliot's italics are enough to dispel the ambiguity. It is Tiresias's *attitude*, as much as his vision, that counts, and when we begin to see the scenes that the poem presents as if through his eyes, the eyes of a being for whom desire has become meaningless, we begin also to understand the true significance of those scenes. Here again, in what follows, we see love reduced to a drab insignificance. A fragment from Sappho (herself an appropriate choice) revives the chain of references to 'the sailor' and then leads into a scene that is largely a repetition of what has gone before. Love is at bottom merely lust, and perfunctory besides. The scene ends with the music of the typist's gramophone, the sort of music heard also from the canoes and punts that throng the river on summer evenings, and the speaker contrasts with it 'The pleasant whining of a mandoline' played by an authentic if not necessarily accomplished musician in the bar where, significantly again, sailors or 'fishmen' gather. These indirect but continuing allusions to the drowned man seem to me to corroborate my suggestion that the speaker is not yet detached from his own affections, even if he has seen through them, but the sudden juxtaposition, after the 'public bar . . . Where fishmen lounge at noon', of the Church of St. Magnus Martyr should intimate to us that they may be beginning to alter, to undergo a process of sublimation and refinement into faith.

This process is postulated rather than described in the poem and I am half inclined to make its status as a postulate my excuse for not discussing it. It would be easy enough to by-pass the question with a vague formula—to say for example that the ἔρως felt by the speaker is becoming ἀγάπη—and it is true that a commentator might be excused if he felt that the only decent formula of this kind would be to quote at length from the literature of Christianity, and perhaps especially from St. Augustine's *Confessions*. I cannot permit myself too many secondary quotations in this sort of commentary, important though I think many of them might be, but on the other hand this incipient alteration in the speaker's attitude is a principal theme in *The Waste Land*—the main theme one could say—and I feel that I must accord it a little more attention than would be contained in a formula. To put the matter bluntly, I think the speaker's motivation is a subject on which the readers of the poem are likely to divide very sharply. On the one hand there will be those who wish to explain his development in psychological terms and on the other there will be those who wish to explain it in Christian terms, as a matter of humiliation and grace. The first of these groups will say that because his love is frustrated in this life he resorts to another life in which it may be satisfied, that he is in a sense running away from himself; and the second group will say that it is through the love that he feels for the dead man, and through the sense of guilt associated with it, that he is brought nearer to God. I do not myself believe that the argument between these two groups necessarily lies outside the field of literary criticism. For instance, I can conceive of a responsible critic arguing that the Christian interpretation of the speaker's gropings towards faith is seriously weakened by the comparative absence of charity from the poem and by the (possibly unavoidable) impression of superciliousness that some sections of it produce. At the same time I feel that a critic should be on his guard against entering into the argument too impetuously, lest he find that he is not criticizing or defending an ingredient in the poem so much as an ingredient in himself. I suppose one might say that it is to the second group, the believers, that the poem is really addressed, and certainly the references to St. Augustine which we shall be considering in a moment tend to confirm such a view. Yet even this is to distort the poem a little for, as I have said, its later sections merely *assume* development in the speaker and are not concerned to describe or justify it. It is for this reason that the critic needs to proceed cautiously. It will not do to criticize *King Lear* by saying that one would not oneself be so foolish as to divide a kingdom between two hypocritical

Early Poems and *The Waste Land*

daughters, casting off the youngest for her honesty. This is not a complete parallel to the problem in *The Waste Land*, but it does suggest the sort of caveat that seems to be necessary. The problem is a complex one and, of course, it needs a much fuller discussion than I have found space for here. I cannot, however, afford to go more deeply into it in an essay like this, the purpose of which is expository rather than critical, and I accordingly return to the text of *The Fire Sermon*, from which I have already digressed too far.

The reference to St. Magnus Martyr is followed by 'The Song of the (three) Thames-daughters', and here it is again the river that we focus upon. At first it is the river that we know today, the industrial artery sweating 'Oil and tar', but an allusion to the Isle of Dogs awakens more remote associations and the picture changes. We see a more brilliant Thames with a colourful barge, in which Elizabeth and Leicester are flirting, floating upon it. I take it that there is an indirect reference here to the barge of that other queen, Cleopatra, and I think we should also notice that a 'narrow canoe' is mentioned just afterwards. Some sort of comparison between the barges and the canoe is evidently intended, though it might be argued that the comparison is too laconic to be seized upon with any firmness, and that it is difficult to decide whether what is meant is a simple contrast between Elizabethan glamour and modern drabness or a parallel between Elizabethan coquetry and modern philandering. But these effects are not mutually exclusive and the successive references to Cleopatra, to Elizabeth and to the 'nymphs' of Richmond seem to hang together quite coherently. The speaker sees a fundamental futility in all love-affairs and flirtations, whatever the trappings in which they are decked out and however remote from his own time they may be. The 'Song' of the Thames-daughters continues in the form of snatches of conversation which hint at the sort of promiscuity in which these daughters have been involved, but the tone of the verse grows more and more impersonal and resigned until it culminates in a deliberately false note:

> *My people humble people who expect*
> *Nothing.*

This liturgical touch prepares us for the quotation from St. Augustine which follows.

The quotation comes from the beginning of the third book of the *Confessions* and the note which Eliot has appended to it, with its mention of 'unholy loves', translates enough of its context to explain how it bears upon the characters and incidents—the lovers on the river, Mrs. Porter, Mr. Eugenides, the typist and the rest—that have preceded it. What the notes do not make clear, and what I feel they might have, is that Augustine 'came' twice to Carthage and that on the second occasion he had travelled to it in order to escape from the misery into which he had been plunged by the death of a friend, one with whom he had enjoyed a friendship which he himself describes as 'delightful to me above all the delights of this my life'. Anyone who begins reading at the fourth chapter of Book IV of the *Confessions* will, I think, agree that this second visit to Carthage is even more revealing when we refer it to the theme of *The Waste Land*, and he is likely to realize also what a huge reference the broken fragment 'To Carthage then I came' really contains.[6] Like Augustine at this stage of his life the speaker is not yet able to accept Christianity, despite the craving for consolation and forgiveness that he endures. At least his repetition of the word 'burning' seems to imply that he is still caught in the trammels of the senses, since in the Fire-Sermon in the *Mahā-Vagga* from which this section derives its title it is chiefly to the organs of sense, and to the perceptions that they report, that the Buddha applies this word. It is for these sensual perceptions, and for the impressions received from them by the mind, the Buddha declares, that 'the learned and noble disciple conceives an aversion', and he goes on to say that 'in conceiving this aversion, he becomes divested of passion, and by the absence of passion he becomes free, and when he is free he becomes aware that he is free'. Augustine has a section on the senses in Book X of the *Confessions* which almost exactly parallels these tenets and it is evidently from it that the second of the references to this work is taken:

> But I . . . entangle myself lifewise in these [merely outward] beauties; but you pluck me out, O Lord, you pluck me out, since your compassion is before my eyes.[8]

What is the point of this 'collocation of . . . two representatives of eastern and western asceticism'? Obviously there is common ground between them in that it is detachment which they are both recommending, but perhaps we are meant to notice that, whereas the Buddhist has virtually to achieve this detachment for himself, the Christian rather feels himself torn up by God from the webs and meshes of the world. With the repeated 'O Lord Thou pluckest', as with the repeated 'burning', we surely feel the agony of the speaker undergoing this avulsion and although by the end of the section the fourfold repetition of 'burning' has died down to the single word that word itself suggests that the agony continues. The original Fire-Sermon was irresistible, as the last paragraph of the translation mentioned in Eliot's note makes clear:

> Now while this exposition was being delivered, the minds of the thousand priests became free from attachment and delivered from the depravities.

Here, however, it is with the equivocal 'burning' that the section concludes. It is obvious that, in the words of *Gerontion*, 'We have not reached conclusion' and that Parts IV and V will not necessarily provide an anticlimax.

Death by Water, in which we see the drowned Phlebas[9] drifting among subaqueous currents, may at first sight appear to be misplaced, and perhaps it would be if its only purpose were to provide us with a picture of the drifting

Early Poems and *The Waste Land*

body. But I think it is intended to do much more than this and that it is perfectly successful, though in a way that is so subtle as to be very nearly indescribable. As other commentators have noted, the section consists of a free translation of the last lines of an earlier poem, *Dans le Restaurant*. In that poem it is evidently intended to contrast with 'the obscene boastful reminiscences of the old waiter'[10] in much the same way that the *voix d'enfants* contrast with the fornication between Sweeney and Mrs. Porter in *The Fire Sermon*. Here, however, its bearing on what has gone before is more tenuous and at the same time more intricate.

I think we could say that the main effect of the section is valedictory rather than descriptive. It is as though the speaker has turned back for a last survey of the pattern of his former life before going forward into the new and the unknown. He sees the friend upon whom his desires were centred not only as someone who has been reft from him but also as someone already acclimatized to the kingdom of Death and perhaps unconscious of the yearning to which his death has given rise. Phlebas rises and falls as he welters among the currents, and there is a sort of resignation or indifference in his serene insentience. The speaker's love is unrequited now, Death having made it so, and it is as if some of the poignancy with which he realizes this has crept in at the end:

> *Gentile or Jew*
> *O you who turn the wheel and look to windward,*
> *Consider Phlebas, who was once handsome and tall as you.*

But the relationship is a barren one and, with this obscurely disturbing appeal, he turns back from it again.

This might seem to suggest that there are only two levels at which the lyric may be read—as a description in the first place and, in the second, as a valediction—but I think there are others and that even as terse a commentary as this can afford to notice one more. Surely, then, the image of the body weltering under water also symbolizes that stage of development to which the speaker himself has now attained. He too, like the drowned sailor, is disembodied, suspended in a condition of being where 'the profit and loss' have ceased to matter, and he too may be said to have 'passed the stages of his age and youth'. Indeed of him we may say that he has already passed the whirlpool also (though we are to see him spinning in it still at the end of the poem). The effect is to suggest that his attitude is one from which expectation has almost disappeared. Here in fact is a measure of that detachment to which *The Fire Sermon* has directed us. For the moment the speaker has achieved it and even if he cannot maintain it at least it will last long enough for him to hear the commands of the thunder.

The general note to Part V, *What the Thunder Said*, mentions the three themes that run through the first half of it. The existence of this note, and the fact that other commentators have analysed the first half of the section in much the same way that I should wish to do, allows me to adopt a more cursory kind of comment here. The references to Miss Weston's book are perhaps denser here than in any other section of the poem and it seems clear that the idea behind the opening paragraphs is what she calls 'The Task of the Hero', the task of redeeming the Waste Land. Miss Weston points out that in one version of the Gawain story the desolation of the land 'is, in some manner, not clearly explained, connected with the death of a knight whose name and identity are never disclosed'.[11] In Eliot's poem this knight is, of course, Phlebas and, as the first paragraph of this last section makes clear, the Hero is no longer Gawain or Perceval or Galahad but Christ himself. As in an Elizabethan tragedy, thunder is presented as the voice of God (thus in the sixth line it is associated with the Crucifixion), and the spring in which it is heard is no longer merely the 'cruellest' season but the season of fertility and rebirth also. In the same way 'He who was living is now dead' refers not so much to Phlebus as to Christ, and when the speaker goes on to say 'We who are living are now dying' he seems to be thinking of a very special sort of death, the death into faith.

In the second paragraph we have again a description of the aridity of the Waste Land, but it is a description that can also refer to the approach to the Chapel Perilous—as well, of course, as to the sterile desert which is the speaker's own spiritual condition. A reference to 'dry sterile thunder without rain' evidently means that though the speaker has meditated upon the doctrines of St. Augustine and the Buddha he has not yet properly absorbed them. His mind knows what the commands of God entail, as it were, but they are not yet assimilated into his emotions and spirit. It is the water of grace, the ability to accept these commands absolutely and with firm conviction, that he craves but so far at least 'there is no water'. Like the Antarctic explorers mentioned in one of the notes he is at the extremity of his strength, and cautious lest the belief towards which he feels himself to be driven should turn out to be hallucinatory, the effect of mere exhaustion. Again, like Cleopas and the other disciple on the road to Emmaus, he cannot yet recognize the Saviour who has appeared and who remains 'wrapt in a brown mantle' of doubt. Yet as he surveys his position, trying to ascertain the probity of the influences that are encouraging him to make the leap of faith, he becomes more and more aware that that leap is, for him, inevitable. The temporal world has lost all meaning: cities rise and fall and now there are hordes of godless men swarming over eastern Europe, hordes whose apostasy itself becomes, for others, an argument in favour of belief. On the other hand, when he turns his eyes inwards upon his own soul it is only to find there a gallery of horrors which repentance and faith alone can dispel. These visions come to him in the violet light previously associated with Tiresias and are thus, I think, intended to represent introspection or self-knowledge at its most scrupulous and luminous. At the same time we

Early Poems and *The Waste Land*

remember that 'the violet hour' is that hour 'when the human engine waits Like a taxi throbbing waiting', and we realize that the speaker's anguish is now verging upon a crisis that is to be decisive. Miss Weston speaks of 'a strange and terrifying adventure in a mysterious Chapel, an adventure which ... is fraught with extreme peril to life'[12] and, with the speaker, it is in that Chapel that we now find ourselves. Contrary to what we might expect, however, it is not fear that he feels: the 'Dry bones' of his tortured fancy, among which the rats' feet rattled 'can harm no one' now. He feels shame only, shame that he should have been willing to say, with Peter, 'I do not know the man'. 'In a flash of lightning' he sees that it is not so much scruple as cowardice that is holding him back and, as the cock that reproved Peter falls silent, there comes 'a damp gust' of the wind that he has waited for, bringing relief at last. The Hero, Christ, has achieved the feat of 'Freeing the Waters' and now the thunder is heard through the falling rain.

Significantly enough it is not the Christian God who speaks: the protagonist has achieved belief but orthodoxy he cannot yet compass. But it is enough that his faith should be absolute at last, even if only fleetingly, and the three commands of the thunder ('Give, sympathize, control') find no resistance as they pass into his consciousness. The first injunction rouses him to a passionate avowal of his love, an avowal that is at the same time a denial of its sufficiency, and the second endows him with a charity that enables him to look outwards upon the tragedies of others as well as inwards upon his own. But with a final irony, and an honesty that I find most impressive, the poem in effect admits that the moment of revelation, like the lightning flash, has faded, and with the last of the thunder's commands his nostalgia and yearning for the love that he has missed reasserts itself:

> *The sea was calm, your heart would have responded*
> *Gaily, when invited, beating obedient*
> *To controlling hands.*

Even as thunder is speaking we are thus returned to the mood of the Hyacinth garden and this transitional passage prepares us for the speaker's relapse into the role of the Fisher King, sitting on the shore with the arid plain behind him. Far from its being an anticlimax this relapse seems to me indispensable to the whole structure and meaning of the poem, for without it the speaker's love for Phlebas would inevitably seem a little shallow and too easily displaced. Moreover, such faith as he has achieved would itself appear in a false light. That faith, the poem seems to be saying, is not an easy chair into which one slumps after a hard day's work, with no prospect of being disturbed, but a continual challenge requiring effort, like the effort of a man trying to walk upright on the deck of a wildly tossing ship. It is true that the speaker returns to his own tragedy, quoting from the *Pervigilium Veneris* (and perhaps from Tennyson)[13] to express his longing for a life that shall be as free and impulsive as the flight of a bird. But he has had his revelation, however brief, and now it is in a mood of expiation rather than meaningless suffering that he accepts the burden of his grief and guilt. That guilt is again suggested by the line from the *Purgatorio* (here also the provenance of the quotation seems to me to go a long way to confirm my interpretation of the poem: *Nostro peccato fu ermafrodito*), and here as in the earlier sections of the poem the weight of the guilt is all but insupportable. Nevertheless if he is to be, with Hieronymo, 'mad againe' it must now be with a holy madness. Like Arnaut Daniel in Purgatory he plunges into the refining fire of repentance, steeling himself to accomplish gradually a more stable detachment from his own desires. 'Give, sympathize, control': these are the admonitions of the thunder and these he must learn to apply. If he can do so, 'peace and peace and peace' may indeed come upon his tortured spirit in the end.

I said at the beginning of this essay that what I wanted to do in it was to offer a simpler and more palpable reading of *The Waste Land* than I had been able to find in the commentaries of others, and I hope that the interpretation may also help to show that the poem is no mere ingenious exercise but an impassioned history. It seems to me to gain rather than to lose when we accept the tragedy of its protagonist as personal, and when we see that personal tragedy as the central impulse from which the more generalized reflections arise. The ἀποθανεῖν θέλω of the epigraph, the speaker's recollection of Madame Sosostris's prediction while he endures Belladonna's frantic questions, Mr. Eugenides's proposal, the 'Burning burning burning burning' of *the Fire Sermon*, Phlebas's body adrift in the sea, the despair of the speaker as he says 'But there is no water', the avowals and regrets that the commands of the thunder wring from him—all these touches seem to me to become much more moving if the sort of interpretation that I have sketched can be accepted. At the same time I ought perhaps to point out again that for a poem of this sort no single exegesis can ever be quite enough, particularly if it is as condensed as I have tried to make mine. For reading *The Waste Land* is rather like looking through a microscope at an object that cannot be reduced to the flat plane of a slide. Continual readjustments are necessary, so that new levels can come into focus, and it is difficult to feel that any one setting is definitive. In the circumstances, then, analysis necessarily becomes a co-operative enterprise. It is as one more adjustment of the eyepiece that I offer this essay.

Notes

1. *Poetry at Present* (Oxford 1930), p. 163.
2. *The Poet and Society* (London 1939), chapter 6.
3. *New Bearings in English Poetry* (London 1932), p. 95. I regret I have not been able to check Dr. Leavis's analysis in the revised edition of this book.
4. *Poetry Direct and Oblique* (London 1934), p. 72.

Early Poems and *The Waste Land*

5. *T.S. Eliot . . . By Several Hands*, ed. B. Rajan (London 1947), pp. 13–14.
6. Thus Augustine's *mirabar enim ceteros mortales vivere, quia ille, quem quasi non moriturum dilexeram, mortuus erat* (IV, 6), to take only one example, can surely be related to lines 60–6, those lines in which the fragments from the *Inferno* occur.
7. See *Buddhism in Translations* by Henry Clarke Warren (Cambridge, Mass. 1915), pp. 351–3.
8. *Confessions*, X, 34.
9. I have not traced this name, but it may well be fictitious. The important point seems to be that, as Miss Weston points out, 'the worship of Adonis . . . was originally of Phoenician origin' (*From Ritual to Romance*, Cambridge 1930), p. 40.
10. Matthiessen, *The Achievement of T.S. Eliot* (2nd ed. New York 1947), p. 150.
11. *Op cit.*, p. 11.
12. *Op. cit.*, p. 165.
13. A song in *The Princess* begins 'O Swallow, Swallow, flying, flying South'.

# 109
T.S. Eliot: The Death of Literary Judgement*

KARL SHAPIRO

There is no passable essay on Eliot at this time (about A.D. 1960) and little chance of there being one. As far as the literary situation goes, nothing could be more useful today, but the literary situation has seen to it that this essay does not exist. The very idea of a summary of Eliot's writings seems a kind of blasphemy, or an act of unpardonable rudeness. For the Literary Situation (whatever that ecclesiastical expression is supposed to mean) is largely Eliot's invention, and for that reason it is all but impossible to discuss. Eliot is untouchable; he is Modern Literature incarnate and an institution unto himself. One is permitted to disagree with him on a point here or a doctrine there, but no more. The enemy at Eliot's gate—practically everybody— searches his citadel for an opening and cannot find one. Eliot has long since anticipated every move; he and his men can prevent ingress or exit. Eliot resembles one of those mighty castles in Bavaria which are remarkably visible, famed for their unsightliness, and too expensive to tear down. Life goes on at the bottom; but *it* is always up there.

The question of Eliot as the chief obstacle to poetry today may not be a real question; it may be precisely the kind of imaginary question which Eliot himself brings up in his writing. Insofar as one tries to deal with it, he is simply playing Eliot's game, with all the odds against him. I do not myself consider the question real, but I know of no way to discuss the ultimate value of Eliot's work without first discussing the exploits of his straw men. Eliot's reputation and the antagonism to it may be false. I propose in this essay to show both the reputation and the opposition to it in another light. That there is something of value in Eliot's poetry and Eliot's criticism is quite possible, even from my pessimistic point of view; though the valuable portion is minuscule and is much different from what has been supposed.

Eliot is both the hero and the victim of a historical predicament. And he himself is as much the author of that predicament as 'history' itself. Eliot created a literary situation deliberately; he and his 'situation' are fabri-

*From *In Defense of Ignorance* (New York, 1960), pp. 35–60.

cations, and very plausible fabrications at that. In other words, Eliot invented a Modern World which exists only in his version of it; this world is populated by Eliot's followers and is not a reality. The Eliot population consists of a handful of critics and professors and a few writers of Eliot's generation, though one would think, reading modern criticism and teaching from modern literary textbooks, that there really is a kingdom of Modern Poetry in which T.S. Eliot is the absolute monarch and Archbishop of Canterbury in one.

You will be thinking that I am using metaphorical language and am attempting to work up a nice critical discussion, the subject of which is the overestimation of T.S. Eliot. I am saying something quite different, namely, that Eliot exists only on paper, only in the minds of a few critics. No poet with so great a name has ever had less influence on poetry. At no point in the career of Eliot has there been the slightest indication of a literary following. For example, W.H. Auden, for a decade or so, set patterns for poetry which were followed by thousands of new poets all over the world. Dylan Thomas did the same, as did Wallace Stevens. Neither Eliot nor Pound ever had any such effect on their readers or on young writers. Eliot's 'influence' is confined purely to criticism. Insofar as Eliot has enjoyed a *poetic* influence, it lies outside literature entirely and is what can only be called a 'spiritual' influence. This spiritual influence is itself calculated and synthetic; and insofar as it fails as a true influence, it removes Eliot's one and only claim to literary power. But here he does not entirely fail.

To deal with Eliot outside the literary situation which he has invented, means to deal with his poetry head-on. It means passing judgement upon it as good or bad poetry or, in some cases, as not poetry at all. But how is one to look at Eliot, if not from his own viewpoint? There is the rub. Eliot has arranged matters in such a way that criticism of his own poetry is impossible.

Eliot has written a small body of poetry which is sacrosanct; he has written his most favourable criticism about poetry which is like his (namely Pound's), and has surrounded both with a full-scale esthetic-social doctrine. What I would like to do is to draw attention to Eliot's poetry—for that is the heart of the matter. For those who do not instinctively and spontaneously reject this poetry, I suppose some form of argument is required. Perhaps this essay will be of some assistance to them. I have in mind students primarily, those who are given Modern Poetry as gospel; I also have the young critic in mind, and also teachers and scholars. Poets do not need these remarks. I have met hundreds of poets in my life but not more than one or two who entertained the reverence for Eliot which they find in the textbooks. As most poets are not intellectuals and are the opposite, they are always stunned by the intellectual pretensions of Eliot and are at a loss to deal with them.

Eliot's preparation of the historical ground upon which he would found his position was the territory of all literature—excluding the Chinese, which was the preserve of Pound. He did not, evidently, intend a personal seizure of intellectual power; Eliot's famous humility testifies to his uneasiness in the face of overwhelming success. His irrational and subservient association with Pound also points to a genuine desire to refuse intellectual leadership, or at least to share it with others.

There was, it appears, a need for an Eliot about 1910. Eliot arrived on the literary scene at the point of vacuum; and he filled this vacuum which literary Nature abhors. Such at least is the accepted view. What is probably nearer the truth is that Eliot appeared at a time when the vitality of the audience was low; and when this is the case, criticism pours into the void. It is the critic in the guise of poet that we have to deal with, not a new kind of poet. For it is criticism which is the twentieth-century substitute for poetry.

The Historical Situation which Eliot exploits under the banner of Tradition was in the beginning the Educational Situation. It was local and Anglo-American, a defense of the Gentleman's Education. I put it vulgarly because that is the way it was. Too many writers have commented on Eliot's fears of being taken for a provincial for me to add my comment. These fears, however, are part of the New England heritage—the worst part—which leads the New Englander to become the Old Englander. Eliot's early life and work follow an almost hypnotic pattern; one might call him that pseudo-American, the type which finally won New England from the immigrant and gave it back to 'history.' The cultural dryness of New England was a by-product of this attitude which Eliot exemplifies even better than Henry James: that of relating America to New England, New England to England. Eliot was simply retracing the path back to Europe, exactly as Pound did, and as so many of our nineteenth-century writers tended to do, all but those specifically American.

The criticism of Eliot and Pound has blighted enormous literary areas, as far as we can tell.

The critics who helped establish Eliot were no less instrumental than Eliot himself in opening the frontiers of the cultural territory. Eliot with his palaver about the Tradition could gather in the entire Indo-European world, leaving North Asia and Africa to his senior. I do not want to go into the story of Eliot's critical rise to fame, but to illustrate what I mean I want to point to two literary critics who from every indication should have become his strongest foes; instead of becoming foes they were easily engaged to take his part in the high venture of Modern Poetic Culture. They are Edmund Wilson and F.O. Matthiessen.

Edmund Wilson may be fairly described as a critic in every way the natural opposite of Eliot. In his early estimate of Eliot in *Axel's Castle*, probably the first work to install Eliot in a high position in the literary mind, he pointed out almost every serious defect of the poet: his 'fear of vulgarity,' his intention to 'depersonalize' literature, his overintellectuality, his obsessive imitativeness, and so forth. Wilson described Eliot as the Puritan-turned-artist and expressed the fear that the extravagant praise of Eliot on all sides

Early Poems and *The Waste Land*

would perhaps unbalance literary judgement, as of course it did. What then attracted Wilson to Eliot? *It was Eliot's influence on literary criticism.* Wilson walked straight into the trap which Eliot had baited for all humanists and run-of-the-mill men of letters. Eliot had written so high-mindedly about the literary past and so dolefully about the present that Wilson was taken in. He even began to praise Eliot's prose style—probably the worst prose style in the history of the English essay, as well as the most personal. What attracted the budding critic Wilson was, of course, the keenness of intelligence, the range of ideas, the feel of authority, and the sense of History. Also, a hopeful critic like Wilson was on the search for a poet to praise, and Wilson thought he had found him. Meanwhile Wilson was popped into the Eliot oven to be turned into a nice little, right little gingerbread man. Fortunately, he escaped, but that chapter does not belong to our chronicle.

F.O. Matthiessen's relationship to Eliot is even more extraordinary than that of the humanist critic who gazes in fascination at the Puritan-turned-artist. Matthiessen, I think, felt the same attraction for New England that Eliot did, the one coming from the West Coast, the other from the Midwest. To the critical and historical mind of Matthiessen, Eliot must have seemed an incarnation of American history. But Matthiessen had some adjusting to do in his own thinking in order to place Eliot in the same high position that Wilson had. He acknowledged his indebtedness to Wilson and also to I.A. Richards, the man who tried, and almost succeeded, in driving the poetic mind into the test tube. Matthiessen could not agree with Eliot's philosophy, his religion, or his politics, and yet he felt he must adulate Eliot! The result was his book on Eliot in which Matthiessen disdains the kind of criticism that deals with the poet's 'ideas' and praises the kind of criticism that deals with the 'forms.' This book, *The Achievement of T.S. Eliot*, was published during the height of the Depression and at a time when Marxism was strong in the United States. Matthiessen was perhaps the most intensely engaged political mind among the English professors of his day, and a leftist; *yet he chose to cut himself off from the politics of Eliot's poetry and criticism to talk about the 'forms.'* This was a split that Eliot had invented for himself and which Eliot evidently kept from being fatal in his own life by various makeshifts of criticism. The false dualisms set up by Eliot between art and social action are symptomatic of the insanity of much modern criticism. In any case, it was Eliot's attractive formulation of these dualisms that neutralized so many critics and led Criticism itself into a squirrel cage where it still performs so brilliantly for its own amusement. Even Eliot's most favorable critics have never been able to resolve his major contradictions, which are central and irreducible conflicts rising from a false view of art as a function of history and culture, and a twisted attitude toward human nature.

Eliot's criticism is not 'one thing' and his poetry another. They are one and the same. Herein lies the only unity of his work and of his 'sensibility.' This unity has been achieved coldly and ruthlessly, on paper. It has only as much relation to life as books can have: experience in Eliot is always and necessarily literary experience. All other experience is vulgar, with the possible exception of the religious experience, which is Eliot's escape hatch. His poems are therefore illustrations of the various stages of his 'position,' just as Pound's poems are illustrations of Pound's politick. Pound is not interested in poetry as poetry but in demonstrating what poetry is for. Eliot is above pedagogy, being closer to philosophy than to history. But the unifying element in Eliot is theology: and it is not inaccurate to describe Eliot as a theologian gone astray. The difference between Eliot's respectability and Pound's notoriety lies here as well. The frequent violence of Eliot's feelings is overlooked because of the 'religious' context. Both his verse and his prose are held together by the main strength of certain theological abstractions. Eliot shows a positive hatred for originality and in fact condemns it in every manifestation; originality is irresponsible freedom to him. It is for this reason that he consigns Blake to limbo while hanging on to Pascal for dear life. Blake, says Eliot, is home-made religion. Eliot stays within the shadow of his theological law, which shelters his politics, his religion, and his esthetics.

How then is one to deal with his poetry without bringing in such terms as 'mythic form,' the 'objective correlative,' the 'auditory imagination,' the 'dissociation of sensibility,' the 'Tradition,' and fifty or sixty other concepts which are supposed to explain his poetry to us? The answer is by dealing with the poetry as poetry, as if Eliot had never published a single line of critical theory or laid down a single law or set up a single guidepost to 'correct' taste. Ignore the criticism, if possible. Eliot's criticism, like all literary criticism, has a place in the seminar room in the philosophy department; let's keep it there. How it ever got out is a biographical question which we will leave to anyone daring enough to violate Eliot's fiat against biography. I take it that Eliot is mainly responsible for the modern taboo against literary biography, one of his less publicized fields of propaganda.

In another section of these notes I have made a distinction between criticism and judgement. The strategic purpose of Eliot's criticism was to prevent judgement; that is the purpose of the criticism which he gave birth to (called the New Criticism), to replace judgement by theory. Eliot's own judgement is seldom shown, governed as it is by precept. His intellectualization of feeling and taste led him to such twisted judgements as the praise of Kipling and the execration of Whitman, the approval of Donne and the disparagement of Milton, and to pronouncements such as 'the novel died' on such and such a date. One of Eliot's followers, taking a suggestion from the master, writes a long, seemingly 'objective' account of the weaknesses of the poetry of D.H. Lawrence. Lawrence had committed the horrible sin of expressing his own feelings in poetry. Instead of following 'the discipline of a rationally constructed imagination,' Lawrence *expresses*. If only, this critic complains, Lawrence had learned to use 'controlled hysteria' like Eliot. And so forth. ('Controlled hysteria' strikes me as an accurate description of Eliot's poetry from an amateur psychology point of view, but the critic in question, R.P. Blackmur, egregiously takes Eliot's tightly buttoned-up pathology to be the normal state of affairs for poetry.)

To Eliot and Pound, with their provincial and educated horror of the unlettered and the spontaneous, the idea of a large or mixed audience was unspeakable. Throughout the criticism of these two leaders of modern taste the audience is constantly defined as a danger to the *status quo*. Pound, for example, in making up his booklist for converts to his criticism is even suspicious of the ballad. He cannot explain to himself that the ballad may be and probably is the product of the 'unliterary' mind; he distrusts Shakespeare for the same reason. Eliot's own plays, of course, are addressed to a good sound upper-middle-class audience, British preferably, even though a couple of his dramatic works have a popular appeal. Eliot must get quite a chuckle out of that.

In discussing Eliot's or Pound's idea of the audience (or what they would call the *function* of literature, in their strangely mechanistic language) one runs into the old danger of bogging down in points of doctrine and definition. It is no exaggeration to say that Eliot's criticism contains a definite plan of action, leading from a theory of poetics to political philosophy and covering all the intermediate stages. I will come back to this matter in my remarks on Yeats and Pound and their part in the religion of modern poetry. As far as the audience is concerned it is enough to say Eliot and Pound have not really had one—Eliot not until a few years ago, Pound never. The public has consistently rejected all of the poetry of 1915–25 from the beginning and has ignored both the poetry and its scales of values. In the voluntary withdrawal of the audience, the critics have created an academic audience, that is, a captive audience. The true audience, when it is allowed to grow, may of course reach all levels of appreciation from the lowest to the highest; it is ever the job of the poet to address himself to the present *condition* of the audience and to the language of that audience. Eliot and Pound have both attempted to find the language of their time: both have failed miserably and have succeeded only in constructing parodistic copies of the language. (This is the cogent argument of William Carlos Williams against both poets.) Eliot's style of deliberate plagiarism is the first symptom of failure to locate the language—in his case a lifelong admission of defeat. Modern poetry is macaronic because, in fact, it is not linguistically modern at all. It is high time we related the Pound-Eliot antiquarianism in ideas to the antiquarianism of their styles. Pound uses more archaisms than the Poet Laureate of Florida.

I am going to deal with only a sample of the most typical and celebrated poems of Eliot's, from 'Prufrock' through the *Quartets*, trying to *judge* these poems as if Eliot had never written any criticism. I judge them from the point of view of writing, on the assumption, which is to me a certainty, that all English-speaking people can appraise their worth as English poetry. This is the way poetry has always been read—without criticism or in spite of it. I disregard, as far as possible, Eliot's talk about the form of this and the form of that. I am confident that my judgments of these poems as poetry, not as sociology or esthetics, is extremely close to the judgments of nearly all readers of modern poetry who have not been conditioned by the criticism.

'The Love Song of J. Alfred Prufrock'—this is probably Eliot's best poem and is a little masterpiece of its kind. It is highly unoriginal in content and in style, based as it is on the rhythms, the attitudes, and sometimes the very lines of minor Symbolist poets like Corbière and Laforgue. Rhythmically it is the most successful of Eliot's poems, possibly because it was conceived as a dramatic unit. The meter is varied within the conventional English line, and the rhyming is superb. There is every indication that at the time of composition (age twenty-three) Eliot still took seriously the customs of English prosody and was trying in earnest (i.e., without irony) to develop this technical side of our poetry. The general tone of the poem is that of polite sophisticated ennui, an essay in self-mockery. The literary allusions in the poem, not counting the epigraph, are of the most obvious nature. This poem does not offend on the side of Culture. The epigraph from Dante purportedly throws a special light on the meaning of the poem; it is the epigraph which critics talk about most and which teachers teach. This quotation is gratuitous, a meaningless decoration; later it becomes the actual method of the Eliot poem. The difficulties of the poem, which are intentional, are not insurmountable, say, to a reader quite conversant with poetry tending toward the baroque or self-conscious. 'Prufrock' is a poem *about* self-consciousness. The split personality of Prufrock creates the chief obstacle to a first understanding of the poem. The other primary difficulty is imagistic, but this is also the main virtue of the poem. The famous opening image of the evening prostrate 'like a patient etherized upon a table' is one of the most brilliant examples of the poetry of exhaustion; very possibly it is a variation of Baudelaire's statement that the sexual act is like a surgical operation. Eliot's poem, however, is humorous rather than vicious and develops a kindly pathos to the very end. The imagery of the poem is all related to suggestion, a watering-down of the extreme suggestiveness of 'effect' of poets like Mallarmé and Poe, and is, in fact, a retreat from official Symbolism. (Eliot would already be conscious of all the 'historical' possibilities of his 'position.') 'Prufrock' is a masterpiece of a 'period,' the high point of Eliot's poetry. It is a true poem and also an experiment in criticism. It is a true poem by virtue of a personal content, which we can only guess at, for Eliot is always more sensitive about the autobiographical than any other writer I know of. But many things in the poem point to the so-called objectification of experience; even after Eliot airs to the public his problem of the personal and the impersonal, Life versus Art. The figure of Hamlet in 'Prufrock' he finds particularly expressive of his own dilemma, even though Prufrock disclaims a true identity with the Prince. But Hamlet is the figure who makes an art of indecision. Indecision leads to thinking things over, soliloquizing, becoming an intellectual. Eliot's poetry all turns to talk. As it goes on through the years it becomes nothing but talk, and talk about the kind of poetry that comes closer and closer to talk. Technically, the poem prefigures all the criticism, with its debates about the personal and the impersonal, the more and more 'objective,' the great struggle toward 'unified sensibility' and what not.

Eliot's failure as a poet is his success as a critic. Prufrock as a character is of no intrinsic interest but he is of high *literary* interest to all. In this poem Eliot has remained close enough to a human footing to make poetry out of a personal complex of crises, private, social, and intellectual. Had he written nothing else he would be remembered for this masterly little poem.

The 'Portrait of a Lady' is also a young poem, written apparently at the time of 'Prufrock.' The 'Portrait,' however, is not a textbook piece; it is too much of a love poem. It is not as good a poem as 'Prufrock,' actually, because it has the tone of adolescence rather than the tone of a prefigured worldliness, as in 'Prufrock.' In the 'Portrait' the woman is made fun of; she is wiser but inferior to the young Eliot; the poem leaves the reader nothing much to dwell upon except its excellence of execution. It appears to be one of Eliot's many exercises in tone. The epigraph in this case is a falsification. Eliot takes three lines from Marlowe's *The Jew of Malta*, the meaning of which he distorts for his own purpose. The lines are these:

> *Thou hast committed—*
> *Fornication: but that was in another country,*
> *And besides, the wench is dead.*

These three lines are actually part of a long involved dialogue; two people are speaking, not one. Eliot does not mean to convey that only one person is speaking, but he must for convenience gloze over the sense of the play. Eliot exegetes can retrace the quotation and explain that a friar is accusing the traitorous Jew, Barabas, of a series of crimes and that the Jew is evading answering; in the same way the Eliot in the poem is evading answering the questions of the woman. Psychologically this kind of thing can become so involved that everything reverts back to the meaning of the *quotation*. This is the crux of the Eliot poem, as we well know: how does the quotation fit the poem? Very shortly the matter is reversed and the question becomes: how does the poem fit the *quotation*? The beauty of the 'Portrait' testifies to Eliot's residual interest in the poem, not in its possible intellectual overtones; the quotation (virtually a misquotation) also indicates the poet's concern about what he writes rather than what he quotes. But the quote is also a loophole for the meaning of the poem, permitting Eliot to evade his meaning or permitting critics to elaborate it.

In both of these poems Eliot displays a mastery of sound and rhythm which marks the poet of genius. The rhyming is dazzling, a mixture of shock (the use of near-comic pairs such as Pole-soul) and the much more subtle effect of nonrhyme, such as we find in 'Lycidas.' It is almost, but not quite, apparent that Eliot at the beginning of his career is playing the weary virtuoso. But this is not sufficient, either for Eliot or for the literary scene. There is not much to be gained by becoming another Anglo-American Laforgue.

The remaining poems of this early style are even more 'French' than the longer ones, but more satisfying evidently to Eliot. 'Preludes' introduces the typical sordid furniture of the Eliot world, a Baudelairean rather than Laforguean world. The poem is a series of images evoking despair and disgust. The popularity of the poem comes from its seriousness, the transference from youthful, well-educated ennui to a genuine, if not very thoughtful, revulsion for all those people 'raising dingy shades in a thousand furnished rooms.' Eliot here imports the clichés of nineteenth century French poetry about the wickedness (i.e., mediocrity) of the modern city. 'Rhapsody on a Windy Night,' a much more convincing poem, dramatizes and symbolizes the horror of the city. Eliot has already found the Culture of the modern city; by simply recording its images (a broken spring in a factory yard, a morsel of rancid butter, the tooth-brush hanging on the wall) he evokes a cultured response—the response of the *avant-garde* reader to society. It is assumed, without having to say so, that the modern city is a degeneration of the Past. *Now he knows what to say*: the housemaids have 'damp' souls; people await the evening paper for want of something better, the old order changeth and Cousin Nancy has taken to smoking; the poet is quietly rejecting both the present and the immediate past—the American past.

The first really literary poem comes in this phase also. (I use the term 'literary' opprobriously.) 'Mr. Apollinax' marks the new Eliot; the Greek epigraph becomes an integral part of the poem, an explanation of it; and there is no attempt to provide links from the reader's experience to the cultural cues. The meter begins to break and the rhymes are now artfully coarsened (afternoon-macaroon). Mr. Apollinax is something of a pagan oracle to Eliot and a Priapic figure, but not to the Boston professors who entertain him. The poem is inferior to the 'Rhapsody' in every way; it is already a culture poem and an exercise in footnoting.

Eliot's reputation to a large extent is based upon the poems of this early period, and rightly so. 'Prufrock,' 'Portrait of a Lady,' 'Preludes,' and the 'Rhapsody' are among his best works. Of these 'Prufrock' is head and shoulders above the rest and is sufficient to justify Eliot's claim as one of the most gifted twentieth-century poets. At the same time it is extremely close to *vers de société*, as the first reviewers were aware (and first impressions are generally valuable in literary criticism), while the other poems mentioned are almost mannerist in their attention to theory and precedent. These are true weaknesses and Eliot is evidently conscious of their defects, the proof being that he deserts these forms for new ones.

In the next phase we find the majority of the poems in pedantic and ironic quatrains. There is one attempt at a 'major' form, as the critics say, in the poem 'Gerontion,' and there are several poems in French, which certainly cannot be judged as English poems. The quatrain poems introduce Sweeney and various minor characters in Eliot's pantheon. In this group there is also the extraordinarily crude anti-church poem named 'The Hippopotamus,' one of those surprising lapses of Eliot's which almost equal his good poems in number. Equally crude is the embarrassing anti-Jewish poem 'Burbank with a Baedeker,' a typical utterance of the modern 'classical' school. Eliot's anti-Semitism, which I am not going to discuss, is connected with his view of American commercial wealth: Bleistein is 'Chicago Semite Viennese' and he is described in disgusting physical detail. It is interesting to note that as Eliot's feelings become more violent and shocking the epigraphic matter becomes more talky and deranged. The quotation affixed to this poem is a hodgepodge of a French poem, a Latin motto, something from Henry James, something from Shakespeare, something from Browning, and something from Marston. It is as obscure as the quatrains are clear. The Chicago Shylock and the British baronet with a Jewish name have taken back Venice, according to this culture lyric. Stylistically and otherwise there is little virtue in the piece.

Stylistically there is little or nothing of value in all the quatrain poems, 'Sweeney Erect,' 'A Cooking Egg,' 'Whispers of Immmortality,' 'Mr. Eliot's Sunday Morning Service,' and the famous 'Sweeney Among the Nightingales.' In these poems Eliot is exploring the possibilities of character symbols; most turn out to be mere caricatures and do not appear again. Sweeney survives as a representation of Eliot's dim view of modern man. Eliot tries humour in the poems, if humour is the proper word (a highly polysyllabic bumbling kind of pseudo-British joking); and this he alternates with scenes of horror and disorder made ironical by the propriety of the meters. The close of the 'Nightingale' poem is said by critics to mark a high point of nobility, why I am not sure, unless it is that Eliot leaves off 'Rachel *née* Rabinovich' and switches to Agamemnon and the Convent of the Sacred Heart. These closing lines, if indeed they are serious, are cheap rather than noble and so poorly articulated that they can barely be pronounced. These poems show a drastic falling-off from the poet's earlier work. (I have said nothing of the complexities of cultural allusion in these poems; most people know them and accept them as part of the rocky road to modern poetry.)

'Gerontion' is usually placed high among Eliot's works; but it is not much better than 'Mr. Apollinax' and is in fact an extension of that poem in its manner. In order to escape a derivative Symbolism, Eliot has settled on the borrowing of quotations. Without a knowledge of the sources the poems sound more or less unified; the quotations themselves remove some of the author's responsibility for what the poems say. Eliot was here working out a method for a kind of poem which would implant certain ideas and images in the reader's mind, almost as if Eliot himself had nothing to do with the poem. The use of quotation without reference has a further advantage: it creates a specialized class of readers; I am quite serious when I say that Eliot is here providing texts for a new academic faculty. In the same way as Pound he is trying to solve an educational problem. But 'Gerontion' is also a personal catechism of the poet's religious hopes and doubts and is part of his spiritual autobiography. Its best feature is the rhetorical accretion of the same grammatical form and the use of meaningless but suggestive names. The theme of the youthless-ageless man, which is Eliot's one contribution to symbology, is advanced again, as in all his earlier poems. There is in 'Gerontion' a careful propoganda for Eliot as a symbolic figure, the poet deep in thought, seated among the ruins of the ages, longing for a salvation which will suit his intellect as well as his desires for spiritual comfort.

The Waste Land is the most important poem of the twentieth century, that is, the one that has caused the most discussion and is said by critics to be the culmination of the modern 'mythic' style. The poem, by Eliot's own admission, is a collaboration with Pound. Pound edited it and removed a third or two thirds of it. The 'continuity,' we can assume, is therefore the work of Pound, who abhorred continuity in his own more ambitious poetry. As everyone knows how to read the poem or can find out by visiting the nearest library, I will say nothing about its meaning. I will speak rather of the success and the failure of the poem. That it is lacking in unity is obvious (assuming, as I do, that unity is a literary virtue). Any part of *The Waste Land* can be switched with any other part without changing the sense of the poem. Aside from the so-called 'mythic' form, which is worthless and not even true—for Eliot misread James Joyce's *Ulysses* when he saw it as a parallel to Homer— the underlying unit of the poem is tonal and dramatic, exactly as a Victorian narrative poem would be. Eliot tries to conceal this indispensable literary method by mixing languages, breaking off dramatic passages, and by dividing the poem into sections with titles. But what really keeps the poem moving is its rhetoric, its switches from description to exclamation to interrogation to expletive, sometimes very beautifully, as in the passages beginning 'Unreal City.' The straight descriptive passages are weak: 'A Game of Chess' is one of the dullest and most meretricious of Eliot's writings, indicating his own dissatisfaction with that kind of verse. The dialogue, on the other hand is generally good. The best moments of all are the image passages, where the images are set in dramatic tonalities: 'What the Thunder Said' is the finest of these. The very worst passages are those which are merely quotes; even Eliot's most abject admirers can find no justification of the last lines of the poem, with its half-dozen languages and more than half a dozen quotations in a space of about ten lines.

The Waste Land, because of its great critical reputation, not because of any inherent worth it might have, is one of the curiosities of English literature. Its critical success was, I dare say, carefully planned and executed, and it was not beyond the realm of possibility that the poem was originally a hoax, as some of the first readers insisted. But hoax or not, it was very shortly made

Early Poems and *The Waste Land*

the sacred cow of modern poetry and the object of more pious literary nonsense than any modern work save the *Cantos* of Pound. The proof of the failure of the 'form' of this poem is that no one has ever been able to proceed from it, including Eliot himself. It is, in fact, not a form at all but a negative version of form. It is interesting to notice that in the conventional stanzas of the quatrain poems Eliot is more personally violent and ugly about his own beliefs; in his unconventional style the voice of the poet all but disappears and is replaced by characters from his reading.

The emergence of Eliot's piety in 'The Hollow Men' and in *Ash Wednesday* takes the form of self-disgust in the one and self-pity in the other. 'The Hollow Men' is in every way a better poem than *The Waste Land*, though the parodistic style again enforces a poverty of statement and language which become the marks of self-imitation in Eliot. *Ash Wednesday* is probably even more laden with gratuitous quotation than *The Waste Land*, but its ecclesiastical imagery and richness of music give the poem a beauty which the poet can finally accept as beauty. Eliot here luxuriates in the emotions of piety and surrender which seemed shameful to his Puritan soul in a purely human situation. The Eliot-God equation, once he has made the daring step, gives him an intellectual emotional balance for the first time in his career. After the publication of this poem, Eliot's former work seems more of a piece and his future work is all laid out for him, everything from church pageants to Christmas-card poems. The *Ariel Poems* are relatively simple and almost narrative. The rest of the poems are shelved under 'fragments,' minor pieces, and unfinished experiments. Eliot's career as a poet virtually comes to a close with *Ash Wednesday*. After that there is criticism, theology, and drama. The *Four Quartets* is the only attempt at what modern criticism calls a 'major' poem—meaning a poem that deals with Culture wholesale. The *Quartets* were hailed by the Eliot critics as his crowning achievement; actually they are evidence of the total dissolution of poetic skill and even a confession of poetic bankruptcy. Eliot is quite open about this in the *Quartets*.

The *Quartets* are Eliot's bid to fame as a 'philosophical poet.' In it he expounds his metaphysics, his poetics, and his own place in the scheme of things. All of this is quite legitimate and not at all surprising; what is disturbing about the poems is their commonplaceness, their drabness of expression, their conventionality, and, worst of all, their reliance on the schoolbook language of the philosophy class. Eliot has traded poetry for the metaphysical abstraction, as in *The Waste Land* he had traded narrative for 'myth.' This development is psychologically consistent, a descent from French Symbolism to Metaphysical complexity-for-the-sake-of-complexity, to pastiche, to the myth-science of *The Golden Bough*, to philosophical abstraction without poetic content. It all ends in the complete abandonment of poetry. When he comes to the drama in earnest he knows, of course, that he must use human language and he begins a new ascent into literature and the voices of poetry. But the *Quartets* lie at the bottom of the literary heap. All the so-called lyric sections, with one or two exceptions, are written with such disregard for the ear that one cannot associate them with the Eliot of 'Prufrock' or the 'Rhapsody.' 'Garlic and sapphires in the mud/Clot the bedded axle-tree' is typical of this diction devoid of both image and music. Eliot, who used to condemn poets like Tennyson for what he called crudeness of feeling, here shows an insensitivity toward language which is marvelous. The more prosy passages are even voided of that kind of poetry which rises from the use of imagery or sound. As for the philosophical development, it fails to reach a state of poetry, and it may fail as philosophy—of this I am no judge. The much-quoted third section of 'East Coker' about everyone going into the darkness, even people in the Almanach de Gotha and the Stock Exchange Gazette, is possibly the best passage of a long, very bad piece of writing; one feels that here there is an acceptance of the badness of the writing, as if good writing no longer held any meaning for the poet. The 'lyric' section that follows contains a stanza ('The whole earth is our hospital/Endowed by the ruined millionaire . . .') which in its vulgarity of thought and expression is hardly superior to 'Only God can make a tree.' For the rest there is a kind of narcissistic figure of the aging Eliot lolling through the poem, the climactic Dante imitation in 'Little Gidding,' and finally the magnificent passage 'Sin is Behovely, but/All shall be well . . .' Unfortunately these glorious lines are not Eliot's but are one of his borrowings. In general, the *Four Quartets* appears to be a deliberately bad book, one written as if to convince the reader that poetry is dead and done with. We should remember Eliot's lifelong interest in the final this and the final that, and at least entertain the possibility that the *Four Quartets* were intended to stand as the last poem in the Great Tradition. Eliot and Pound have both shown themselves capable of such arrogance.

I have now said all the wicked things I can think of about Eliot and it remains at last to say something favorable. At the beginning of these remarks I mentioned one phase of Eliot's work in which I regard him as a true poet and a man of rich spiritual insight. While I cannot feel that Eliot has contributed anything to the spiritual advancement of our age, I am convinced that he tried. But why is it that his own poems are rubrics rather than works of art? What are they for? What are they trying to say? Is it really all just sociology, reactionary politics, bitterness, spite and despair? I think not. I have spoken of the apparently deliberate erosion of his great gifts, leading to the final desertion of poetry. And I have touched on Eliot's lapse into religion. Here is a capital puzzle for the critic.

My solution to the puzzle is this. The motivating force in Eliot's work is the search for the mystical center of experience. This search in his case has been fruitless and increasingly frustrating. Eliot's entire career is a history of his failure to penetrate the mystical consciousness. He begins as a youth with Symbolism when it is already a dying religious-esthetic *mystique*. He moves from Symbolism to the Metaphysical poets of the seventeenth century.

(Neither the dictionary nor modern criticism explains what it is that interested Eliot in these poets, for it certainly was not extreme metaphorical technique or what the textbook calls the conceit.) Eliot was fascinated by the Metaphysical poem because it is virtually a demonstration of prayer. Nearly all the Metaphysical poets were Divines, men deeply troubled by the new scientific knowledge. What Eliot studied in their poetry was the possibility of fusing sacred with secular knowledge in poetry. Metaphysical poetry lies close to absurdity because it is premised on this peculiar dualism. We recall also that Eliot associated the fairly recent French poet Laforgue with the English Metaphysicals, for at one time it seemed to Eliot that a keen enough wit might serve as a key to the door that refused to open. But neither Symbolism nor Metaphysical sacred poetry offered a way to Eliot, even when he tried a fusion of the two. Third, he attempted secular mythology as a way to penetrate the mystical consciousness. It was in this phase that he wrote *The Waste Land*, a poem which is a jumble of sacred and 'profane' myths, adding up to nothing.

Meanwhile, both Eliot and Pound had discovered T.E. Hulme, whose essays provided written authority for them both, in different ways. Every major doctrine of Eliot's can be found in Hulme's *Speculations*, the most basic the one that relates fundamental Christian doctrine to a theory of society and a theory of poetics. Hulme formulated for Eliot the attack on Romanticism and the attack on mysticism (for the Romantic and the mystical are always related, while the Classical and the orthodox are related in their ways, at least in the critical mind). Hulme pointed the way for Eliot to orthodoxy in letters and to ritual and dogma in the spiritual realm. I consider Hulme's book as the *Mein Kampf* of modern criticism and a thoroughly evil work; and it was Eliot's undoing. For after the assimilation of Hulme, the rest is elaboration. Except for one thing: the search for the mystical center of experience goes on. Eliot worries it in Dante, in the Hindu scriptures, in St. John of the Cross, and in Julianne of Norwich. But poets of more recent vintage who come closer to mysticism infuriate Eliot, and he pours out his scorn on Blake, Lawrence, Whitman and our own Transcendentalists. Yet it is eternally to Eliot's credit that he does not fake the mystical (as he seems to accuse Blake of doing) and it is also to his credit that he does not relapse into magic and spiritualism, as Yeats did. It appears that Eliot is not even acquainted with esotericism; at least he does not even seem to be conscious of the esoteric meaning of the Tarot, which he uses in *The Waste Land* for 'fortunetelling.'

The failure to achieve mystical consciousness (which indeed is one of the rarest achievements in mankind) drove Eliot back to metaphysics proper and to religion proper. This in my view is the great failure of Eliot. Eliot ends up as a poet of religion in the conventional sense of that term. And once having made the religious commitment he tried to visualize a religion-directed society; he thus becomes an official of the most conservative elements of society and a figurehead for all that is formalized and ritualized. Yeats's fascination for the Byzantine betrays the same spiritual conservatism, as does Pound's fascination for the corporate state and the leadership principle. And Eliot ends his quest with his caricature of the modern poet-priest or psychiatrist-priest who alone has power to allay the Eumenides. Witch-hunting runs through Eliot from beginning to end.

Eliot is a poet of religion, hence a poet of the second or third rank; he is a thoroughgoing anachronism in the modern world, a poet of genius crippled by lack of faith and want of joy. I believe in Blake's proverb that 'the road of excess leads to the palace of wisdom.' Had Eliot ever set foot on that road he might have been as great a seer as Whitman or Rimbaud or even Dylan Thomas.

110
The Defeatism of *The Waste Land**

DAVID CRAIG

T.S. Eliot's *The Waste Land* is one of the outstanding cases in modern times of a work which projects an almost defeatist personal depression in the guise of a full, impersonal picture of society. Lawrence's *Women in Love* is a much more substantial case of the same thing, but the response it demands is much less easy. Both, however, in my experience, encourage in readers, especially young students, a sort of superior cynicism which flatters the educated man by letting him feel that he is left as the sole bearer of a fine culture which the new mass-barbarians have spurned and spoiled. Eliot has characteristically slid out of responsibility in the matter by means of his remark that *The Waste Land* pleased people because of 'their own illusion of being disillusioned'.[1] But, I suggest, the essential (and very original) method of his poem and the peculiar sense of life which it mediates are such that they invite that very response—and get it from the most considerable critics as well as from young cynics.

Before considering *The Waste Land* itself, it will be as well to quote a case of that view of the modern 'plight' which the poem has licensed, or seemed sufficient grounds for. Summing up the social state of affairs which he sees as the basis for the poem's 'rich disorganisation', F.R. Leavis writes: 'The traditions and cultures have mingled, and the historical imagination makes the past contemporary; no one tradition can digest so great a variety of materials, and the result is a break-down of forms and the irrevocable loss of that sense of absoluteness which seems necessary to a robust culture.'[2] This is suggestive, and 'that sense of absoluteness' implies a more felt idea of what modern rapid change has done to us than is usual in admirers of 'the organic community'. But consider what it leads on to:

In the modern Waste Land

> *April is the cruellest month, breeding*
> *Lilacs out of the dead land,*

**Critical Quarterly* 2 (1960), pp. 241–52.

Studies of *The Waste Land* and poems

> but bringing no quickening to the human spirit. Sex here is sterile, breeding not life and fulfilment but disgust, accidia, and unanswerable questions. It is not easy today to accept the perpetuation and multiplication of life as ultimate ends.[3]

The logic of this is by no means consecutive: the critic is moving with shifts which seem not quite conscious, between life itself and the poem treated as a report on life. When he writes, 'Sex here is sterile', although the immediate reference of 'here' seems to be the world of the poem, the quick shift to 'today', which must refer directly to real life here and now, suggests that Dr. Leavis considers the experience in *The Waste Land* a self-evident, perfectly acceptable version of the world we and the poet live in. That is the kind of assumption, and the pessimistic thought behind it, which I wish to challenge.

The technique of *The Waste Land* is very various; it gives the impression (compared with, say, Pound's *Cantos*) of rich, or intensely-felt, resources both of literature and of life direct. But one method stands out: that way of running on, with no marked break and therefore with a deadpan ironical effect, from one area of experience, one place or time or speech or social class, to another. Section II, 'A Game of Chess', throws shifting lights on the woman protagonist by changes of style. At first Cleopatra is present, but a Cleopatra who lives in an indoor, lifelessly ornate setting:

> *The Chair she sat in, like a burnished throne,*
> *Glowed on the marble, where the glass*
> *Held up by standards wrought with fruited vines*
> *From which a golden Cupidon peeped out*
> *(Another hid his eyes behind his wing)*
> *Doubled the flame of sevenbranched candelabra*
> *Reflecting light upon the table as*
> *The glitter of her jewels rose to meet it . . .*

By this point she has become Belinda from *The Rape of the Lock*, living in a world of 'things', make-up, dress, *bijouterie*—in Veblen's phrase, conspicuous consumption. But the modern poet does not have a mocking relish for the woman, as did Pope:

> *This casket India's glowing gems unlocks,*
> *And all Arabia breathes from yonder box.*
> *The tortoise here and the elephant unite,*
> *Transform'd to combs, the speckled and the white.*
> *Here files of pins extend their shining rows,*
> *Puffs, powders, patches, Bibles, billet-doux.*

By the end of the equivalent passage in *The Waste Land*, the woman is not even Belinda, moving with assurance in her idle, expensive world. She is a neurotic who cannot stand being alone with her own thoughts—a type psychologically and socially akin to Eveline Hutchins who kills herself at the end of John Dos Passos's trilogy *U.S.A.* The change is given in the shift from a quite richly 'literary' diction—

> *Under the firelight, under the brush, her hair*
> *Spread out in fiery points*
> *Glowed into words, then would be savagely still—*

to a bitty, comparatively unshaped, modern spoken English (though the repetitiveness is cunningly stylised):

> '*My nerves are bad to-night. Yes, bad. Stay with me.*
> '*Speak to me. Why do you never speak? Speak.*
> '*What are you thinking of? What thinking? What?*
> '*I never know what you are thinking. Think.*'

The effect is of landing up with final disenchantment face to face with the unpleasant reality of life today.

There is then, in mid-section, a change of social class, from wealthy life ('The hot water at ten./And if it rains, a closed car at four') to ordinary ('When Lil's husband got demobbed, I said . . .'). But life is fruitless here too, and the poet's aloof revulsion is conveyed by similar means. The working-class women in the pub talk about false teeth, abortions, promiscuous sexual rivalry between the wives of Great War soldiers, in a lingo which sprawls over any kind of formal elegance of metre or rhyme; and the poet does not intrude on the common speech until the closing line:

> *Goonight Bill. Goonight Lou. Goonight May. Goonight*
> *Ta ta. Goonight. Goonight.*
> *Good night, ladies, good night, sweet ladies, good night, good night.*

'Sweet ladies'—the irony is, to say the least, obvious. As well as the effect of 'sweet' there is the reminiscence of the innocently hearty student song (this seems more relevant than Ophelia's mad snatch in *Hamlet*). The effect is identical with what he does by incorporating Goldsmith's ditty from *The Vicar of Wakefield* at the end of the typist's dreary seduction in 'The Fire Sermon':

> '*Well now that's done: and I'm glad it's over.*'
> *When lovely woman stoops to folly and*
> *Paces about her room again, alone . . .*

This technique, which is typical of the transitions of tone and of the collation of two cultures which occur throughout the poem, seems to me unsatisfactory in two ways. The irony is no finer than ordinary sarcasm—the simple juxtaposing of messy reality and flattering description (as in a common phrase like 'You're a pretty sight'). The pub women and the typist have been made so utterly sour and unlovely that the poet's innuendo, being unnecessary, does no more than hint at his own superior qualities. Secondly, using earlier literature to embody the better way of life which is the poet's ideal depends on a view of the past which is not made good in the poem (it hardly could be) and which the reader may well not share—unless he is pessimistic. Consider some further instances. The Thames as it is now given thus at the beginning of 'The Fire Sermon':

> *Sweet Thames, run softly till I end my song.*
> *The river bears no empty bottles, sandwich papers,*
> *Silk handkerchiefs, cardboard boxes, cigarette ends*
> *Or other testimony of summer nights . . .*

The life evoked here is unpleasant—but so is the poet's attitude, notably the pointed but prudishly or suggestively tacit hint at contraceptives. At the same time, for us to respond as the poet means, we have to accept his glamourising view of Spenser's London, Elizabethan England with its pure rivers and stately ways. The same suggestion occurs in the lyrical passage which is meant to parallel the Rhinemaidens' song from *Götterdämmerung*. Modern:

> *The river sweats*
> *Oil and tar*
> *The barges drift*
> *With the turning tide . . .*
> *The barges wash*
> *Drifting logs*
> *Down Greenwich reach*
> *Past the Isle of Dogs.*

Renaissance:

> *Elizabeth and Leicester*
> *Beating oars*
> *The stern was formed*
> *A gilded shell*
> *Red and gold*
> *The brisk swell*
> *Rippled both shores . . .*

The poet's meaning is clear: modern civilisation does nothing but spoil what was once gracious, lovely, ceremonious, and natural.

Here it must be said that the poet's comparative view of old and modern culture is not quite one-sided. As Hugh Kenner suggests, it may not be implied that Spenser's nymph-world 'ever existed except as an ideal fancy of Spenser's',[4] and as Cleanth Brooks suggests, the Elizabeth passage has 'a sort of double function': historically, Elizabeth flirted so wantonly with Leicester, in the presence of the Spanish bishop de Quadra, that Cecil at last suggested that as there was a bishop on the spot, they might as well be married there and then (Froude's *Elizabeth*, quoted in Eliot's note). As Brooks says, the passage 'reinforces the general contrast between Elizabethan magnificence and modern sordidness: in the Elizabethan age love for love's sake has some meaning and therefore some magnificence. But the passage gives something of an opposed effect too: the same sterile love, emptiness of love, obtained in this period too: Elizabethan and the typist are alike as well as different.'[5] In the whole poem, however, it is certainly old magnificence which is given the advantage, and it is as well to say straight out that this is an absurdly partial outlook on culture—groundlessly idealising about the old and warped in its revulsion from the modern. If magnificence is desired, modern life can supply it well enough, whether the show of Royalty or big-business ostentation. And if one thinks of the filth, poverty, superstition, and brutal knockabout life invariable in town or country four centuries ago, one realises how fatuous it is to make flat contrasts between then and now. History, reality, are being manipulated to fit an escapist kind of prejudice, however detached the writer may feel himself to be.

As one would expect, the cultural warp has as strong an equivalent in the poet's way of presenting personal experience. Consider the attitudes implied in the seduction of the typist. In this most cunningly-managed episode, one is induced to feel, by means of the fastidiously detached diction and movement, that a scene part commonplace, part debased, is altogether unpleasant. The experience is a more intimate meeting between people than Eliot deals with directly anywhere else in his work, but here is the style he finds for it:

> *He, the young man carbuncular, arrives,*
> *A small house agent's clerk, with one bold stare,*
> *One of the low on whom assurance sits*
> *As a silk hat on a Bradford millionaire.*
> *The time is now propitious, as he guesses,*
> *The meal is ended, she is bored and tired,*
> *Endeavours to engage her in caresses*
> *Which still are unreproved, if undesired.*
> *Flushed and decided, he assaults at once;*
> *Exploring hands encounter no defence;*
> *His vanity requires no response,*
> *And makes a welcome of indifference.*

The unfeeling grossness of the experience is held off at the finger-tips by the analytic, unphysical diction—'Endeavours to engage her in caresses'—and by the movement, whose even run is not interrupted by the violence of what is 'going on'. The neat assimilation of such life to a formal verse paragraph recalls Augustan modes. But if one thinks of the sexual passage concerning the 'Imperial Whore' in Dryden's translation of Juvenal's sixth Satire, or even the one concerning the unfeeling Chloe in Pope's *Moral Essay* 'Of the

Characters of Women',[6] one realises that the Augustans did not stand off from the physical with anything like Eliot's distaste. Eliot's style is carefully impersonal; it enumerates with fastidious care the sordid details:

On the divan are piled (at night her bed)
Stockings, slippers, camisoles, and stays.

But here one has doubts. This is given as a typical comfortless modern apartment, suggesting a life which lacks the right pace, the right sociableness, the right instinctive decency for it to merit the name of civilisation. (Were Elizabethan houses and habits any better?) But the touch in the second line feels uncertain: is the heavily careful art with which the line is built up not too contrived for the rather ordinary modern habit it is meant to satirise? When we come to 'carbuncular'—an adjective which, placed after the noun and resounding in its slow movement and almost ornamental air, is deliberately out of key with the commonplace life around it—I think we begin to feel that Eliot's conscious literariness is working, whatever his intention, more to hold at arm's length something which he personally shudders at than to convey a poised criticism of behaviour.[7] There is a shudder in 'carbuncular'; it is disdainful, but the dislike is disproportionately strong for its object; queasy emotions of the writer's seem to be at work.[8] The snobbery is of a piece with this. 'He is a nobody—a mere clerk, and clerk to a *small* house agent at that. What right has *he* to look assured?' That is the suggestion; and we are also left wondering what warrant the poet has for uniting himself with some class finer, it seems, then the provincial bourgeoisie. And the passage ends with the snatch of Goldsmith, 'When lovely woman stoops to folly':

She smoothes her hair with automatic hand,
And puts a record on the gramophone.

Here the nerveless movement and the ordinariness of the detail are deftly managed. And the human poverty of the scene has never been in doubt. But the writer's means of conveying *his valuation* of it are surely objectionable. One may agree or not that modern civilisation has its own kind of health; one may agree or not that the petty bourgeoisie are a decent class. But one must surely take exception to a method which seeks its effects through an irony which is no more than smart sarcasm. It is amazing that Dr. Leavis should speak of 'delicate collocations',[9] when the contrasts are regularly so facile in their selection of old grandeur and modern squalor.

To put the matter in terms which refer directly to life: if, as Brooks says, 'the same sterile love, emptiness of love, obtained in this period too', then why does the criticism work so consistently against contemporary civilisation? And when Dr. Leavis says, 'Sex here is sterile', does he really mean that love between men and women has deteriorated as a whole? (One remembers similar extraordinary suggestions about intercourse now and formerly in *Lady Chatterley's Lover*.) The historian tells us that in Renaissance England,

> Wife-beating was a recognised right of man, and was practised without shame by high as well as low. Similarly, the daughter who refused to marry the gentleman of her parents' choice was liable to be locked up, beaten, and flung about the room, without any shock being inflicted on public opinion. Marriage was not an affair of personal affection but of family avarice, particularly in the 'chivalrous' upper classes.[10]

I think we may take it that the comparison of cultures to the advantage of the older is either impossible, pointless, or else feasible only by specific fields and not overall.[11] The question remains why critics have surrendered so gratefully to an almost nastily despairing view of the civilisation we live in. This occurs in Leavis's *New Bearings* and Edmund Wilson's *Axel's Castle*.[12] It is seen at its most irresponsible in Hugh Kenner's glib explication of the pub scene: 'If we move from the queens to the pawns, we find low life no more free or natural, equally obsessed with the denial of nature, artificial teeth, chemically procured abortions, the speaker and her interlocutor battening fascinated at second-hand on the life of Lil and her Albert, Lil and Albert interested only in spurious ideal images of one another.'[13] 'Battening fascinated at second-hand' means no more than 'listening with interest to the tale of someone else's experiences': Mr. Kenner's condemnation comes from the general atmosphere of moral depression which the poem generates rather than from anything established by the dramatic speech of that scene—here the critic's sourness outdoes the poet's. And the reference to false teeth, lumped with abortions, as though false teeth were not simply an admirable achievement of medical science in giving comfort where nature has broken down, is a glaring case of that blind dislike of science which nowadays has become an intellectual's disease. It is primitivist; and it thoughtlessly ignores the experience involved.

Dr. Leavis's adherence to the old culture is much more scrupulously worked out, and must be considered by itself. A key term in that part of *New Bearings* (as in his early *Scrutiny* editorials) is 'continuity':

> In considering our present plight we have also to take account of the incessant rapid change that characterises the Machine Age. The result is breach of continuity and the uprooting of life. This last metaphor has a peculiar aptness, for what we are witnessing today is the final uprooting of the immemorial ways of life, of life rooted in the soil . . . There are ways in which it is possible to be too conscious; and to be so is, as a result of the break-up of forms and the loss of axioms noted above, one of the troubles of the present age. . .[14]

Now it would be foolish to burke the truth that the rapid disruption started by the Industrial Revolution undermined, and actually demoralised, the masses who were uprooted from the country and flung into the towns. But there are ways and ways of viewing this change—defeatist ways and constructive ways. The description of the old village culture which opens

Engels's *Condition of the Working Class in England in 1844*[15] is remarkably similar to the main 'line' of *Scrutiny*; it belongs to the same humane tradition of protest at the harrow of industrialism. But realisation of such sufferings and social deterioration may lead on to a practical will to reconstruct, using the new social instruments, or it may lead on to a really helpless fixation on the past which comes from a distaste for the raw difficulties and uncomeliness of the life around us. An outlook which assumes the fineness of the older culture belongs to the defeatist class. Dr. Leavis of course cannot back up his assumptions in a book mainly on modern poetry. But if we are to keep our thought grounded, we must notice that the obverse could be stated to every one of the advantages he sees in the 'organic' culture. Marx and Engels no doubt went too far the other way when they referred summarily to 'the idiocy of rural life'.[16] But when we speak of immemorial ways of life, we must remember how cramped a range of vocations they offered: consider the release of wider human talents made possible by the growth of technology and of organisation (both treated as evils by the *Scrutiny* critics). The village life was socially healthy in various ways, but it also ground down people cruelly: consider the lives of Burns and Gorky. When 'axioms' are mentioned, we must remember that they reflected fixed habits which held human possibilities in rigid bounds. I have suggested that it is futile to draw up an overall comparison between the old and contemporary types of culture. This is partly because we are now as we are; we have the means we now have; it is these alone that we can use. Therefore the only positive course is to co-operate with the hopeful present trends. No-one saw more piercingly into the anti-human effects of industrial labour as it once was than Marx; but he knew that that was the very means by which we must win through to the *new* good life. He gives this balance of possibilities in passage such as these from *Capital*, vol. 1:

> Modern Industry, on the other hand, through its catastrophes imposes the necessity of recognising, as a fundamental law of production, variation of work, consequently fitness of the labour for varied work, consequently the greatest possible development of his varied aptitudes ... Modern Industry, indeed, compels society, under penalty of death, to replace the detail-worker of today, crippled by lifelong repetition of one and the same trivial operation, and thus reduced to the mere fragment of a man, by the fully developed individual, fit for a variety of labours, ready to face any change of production, and to whom the different social functions he performs, are but so many modes of giving free scope to his own natural and acquired powers.

(As a step towards this he then cites the setting up of agricultural and technical schools.) And again:

> However terrible and disgusting the dissolution, under the capitalist system, of the old family ties may appear, nevertheless, modern industry, by assigning as it does an important part in the process of production, outside the domestic sphere, to women, to young persons, and to children of both sexes, creates a new economical foundation for a higher form of the family and of the relations

between the sexes . . . the fact of the collective working group being composed of individuals of both sexes and all ages, must necessarily, under suitable conditions, become a source of humane development . . .[17]

The Waste Land, then, seems to me to work essentially against life, for the range of opinions it mobilises, that come welling up in response to it, are all negative. In the final section Eliot uses the philosophy of F.H. Bradley. The lines

> *I have heard the key*
> *Turn in the door once and turn once only*
> *We think of the key, each in his prison*
> *Thinking of the key, each confirms a prison . . .*

he himself glosses from Bradley's *Appearance and Reality*:

> My external sensations are no less private to myself than are my thoughts or my feelings. In either case my experience falls within my own circle, a circle closed on the outside; and, with all its elements alike, every sphere is opaque to the others which surround it . . . In brief, regarded as an existence which appears in a soul, the whole world for each is peculiar and private to that soul.[18]

This thought of Bradley's has led on to that barren line of philosophy which includes John Wisdom's *Other Minds*. To say what must suffice here: if our sensations, thoughts, and feelings are perfectly private and the sphere of each person's life 'opaque', how is it that speech and literature are intelligible—and intelligible so fully and intimately that to reach understanding with a person or appreciate a piece of writing can seem to take us inside another existence? That the question of whether one mind can get through to another should even have arisen seems to me a perversion of thought. (Historically, it is perhaps a cast from the anti-co-operative state of existence brought about by entrepreneur capitalism. It seems similar to the helplessly solipsistic 'denial of objective truth' which Lenin refutes in *Materialism and Empirio-Criticism*. In each case the individual ego relies less and less on anything outside itself.)

The obscurity of *The Waste Land* is significant likewise, for though the trained reader no longer jibs at it, it is certainly impossible that it should ever become popular reading as did earlier important literature (Burns, Byron, George Eliot, D.H. Lawrence). Dr. Leavis writes on the issue of 'minority culture' which this raises: 'that the public for it is limited is one of the symptoms of the state of culture which produced the poem. Works expressing the finest consciousness of the age in which the word "high-brow" has become current are almost inevitably such as to appeal only to a tiny minority'.[19] The argument that follows is dubious at a number of points. In the first place, Lawrence expressed many sides of the 'finest consciousness of the age' and he has been read in the cheap editions by the million (as has Gorky in the Soviet Union and James T. Farrell in the United States). The usual obstinately pessimistic reply is that 'They only read Lawrence for the sex, or the love story'. But this is only reaching for another stick to beat the times, for is it not good that a major writer should have devoted himself to the universal subjects of love and sex? Dr. Leavis goes on to say that the idea that the poem's obscurity is symptomatic of our cultural condition 'amounts to an admission that there must be something limited about the kind of artistic achievement possible in our time'. But if this were so, how account for the work of Lawrence and of the many other considerable novelists of our time? Finally his question 'how large in any age has the minority been that has really comprehended the masterpieces?' contains an equivocation—'really'. If one sets the highest standard, of course 'real' (that is, full) comprehension is attained by few; but if the numbers of even the *total* public reached are small, as has happened with *The Waste Land*, then there is indeed a significant difference between its meaningfulness and appeal for readers and that which the major novelists have regularly achieved (George Eliot, Hardy, Lawrence, Tolstoy, Gorky, Farrell). *The Waste Land*, in short, is *not* the representative work of the present age, and to make it so implies that pessimistic view of the present age which I have already challenged.

What has been made of *The Waste Land* illustrates two more issues important in our times. It is significant that Dr. Leavis should meet the charge that the poem is a 'dead end', literarily and morally. When he says, 'So complete and vigorous a statement of The Waste Land could hardly . . . forecast an exhausted and hopeless sojourn there',[20] he implies a proper distinction between Eliot's quality of art and that of Pound's *Cantos* or Joyce's *Ulysses*—both recognisably from the same line of art distorted by the break-up of cultural forms. *The Waste Land*, it is true, does not cut life into bits and juggle them into patterns interesting only for their intricacy, or meaningful only to their manipulator. At the same time there turns out to be little that Dr. Leavis can plead convincingly when he has to say what way beyond The Waste Land Eliot found. He quotes some bracing sermons from the *Criterion*: 'a tendency—discernible even in art— towards a higher and clearer conception of Reason, and a more severe and serene control of the emotions by Reason', and 'the generation which is beginning to turn its attention to an athleticism, a *training*, of the soul as severe and ascetic as the training of the body of a runner'.[21] The vague 'dedication' of this recalls the loftiness with no definite direction which characterised the more serious of the *fin de siècle* writers, notably Yeats, when they were being Hellenic or religiose. Its abstractness, its lack of reference to any social facts, suggests Eliot's inveterate drift away from anything progressive in society with which he might have co-operated in a practical way.[22]

The wider affiliations of such defeatism come out in the agreement Eliot and Leavis reach on 'eastern Europe'. Eliot's note introducing the final section of the poem says: 'In the first part of Part V three themes are employed: the journey to Emmaus, the approach to the Chapel Perilous (see

Miss Weston's book) and the present decay of eastern Europe'.[23] This is very bland. The final phrase has that characteristic air of stating the unanswerable—he would explain further if he wished but he does not condescend to. Actually it must have behind it the most reactionary politics. How did Bela Kun's Communist régime in Hungary, for example, represent decay? or is Eliot sympathising with the Russian Tsars?[24] Dr. Leavis's interpretation is still more unacceptable: 'These "hooded hordes", "ringed by the flat horizon only", are not merely Russians, suggestively related to the barbarian invaders of civilisation . . .'[25] Eliot's poem, we need only recall, was being written when the civilised armies of Britain, America, France and Japan were invading Russia on twenty-three fronts.[26] But there is nothing with which the pessimistic liberal *can* associate himself—neither the new civilisation which is being founded in the East nor the ordinary life of the West which he is so ready to write off.[27]

Notes

1. T.S. Eliot, *Selected Essays* (ed. 1951), 'Thoughts after Lambeth', p. 368.
2. *New Bearings in English Poetry* (ed. 1950), pp. 90–1.
3. *New Bearings*, p. 93.
4. *The Invisible Poet: T.S. Eliot* (New York, 1959), p. 165.
5. Cleanth Brooks, Jr., '*The Waste Land*: An Analysis': *Southern Review* (Louisiana State University, Summer 1937), Vol. 3, No. 1, p. 123.
6. Dryden, 'The Sixth Satyr' of Juvenal, 11, 161–89; Pope, 'Of the Characters of Women', 11, 157–70.
7. Compare Lawrence's analysis of Thomas Mann: 'Thomas Mann, like Flaubert, feels vaguely that he has in him something finer than ever physical life revealed. Physical life is a disordered corruption against which he can fight with only one weapon, his fine aesthetic sense, his feeling for beauty, for perfection, for a certain fitness which soothes him, and gives him an inner pleasure, however corrupt the stuff of life may be . . . And so, with real suicidal intention, like Flaubert's, he sits, a last too-sick disciple, reducing himself grain by grain to the statement of his own disgust, patiently, self-destructively, so that his statement at least may be perfect in a world of corruption.' (See *Pheonix*, ed. Edward D. Macdonald, 1936, p. 312).
8. Compare 'The young are red and pustular' (from 'Mr. Eliot's Sunday Morning Service': *Collected Poems*, 1909–1935, ed. 1946, p. 53).
9. *New Bearings*, p. 112.
10. G.M. Trevelyan, *A Shortened History of England* (Pelican ed., 1959), p. 196.
11. An interesting suggestion has been made by the Communist Party Historians' Group that, as it is desirable that history should be taught as 'a matter of cause and effect, and, too, of human progress; as opposed to the view that history has nothing to teach, no meaning nor pattern', it should be taught through the history of technique 'because progress in this field is clear . . . there is never total retrogression'. ('The Teaching of History': *Marxism Today*, January 1959, p. 30).
12. (New York, 1936), p. 106.
13. *The Invisible Poet*, p. 156.
14. *New Bearings*, pp. 91, 93–4.
15. See Marx and Engels *On Britain* (Moscow, 1953), pp. 35–8.
16. *The Manifesto of the Communist Party* (Moscow, 1957), p. 55.
17. Trans. Moore and Aveling (New York, Modern Library), pp. 534, 536.
18. Note to 1.411: *Collected Poems*, p. 84.
19. *New Bearings*, p. 104.

Studies of *The Waste Land* and poems

20. *New Bearings*, pp. 113–14.
21. *Ibid.*, p. 114.
22. Compare Edmund Wilson's sensible criticism of Eliot's set of reactionary slogans, Royalist, classicist, and Anglo-Catholic: see 'T.S. Eliot and the Church of England', *The Shores of Light* (1952), [pp. 437–41.]
23. *Collected Poems*, p. 82.
24. Various touches suggest that he moves naturally amongst upper-class émigrés, e.g.
    Bin gar keine Russin, stamm' aus Litauen, echt deutsch.
    And when we were children, staying at the arch-duke's . . .
    (Section 1: Poems, *p. 61)*
25. *New Bearings*, p. 101.
26. This episode is summarised and placed by R. Palme Dutt in his *World Politics, 1918–1936* (1936), pp. 45–6.
27. Compare L.C. Knights, who argues straight from the debased mass madia to the mentality of the people themselves: 'Those Elizabethans who never got beyond Deloney, even those who remembered nothing of *King Lear* beyond the action and a couple of bawdy jokes, were not doomed to pass their lives in the emotional and intellectual muddledom of the readers of the *Daily Mail*'. ('Elizabethan Prose': see *Drama and Society in the Age of Johnson*, ed. 1951, pp. 313–14).

111
Eliot: The Poetics of Myth*

ROY HARVEY PEARCE

In 1932 Pound, as was his habit, set his readers straight about the meaning of his own work and Eliot's:

> [Mr Eliot] displayed great tact, or enjoyed good fortune, in arriving in London at a particular date with a formed style of his own. He also participated in a movement to which no name has ever been given.
> That is to say, at a particular date in a particular room, two authors, neither engaged in picking the other's pocket, decided that dilutation of *vers libre*, Amygism, Lee Masterism, general floppiness had gone too far and that some counter-current must be set going.[1]

In Eliot's work the counter-current, as Pound testified later in the same essay, did not really begin to move until that (apocryphal?) particular date in a particular room. Still, there were sufficient anticipatory and prefigurative signs of the movement.

The protagonists of the poems collected in *Prufrock and Other Observations* (1917) are such as to manifest the very exhaustion of the ego which set Pound and Eliot to searching for a new (or, as they came to insist, renewed) poetic mode. The 'Lady' whose 'Portrait' Eliot draws is like someone out of E.A. Robinson; but there is in this poem none of the precision and self-defeating honesty of Robinson's best portraits. Observing his Lady, listening to her, meditating her fate, the poet concludes:

> *Well! and what if she should die some afternoon,*
> *Afternoon grey and smoky, evening yellow and rose;*
> *Should die and leave me sitting pen in hand*
> *With the smoke coming down above the housetops;*
> *Doubtful, for a while*
> *Not knowing what to feel or if I understand.*

This is honest enough, but really not very clear. Indeed, such clarity as the poem has resides in its epigraph, from *The Jew of Malta*:

*From *The Continuity of American Poetry* (Princeton, New Jersey, 1961), pp. 296–318.

290

> *Thou hast committed—*
> *Fornication; but that was in another country,*
> *And besides, the wench is dead.*

We gather that it is that other country which the poet cannot understand. Obviously lacking in 'Portrait of a Lady' is the motivating force, the sense of the human situation, which will make for continuity and integral, not to say organic, form. Eliot could not (would not?) endow the speaker with such insight into motivation as would make of the poem that sort of whole composition in which one part leads to and demands the next. In short, from the very beginning the autobiographical mode, much less the narrative, has simply not been Eliot's *métier*.

If it be objected that the whole of Eliot's work is the record of a spiritual autobiography, I would grant the objection and then point out that spiritual autobiographies derive their motivating force not from the lesser spirits whose autobiographies they are but from a greater spirit which informs the lesser—from history, or myth, or God. As a matter of fact, in the long run Eliot's sense of that greater spirit, being increasingly motivated thus, is much surer than Pound's; for in Pound that greater spirit tends, in spite of his efforts in the *Rock-Drill Cantos* and later, increasingly to reflect merely 'the cultural' and can be formulated and objectified in terms whose adequacy no one but Pound can judge.

As 'The Love Song of J. Alfred Prufrock' is in every way the other side of the coin from 'Portrait of a Lady,' it manifests the fact that the countercurrent was moving even before Pound began to have his influence on Eliot. The epigraph from Dante defines the limiting situation of the poem. From the beginning we are given the self-portrait of a man who knows his own inadequacy to draw it and suffers accordingly. The 'metaphysical' conceits in the poem are appropriate to this man for whom formal ratiocination must take the place of simple, spontaneous thought, analysis the place of the exercise of the sensibility. Prufrock's is yet another exhausted ego, able to celebrate, in pathetic irony, only its own exhaustion. Choosing such a one for his protagonist, Eliot can in bitter pity reveal to us Prufrock's abject inferiority to even 'the women [who] come and go / Talking of Michelangelo,' not to say the Hamlet who, in so far as he can bring himself to have one, is his ego ideal. The poet surely is not Prufrock; yet Prufrock is surely an aspect of the poet's sensibility, one which must carry its self-exhaustion to the end, so that there will be achieved that spiritual vacuum which only a greater spirit can fill. The formal achievement of this poem, since it has come to be archetypal for the formal achievement of so many other poems, is one which we too easily fail to see: In 'Prufrock' Eliot measures the failure of a modern sensibility in the very terms which, so he believes, will, after the failure has been measured and faced up to, constitute its means to success. One's residual impression is neither of a protagonist, a poem, nor a poet, but of a force which teaches the last to care enough for the first so that he can destroy him in the second. As early as 'Prufrock,' then, Eliot knew how to care and not to care.

For the poet writing in this mode, the formal problem is one of sustaining the nice tension between caring and not caring—looking to that restoration of modern man from the ruins of nineteenth-century egocentrism, while yet not strengthening his ego so much as to set him once more on his way to his own ruination. Eliot's search for the means to this end is well known, as are the means themselves. The search and the means discovered are recorded in a vast literature of exegesis and redaction. Techniques, models, sources, parallels, and the like—Eliot had recourse to them, because only they could furnish him the means of defining, as opposed to creating or re-creating, the modern ego. Indeed, he has gone so far as to minimize his own ultimate role as the maker of his poems, as though this might smack of that fatal egocentrism. The emphasis in his criticism, and that which his has so greatly influenced, has been on the poet as 'craftsman,' not 'maker.'

The history of Eliot's poetry before his major achievement, 'The Waste Land' (1922) is the history of a technique, a technique which would make possible the restoration of the idea of man as the creature, not the creator, of his world. In the course of events, that world would turn out not to be his after all. Most important here are the Sweeney poems and the kind they exemplify: hyperallusive, written in a quatrain imitated from Gautier, with a diction modeled after Laforgue's; in a tone recalling Donne's; and intended to carry over some of the disciplined rigor and inclusiveness of sensibility of all the poets whose work they echo. The Eliot of the Sweeney poems, as we have been often told, is the poet of the unification (following upon the dissociation) of the modern sensibility. But he would show that the means whereby to strive for that unification have been given to him and are by no means his alone. At one extreme is 'Burbank with a Baedeker: Bleistein with a Cigar.' Here, beginning with his inordinately complex epigraph (drawing from at least five writers), Eliot views with rather heavy-handed irony the descent into meaninglessness of one European tradition. At the other extreme, is 'Sweeney among the Nightingales,' in which the American, savage and vulgar in his blind egocentrism, is defined in relation to a larger, alien kind of order in which he cannot participate. Such poems are dazzling, to be sure; but they suffer from their own sort of over-insistence and do not quite avoid the ambiguous dangers of their kind. For their protagonists are so exhausted of their egos as not to be persons at all, just functions of their creator's understandable anxiety about the state of the world and those who inhabit it.

'Gerontion' (1920), which seems originally to have been intended to be part of 'The Waste Land,'[2] is the first of Eliot's great poems in the mode he has made both his own and his culture's. Here Eliot begins to move from denial for the sake of denial to denial for the sake of affirmation. The mode is one in which the effect is not of creating but of being created. This is the basic style of the poem of the counter-current and compares with that of, say, Emerson's poems as do the *Cantos* with *Song of Myself*. In 'Gerontion,' as in 'Prufrock,' there is a delicately balanced portrayal of a protagonist against the backdrop of his world; still, he exists only in so far as he can 'use' the elements of that backdrop in composing his so wearily pathetic song of himself. As the poem develops, the backdrop comes to have much more substantiality than does he who places himself (or should one say: is placed?) against it. The form of the poem is set initially by the tension of protagonist against background and finally by the collapse of that tension, as the protagonist loses himself in the background. The title indicates that the modern ego is characteristically that of an old man (like Tiresias in 'The Waste Land'), living out his dry days, bravely allowing his sense of the past to tell him what he is and, in the telling, to overwhelm him. He dreams of the juvenescence of the year in which 'Came Christ the tiger.' This Christ is not yet God; he is rather the Christ-figure of 'The Waste Land': one among several who manifest that gift of grace and order for which modern man yearns and which he yet fears. In this poem Eliot comes to see that his problem, modern man's problem, is one of a history, his own, which man cannot forget. The cluttered memories which fill the old man's mind are fused into a single pattern because, adding up to his history, they define the single pattern of his life. We do not look for him to initiate his thoughts and work them through; he is his thoughts; he is, in the end, *only* his thoughts, his memory, his history.

Here, most clearly, the Adamic principle of nineteenth-century American poetry is foresworn; or rather, here Adam is taken to be modern man's ancestor in historical fact, not an ever-contemporary, ever-possible image after which he must model himself:

> *After such knowledge, what forgiveness? Think now*
> *History has many cunning passages, contrived corridors*
> *And issues, deceives with whispering ambitions,*
> *Guides us by vanities. Think now*
> *She gives when our attention is distracted*
> *And what she gives, gives with such supple confusions*
> *That the giving famishes the craving.*

This, as it has often been observed, was the lesson into which Henry Adams (whose work is alluded to in 'Gerontion') educated himself. He too came to believe that the American ego, like that of all modern men, was about to exhaust itself and its potential for creativity. With Eliot, he too could say, 'We would see a sign!' The sign would not only signify the destiny of man, now ready to face fully up to his fate; it would *be* that destiny and that fate. In 'Gerontion' the ego learns to submit itself to history, so to achieve a modicum of definition and understanding. But beyond 'Gerontion' there are

'The Waste Land,' 'Ash Wednesday,' and *Four Quartets*. Beyond history, there is myth, and then—but only then—God's Word. Part of Eliot's greatness as a poet is the result of his extraordinary honesty with himself and his language. Having always been superbly conscious of what he has been about, Eliot early furnished the appropriate glosses. The first is from 'Tradition and the Individual Talent' (1919): 'What happens [to the poet] is a continual surrender of himself as he is at the moment to something which is more valuable. The progress of an artist is a continual self-sacrifice, a continual extinction of personality.'

The second is from his essay on William Blake (1920):

> Had [Blake's gifts] been controlled by a respect for impersonal reason, for common sense, for the objectivity of science, it would have been better for him. What his genius required, and what it sadly lacked, was a framework of accepted and traditional ideas which would have prevented him from indulging in a philosophy of his own, and concentrated his attention upon the problems of the poet . . . . The concentration resulting from a framework of mythology and theology and philosophy is one of the reasons why Dante is a classic, and Blake only a poet of genius. The fault is perhaps not with Blake himself, but with the environment which failed to provide what such a poet needed; perhaps the circumstances compelled him to fabricate, perhaps the poet required the philosopher and mythologist. . . .

The third is from his essay on *Ulysses* (1923):

> In using the myth, in manipulating a continuous parallel between contemporaneity and antiquity, Mr. Joyce is pursuing a method which others must pursue after him. They will not be imitators, any more than the scientist who uses the discoveries of an Einstein in pursuing his own, independent, further investigations. It is simply a way of controlling, of ordering, of giving a shape and a significance to the immense panorama of futility and anarchy which is contemporary history. . . . Instead of narrative method, we may now use the mythical method. It is, I seriously believe, a step toward making the modern world possible for art. . . .[3]

With such glosses Eliot projects the technique of his poetry into poetics.

The idea of a poetry grounded in myth entailed the idea of a poetry ordered and controlled by protagonists who were no more than, or as much as, *personae*—the alternative depending upon the reader's prior commitments. The *personae* of poems in the Adamic mode are in conception diametrically opposed to those in poems in the mythic mode. Whereas in the former, a *persona* is simply one of the shape-shifting forms the poet can assume, in the latter, a *persona* is a role—its design grounded in an order of being beyond any poet's shape-shifting powers—which the poet must discipline himself into playing. In the former, the protagonist must learn to take off his mask; in the latter, he must learn to put it on. Pound's *personae* (he gave this name, of course, to an early collection of his poems) are different from Browning's, who is said in this to be his great master, primarily as they are to be distinguished one from another. They are different too from Whitman's, since they derive from the poet's need to discover himself as possibly someone else, not from his need to discover everyone else as ultimately projections of himself, or of an inexhaustible communal self. Thus with Eliot's *personae* too—but in a more extreme sense than with Pound's. For Eliot—and surely this is an aspect of his final superiority to Pound—has been able to look outward, not inward, behind the *personae* which he believes it is man's inevitable obligation to assume. He has discovered for us again and again that he can make sense out of the obligation only if he can know truly who has put it upon man. Such knowledge is mythic knowledge; for the obligation, as Eliot's late poems understand it, comes from God; and the record of man's bearing up under it is part of that matrix of transhistorical narrative which is myth.

Thus Eliot's is *the* poetics of the counter-current. It constitutes a theory of the mythic poem; and a considerable portion of its force as theory is the product of a certain over-determination in the sensibility of its originator and those for whom he speaks. For the mythic poem—like its counterpart, the Adamic poem—is an over-determined poem. It asks too much of both its protagonists and its readers; for it asks them that they reject utterly the principle of personality (to recall the social scientist's terms) and as utterly opt for the principle of culture. It boldly faces the possibility (for by the time of the First World War it surely was at least a possibility) that the life-style projected by the Adamic poem might not be capable of coming to grips with the problems set for it by history, tradition, and orthodoxy. Rather, that style made for the shaping of personalities whose sense of the power of their own egos dulled, even obliterated, their sense of the power of the culture—the history, tradition and orthodoxy—which in such great part had made them what they were. They had thus broken off the continuity between their past and their present; and so, strictly speaking, the narrative whereby they might grasp that continuity was by now impossible. The extremity of the situation into which they had got themselves called for extreme measures. Now, in all his agony, modern man might see how the very loss of that continuity argued all the more for the need for its recovery. The only means, a means which Eliot quite frankly realized was extreme, was that surrender of the self whereby the hope for an immanent narrative was resigned in favor of a hope for a transcendent myth. Thus over-determination was quite consciously acknowledged to be the price for making the modern world possible for art.

In the light of such concerns, Eliot's relation to Whitman, like Pound's, marks an impasse, or crossroads, in the continuity of American poetry.[4] Eliot's pronouncements on Whitman indicate that the latter was the demon whose achievement it was to torment any American who would dare write poetry in any mode but his. Whitman wanted, so it seemed in retrospect, to transmute the forms of ordinary discourse into verse; his chief means of doing so was to emphasize and reinforce their rhythms by an extraordinarily varied and subtle use of parallelism and repetition. Eliot could not avoid being 'influenced' by Whitman in this matter—either directly or indirectly (indirectly as Whitman, like Poe, in effect tutored the French symbolist and post-symbolist poets who, as is well known, so much influenced Eliot). Moreover, as we shall see, when Eliot thought of Pound's achievement, he perforce thought of Whitman's. He would seem to have been aware of Pound's concern to do right what Whitman, for all his noble intentions, had done wrong.

Consider this single pair of examples. First, from Whitman's 'Song of the Open Road':

> *Allons! to that which is endless as it was beginningless,*
> *To undergo much, tramps of days, rests of nights,*
> *To merge all in the travel they tend to, and the days and nights they tend to,*
> *Again to merge them in the start of superior journeys,*
> *To see nothing anywhere but what you may reach it and pass it,*
> *To conceive no time, however distant, but what you may reach it and pass it,*
> *To look up or down no road but it stretches and waits for you, however long but it stretches and waits for you,*
> *To see no being, not God's or any, but you also go thither,*
> *To see no possession but you may possess it, enjoying all*
> *without labor or purchase, abstracting the*
> *feast yet not abstracting one particle of it...*
>
> *(Section 13)*

Compare:

> *To arrive where you are, to get from where you are not*
> *You must go by a way wherein there is no ecstasy.*
> *In order to arrive at what you do not know*
> *You must go by a way which is the way of ignorance.*
> *In order to possess what you do not possess*
> *You must go by a way of dispossession*
> *In order to arrive at what you are not*
> *You must go through the way in which you are not.*
> *And what you do not know is the only thing you know*
> *And what you own is what you do not own*
> *And where you are is where you are not.*
>
> *('East Coker,' III)*

There is in the passage from Eliot not only an echo of Whitman's phrasing but, more important, an echo of the metering of syntax—this last an aspect of Eliot's notion of the 'music of poetry.' ('My words echo / Thus, in your mind,' he wrote in 'Burnt Norton.') However it got to Eliot, the influence is obvious enough. The very obviousness lends all the more significance to the fact that Eliot 'uses' the Whitmanian style to deny the cogency and truth of what Whitman would say. Unlike Whitman's vocabulary even in this, for him, relatively 'contemplative' passage, Eliot's is here stripped bare, so that the repetitions are all the more insistent and the insistence all the more powerful. The Whitmanian mode is made to negate itself and generate its opposite; a wholly personal style takes on a grand impersonality. Where Whitman, as always, would 'merge all' in the image of himself, Eliot would order all so that, as the poem develops, he might catch a glimpse of the image of the Other. By the time of the *Quartets*, Eliot's mythic poetry had achieved the status of ritual, thus projecting in all its purity and inclusiveness the one myth which was, in its oneness, by definition not a myth. He had managed to use the Whitmanian sensibility, among many others, as a means of discovering that the Whitmanian 'content' involved an egocentric predicament so terrible that it could be resolved only by beginning all over again, at the beginning, with the Whitmanian ego and its basic style, and reaching out toward that Other to whose existence its predicament had blinded it. Thus in 1928, commending Pound's verse as genuinely 'original,' Eliot found it necessary to claim that Whitman, another originator, was only a great writer of prose and that the content of his work was in 'large part . . . claptrap.'[5] This is but a way of saying that Whitman's poetics was deficient because it kept him from achieving that orthodox, classical, even royalist view of life—deriving from what I have, following Eliot, called the mythic—which, as it should have made for the continuity of American life, so should have made for the continuity of American poetry. Eliot has been happier with Poe, whose torment he can interpret as a product of his being alienated by the sort of life in which Whitman seemed so much at home.

For Eliot the deficiency of American life—a deficiency characteristic of all mass-democratic life—was directly responsible for the deficiency of American poetry. The difference between him and his forebears in the continuity, however, lies not in the fact that he has discovered such a deficiency, for certainly they did too. Rather, it lies in the fact that he cannot, as they could, conceive of anything immanent in that life which might remedy the deficiency. He would attune himself to its rhythms, but he would then change them so that they would be in concord with something outside of American life—indeed, outside of all 'merely' human life. Pound has gone to history for his source of mythic renewal. Eliot has gone through history, so to go beyond myth.

The mythic poem, reflecting the grave lucubrations of its author, has deliberately asked too much of its readers. But, as Eliot's public career shows, it has also asked too much of itself: that it establish the transhistorical scaffolding upon which a strictly historical narrative of the origin and destiny of modern man might be erected; that, through it, tradition and a sense of the past might be recovered; that, in opposition to the Adamic poem and its rejection of the past for the present, it might show how the past and the present are inextricably involved in a single continuum. The mythic poem can indeed do all these things, but its maker cannot stop there. Being what he is, having to reject even the minimal claims of the Adamic poem, he too has created his own extreme situation, wherein he has had finally to reject the very history toward the reestablishing of whose force and meaning he originally directed his poetry. Rejecting history means to a degree rejecting also the very men whose history it is. If 'Gerontion' demanded 'The Waste Land,' then surely 'The Waste Land' demanded 'Ash Wednesday' and the *Four Quartets.*

'The Waste Land' has become such an assured part of the twentieth-century consciousness, one of the major vehicles for its sensibility, that we easily forget the transformation it worked. Realizing some of the possibilities latent in 'Gerontion,' it in effect at once proposed and confirmed a new basic style so powerful that the older basic style, charged deeply with egocentrism, would no longer be viable unless it met the challenge Eliot put to it.

The disparate materials of which 'The Waste Land' is composed are designed to lose their disparateness in the composing. Tiresias, the Fisher-King, Phlebas, the Thames maidens, and the rest—each participates in the life of the other, and so contributes to the single-minded effect of the poem: not because of what he is but because of what he manifests, negatively or positively, for good or for bad. Even the reader is made out to be one of the poem's *personae.* 'The Waste Land,' in so far as it succeeds in its intention, offers us everything—locales, *personae*, motifs, structure—everything but a poet assured in his ability to make a poem. Certainly the poet is there, as his wit, intelligence, and imagination are there. But he can *pretend* not to be, except as he is but one bootless protagonist among many such. This, in any case, is a principal attribute of his particular kind of make-believe: that the poet is there only so that he may compose a poem which, in the light of his ultimate vision, will make his existence unnecessary.

He makes Tiresias, his principal protagonist, into a shape-shifter, unstable, uncertain of the powers of his own sense and sensibility, his creativity lying in his wise passiveness. Tiresias is not at the center of the history which the poem epitomizes; he does not have the power to be at the center of anything. Nor is the effect that of Eliot's *giving* him such a power. Rather, Eliot's studies and his meditations appear to have taught him that such a protagonist must have existed at various times, his intelligence and his power for action determined by the situation in which he was placed. So it is with all the other materials—fragments of folk-lore, *belles-lettres*, myth, cultural history, and the like—which fill out the poem. The poet's genius is in so insistently seeming to have none. Even his 'modern' Tiresias, who opens the poem, is not endowed with the ability to 'do' anything. The poem, taken as a pronouncement on the nature of man, argues against the possibility of what I have called, in reference to Emily Dickinson, authentic autobiography. For such a possibility would inevitably argue the significance of the existence of the poet as a radically free self. The development of 'The Waste Land' is such as theoretically to do away with that self, actually to put it in its place, low in the scale of things. The poet ostentatiously removes himself from his poem. Such ostentation derives from his actual creative role, to be sure; still, it is such as to urge that we minimize his relevance to his creation.

Eliot's method in 'The Waste Land' is constantly to define the persons in the poem in terms of that which they are not. They cannot even directly conceive of that which they are not; they do not have the power to set going within themselves that process of action and reaction whereby they may begin to establish their own identity. They are denied even that last resort of the self-reliant, suicide. 'The Waste Land,' thus, cannot be self-contained. For if it were, it would *a fortiori* argue for the possibility that somehow one or another of its protagonists might in and of himself do or make something. That enormous range of allusiveness which has set so many exegetes to work is accordingly the central technique of the poem, as it is the means of preventing the self-containment which any single poem, written by any single man, might achieve merely by virtue of its singleness. This, of course, is the major technique of the *Cantos*, too, but with this difference: that Pound will so control the allusive quality of his poem that it will be sufficient unto itself and will thereby manifest the power of him who has made it so; hence the poet will set himself up, epically, as a hero whose condition of life is one toward which, in reading the poem, his reader may aspire.

In 'The Waste Land' Eliot sees more clearly than Pound ever has the direction in which a poet of his commitments must move. For example, there is the exquisitely contrived mélange of allusions at the end of 'The Burial of the Dead'—

> ... 'Stetson!
> *'You who were with me in the ships at Mylae!*
> *'That corpse you planted last year in your garden,*
> *'Has it begun to sprout? Will it bloom this year?*
> *'Or has the sudden frost disturbed its bed?*
> *'Oh keep the Dog far hence, that's friend to men,*
> *'Or with his nails he'll dig it up again!*
> *'You! hypocrite lecteur!—mon semblable,—mon frère!'*

The protagonist's friend Stetson, met on a London street, is identified as one who fought at the Battle of Mylae. This battle must be a mythic analogue to Jutland, surely; but the reference is to the battle at which Carthage was defeated and so serves to put the immediate fact of Jutland into deeper perspective. Then, as though the poet were trying to report the result of the battle, there is a corpse, treated half-graphically as buried in a vegetation ritual: so that the fact of death is not treated directly, but in the context of a ceremony which begins to make it meaningful. Then there is the twisted quotation from Webster, which, because of its source and provenience, at once marks the botching of a ritual and draws our attention to the poet's role

Early Poems and *The Waste Land*

as recorder, not creator. Then, if the reader, drawing a deep breath, has perhaps begun to sense how the carefully wrought consolidation of allusions does indeed argue for the creative presence of the poet, the last line transforms this argument into one for rather the creative presence of the reader. Yet, even this is managed indirectly, through an allusion to Baudelaire; so that the reader is not allowed to keep that private identity deriving from his sense of being 'involved' in the poem. Or rather, such private identity as the reader has is made out to be a product of his discovering something whose power, import, and significance derive from a source other than himself.

Strictly speaking, there is no individual action which can be *imitated* in this mythic poem. There is potentially a communal action, a ritual, but it is as yet one which can only be observed. Eliot is still the poet as philosophical anthropologist. The poems of the participative ritual were to come later. 'The Waste Land' made their coming inevitable. Interpreting the history of culture as a history of ritual forms, it postulated the existence of that single transcendent ritual in which alone the person would discover the power whereby he might move and act and be.

Such ritual, not directly participated in because considered as an historical-cultural rather than a theological fact, becomes explicitly the technique of 'The Waste Land' in the final part of the concluding section, 'What the Thunder Said.' There are the ritual words, listened to from afar and registered in a 'dead' language: *Datta, Dayadhvam, Damyata—Give, Sympathize, Control.* (True enough, these words are proved not *really* to be dead, for they have much to signify for us. The point, however, is that Eliot cannot find the properly ritualistic words in the language of any culture presently 'alive.') *Make,* much less *Create,* is not part of the poet's vocabulary. He has only the fragments which he has shored against his ruins, the materials out of a world now known to be mythic, transhistorical. Eliot comments thus on these last lines in his Notes: 'Cf. . . . F.H. Bradley, *Appearance and Reality,* p. 346. "My external sensations are no less private to myself than are my thoughts or my feelings. In either case my experience falls within my own circle, a circle closed on the outside; and, with all its elements alike, every sphere is opaque to the others which surround it. . . . In brief, regarded as an existence which appears in a soul, the whole world for each is peculiar and private to that soul."'

It has been customary to ascribe much of Eliot's concern for the limitation, isolation, and untrustworthiness of the self—the simple, separate person—to his reading of Bradley. This may well be so. But there is a larger dimension in which Eliot's poetry must be placed, that of the continuity of American poetry against which he so magnificently set himself and which, by virtue of doing so, he forever changed. The private world of the Adamic poet was a closed circle too; but it was said to include within itself all possible worlds. That possibility, it was believed, had simply to be brought to fruition by the creative act. But for the mythic poet, man's private world was so narrow and constrained that it had to be transcended. The power to such transcendence could not possibly reside within man—nor, as it develops in Eliot's later poetry, within history.

This, then, is the meaning of 'Ash Wednesday' (1930): 'Teach us to care and not to care.' 'Ash Wednesday' is an acolyte's poem. He would still learn to give, sympathize, and control; but now he grants fully that the way to such powers is the way of positive denial and discipline. He would learn to know and to love the world for what it is, so as to be able to renounce it fully. The fragmented, futile, anarchic world is to be transcended; history is to be comprehended mythically and thus also be transcended. But now the myth is mythic only to those of Eliot's readers who cannot assent to it. We are caught up in the paradox of mythic consciousness—that for those who believe in what we outsiders call a myth, it is not myth. The mythic truth of 'The Waste Land' was a truth pertaining to that area in the psychic cosmos at which historical process was touched and stabilized by a supervening theistic order. The fragments of history, understood mythically, manifested the fragmented consciousness of modern man. But in 'Ash Wednesday' mythic understanding itself is transcended, because it is discovered to be available to man directly, not mediated by the fragments of history. Myth begins to be absorbed into Christian doctrine and so gradually is bereft of its quality as myth. The poet now would drain himself of even his historical consciousness. He would leave behind even his image of himself as the myth-maker of 'The Waste Land':

> *At the first turning of the third stair*
> *Was a slotted window bellied like the fig's fruit*
> *And beyond the hawthorn blossom and a pasture scene*
> *The broadbacked figure drest in blue and green*
> *Enchanted the maytime with an antique flute.*
> *Blown hair is sweet, brown hair over the mouth blown,*
> *Lilac and brown hair;*
> *Distraction, music of the flute, stops and steps of the mind over the third stair,*
> *Fading, fading; strength beyond hope and despair*
> *Climbing the third stair.*
>
> *Lord, I am not worthy*
> *Lord, I am not worthy*
>   *but speak the word only.*
>   *(III)*

Thus the structure of 'Ash Wednesday' is tied to a continual, if at times only implicit, reference to the Christian doctrine which tells how through time man may transcend time. This is the opening of Section II:

> *Lady, three white leopards sat under a juniper-tree*
> *In the cool of the day, having fed to satiety*

Early Poems and *The Waste Land*

> *On my legs my heart my liver and that which had been contained*
> *In the hollow round of my skull. And God said*
> *Shall these bones live? shall these*
> *Bones live?*

The three white leopards and the lady—these are not quite Christian symbols, but almost. It is crucial for the meaning of the poem that at this stage they be not quite, but almost. For they exist somewhere between history and God. They are part of the poet's private myth—the myth which, by means of his prayerful discipline, he has come to envisage—and they lead to something beyond myth. The structure of the poem and its action work so as to make the poet's readers grant him the him the need and the power (a boon of his prayer) to make such a myth, but only in order to transcend it.

The poem, in fact, registers the dialectic of that prayer; it evokes a series of psychic states whereby the poet moves from 'Because I do not hope to turn again' to 'Although I do not hope to turn again.' 'Because' signifies that the poet is confined and constrained by the myths of his world. 'Although' signifies that he accepts his confinement and constraint and therein is on his way to the single myth, the only myth, the myth beyond myth, Truth. He no longer acts 'because'; he acts in spite of, 'although.' He grants his sad condition in his sad world, and so comes directly to apprehend and to confront his deepest need. The form and the rhythm of the poem are expressive of the poet's discovery and acceptance of his need. It is, in short, a need not to be himself, not to be in history, not to be bound even to the mythic structures of history.

The ruins of the self begin to be reconstituted into a whole; the principle of the reconstitution is not generally but particularly mythic. It finds its vital center in an absolute beyond myth—that revealed by Christian dogma. The poet must be lost, and his world and his history with him, so that he can be found:

> *And the lost heart stiffens and rejoices*
> *In the lost lilac and the lost sea voices*
> *And the weak spirit quickens to rebel*
> *For the bent golden-rod and the lost sea smell*
> *Quickens to recover*
> *The cry of quail and the whirling plover*
> *And the blind eye creates*
> *The empty forms between the ivory gates*
> *And smell renews the salt savour of the sandy earth*

This passage is from the last section of the poem. It comes at a point in the poet's meditations when he has begun truly to discover what he had long known: that only through abject submission and the surrendering of all that makes him a man might he transform his humanity—or rather, might he be granted the power to work the transformation. Only the blind eye can create. This is the only sort of creation proper to him who would learn to give, sympathize, and control. The insistent repetitions of the poem, held together merely by their loose parallelism, not controlled by the usual analytic devices of language—such repetitions insistently register the movement of the human spirit in the process of exhausting itself of its humanity, so to be filled with something larger. 'And let my cry come unto Thee' the poem concludes.

The weakness of 'Ash Wednesday,' if indeed it is a weakness, derives from its excessively meditative, disciplined manner. We are allowed to see how the poet disciplines himself into the discovery of a yet larger disciplinary force. This is at once a progress of the soul and a psychomachia. Yet there is nothing in the poem which we can conceivably imitate or recognize—nothing like the clearly etched allegorical figurations in medieval poetry. Likewise there is not much we can see.

Murder in the Cathedral (1935) marks the point at which Eliot holds in view at once the two kinds of poetry he was later to write: the extended meditation (*Four Quartets*) and the drama (*The Family Reunion, The Cocktail Party, The Confidential Clerk,* and *The Elder Statesman*). It is a kind of morality play, in which the element of dramatic conflict is subordinate to the supernatural force that makes the conflict meaningful. Eliot has not yet achieved that mastery of dramatic verse which, as in the later plays, renders language as a mode of action, almost beyond the limits of discourse; nor has he achieved that mastery of meditative verse which renders language as a mode of prayer, likewise almost beyond the limits of discourse. The main speeches have a quality somewhere between prayerful meditation and analysis. Unlike those in *Four Quartets*, they are not sufficiently counterpointed by lyric passages which will serve to mitigate the effect of analysis and so make them wholly prayerful. But the theme of renunciation of the earthly and human, thus of the strictly linguistic, is there:

> . . . *Neither does the agent suffer*
> *Nor the patient act. But both are fixed*
> *In an eternal action, an eternal patience*
> *To which all must consent that it may be willed*
> *And which all must suffer that they may will it,*
> *That the pattern may subsist, that the wheel may turn and still*
> *Be forever still*
>
> *(Part I)*

Here is that still point in the turning circle celebrated in the *Quartets*. But it is to be talked about, not yet to be apprehended, perhaps because these are the words of one of the tempters in the play.

To a degree, then, both 'Ash Wednesday' and *Murder in the Cathedral* are

Early Poems and *The Waste Land*

but records of the poet's spiritual exercise—steps, albeit necessary ones, toward the vision of *Four Quartets* (1943). 'Vision' is perhaps the wrong word; certainly, it is inadequate. Yet there is no essentially 'humanistic' word which can quite describe the *Quartets*, since they do not constitute a 'humanistic' poem. Systematically, Eliot explores sensory modes, but only to point to their transcendence; for the real subject of the poem is just beyond its limits. The transcendence, which at most can only be hinted at, is managed by the essentially 'musical' form of the poem. Words, images, concepts, rhythms—all are subordinated to a musical whole. *Seriatim*, they 'mean.' In the ensemble, they point beyond 'meaning.' There must be for the concord of language something analogous to, but not 'technically' imitative of, the concord of music. (This is the doctrine of his essay, 'The Music of Poetry,' 1942.) In a poem so conceived, words 'mean' only so that, when taken together, they may 'be.' This is the semantics of ecstasy.

Eliot is on surer grounds than most modern poets who conceive thus of their work. For the principle of being, as he makes his later poetry insist, is not man the creature but God the creator, Who is not bound by the limits of language, for Whom all is of necessity in concord. Eliot demonstrates, at however great a cost, that it is yet possible to write a poem in which it is the glory of the self to put its power for making poetry at naught; that a poem can be a means of pointing to the transcendence not only of humanity, but of human history and its potential for myth; that to be human might well mean to grant that to be human is to be next to nothing. He thus takes his place with the great religious poets of the Anglo-European tradition, against whose work, in a sense, so many American poets in their ineluctable egocentrism had set themselves. What marks him as somewhat different from the poets of the Anglo-European tradition is the very insistence and self-consciousness of his drive toward the religious poem: the progress of an American soul which, tearing the last shred of antinomianism out of itself, comes to grant that in the end nothing will be left, and is glad. Something *is* left, to be sure; the fact that there is a poem shows this. But we are exalted by our sense that, just one stage further, even this might be gone. In the *Quartets* we are told that the further stage is to be reached only by Saints—creatures of an order which the American mind, in its compulsive search for evidences of its own election in this world or another one, has been constitutionally unable to comprehend. Meantime, the poet can rest content with the narrow lot that his humanity bestows upon him, because he knows how to measure its narrowness and discovers exactly how much he has when the measuring is done. He has very little; but he knows there is more, beyond measuring. The mythic poem achieves its proper end: by its mythic force to transcend its mythic substance, to negate itself as myth, and to establish itself as a mode of acknowledging in all triumphant humility the existence of God from Whom all myths flow.

In retrospect, then, Eliot's early poetry seems not only to lead to but to require the *Quartets*. In 'The Waste Land' the technique is, through the use of allusive materials, constantly to shift perspectives on the contingent and substantial. In 'Ash Wednesday' the technique is, through the use of the repetitions inherent in disciplined meditation, to eliminate the contingent and substantial. In the *Quartets* the technique is, through the use of essentially musical forms, to transform the contingent and substantial into a mode of truth whose substance consists precisely in its non-contingency. Each of the four poems which make up the *Quartets* has the same form: a meditation on a 'philosophical' problem, which develops into an autobiographical recollection—one existing only to demonstrate its inadequacy to generate its own meaning; a lyric commentary, which develops into a 'psychological' meditation; another lyric, this one registering the victory implicit in the insight thus far gained; and a final meditation, rather impersonally autobiographical. In each case, the final meditation centers on the substantial problem of the particular poem; the problem has been solved, however, and now is in its solution known as an aspect of man's necessary relation to God. The problem throughout the poem, however, is the same—that of time, change, language, particularity, and universality: in all, the nature and destiny of that which, being bound to time and place, is specifically human.

The poet is unflinching in his confrontation of man's estate. Casting aside the individual, he searches for understanding in the communal. He makes his situation archetypal for every man and then rejects the archetype. It is given to the poet to know that a community subsists above all in its language. And yet he who knows language best discovers in the knowing that it is not enough:

> *Words move, music moves*
> *Only in time; but that which is only living*
> *Can only die. Words, after speech, reach*
> *Into the silence.*

and

> *So here I am, in the middle way, having had twenty years—*
> *Twenty years largely wasted, the years of* l'entre deux guerres—
> *Trying to learn to use words, and every attempt*
> *Is a wholly new start, and a different kind of failure . . .*

and

> *. . . all these are usual*
> *Pastimes and drugs, and features of the press:*
> *And always will be, some of them especially*
> *When there is distress of nations and perplexity*
> *Whether on the shores of Asia, or in the Edgware Road.*
> *Men's curiosity searches past and future*
> *And clings to that dimension. But to apprehend*

Early Poems and *The Waste Land*

> *The point of intersection of the timeless*
> *With time, is an occupation for the saint—*
> *No occupation either, but something given*
> *And taken, in a lifetime's death in love,*
> *Ardour and selflessness and self-surrender.*
> *For most of us, there is only the unattended*
> *Moment, the moment in and out of time . . .*

and

> *Every phrase and every sentence is an end and a beginning.*
> *Every poem an epitaph. And any action*
> *Is a step to the block, to the fire, down the sea's throat*
> *Or to an illegible stone: and that is where we start.*
> *We die with the dying:*
> *See, they depart, and we go with them.*
> *We are born with the dead:*
> *See, they return, and bring us with them.*

These passages are all from the fifth, and final, sections of the poems which make up the *Quartets*, in which the explicit theme of the poems centers on the faith that there is available to man—how little available is no matter—that understanding which comes when poetry is a means to communion. Thus these passages manifest aspects of the victory earned in each of the poems, and also the cost of the victory, as earlier sections of the poems manifest the means whereby it might be achieved and the quality of insight gained in the achieving. The quality of insight, marked by the lyrics which appear in the second section of each of the poems, cannot be held on to, but only recalled while its 'meaning' is searched out. The lyrics are too 'poetic' and the meditations which follow them too 'prosaic,' so that the 'meaning' of the poem develops as the reader feels himself caught between the tug of the poetic and the prosaic. The effect is to make the reader overwhelmingly conscious of the inadequacy of language to define, or even to suggest, the truth on which its very existence depends. Man's fate is again and again to learn this lesson, again and again to learn that language and his proud use of it—whereby he *is* man—is only a primer of consciousness. Man can never get beyond the first lesson. In his end, as the poem says repeatedly, is his beginning. But it is his by virtue of not being his, by virtue of being utterly beyond him. Yet if only he could reach it! Then he would know that it was the beginning of all men and all things, and also their end. This knowledge—this faith gained by Ash Wednesday meditations in the Waste Land—sustains the poet and makes his work possible. He would have us believe that it makes him possible, as it makes possible his conceiving of himself as possible.

Moreover, it makes all men possible. 'My words echo / Thus, in your mind,' says the poet in 'Burnt Norton,' telling us that his gift of language, his sensibility, is genuine only as much as he is able to make it summon up for us the Word which is beyond words—the Word which, through words rendered into music, he would evoke. This is the ultimate development of 'You! hypocrite lecteur!—mon semblable,—mon frère!' The task of the poet is, through a continuing exhaustion of his own sensibility, to let himself be filled (as much as any mortal can be) with such knowledge as will let him know the ground of his own possibility, a ground beyond language, beyond history, beyond myth, and therefore the ground of them all. The cost of such knowledge? Further knowledge—that poetry, even mythic poetry, like humanity, even mythic humanity, is but a necessary evil. After such knowledge, in the words of 'Gerontion,' what forgiveness indeed? Eliot's triumph, then, was, in conceiving of the mythic poem and our need for it, to confront with all honesty not only the meaning of the poem for us but also the meaning of the need.

Yet beyond the mythic poem at its most powerful there was yet a 'purer' form, the poem as drama. Eliot's plays are not our concern here. Still, I think that his statement of his rationale for them, in the essay 'Poetry and Drama,' 1951, should concern us, since it indicates with what magnificent self-consciousness he has been willing to follow out his commitments to the very end. The end of 'poetic drama' is impossible of achievement, he says, because it essays to do so much:

> . . . beyond the nameable, classifiable emotions and motives of our conscious life when directed towards action—the part of life which prose drama is wholly adequate to express—there is a fringe of indefinite extent, of feeling which we can only detect, so to speak, out of the corner of the eye and can never completely focus. . . . This peculiar range of sensibility can be expressed by dramatic poetry, at its moments of greatest intensity. At such moments, we touch the border of those feelings which only music can express. We can never emulate music, because to arrive at the condition of music would be the annihilation of poetry, and especially of dramatic poetry. Nevertheless, I have before my eyes a kind of mirage of the perfection of verse drama, which would be a design of human action and of words, such as to present at once the two aspects of dramatic and of musical order.

Noting the equations—human action: dramatic; word: musical—we understand how completely Eliot would move beyond language to ritual form. For 'ritual' is a word designating actions at their most formal, in which meaning is completely absorbed into form; and it has been maintained, moreover, that rituals 'precede' myths and make them necessary. Thus it would appear that Eliot has deserted poetry for poetic drama, because only in the latter can he hold steadily in view his 'mirage.' Only it *really* is not a 'mirage.' For the essay 'Poetry and Drama' ends with these words: '. . . it is ultimately the function of art, in imposing a credible order upon ordinary reality, and thereby eliciting some perception of an order *in* reality, to bring us to a condition of serenity, stillness, and reconciliation; and then leave us, as Virgil left Dante, to proceed toward a region where that guide can avail us no farther.'

Notes

1. Quoted from *The Criterion*, July 1932, in Espey, *Ezra Pound's Mauberly*, p. 25. The actual meeting seems to have taken place late in 1914, when Conrad Aiken, who had succeeded in getting Miss Monroe to publish 'Prufrock' in *Poetry*, either took Eliot to Pound or gave him a letter of introduction. (See Aiken's and Eliot's recollections as quoted in Charles Moorman, *Ezra Pound* [New York, 1960], pp. 165–168.)
2. See Grover Smith, *T.S. Eliot's Poetry and Plays* (Chicago, 1956), pp. 65–66.
3. The first of these essays, printed originally in *The Egoist*, has been widely reprinted, of course. The second, called originally 'The Naked Man' for its publication in the *Athenaeum*, is reprinted in the *Selected Essays*. The third, printed originally in *The Dial* as '*Ulysses*, Order, and Myth' has been reprinted, so far as I know, only in M. Schorer, J. Miles, and G. Mackenzie, eds., *Criticism: The Foundations of Modern Literary Judgement* (New York, 1948), pp. 269–271.
4. See S. Musgrove, *T.S. Eliot and Walt Whitman* (Wellington, New Zealand, 1952). The example I give below is from this book, pp. 54–55.
5. *Selected Poems of Ezra Pound* [1928], 'Introduction,' p. 10. Cf. his earlier claim that Whitman was outdated, that his undoubted skill in versification was unrelated to his political, social, religious, and moral ideas, which were 'negligible.' (*Nation and Athenaeum*, XV [1926], p. 426 and XLI [1927], p. 302.)

112
T.S. Eliot: The Retreat from Myth*

LILLIAN FEDER

For T.S. Eliot, Pound's hell, at least his depiction of it in Cantos XIV and XV, though 'in its way admirable,' lacks the essential component of evil. 'Mr. Pound's Hell,' Eliot says, 'for all its horrors, is a perfectly comfortable one for the modern mind to contemplate and disturbing to no one's complacency.' These critical comments disclose less about Pound's mythical construction of the horrors of modern society than they suggest about Eliot's own 'mythical method.' His most revealing remark in this connection is that 'a Hell altogether without dignity implies a Heaven without dignity also.' Eliot's dissatisfaction with Yeats's approach to myth is based on the same criterion: regarding him as an 'equally interesting example of the modern mind,' Eliot remarks on Yeats's use of 'folklore, occultism, mythology and symbolism, crystal-gazing and hermetic writings,' and concludes that Yeats's was the 'wrong supernatural world. It was not a world of spiritual significance, not a world of real Good and Evil, of holiness or sin, but a highly sophisticated lower mythology.'[1] Here Eliot clearly indicates that the 'mythical method' which he had recommended in an earlier essay as 'a step toward making the modern world possible for art,'[2] can be effective only when it expresses the Christian ethos.

Certainly pagan myth and Christian theology are often connected in his own poetry, but it is not the mere presence of the two that is particularly new or interesting. Both have been abundantly explicated and discussed, but no one has elucidated the unique way in which they function in his poetic development. In his early poetry, ancient myth is one of his most important means of conveying unconscious feelings and drives. It creates an essential thematic and stylistic quality of *The Waste Land*: the suggestion and evocation of unconscious conflicts which are never fully expressed or resolved. At the very moment when a mythical persona discloses or a mythical image implies deep human emotion or experience, these are diverted into a Christian framework of sin, suffering, and potential repentance through allu-

*From *Ancient Myth in Modern Poetry* (Princeton, New Jersey, 1971), pp. 121–36.

sions to or imitation of traditional ritual. In *The Waste Land* myth functions chiefly in relation to ritual, a subject that will be developed more fully in the next chapter. However, a significant clue to the purpose and nature of Eliot's ritual effects must be sought in his use of myth to convey man's struggle and failure to gain self-knowledge—a conflict resolved only in the conversion of personal into religious experience, the transformation of mythical insight into ritual observance.

There is no doubt that Eliot considered myth a means of reaching beneath the level of present and conscious experience. In a review of Stravinsky's *Le Sacre du printemps*, he says: 'In art there should be interpenetration and metamorphosis. Even the Golden Bough can be read in two ways: as a collection of entertaining myths, or as a revelation of that vanished mind of which our mind is a continutation.'[3] His conception of poetry, moreover, is based on the assumption that it contains and expresses unconscious levels of experience:

> What I call the 'auditory imagination' is the feeling for syllable and rhythm, penetrating far below the conscious levels of thought and feeling, invigorating every word; sinking to the most primitive and forgotten, returning to the origin and bringing something back, seeking the beginning and the end. It works through meanings, certainly, or not without meanings in the ordinary sense, and fuses the old and obliterated and the trite, the current, and the new and surprising, the most ancient and the most civilized mentality.[4]

Eliot employs myth as well as sound to probe 'far below the conscious levels of thought and feeling,' but, in doing so, he does not seek any new insight into human emotion, suffering, conflict, or aspiration. In fact, he avoids such revelation when it seems about to emerge, for his aim is to disclose not human but 'supernatural realities.' The conflict implicit in 'The Love Song of J. Alfred Prufrock' and *The Waste Land* is stated directly in a critical essay written some years after these poems: 'Either everything in man can be traced as a development from below, or something must come from above. There is no avoiding that dilemma: you must be either a naturalist or a supernaturalist.' For Eliot there is no real choice: 'If you remove from the word "human" all that the belief in the supernatural has given to man, you can view him finally as no more than an extremely clever, adaptable, and mischievous little animal.'[5] It is this view of man that consistently determines Eliot's approach to myth: to the 'lower mythology' which for him expresses man's cleverness and adaptability and, at best, his dissatisfaction with his limited nature and his yearning for completion 'from above,' and to the more advanced mythology of Dante, which offers the 'pure vision' of the supernatural.[6]

Even as early a poem as 'Prufrock,' written years before Eliot's formal conversion to the Anglican Church, has an implicit Christian point of view. The Hell of Dante sets the mood of the poem through the epigraph spoken by Guido da Montefeltro. The lines

> *If I thought that I were making*
> *Answer to one that might return to view*
> *The world, this flame should evermore cease shaking.*
> *But since from this abyss, if I hear true,*
> *None ever came alive, I have no fear*
> *Of infamy, but give thee answer due.*[7]

establish not only the fact that Prufrock, like Guido, is trapped in Hell, but that Hell—which Eliot, in an essay on Dante written in 1929 but certainly illuminating in relation to 'Prufrock,' defines as 'not a place but a *state*'—is the mythical structure beneath the ordinary details of Prufrock's memories and fantasies. To Eliot, 'man is damned or blessed in the creatures of his imagination as well as in the men who have actually lived; . . . Hell, though a state, is a state which can only be thought of, and perhaps only experienced, by the projection of sensory images.'[8] Prufrock is damned by the creatures of his own imagination, all of whom are projections of his own narcissism and despair.

These are expressed mainly in realistic terms, but beneath the streets and drawing room lies the mythical underworld transformed by a Christian perspective into a state extremely uncomfortable 'for the modern mind to contemplate.' The myth is almost totally submerged in this poem but, as Prufrock talks to himself, the rituals which rise to the surface of his consciousness in distorted and even comic form clarify the mythical structure of his 'visions and revisions.'[9] For Eliot a true Hell implies the existence of Heaven; thus Prufrock, immobilized by neurotic terror in the hell of his own soul, gropes toward the 'overwhelming question,' the possibility that the world he knows has some meaning beyond its present chaos and despair. Like many of Eliot's personae, Prufrock is a quester, but his acceptance of his damnation precludes his possibility of escape. In the epigraph Guido da Montefeltro says he will respond to a question only because he assumes the seeker is doomed. Prufrock approaches the overwhelming question without belief or hope; in the end he is tormented not by his society or his way of life, but by a mythical ideal which has replaced his brief and unrealized glimpse at the possibility of heaven: the 'mermaids singing, each to each,' teasing the lonely inhabitant of hell with a suggestion of joy he cannot experience. Prufrock's interior monologue, his brief and pathetic effort to unite his timidity and desire, his apathy and yearning, in a fantasy of love, leads him to the overwhelming question, which implies a 'world of spiritual significance' that can be encountered only through religious ritual; in Chapter IV it will be demonstrated that Prufrock's retreat from this one possibility of action, which is, of course, symbolic, is the key to his final damnation.

In 'Mr. Apollinax' Eliot uses ancient myth to suggest submerged personal feelings within the individual which have an unacknowledged effect on human society. There is, in this poem, neither revelation for the characters nor resolution in ritual, merely the ominous and ironic indication that a hidden world, 'submarine and profound,' confronts us even as we turn away from its meaning. Mr. Apollinax, whom Grover Smith identifies as Bertrand Russell,[10] is far more than an individual portrait. Admired, as the epigram indicates, for his paradoxes, he is himself an embodiment of the paradox of man: Fragilon and Priapus, inventive mind and wild, demanding body. The essential character of Mr. Apollinax emerges from his unconscious in mythical images. At a tea party in the United States, the new world, he reminds us of the most ancient and continuous elements of the human soul—lust and violence, both expressed in images of superhuman aspiration. He contains all that is man, in his formation and development, his inheritance from the past, and his life in the present.

Much is revealed in his laughter, with which the poem begins:

> *When Mr. Apollinax visited the United States*
> *His laughter tinkled among the teacups.*

This is his social manner, but soon the deeper self emerges:

> *He laughed like an irresponsible foetus.*
> *His laughter was submarine and profound*
> *Like the old man of the sea's*
> *Hidden under coral islands*
> *Where worried bodies of drowned men drift down*
>   *in the green silence,*
> *Dropping from fingers of surf.*

Now his laughter bursts upon the pretentious tea party as the very force of life—elementary, pre-human, rich as a sea-god's and suggestive of beauty and death. The observer imagines Apollinax's head 'rolling under a chair.' He sees it 'grinning over a screen / With seaweed in its hair.' After the wild laughter, Apollinax exhibits a grin of vast experience and pleasure. The final mythical image he suggests is of a centaur:

> *I heard the beat of centaur's hoofs over the hard turf*
> *As his dry and passionate talk devoured the afternoon.*

Even his intelligent and rational conversation conveys the force of his unconscious drives. The centaur implies more than the obvious presence of the human and animal in man; it is a projection of the desire to transcend conflict in fusion, to impose human reason on animal power. The integrity of Mr. Apollinax lies in the very qualities that shock his hosts: 'He must be unbalanced,' they conclude. They are neither informed nor enlightened by his presence, but his vitality disturbs them.

Mr. Apollinax, 'clever, adaptable, and mischievous,' is Eliot's most elegant and attractive mythical creation of 'natural' man; Sweeney, his most repulsive. Like Apollinax, Sweeney is characterized both as an individual

Studies of *The Waste Land* and poems

and a representative of continuous instinctual drives, the unconscious forces in man and society. The initial shock on reading the epigraph of 'Sweeney Among the Nightingales'— '*ὤμοι, πέπληγμαι καιρ⌢ αν πλμγὺν ἔσω*,' the cry of the dying Agamemnon in Aeschylus' tragedy—preceding 'Apeneck Sweeney,' soon wears off as Eliot convinces one that Sweeney participates in mythical experience as authentic as that of Oedipus or Agamemnon. F.O. Matthiessen refers to Eliot's comment that 'all he consciously set out to create in "Sweeney Among the Nightingales" was a sense of foreboding.' Matthiessen sees 'wider implications' in the 'sympathetic feeling for Sweeney' created by the suggestion that his fate will be similar to Agamemnon's.[11] Actually, Eliot's statement contains 'wider implications' than Matthiessen's interpretation of it or the poem. The complicated mythical structure of 'Sweeney Among the Nightingales' creates 'a sense of foreboding' not only about the fate of Sweeney but of mortal life. Implicit in the myths of Oedipus, Agamemnon, Orion, and the horned gate is the inevitability of violence and destruction as part of man's experience on earth. Sweeney, the prototype of the most basic human drives, neither restrained by social, nor tempered by spiritual, experience, is closer than most men to the primitive, destructive forces which myth delineates. 'Among the nightingales,' he embodies the knowledge of conflict and death which Oedipus possessed near the end of his life, as he rested in a grove sacred to the Furies and listened to the song of the nightingales (*Oedipus at Colonus*, l. 18). Sweeney 'guards the hornèd gate' because this awareness, unconscious and universal, is present in true dreams.

The poem suggests the preparation for Sweeney's murder by 'Rachel *née* Rabinovitch' and 'the lady in the cape.' As Sweeney sits with them in a cafe, he grows suspicious, and soon he leaves. For the moment he is spared, but the last two stanzas make it clear that he is indeed destined to act out a mythical role as the victim of treachery and violence:

> *The host with someone indistinct*
> *Converses at the door apart,*
> *The nightingales are singing near*
> *The Convent of the Sacred Heart,*
>
> *And sang within the bloody wood*
> *When Agamemnon cried aloud*
> *And let their liquid siftings fall*
> *To stain the stiff dishonoured shroud.*

The song of the nightingales, the symbol of recurrence in the title and the poem, first associated with the suffering and knowledge of Oedipus, now seems to echo the tranquillity of the convent and to suggest the permanence of its values. These exist, however, within a world of continuous hatred and violence, which still contains 'the bloody wood' where kings were killed who

Early Poems and *The Waste Land*

exemplified in myth what Sweeney enacts in contemporary society.

The Waste Land marks the height and essentially the end of Eliot's use of classical myth in his poetry to symbolize individual and general unconscious feeling and conflict. In later poems he does employ classical myth, though more sparingly, and he combines pagan allusions with Christian ones, but never again is myth so intrinsic to the theme and structure of his poetry. In the 'Notes' to *The Waste Land* Eliot informs the reader that Tiresias, 'although a mere spectator and not indeed a "character," is yet the most important personage in the poem, uniting all the rest . . . What Tiresias *sees* in fact, is the substance of the poem.' Eliot's emphasis on the sight of the blind prophet is a perhaps unnecessary indication that it is his insight, his awareness of what lies beneath his and others' conscious perception, that unifies all the elements of the poem.

Yet it is not the myth of Tiresias but the Grail legend that provides the dominant symbolism of *The Waste Land*. Eliot's referrences in the 'Notes' to Jessie Weston's *From Ritual to Romance* and Frazer's *The Golden Bough*, and to the 'great anthropological interest' of Ovid's tale of Tiresias' metamorphosis from male to female and his return to his original state, suggest that in his view it is their connection with ancient religious rituals that unites the Greek myth and the medieval legend. More important perhaps is Tiresias' power to see, comprehend, and predict what is dark to other men. His the unconscious mind of the poem, containing secret knowledge of male and female, gods and mortals, past and future. It is he who perceives the structure of the Grail legend beneath the surface of modern society.

Eliot's use of Jessie Weston's interpretation of the Grail legend as his main symbol of a quest for some source of recovery from the sterility of modern life has been discussed by many critics, whose chief aim has been to explain his various and sometimes cryptic allusions.[12] In so doing they seem to have missed important thematic and structural elements of the poem that are directly related to Eliot's choice of a legend which, at least as Miss Weston interprets it, originates in ancient fertility rites with their attendant myths and is later adapted to Christian myth, symbol, and ritual observance. In adapting this legend, Eliot employs symbols which emerge from its ancient mythical origins to depict modern man's dissatisfactions and inner struggles; his mythical commentary is ironic and tragic, offering neither consolation nor resolution, only the conversion of suffering into a ritual quest for divine sustenance.

In discussing certain similarities in Eliot's and Jung's use of myth, Elizabeth Drew sees a parallel in Eliot's concept of rebirth and Jung's 'archetype of transformation.' The 'I' of *The Waste Land*, she says, 'is agonizingly aware, in the imprisonment of his personal waste land, that the possibilities of rebirth cannot be dismissed as an historical anachronism; that the truth of the experience is eternally present and that the living of it plunges the whole man into a process of disintegration and conflict.' Miss Drew also reveals similarities in the images used by Jung and Eliot to symbolize unconscious experience, especially the image of water.[13] These parallels are interesting but not surprising since both Jung and Eliot use traditional mythical and literary sources; moreover, in *The Waste Land* Eliot is not quite consciously straining toward a religious position similar to that which is the basis of Jung's psychology. Miss Drew assumes, as does Jung, that the 'change of consciousness' brought about through the archetypes of transformation effects 'an integration of personality.' Actually, it can be shown that the mythical experience depicted in *The Waste Land* is similar to the Jungian plunge into archetypal consciousness because it leads not to self-knowledge or the resolution of personal conflict, but to a transformation of uncertainty into faith, of human weakness into reliance on supernatural omnipotence. Such a transformation may provide 'integration,' but only through a belief that the self can merge with a divine principle.

This process evolves gradually in the mythical structure of the poem, which is first indicated in the epigraph spoken by the Sibyl of Cumae in the *Satyricon* of Petronius. The prophetess is associated with the most ancient and honored of rituals, yet in the context of the *Satyricon* and in the story told by Trimalchio, whom Eliot quotes, she is debased both by the scornful attitude of the narrator and the particular myth he tells. The Sibyl, hung in a jar, responds to the children who ask her what she wants, 'I wish to die.' This is the Sibyl who led Aeneas to the underworld, where his spirit was restored and his dedication to his mission renewed. Now, in a degenerate time, her powers limited, she can only wish for death. The epigraph creates the atmosphere of cynicism and despair with which *The Waste Land* begins; the old rituals of renewal, like the Sibyl who once assisted in their performance, have been tainted by the weakness and corruption of man.

Thus April, the month of rebirth, is 'the cruellest month,' promising renewal and indeed 'breeding / Lilacs' but along with them 'Memory and desire.' As the earth stirs, man becomes aware of a drive for renewal within his own soul, a yearning to overcome the limitations of his separate being and to feel himself reborn as the earth is restored. Yet his memories and experience seem to deny such fulfillment. Eliot's first allusion to a religious source in this poem is explicit: he refers in a note to Ezekiel 2 and Ecclesiastes 12 in connection with lines 20 and 23, but in the entire passage from line 19 to line 30, he echoes the preacher and the prophet to intensify and extend the feelings of sterility and despair which darken man's memory and his life in the present.

Momentarily, the possibility of human love, 'the hyacinth girl,' seems to offer salvation, but the very symbol in which this hope is expressed reveals its limits. The 'hyacinth garden' calls to mind Frazer's description of both the mythical figure Hyacinth as representative of 'the vegetation which blooms in the spring and withers under the scorching heat of the summer sun' and the 'sad flower' which was 'an omen of death.'[14] Eliot suggests that human love cannot offer fulfillment, for it is itself involved with and subject to death.

The protagonist of *The Waste Land* then turns to a new source of regeneration, a contemporary and debased form of an old myth and ritual, 'the lower mythology' of the fortune teller. The Tarot pack, originally used 'to predict the rise and fall of the waters which brought fertility to the land,'[15] is now employed by Madame Sosostris, the 'famous' and tainted clairvoyante. After telling the protagonist that his is the card of 'the drowned Phoenician Sailor,' she announces that she cannot find the 'Hanged Man,' whom Eliot associates 'with the Hanged God of Frazer,' a figure sacrificed in various forms and cultures so that his spirit might insure fertility to the earth and its inhabitants. She offers the advice, 'Fear death by water,' but does not see the connection between the missing 'Hanged Man' or god and the prophetic meaning of the 'drowned Phoenician Sailor' for the protagonist.

Like most prophetic statements, this one is ambiguous and cryptic, revealing as much about the character of the recipient as about his fate. The prophecy confirms the protagonist's fear of death and at the same time reveals his yearning to participate in a rite of rebirth. Since the hanged god is not to be found in his society, he himself will imitate the prototypal sacrificial figure, drowning only to be recovered, dying to be reborn. This is the first hint of a wish to merge with divinity, which is later realized in the poem. The prophecy is fulfilled in Part IV in the drowning of Phlebas the Phoenician, 'a type of fertility god,'[16] with whom the speaker identifies as sacrificial victim and example. Only after this 'death by water' does the 'Hanged God' appear; in a note Eliot associates him with 'the hooded figure in the passage of the disciples to Emmaus in Part V,' a clear indication that he is also Christ.

The continual merging of characters with one another and all of them with the speaker or protagonist is intrinsic to the theme of *The Waste Land*. Eliot emphasizes this technique in a note: 'Just as the one-eyed merchant, seller of currants, melts into the Phoenician Sailor, and the latter is not wholly distinct from Ferdinand Prince of Naples, so all the women are one woman, and the two sexes meet in Tiresias.' Since, moreover, all the figures merge in the mind of Tiresias, they are all part of a universal consciousness whose fate is projected in the symbols of the Tarot pack.

Among these is 'the man with three staves,' whom Eliot associates 'quite arbitrarily with the Fisher King.' His role in *The Waste Land* reflects Jessie Weston's theory that he is 'the essential centre' of the entire ritual of fertility on which the Grail legend is based, 'a being semi-divine, semi-human, standing between his people and land, and the unseen forces which control their destiny.'[17] It is toward the maimed Fisher King, who symbolizes 'the Divine Principle of Life and Fertility,'[18] combining the attributes of ancient fertility god and Christian healer, that the quest of the protagonist is directed. Jessie Weston points out that in many versions of the Grail legend the duty of the hero is to ask the proper question of the Fisher King: in one version he asks 'concerning the Grail,' in another 'whom it serves.' When the proper question is asked, the maimed king is healed and thus the land is restored; when the question is not asked, the king remains sick or dies, and the land suffers.[19] Questions about the meaning of their own lives or of life itself are implicit in the conflict and despair of the protagonist and the other characters of *The Waste Land*. These feelings expressed in myth throughout the poem are ultimately enacted in a ritual quest for the restoration of health to man and the earth.

The unfulfilled desire for human love symbolized in the allusion to the myth of Hyacinth has already been discussed. Other mythical references repeat and intensify this experience. In Part II the failure of romantic love is revealed in human society on both its highest and lowest cultural and economic levels. In the first scene Eliot evokes Shakespeare's most magnificent description of Cleopatra and alludes to Vergil's Dido only to flatten and demythify the composite portrait. This lady, 'Belladonna,' has all the external trappings of a great queen and none of her mythical power. The symbol of overwhelming physical beauty and sexual appeal is itself reduced in this portrait of a modern upper-class woman, nervous, frightened, vainly seeking some purpose in her superficial life. She is surrounded by reflections of her own despair:

> *Above the antique mantel was displayed*
> *As though a window gave upon the sylvan scene*
> *The change of Philomel, by the barbarous king*
> *So rudely forced; yet there the nightingale*
> *Filled all the desert with inviolable voice*
> *And still she cried, and still the world pursues,*
> *'Jug Jug' to dirty ears*
> *And other withered stumps of time*
> *Were told upon the walls; staring forms*
> *Leaned out, leaning, hushing the room enclosed.*

In this representation even the myth of Philomel has lost its power and its dignity. Its ancient meaning—the conversion of pain to beauty, death to perennial life—is gone: in the past the nightingale may have 'Filled all the desert with inviolable voice,' but now it sings, '"Jug Jug" to dirty ears.' It is one of the 'withered stumps of time.' The myth serves a double purpose here: it expresses one of the themes of *The Waste Land*, the effect of the sterility of modern life on traditional values, and, more important, it suggests the inadequacy of myth to do more than depict contemporary apathy and despair. Eliot presents the Philomela myth in a static picture 'displayed' over an 'antique mantel'; it does not function either to reveal or to transcend the sources of alienation and spiritual death. The woman whose home it adorns asks, 'What shall I do now? What shall I do? . . . What shall we do tomorrow / What shall we ever do?' The mythical exposure of violation and sterility ends in a frantic quest.

In 'The Fire Sermon,' another scene reveals the failure of human love to provide sustenance in a sterile world. Here the presence of Tiresias, who announces that he 'Perceived the scene, and foretold the rest—' suggests the depth of unconscious agony beneath the sordid and trivial life of the typist and her 'carbuncular' lover, but the seer offers no revelation. The young woman looks not at her inner self, but 'in the glass':

> *Hardly aware of her departed lover;*
> *Her brain allows one half-formed thought to pass:*
> *'Well now that's done: and I'm glad it's over.'*

The consciousness of Tiresias drifts away from the mechanical sound of the gramophone to music which evokes an enchanted world of love and beauty: 'This music crept by me upon the waters.' As he incorporates the character Ferdinand, remarking on a song of Ariel in *The Tempest* (1.391), he brings this memory to the contemporary city. It leads him away from the ugliness he has witnessed to a place

> *Where fishmen lounge at noon: where the walls*
> *Of Magnus Martyr hold*
> *Inexplicable splendour of Ionian white and gold.*

The mythical seer whose mind encompasses all the suffering of the waste land seeks the 'fishmen' and the church, a scene of momentary relief and a suggestion that even in the barren 'city' and its maimed inhabitants there is a remnant of 'splendour' and hope.

The music continues in the sound of the river, which Eliot mythicizes; three 'Thames-daughters,' like the Rhine-daughters of the *Götterdämmerung*, sing of the failure of love, of violence and ugliness, all without meaning:

> *I can connect*
> *Nothing with nothing.*

The shift from this mythical scene of unrelieved despair to a quotation from St. Augustine's *Confessions* and the Buddha's Fire Sermon, which Eliot compares with the Sermon on the Mount, serves as a religious commentary on man's sin, suffering, and possible repentance.

In the last two sections of *The Waste Land* the central myth of sterility and rebirth is expressed almost entirely through allusions to and imitation of ritual. Like all the action of *The Waste Land*, this takes place within the consciousness of the protagonist who merges with all the characters as the impotent Fisher King, waiting for the proper question. The rich and varied mythical structure of the poem reveals man's inability to understand or resolve his central conflicts; the poetic reconstructions of ritual indicate that his only possibility of salvation lies in the enactment of a symbolic quest.

The study of Greek and Roman myth as a vehicle expressing unconscious conflict in Eliot's poetry properly ends with *The Waste Land*. Though some allusions to ancient myth occur in connection with Christian ritual in his later poems, and Greek mythical themes and characters are the essential structural background of most of his plays, he did not use pagan myth extensively in the poetry he wrote after his conversion to the Anglican Church. In certain respects, Eliot rejected the full implications of myth even as he used it in his poetry; here mythical figures and symbols express yearning for love and purpose and the pain of impotence and frustration within men's souls, but these feelings reveal little about the nature of human beings, except their need for 'something outside themselves.'[20]

In using myth Eliot neither sought nor attained insight into his own unconscious mind, as did Yeats; nor does myth develop in Eliot's poetry, as it does in Yeats's, into an instrument for approaching the deepest and most fearful aspects of inner and external reality. For Eliot myth essentially provides 'an escape from emotion . . . an escape from personality.'[21] In an essay on Matthew Arnold, in which he comments on the statement: 'Poetry is at bottom a criticism of life,' Eliot remarks: 'At the bottom of the abyss is what few ever see and what those cannot bear to look at for long. . . . We bring back very little from our descents.'[22] Classical myth was for a long time a guide to the 'abyss' for Eliot, but he could use it effectively only as an impersonal means of expression, which inevitably led to imitation of traditional ritual.

Notes

1. *After Strange Gods*, pp. 43–46.
2. See Chapter I, p. 26 and footnote 27 to that chapter.
3. 'London Letter,' *Dial*, LXXI (October 1921), 453.
4. 'Matthew Arnold,' *The Use of Poetry and the Use of Criticism* (London, 1933), pp. 118–19.
5. 'Second Thoughts About Humanism,' *Selected Essays, 1917–1932* (New York, 1932), p. 397.
6. 'Dante,' *The Sacred Wood* (1920; reprint, London, 1964), pp. 162–63.
7. *The Divine Comedy*, I: *Hell*, trans. Dorothy L. Sayers (Harmondsworth, Middlesex, 1949), p. 241.
8. 'Dante,' *Selected Essays, 1917–1932*, pp. 211–12.
9. 'The Love Song of J. Alfred Prufrock,' *Collected Poems 1909–1962* (New York, 1963). All quotations from and page references to Eliot's poetry are from this edition.
10. *T.S. Eliot's Poetry and Plays* (Chicago, 1956), p. 32.
11. *The Achievement of T.S. Eliot*, 3rd ed. (New York, 1958), p. 129.
12. See, for example, Grover Smith, *T.S. Eliot's Poetry and Plays*; Cleanth Brooks, 'The Waste Land: Critique of the Myth,' *Modern Poetry and the Tradition*, pp. 136–72; and George Williamson, *A Reader's Guide to T.S. Eliot*, 2nd ed. (New York, 1966).
13. *T.S. Eliot: The Design of His Poetry* (New York, 1949), pp. 63–65. Miss Drew approaches the body of Eliot's poetry from a Jungian point of view as exemplifying an 'integration of the personality' (p. xiii). Other studies of Eliot from the perspective of Jungian psychology are: Genevieve W. Foster, 'The Archetypal Imagery of T.S. Eliot,' *PMLA*, LX (June 1945), 567–85; and P.W. Martin, *Experiment in Depth, A Study of the Work of Jung, Eliot, and Toynbee* (New York, 1955).

14. *The New Golden Bough, A New Abridgment of the Classic Work by Sir James Frazer*, ed. Theodore H. Gaster (New York, 1959), pp. 320–21.
15. Jessie L. Weston, *From Ritual to Romance* (1920; reprint, New York, 1941), p. 76.
16. Brooks, *Modern Poetry and the Tradition*, p. 142.
17. *From Ritual to Romance*, p. 129.
18. *ibid.*, p. 108.
19. *ibid.*, pp. 13–15.
20. T.S. Eliot, 'The Function of Criticism,' *Selected Essays, 1917–1932*, p. 15.
21. T.S. Eliot, 'Tradition and the Individual Talent,' *Selected Essays 1917–1937*, p. 10.
22. *The Use of Poetry and the Use of Criticism*, p. 111.

113
Maps of the Waste Land*

BERNARD BERGONZI

In 1956 Eliot wrote, apropos of John Livingstone Lowes' *Road to Xanadu*, 'poetic originality is largely an original way of assembling the most disparate and unlikely material to make a new whole.' 'Assembling' is not a word one usually applies to writing poetry, but it is very relevant to Eliot's own methods. C. K. Stead has shown how the separate parts of 'The Hollow Men' were previously published in different combinations, until Eliot finally shuffled them into the right order. And we have his own account of how 'Burnt Norton' was made up of fragments discarded from *Murder in the Cathedral* during the course of production. Eliot's basic method of composition was more traditionally Romantic than is often realised, with a frank reliance on unconscious sources of inspiration to produce brief poetic passages, or perhaps just single lines, of great isolated intensity. The next, and equally arduous, stage in the assembling of a whole poem was akin to the methods of an artist in mosaic or collage. Fragments or phrases not suitable for one poem would be carefully kept, sometimes for years, until they could be used in another. It is this aspect of Eliot's art that is most fascinatingly revealed in the long-lost manuscripts of *The Waste Land*, a poem whose most crucial line is certainly '*These fragments I have shored against my ruins.*'

For a long time readers have wistfully assumed that if only those legendary manuscripts would turn up then the worst difficulties might be resolved, since Eliot's *ur*-version must have been more lucid and coherent than the final product of Ezra Pound's ruthless editing. That notion, at least, is now dispelled. The first draft of *The Waste Land*, brought back by Eliot from his rest-cure at Lausanne in the autumn of 1921, was, as he once deprecatingly told an interviewer, 'just as structureless, only in a more futile way.' The original manuscript consisted of several extended sections—in blank verse, quatrains and heroic couplets—plus a number of shorter fragments, that Eliot hoped could be somehow 'worked in.' If Eliot's original design had a unity it was of a very loose kind, for the work that he brought back from

---

**Encounter (April 1972), vol. xxxvii, no. 4, pp. 80–3.

Lausanne was essentially a set of separate poems; even after *The Waste Land* was published in 1922 reviewers tended to refer to it as 'poems' rather than 'a poem.' Mrs Eliot's admirable edition[1] shows clearly the streamlining effect of the editorial cuts, by no means all of which were made by Pound, as Eliot modestly implied. It was a pencil stroke in Eliot's own hand that excised the original opening, a low-pressure chatty passage about Boston low-life, thereby ensuring that the first line was 'April is the cruellest month' rather than 'First we had a couple of feelers down at Tom's place.' Most of the material that was cut out, whether by Eliot himself, or by Pound, deserved to go. But I think Eliot was mistaken when he removed, at Pound's suggestion, the original epigraph from Conrad's *Heart of Darkness*:

> Did he live his life again in every detail of desire, temptation, and surrender during that supreme moment of complete knowledge? He cried out in a whisper at some image, at some vision—he cried out twice, a cry that was no more than a breath—'The horror! the horror!'

If *The Waste Land* had been prefaced with this quotation it might have been evident from the beginning that the poem is, at bottom, an anguished reliving of subjective experience, and not the 'impersonal' meditation on cultural decline that so many commentators—whether sympathetic or unsympathetic—have assumed it to be. Conrad's lines point to the real subject of the poem; the word 'surrender' had a peculiar significance for Eliot, and Conrad's use of it seems to be echoed later in *The Waste Land*, in 'The awful daring of a moment's surrender' (and perhaps in 'Tradition and the Individual Talent', where Eliot says of the poet, 'what happens is a continual surrender of himself as he is at the moment to something which is more valuable ').

There is one other place where Pound's excisions may have been misdirected. Part IV, 'Death by Water', was originally much longer. After a very inferior set of opening quatrains, the verse develops into a mostly wellwritten account of a disastrous voyage by a New England fishing vessel, with deliberate echoes of Tennyson's and Dante's Ulysses. There are striking anticipations of the Quartets of twenty years later:

> *Kingfisher weather, with a light fair breeze,*
> *Full canvas, and the eight sails drawing well.*
> *We beat around the cape and laid our course*
> *From the Dry Salvages to the eastern banks.*
> *A porpoise snored upon the phosphorescent swell,*
> *A triton rang the final warning bell*
> *Astern, and the sea rolled, asleep.*

Later in this section the verse becomes more intense, recalling the quotation from Conrad, and looking back momentarily to the final lines of 'Prufrock':

> *One night*
> *On watch, I thought I saw in the fore cross-trees*

> *Three women leaning forward, with white hair*
> *Streaming behind, who sang above the wind*
> *A song that charmed my senses, while I was*
> *Frightened beyond fear, horrified past horror, calm,*
> *(Nothing was real) for, I thought, now, when*
> *I like, I can wake up and end the dream.*
> *—Something which we knew must be a dawn—*
> *A different darkness, flowed above the clouds,*
> *And dead ahead we saw, where sky and sea should meet,*
> *A line, a white line, a long white line,*
> *A wall, a barrier towards which we drove.*

Not all the deleted lines are as good as this. Some cutting, particularly of the sailor's talk, was probably required, but it is a pity that the whole section had to go; the parallel between the New England fishermen and Phlebas the Phoenician was effective, and the Phlebas passage by itself (an adaptation from the closing lines of one of Eliot's French poems of 1918, 'Dans le Restaurant') stands rather too abruptly. Eliot, in fact, wanted to delete that too, when the first part of 'Death by Water' went, but Pound dissuaded him. Characteristically, though, Eliot hung on to a couple of phrases from the deleted lines, which later turned up in 'The Dry Salvages' and 'Marina.'

On the other hand, Pound's editing greatly improved 'The Fire Sermon.' This section originally opened with a long set of Popean couplets, which were adroit enough in their way, but which only reiterated points made more tersely elsewhere about the emptiness of fashionable life. As an exercise in the smart neo-classicising of the twenties—there are musical parallels in Stravinsky or Prokofiev—they have a certain curiosity value, but it wasn't really Eliot's kind of thing. Nor, for that matter, were the quatrain poems, like 'Sweeney Erect', that he wrote between 1917 and 1919, largely as a result of reading Gautier under Pound's influence. In the first draft of 'The Fire Sermon' the account by Tiresias of the seduction of a bored typist by the 'young man carbuncular' was told in a long sequence of such quatrains. Pound's cuts boldly ignored the rhyme scheme, so that the lines ended up as the section of continuous and irregularly rhyming verse that appeared in the published version. One of the minor puzzles in that version is the peculiar syntax of the lines,

> *the evening hour that strives*
> *Homeward, and brings the sailor home from sea,*
> *The typist home at teatime, clears her breakfast, lights*
> *Her stove, and lays out food in tins.*

It now looks as if this elision was the result of inadequate suturing after the editorial cuts. The manuscript read

> *The typist home at teatime, who begins*

> *To clear away her broken breakfast, lights*
> *Her stove, and lays out squalid food in tins.* . . . .

Pound's marginal comment on these lines was 'verse not interesting enough as verse to warrant so much of it.' Certainly the taut and rapid final version is a vast improvement on the laboured quatrains. At first there was a good deal more about the young man, whom Eliot seems to have regarded with immense distaste but with a certain novelistic interest, describing him as a layabout who frequents the Café Royal, and a crude but confident womaniser. If some readers find these lines deplorably snobbish and anti-life, one can only say that the original version was far more so; the young man's departure might have read like this, were it not for a cautious comment by Pound:

> *—Bestows one final patronising kiss,*
> *And gropes his way, finding the stairs unlit;*
> *And at the corner where the stable is,*
> *Delays only to urinate, and spit.*

Eliot was much closer to his central concerns in some fragmentary and unused lines about London, seen, as elsewhere in *The Waste Land*, as a Baudelairean inferno. A line, cancelled by Eliot himself, which read 'London, your people is bound upon the wheel,' reflects one of the central configurations of his imagination: 'I see crowds of people, walking round in a ring' and 'Here we go round the prickly pear.'

The most interesting material lies not so much in the cancellations as in the early fragments, in some cases written several years before the 1921 draft, from which Eliot extracted lines or images for use in *The Waste Land*. 'The Death of Saint Narcissus' is one such which provided the source for 'Come in under the shadow of this red rock.' Perhaps the most powerful lines in *The Waste Land* are those beginning 'A woman drew her long black hair out tight,' and in this edition there is a draft of them which Mrs Eliot suggests, on the evidence of handwriting may have been written in 1914, or even before. In another manuscript of the same early date, we find a version of the opening lines of 'What the Thunder said', astonishingly combined with a Laforguean conclusion in the manner of Eliot's first poetic exercises written at Harvard in 1909:

> *After the ending of this inspiration*
> *And the torches and the faces and the shouting*
> *The world seemed futile—like a Sunday outing.*

Such pivotal lines look both forward and back, emphasising the imaginative unity of Eliot's work. So, too, does a seemingly later fragment called 'The Death of the Duchess.' I found this exciting, because it provided the missing link between two passages of Eliot's verse which have always struck me by their resemblances, although quite separate in time: the edgily dramatic speech of the two neurotic women in 'Portrait of a Lady' (1910) and 'A Game of Chess' in *The Waste Land* (1921). 'The Death of the Duchess' takes its point of departure from *The Duchess of Malfi*, in the scene where the Duchess is surprised in her bed-chamber by her evil brother Ferdinand. This draft by Eliot contains most of the lines later incorporated into the middle section of 'A Game of Chess', while being an unmistakable attempt to recapture, perhaps even imitate, the manner of 'Prufrock' and 'Portrait of a Lady.' There is a similar nervous but intense sexuality:

> *With her back turned, her arms were bare*
> *Fixed for a question, her hands behind her hair*
> *And the firelight shining where the muscle drew.*

At one place Pound has scribbled in the margin, 'cadence reproduction from Prufrock or Portrait of a Lady.'

When the *Waste Land* manuscripts were first discovered I feared that they might disintegrate the poem as we have always known it. But Mrs Eliot's edition reassuringly makes this look unlikely: *The Waste Land*, in its final version, is so obviously superior to the drafts—apart from the special case of 'Death by Water'—that they are not likely to affect our reading of it. What they can provide is the traditional Romantic pleasure of seeing how a great poet's mind works.

Gertrude Patterson's book[2] is an intelligent but scrappy study of Eliot's early poems up to *The Waste Land*, the manuscripts of which she was able to inspect in the New York Public Library. She is absolutely right to emphasise the element of assemblage or collage in Eliot's method of composition, and the way in which his multiple perspectives recall the contemporary work of the Cubist painters. But her account of Eliot's early career contains the customary amount of slightly inaccurate literary history that seems inevitable in his commentators, though Mrs Eliot has at last set the record straight in the biographical introduction to her edition. There is too much not very relevant material in Miss Patterson's book, notably about Ezra Pound and the Imagist movement, which tends to blur the fact that Eliot wrote some of his finest poems—'Prufrock', 'Portrait of a Lady', 'Preludes', 'Rhapsody on a Windy Night'—several years before he had heard of Pound or Imagism. Pound may have been, as Eliot generously acknowledged in the dedication to *The Waste Land*, *il miglior fabbro*; but it was the unknown young Harvard graduate student of 1910 and 1911 who was the greater innovator.

Notes

1. *The Waste Land: A Facsimile and Transcript of the Original Drafts*. Edited by Valerie Eliot. Faber & Faber.
2. *T.S. Eliot: Poems in the Making*. By Gertrude Patterson. Manchester University Press.

114
The Word Within a Word*

DENIS DONOGHUE

The publication of the first drafts of *The Waste Land*[1] has not greatly eased the difficulty of reading the poem. We now know that the poem issued, however circuitously, from the unhappiness of Eliot's first marriage—though certain lines and passages in the first drafts were written before 1915—but we hardly know what to make of that fact, unless it prompts us to say that the dominant feeling in the poem is not universal despair but particular guilt, and that the specific movement of feeling through the words corresponds, however obscurely, to the act of penance. Some readers of *The Waste Land* feel that Eliot is saying: 'God, I thank thee that I am not as the rest of men, extortioners, unjust, adulterers, or even as this small house-agent's clerk.' But this sense of the poem is unworthy, false to its spirit as a whole, though there are a few passages which support it. The area of feeling which the poem inhabits is the general provenance of guilt, fear, dread; the presence of disgust, including self-disgust, is not surprising. The first drafts show, and this is more to the point, that the poet's original sense of his poem made it, even more than the final version, a medley. Pound's criticism tightened the poem, but did not otherwise alter its movement. One characteristic of the poetry remains. Eliot's poems often try to escape from the emotional conditions which incited them, not by willing its opposite but by working through a wide range of alternative conditions. The poems find safety and relief in numbers. One mood is answered not by another, equal and opposite, but by a diversity of moods. It is the diversity that saves. The medley of poems which eventually became *The Waste Land* was designed, it appears, with this diversity in view. To the charge that Eliot's poem is the work of a Pharisee, therefore, I would not reply that on the contrary it is the work of a publican, but rather than it effects a movement of feeling to make penance possible. Diversity, number and allusion are the auspices under which the poem moves.

I want to suggest now that this sense of the poem is related to our recognition of its character as a distinctively American work. Specifically, the

*From A.D. Moody (ed.), *'The Waste Land' in Different Voices* (London, 1974), pp. 185–201.

poem is, in Hawthorne's terminology, a romance. In the Preface to *The House of the Seven Gables*, Hawthorne distinguished between romance and novel. The novel aims at minute fidelity to the probable, but the romance, claiming 'a certain latitude', proposes to present 'the truth of the human heart' under circumstances 'to a great extent of the writer's own choosing or creation'.[2] There has always been an implication, in later comments on the romance, that it is the form of fiction most congenial to those feelings for which social correlatives are not available; or, if available, seriously inadequate. It is a commonplace that the romance, in Hawthorne's sense, holds a special position in American literature and that it is particularly serviceable to the writer who feels his imagination driven back upon its own resources. One of the tenable generalizations we continue to make about English literature is that its position is not desperate in this regard. The English writer generally thinks himself ready to establish his feelings in a particular setting and to let it develop and take its chance there. He declares a certain confidence in representing the life of feeling in terms of man, Nature, and society. Nearly everything is allowed to depend upon the relation of man to the society in which he lives, the relation of person to person and to place. We say that English literature is personal, meaning that it is social, historical, and political. We do not say this of American literature. The question of locality is important to American writers, not least to Hawthorne in *The House of the Seven Gables*, but in American literature generally, and especially in the literature of the nineteenth-century a shadow falls between person and place. The feelings in the case are rarely entrusted to that relation, or indeed to any other: there is an impression that such feelings cannot hope to be fulfilled in such relations. There is a remainder of feeling which cries for release in dream, nightmare and fantasy. I want to pursue the notion that *The Waste Land* is best understood as an American romance.

It may be useful to recall Eliot's sense of American literature. He rejected the assertion that there is an American language distinct from English: in his view, both languages use the same notes, even if the fingering is sometimes different. He was not of Mencken's party in that argument. As for the literature, he registered New England as a moral presence, a regiment in the army of unalterable law, but he was not intimidated by it. He reflected upon the complex fate of being an American when he read Hawthorne and, still more, Henry James, who embodied one of the great possibilities consistent with that fate. In an essay on James he wrote that 'it is the final perfection, the consummation of an American to become, not an Englishman, but a European—something which no born European, no person of any European nationality, can become.'[3] Of the relation between Eliot and Whitman it is enough to say that Whitman is audible, for some good but more ill, in the third section of 'The Dry Salvages', providing Eliot with a somewhat insecure tone. Of Mark Twain Eliot is on record as saying in praise that he was one of those writers who discover 'a new way of writing, valid not only for themselves but for others',[4] but I cannot recall any occasion on which Eliot moved in Twain's direction, despite 'the river with its cargo of dead negroes' in 'The Dry Salvages'. The question of his relation to Poe is far more interesting, because it is strange that he should have had any interest in such a writer. In fact, he did not admire Poe's poems, he thought them adolescent things; Poe had never grown up. But there were two aspects of the matter which he could not ignore. The first concerned Poe's style of incantation which, Eliot said, 'because of its very crudity, stirs the feelings at a deep and almost primitive level'.[5] Eliot had his own style of incantation, and he was greatly taken by Poe as a master in the singing style. The second consideration was that Poe's work, fruitless in the English and American traditions, had entered the sensibilities of the great French poets and especially of Baudelaire, Mallarmé and Valéry. Eliot was interested in this event, and he pondered it. There is almost a suggestion that Poe had somehow achieved the final perfection of an American by becoming a European, reincarnated in Baudelaire, Mallarmé and Valéry. Eliot was strongly engaged by Poe, as by Swinburne, for a similar reason, the call of one verbalist to another.

The great interest of American literature arises, it is commonly agreed, from the sense of American feeling as making a new start, every day, with little or nothing regarded as capital saved from yesterday. The world is all before the American writers. So these writers naturally think of making everything new, they do not feel overwhelmed by the weight of previous achievement. American writers burn their bridges behind them, relegating the previous, as James said of his compatriots generally in *The American Scene*, to the category of wan misery. If *The Waste Land* is written by an American who has set out to make himself a European, its chief labour toward that perfection is the assumption of the burden of history. The allusions in Eliot's poem show not the extent of his learning but the gravity of the whole enterprise, the range of those responsibilities he is ready to accept in such a cause. What most of the allusions say is: 'there have been other times, not utterly lost or forgotten; we ourselves were not born this morning.'

We may press the argument a little further. If English literature is devoted to the relation between person, place, and time, it acts by a corresponding syntax of prescribed relations. The first result is that the chief function of one word is to lead the mind to the next. No detail in *Middlemarch* is as important as the entire network of relations, word by word, sentence by sentence: the reader's mind is not encouraged to sink into the recesses of a word, but to move forward until the prescribed affiliations are complete. The modesty with which a word sends the reader's mind running to the next is the verbal equivalent of dependency in a given society, as one person accepts his enabling relation to another. But the modern revolution in such American poems as *The Waste Land* and *Hugh Selwyn Mauberley* depends upon a different sense of life and therefore upon a different syntax. One's first reading of these poems leaves an impression of their poetic quality as residing in their diction: the animation of the verse arises from the incalculable force of certain individual words or phrases which stay in the mind without necessarily attracting to their orbit the words before or after. The memorable quality of those phrases seems to require a clear space on all sides, and it has little need of before and after. I take this to mean that the relations to which the words of an American poem refer are not prescribed or predictive but experimental. Around each word there is a space or a void in which nothing is anticipated, nothing enforced. Every relation must be invented, as if the world had just begun. Harold Rosenberg has argued that this is the chief characteristic of modern French poetry, though he offers a different explanation. 'Lifting up a word and putting a space around it has been the conscious enterprise of serious French poetry since Baudelaire and Rimbaud'; and a little later he speaks of 'the space around words necessary for consciousness'.[6] In Eliot's early poems an American is trying to make himself a Frenchman, perfecting himself in the creation of Jules Laforgue; an enterprise capable of producing, in the longer run, the magisterial achievement of making himself a European. The space around the words is necessary for consciousness, and it puts at risk the continuity of relations, as between one person and another. In Eliot, consciousness is the most available form of virtue, to be conscious is to be holy: an equation which causes great difficulty in the later plays, and especially in *The Cocktail Party*. But the words thus surrounded by empty space receive a corresponding halo of significance, they compel the imagination not by their relation but by their isolation. Such words take unto themselves a force of radiance, an exceptional power which Eliot in the later plays ascribes to saints and martyrs. Martyrdom is Eliot's favourite version of the Sublime.

There is a passage in *Writing Degree Zero* where Roland Barthes offers virtually the same distinction between what he calls classical language and modern language. In classical language the meaning is continuous, linear, it is always deferred until the end. So the mind, like the eye, runs along beside the words, and the movement is gratifying. But in modern poetry it is the word 'which gratifies and fulfills like the sudden revelation of a truth'. The word has lost its prescribed relations, but for that very reason it has acquired a magical power, it has become complete in itself, a revelation in its own recesses. Giving up its old dependency, the word acquires Sibylline presence; it stands there like Rilke's archaic torso of Apollo. It is a mark of such words that we cannot read them, but they read us, they affront us by presenting their significance in relation to themselves. Barthes says of such words that they 'initiate a discourse full of gaps and full of lights, filled with absences and over-nourishing signs, without foresight or stability of intention, and thereby so opposed to the social function of language that merely to have recourse to a discontinuous speech is to open the door to all that stands above Nature'. Classical language 'establishes a universe in which men are not alone, where words never have the terrible weight of things, where

Early Poems and *The Waste Land*

speech is always a meeting with the others'. Modern language presupposes a discontinuous Nature, 'a fragmented space, made of objects solitary and terrible because the links between them are only potential'. I would say that the links between them must be invented and are then fictive rather than prescribed or agreed: they have the freedom of fiction and, paying the price, the loneliness of being arbitrary. Such words, since they cannot be continuous with Nature, must be above or below it, two conditions about equally lonely. They are exceptions deprived of a rule. These words become names because of their oracular power, but what they name cannot be defined; they are like Stetson in *The Waste Land*, whose chief character is that he does not answer, though he instigates, the questions addressed to him. Stetson is the name for the interrogation, but he is under no obligation to reply. *The Waste Land* is the name of another interrogation, and its words are less answers than hints and guesses. Barthes says of these modern words generally—'words adorned with all the violence of their irruption, the vibration of which, though wholly mechanical, strangely affects the next word, only to die out immediately'—that they 'exclude men: there is no humanism of modern poetry'.[7] Stetson is not related to his interrogator or to London or even to Mylae, he is an oracle who stirs a nervous quiver of interrogation, and dies out in a line from Baudelaire.

Classical language, then, is a system organized on the assumption that Nature is continuous; hence the primacy of syntax. Classical poems stand in apposition to a seamless web of relations which we agree to call Nature: when the web is domestic we call it Society. The poems testify to those webs by enacting them in miniature. The long poem is valued as an extended ritual, offered to Nature in the grandest terms, a celebration of prescribed relations. The reader may still be surprised, because he does not know at any moment which of the indefinitely large number of relations the writer will enact, but he knows that one of them will be invoked. Each word is faithful to the others. But in modern poems, according to this distinction, the words are independent and therefore lonely. In *The Waste Land* we respond most deeply to the individual words and phrases with a sense of their exposure. The words are not obscure, because we know what the dictionary says of them and, mostly, we know where they come from. But they are Sibylline because of the darkness between them: they challenge us to provide them with a continuous syntax and they mock our efforts to do so; that was not what they meant at all. The whole poem looks like the sub-plot of a lost play; what is lost is the main plot, Nature as a significant action. The attempt to specify the form of *The Waste Land* is doomed because the form is not specific, it is not—to use Blackmur's word—predictive. The poem cries for its form: what it shows forth in itself is not form but the desperate analogy of form, tokens of a virtual form which would be valid if there were such a thing. What holds the several parts of the poem together is the need, which is at once the poet's need and our own, to keep life going, including the life of the poem in the dark spaces between the words. The problem is not that the poem lacks form but that it has a passion for form, largely unfulfilled, and—to make things harder—the memory of lost forms. Those lost forms would not answer the present need, even if they could be recovered: this is what Blackmur meant by saying of Eliot's early poems and *The Waste Land* that 'they measure the present by living standards which most people relegate to the past'.[8] What is present and vivid to us in the poem is the cry for form, the loud lament of that disconsolate chimera, and the cry is so pure that it almost makes up for what is merely lost. If the poem proliferates in little forms, it is because these are variations on an absent theme, a theme of which only the variations are known. The variations are recited from many different sources, and with increasing urgency toward the end of the poem, the sources being older versions of form, present now as broken images. In their bearing upon the reader, these images tell upon his conscience, forcing him to live up to the exactitude of the poem and to reject false consolations. If the poem is to be read as prolegomena to penance, it is also, in its bearing upon the reader, an incitement to scruple.

So Blackmur on another occasion spoke of Eliot's task as a poet: 'he has in his images to remind reason of its material, to remind order of its disorder, in order to create a sane art almost insane in its predicament.' He has 'to make a confrontation of the rational with the irrational: a deliberate reversal of roles'.[9] But in fact Eliot had to make a double confrontation, the violence going both ways. He had to confront the rational with the irrational, with what is below Nature, and the images used for this violence are mostly those he associated with Conrad's hollow men and *Heart of Darkness*. In the passage which Eliot wanted to use as the epigraph to *The Waste Land* before he came upon Petronius' Sibyl, Conrad's Marlow says of Kurtz:

> Did he live his life again in every detail of desire, temptation, and surrender during that supreme moment of complete knowledge? He cried in a whisper at some image, at some vision—he cried out twice, a cry that was no more than a breath—'The horror! the horror!'

The confrontation of the rational with the irrational is propelled by the assumption that complete knowledge is possible and its horror inescapable. So I have always believed that the reader of *The Waste Land* ought to take Tiresias seriously as the name of such a possibility, and such a horror. But the other confrontation is equally valid: the irrational is confronted with the rational in all those ways for which, in the poem, the rational imagination is represented by Shakespeare, Spenser, St Augustine, and, in the first version, by a passage from Plato's *Republic* which Pound deleted: 'Not here, O Ademantus, but in another world.'[10] The line comes from a famous passage in Book IX where Glaucon says that the city which has been described is merely verbal, it does not exist anywhere on earth; and Socrates answers, 'Well, perhaps there is a pattern of it laid up in heaven for him who wishes to contemplate it and so beholding to constitute himself its citizen.'[11] The

Early Poems and *The Waste Land*

contemplation of the City of God is also complete knowledge, above Nature, its sublimity compelling to the citizen, and its finality is asserted in the repeated Sanscrit word with which the poem ends. A Tiresias would see the City of God as clearly as the Unreal City, its malign counterpart. So the poem moves between *Heart of Darkness* and 'heart of light'. Words stand between reason and madness, touched by both adversaries.

We need an authoritative example; from Section III of *The Waste Land*, 'The Fire Sermon':

> *But at my back in a cold blast I hear*
> *The rattle of the bones, and chuckle spread from ear to ear.*
>
> *A rat crept softly through the vegetation*
> *Dragging its slimy belly on the bank*
> *While I was fishing in the dull canal*
> *On a winter evening round behind the gashouse*
> *Musing upon the king my brother's wreck*
> *And on the king my father's death before him.*
> *White bodies naked on the low damp ground*
> *And bones cast in a little low dry garret,*
> *Rattled by the rat's foot only, year to year.*
> *But at my back from time to time I hear*
> *The sound of horns and motors, which shall bring*
> *Sweeney to Mrs Porter in the spring.*
> *O the moon shone bright on Mrs Porter*
> *And on her daughter*
> *They wash their feet in soda water*
> Et O ces voix d'enfants, chantant dans la coupole![12]

It is useless to ask of that passage such questions as the following: who is speaking? what is the point of his narrative? whose white bodies lay naked on the ground? Such questions assume that there is a world-without-words to which Eliot's words pay tribute, as, in common usage, the word 'box' acknowledges the existence of a certain object which does not depend upon a word for its existence. A reader determined to give some kind of answer might say, to the first question: Tiresias; but he somehow includes the Buddha, Ferdinand Prince of Naples, Ovid and Verlaine. And to the second he might say: Well, the narrative is merely ostensible, we are not meant to think of it as a story, the words in that order make a kind of landscape in the reader's mind, Marshall McLuhan calls it psychological landscape, which is at once subject and object; it has to do with Eliot's theory of the objective correlative or Santayana's theory of the correlative object. And the answerer might say to the third question: The king my brother and the king my father, I suppose, but again the point is verbal and atmospheric rather than denotative. Questions more in accord with the nature of the passage would include the following: what is going on, when 'rat's foot' is preceded by the punning rhyme, 'rattled'? What is going on when the speaker, whoever he is, quotes several fragments from Ovid, Verlaine, the Grail Legend, Australian popular song, Marvell, *The Tempest*, John Day, and Middleton? Why does the passage suddenly change its tone at that first insistent rhyme, 'year' with 'hear'? Why are we given 'wreck' instead of 'wrack' in the quotation from *The Tempest*? These questions are not likely to set anyone's heart astir, but they are more in accord with Eliot's poem because they do not call another world in judgement upon the words. The questions keep strictly to language, and in this respect they follow the rhetoric of the poem. Symbolist poetry yearns for a world governed by the laws of Pure Poetry; internal laws, marking purely internal liaisons between one word and another, without any reference to Nature as a court of appeal. In such a world, time would take the form of prosody. In the passage from 'The Fire Sermon' no effect is allowed to escape from the words, to leave the medium of language. The images and figures do not leave the poem, they refuse to leave a setting which is assertively verbal. It is permissible to say that the speaker here and throughout the poem is Tiresias; but that is like saying that something is the speech of God, it merely replaces one problem by another. The words of the Sermon are not completed by our conceiving for their speaker a personal identity. It is more useful to imagine a possible state of feeling which is secreted in the words. The best way to read the lines is not to ask that each phrase give up its meaning, as if that meaning were then to replace the words; but to ask what quality, in each sequence, the phrases share. That quality may be found to attach itself to a state of feeling which cannot be given in other terms. Not a seamless narrative, but a set of lyric moments, each isolated for consciousness.

It is customary to say that the explanation for this use of language is to be found in the works of F.H. Bradley and in Eliot's thesis, *Knowledge and Experience in the Philosophy of F.H. Bradley*. I quote a few sentences in which Eliot summarizes Bradley's argument: kinship between Eliot's prose and Bradley's has been noted. 'It is only in immediate experience that knowledge and its object are one.' 'We have no right, except in the most provisional way, to speak of *my* experience, since the I is a construction out of experience, an abstraction from it; and the *thats*, the browns and hards and flats, are equally ideal constructions from experience, as ideal as atoms.' 'The only independent reality is immediate experience or feeling.' '"My" feeling is certainly in a sense mine. But this is because and in so far as I am the feeling.' 'Experience is non-relational.'[13] These sentences refer to Bradley's general philosophical position but more especially to certain passages in his *Essays on Truth and Reality*, including this one:

> Now consciousness, to my mind, is not original. What comes first in each of us is rather feeling, a state as yet without either an object or subject.... Feeling is

> immediate experience without distinction or relation in itself. It is a unity, complex but without relations. And there is here no difference between the state and its content, since, in a word, the experienced and the experience are one.[14]

In Eliot's version, 'feeling is more than either object or subject, since in a way it includes both'. Furthermore,

> In describing immediate experience we must use terms which offer a surreptitious suggestion of subject or object. If we say presentation, we think of a subject to which the presentation is present as an object. And if we say feeling, we think of it as the feeling of a subject about an object. . . . It may accordingly be said that the real situation is an experience which can never be wholly defined as an object nor wholly enjoyed as a feeling, but in which any of the observed constituents may take on the one or the other aspect.[15]

Perhaps this is enough to suggest what Eliot means when he speaks of 'the continuous transition by which feeling becomes object and object becomes feeling'. The language of 'The Fire Sermon' is surreptitious in the sense that its objectivity is merely ostensible. The rat creeping through the vegetation has only as much to do with animal life as is required to incite a certain feeling in the speaker. The rat has crept into the words and lost itself there; what transpires in the words is a certain feeling, in this case more subject than object. The meaning of a phrase, a line, a word, in 'The Fire Sermon' is every impression that attaches itself to those sounds under the pressure of consciousness; an assertion which reminds us that the famous Chapter XIV of Bradley's *Essays on Truth and Reality* is called 'What is the real Julius Caesar?' The real *Waste Land* is a sequence of those impressions, incited by the sequence of words: the impressions are different for each reader.

There is nothing unorthodox in this, from the standpoint of a philosophical idealist. It would be possible to quote Susanne Langer or Cassirer just as relevantly as Bradley. It is also orthodox Symbolism, of the kind which Valéry treats in 'Analecta, Tel Quel II', where he says that 'the self flees all created things, it withdraws from negation to negation: one might give the name "Universe" to everything in which the self refuses to recognize itself'. The self refuses to recognize itself in any part of the objective world, so called, until the world is transformed into subjective terms, every apprehended object become subject. But the self is always willing to recognize itself in language and symbols. Thinking of Eliot's poem, one might give the name 'language' to that alone in which the self recognizes itself. As for Eliot himself recognition may be willing or desperate: willing if we emphasize the luxury of the words, the gypsy phrases and cadences, the impression that man who passes his entire life among such words is the happiest of men; desperate, if we emphasize the allusions, and Eliot's need of them, the accepted weight of responsibility, those fragments shored against his ruin. The allusions are Eliot's insignia, and they have this further point; they give his sensibility other ground than itself, ground in history, literature, religion, revelation, through the words, the ground of our beseeching.

For while the self flees every created thing and refuses to recognize itself anywhere but in words, it needs something besides itself. Perhaps language is enough, but we must leave that question open. In a chapter on solipsism Eliot writes:

> The point of view (or finite centre) has for its object one consistent world, and accordingly no finite centre can be self-sufficient, for the life of a soul does not consist in the contemplation of one consistent world but in the painful task of unifying (to a greater or less extent) jarring and incompatible ones, and passing, when possible, from two or more discordant viewpoints to a higher which shall somehow include and transmute them.[16]

In *The Waste Land* Eliot calls this higher perspective Tiresias: 'we are led to the conception of an all-inclusive experience outside of which nothing shall fall', he says in the thesis on Bradley.

A year after the publication of *The Waste Land* Eliot reviewed Joyce's *Ulysses*, and proposed there a distinction which depends upon the idea of greater and lesser perspectives. In this distinction between two methods of fiction, 'narrative method' is based upon the commonly accepted separation of subject and object. The personal equivalent is the notion of a literary character, cut out from his surroundings and endowed with certain qualities. The medium is words, but most of them are common and they are placed in accepted arrangements. Books based upon these arrangements are called novels, so the novel as a form of art came to an end, according to Eliot in 1923, with Flaubert and James. (He later repudiated this obituary, by the way.) The 'mythical method' of fiction, on the other hand, is based upon immediate experience, the primacy of feeling, the idea of subject and object melting into each other beyond positivist redemption, and at last transcended in a quasi-divine perspective, Tiresias in *The Waste Land*, the Homeric archetype in *Ulysses*. But we should not identify Tiresias with the ultimate form of consciousness. It is necessary to think of language (Valéry's 'Saint Langage' in 'La Pythie') as issuing from a perspective grander even than Tiresias', since Tiresias can only see the world as one alienated from it: he does not give or sympathize, he does not participate in the suffering and transformation of 'What the Thunder Said'. It is necessary for the poem, and for poetry, to go beyond the phase of consciousness which Eliot calls Tiresias. The 'going beyond' has no name, it is the action of the poem itself. Instead of common words in common places there is language itself, construed now as a great treasury of images and figures and, increasingly in Eliot, identified with the Word of God. Using language in this way, it seems natural to have Ferdinand Prince of Naples, the Phoenician sailor, the one-eyed seller of currants, and all the women in the world becoming Tiresias. For Eliot, as for Bradley, there is no question of a Wordsworthian liaison between man and Nature. The only part of Bradley's *Appearance and Reality* which Eliot chose to quote in his notes to *The Waste Land* disengages itself

Early Poems and *The Waste Land*

from any such hope. In Ch. XXIII Bradley says that 'we behave as if our internal worlds were the same'. But we err:

> Our inner worlds, I may be told, are divided from each other, but the outer world of experience is common to all; and it is by standing on this basis that we are able to communicate. Such a statement would be incorrect. My external sensations are no less private to myself than are my thoughts or my feelings. In either case my experience falls within my own circle, a circle closed on the outside; and, with all its elements alike, every sphere is opaque to the others which surround it. . . . In brief, regarded as an existence which appears in a soul, the whole world for each is peculiar and private to that soul.[17]

Perhaps our first impression here is wonder that such a view of the mind's predicament could ever have secreted, in Bradley's pupil, a major poem. But the second impression is better, that for such a poet language is the only possible home: either language or that metalanguage we call silence. But we are in danger of confounding the pupil with his master. Just as Bradley cleared himself of a charge of solipsism by arguing, in *Appearance and Reality*, that 'we can go to foreign selves by a process no worse than the construction which establishes our own self',[18] so Eliot cleared himself of a charge of philosophy by becoming a poet; that is, by attending to all the affiliations of words, including their old hankering after objects. Against the persuasion of his idealism, there are the deep persuasions of Dante, Shakespeare, Virgil; and there is eventually the persuasion of Christian belief in which time is redeemed and the higher dream is made flesh. Perhaps these are the necessary qualifications to make while returning to the poem. Without them, we are in danger of turning the poem into a set of more or less interesting ideas; forgetting that to Eliot, as to Bradley, 'a mere idea is but a ruinous abstraction'; forgetting, too, that it was Eliot who praised Henry James for possessing a mind so fine that no idea could violate it. With the passage from 'The Fire Sermon' in front of us again, we see that what came first was not an idea but feeling, 'a state as yet without either an object or subject'. The nearest expressive equivalent is rhythm, at this stage not yet resolved in words. In 'The Music of Poetry' Eliot reported that in his own experience 'a poem, or a passage from a poem, may tend to realize itself first as a particular rhythm before it reaches expression in words, and that this rhythm may bring to birth the idea and the image'.[19] An account of our passage would be a blunt affair if it did not point to the changes of rhythm as among the chief moments; where the echo of Marvell's 'To His Coy Mistress' imposes a new and deeper tone upon the verse; and from there until the line from Verlaine the transitions become more abrupt. Eliot remains true to the original feeling by remaining true to its rhythm. The words, when they are found, maintain a double allegiance: they are required to define the rhythm of the first feeling, and they must also allow for the melting of one experience into another.

The first consequence is that, to a reader sceptical of idealist assumptions, many of these lines appear wilfully arch and secretive: they appear to go through the motions of grammar and syntax without committing themselves to these agencies. They are neither one thing nor the other, neither wholly subject nor wholly object: without proposing themselves as paradoxes, they are paradoxical. A further result is that, in verse of this kind, incidents drawn from whatever source cannot have the status which they would have in a novel or in another poem. In the *Metamorphoses* Ovid tells the story of the rape of Philomela by King Tereus of Thrace. Eliot recalls the story in 'A Game of Chess'. Trico's song in Lyly's *Alexander and Campaspe* has the lines:

> *Oh, 'tis the ravished nightingale.*
> Jug, jug, jug, jug, tereu*! she cries.*

Matthew Arnold's 'Philomela' is one story, John Crowe Ransom's is another, the story is diversely told. How it appears in the mind of God, there is no knowing; what is the real Philomela is a hard question. How it appears in the inordinate mind of Tiresias is given in *The Waste Land*:

> *Twit twit twit*
> *Jug jug jug jug jug jug*
> *So rudely forc'd.*
> *Tereu*

—being the twit of the swallow, the Elizabethan nightingale-call and, by curious association, the word for 'slut', a fine phrase of justice from Middleton's *A Game at Chess*, and lastly the simple vocative, 'Tereu'. Ovid's story is given, indeed, but only the gist of it, the story insofar as it survives transposition in the inclusive consciousness of tiresias. In that strange place, one image melts into another; hence Eliot's idiom of melting, transition, becoming deliquescence, and so forth.

To resume a long story: it is easy to think of Eliot as he thought of Swinburne: 'only a man of genius could dwell so exclusively and consistently among words.' In Swinburne, as in Poe, words alone are certain good. But it is well to qualify that report by adding another, from 'The Music of Poetry', where Eliot speaks of the poet as occupied with 'frontiers of consciousness beyond which words fail, though meanings still exist'. In the plays this exorbitant work is done by miracle, 'the way of illumination'. Tiresias is the Unidentified Guest, until he too is transcended in Celia. The effort of the plays is to allow people to live by a holy language. Language, the ancient place of wisdom, is guaranteed by conscience and consciousness, as in *Four Quartets*. That is why, at last, 'the poetry does not matter'. The procedures of *The Waste Land*, which were sustained by the force of language itself, are transposed into the idiom of characters acting and suffering: transitions and perspectives, verbal in *The Waste Land*, take more specific forms in the later poems and plays, the forms of personal action, chances and choices. The frontier of consciousness is not the place where words fail but where self dies, in the awful surrender of faith. Bradley is not repudiated, but he is forced to accommodate himself to the Shakespeare of *A Winter's Tale* and *The Tempest*: that is one way of putting it.

I have been arguing that it is characteristic of Eliot's language in *The Waste Land* to effect an 'absence in reality', and to move words into the resultant vacuum. At first, the words seem to denote things, *sensibilia* beyond the lexicon, but it soon appears that their allegiance to reality is deceptive, they are traitors in reality. So far as the relation between word and thing is deceptive, so far also is 'objective' reality undermined. The only certainty is that the absence in reality has been effected by the words, and now the same words are enforcing themselves as the only presences. What we respond to is the presence of the words. In this way the words acquire the kind of aura, or the kind of reverberation, which we feel in proverbs; with this difference, that proverbs appeal to our sense of life, an inherited wisdom in our sense of things; Eliot's words appeal to primordial images and rhythms which can be felt, though they cannot well be called in evidence. I cannot explain this use of language except by suggesting that if the common arrangements of words issue from the common sense of time, Eliot's arrangements issue from the quarrel between time and myth: I assume that myth is a way of breaking the chain of time, the chain of one thing after another. Eliot is using words as if their first obligation were neither to things nor to time. Philip Wheelwright has called this kind of imagination 'archetypal', the imagination 'which sees the particular object in the light of a larger conception or of a higher concern'. Nearly everything in Eliot's language can be explained by his feeling that the truth of things resides in an indeterminate area: neither subject nor object, but a state compounded of both; neither time nor eternity, but a state in which the double obligation is registered; neither man nor God, but a being, conceivable in words but not in fact, who is vouched for not in identifiable speech but in language itself, eventually to be invoked as Logos. I am not indeed maintaining that the word 'rat', in 'The Fire Sermon', has ceased to observe all relation to a certain rodent, but rather that the word is a double agent, it accepts the friction between reality and language, but it does not give total allegiance to either party. On one side stands the world of things; on the other, a rival world of dissociated forms, Platonic cities. Between these worlds stands the individual word, maintaining a secret life, double allegiance or double treachery.

It is characteristically American of Eliot to place these inordinate burdens upon language and the poetic imagination. The imagination must do nearly everything because reality cannot be relied on to do much. In the relation between reality and the imagination, he has established conditions extremely favourable to the imagination. This is only another way of saying that language commands the otherwise empty space between consciousness and experience, consciousness and action, consciousness and the earth.

Studies of *The Waste Land* and poems

Notes

1. *Facsimile*, 31.
2. Nathaniel Hawthorne, *The House of the Seven Gables* (Centenary edition, Ohio State University Press, 1965), vol. II, 1.
3. 'Henry James', reprinted in *The Shock of Recognition*, ed. Edmund Wilson (New York, 1955), vol. II, 855.
4. 'American Literature and the American Language', reprinted in *To Criticize the Critic*.
5. 'From Poe to Valéry', reprinted in *To Criticize the Critic*.
6. Harold Rosenberg, *The Tradition of the New* (London, 1970 reprint), 86, 89.
7. Roland Barthes, *Writing Degree Zero*, translated by Annette Lavers and Colin Smith (London, 1967), 54–5.
8. R.P. Blackmur, *Form and Value in Modern Poetry* (New York, 1957).
9. R.P. Blackmur, *Anni Mirabiles 1921–1925* (Washington, Library of Congress, 1956), 31.
10. *Facsimile*, 31.
11. *The Republic*, book IX, 592–A–B, quoted from the Loeb edition in *Facsimile*, 128.
12. *Collected Poems 1909–1962*, 70–71.
13. *Knowledge and Experience in the Philosophy of F.H. Bradley* (London, 1964), 19, 30, 31, 27.
14. F.H. Bradley, *Essays on Truth and Reality* (Oxford, 1914), 194.
15. *Knowledge and Experience*, 22, 25.
16. *Ibid.*, 147–8.
17. F.H. Bradley, *Appearance and Reality* (London, 1902), 346.
18. *Ibid.*, 258.
19. *On Poetry and Poets*, 38.

115
The Waste Land as a Dramatic Monologue*

ANTHONY EASTHOPE

Few poems have hit their original audience with such force as did *The Waste Land* on its publication in 1922, and some of these first readers christened themselves 'Wastelanders' as an earlier generation had called themselves 'Ibsenites'. Yet even a poem as strange and brilliant as this surprisingly soon came to be assessed in conventional terms, conventional both in the sense of normal and of agreed. During the 'thirties influential voices, particularly those of F.R. Leavis, F.O. Matthiessen and Cleanth Brooks,[1] united to establish what may fairly be called a consensus about the meaning of the poem. Symbols of drought and rain, of sterility and rebirth, developed—as the Notes indicate—from *The Golden Bough* and from Jessie L. Weston's account of the Grail legend and the Tarot cards, suggest that under the accidents of civilisation mankind lives essentially, as Leavis puts it, in a 'harmony of human culture with the natural environment'.[2] By nature man is bound to the soil; but the development of modern life, industrialism, the city, imaged in the poem by the contemporary scene, has cut him off from his roots and brought him to a state of self-consciousness, boredom, automatism, and spiritual sterility. This would be a raw paraphrase but gives the substantial content of the exegesis it summarises. It is more or less in these terms that, as Robert M. Adams recently acknowledged, 'Eliot imposed himself on the literary conscience of my generation'.[3] And it is rather in these terms that *The Waste Land* is discussed when set as a text for schools.

To be sure the poem does not *state* its meaning in so many words; but it is no impossible task for a post-symbolist poetic to draw the meaning from its realisation in the poem. Following Mallarmé's principle that to name is to destroy while to suggest is to create, it was argued that the meaning was better communicated the less explicitly it was stated. One sees the method at work when F.O. Matthiessen replaces naming ('rhetorical proclamation') with suggestion ('presented') in this description of *The Waste Land*:

*English Studies, vol. 64, nos. 1–6 (1983), pp. 330–44.

> If, in severest analysis, the kind of poetry Eliot is writing gives evidence of social disintegration, he has expressed that fact precisely as the poet should, not by rhetorical proclamation, but by the very feeling of contemporary life which he has presented to the sensitive reader of his lines.[4]

In this understanding the poem did not offer its meaning discursively: the poem was said to be a 'projection of awareness',[5] and, in a later, extreme formulation, 'a pure, non-discursive Image'.[6] To this extent the poem became something impossible to controvert: to read it was to accept its method; to do that was to submit one's own experience to its (embodied) 'meaning'.

Against this consensus there have been voices raised, particularly by those worried about the unity of the poem. If *The Waste Land* were the equivalent of a direct experience, how did it cohere? If it was unified, how could we *know* it was? Taking up the assertion that the poem presented its meaning directly as a 'stream of consciousness', Graham Hough made this demur:

> The advantage of the 'stream of consciousness' technique is that it allows a flood of images, more or less emancipated from narrative or logical continuity, while still preserving a psychological continuity—the continuity of inhering in a single consciousness. *The Waste Land* conspicuously forgoes this kind of unifying principle.[7]

He concludes that while this technique may achieve 'a startling concentration and brilliance of the individual image' it is a rhetoric inadequate for anything but 'very special effects—states of madness and dream, for example'[8] and certainly inadequate as organising principle for a poem of the intended scope of *The Waste Land*. Barbara Everett has denied the poem any organising principle whatever:

> The only rhetorical rule is the extreme discreteness of its mixed and broken formalism: hardly a word in the whole that does not rest within a local convention, but hardly a convention that is not violated and confused. All the attempts to rectify the poem by imposing upon it unifying categories that improve this situation merely distort its essential medium. *The Waste Land* has neither 'story' nor 'narrator' nor 'protagonist' nor 'myth' nor 'themes' nor 'music' nor 'locale': these are exact and technical terms which the poem includes only to fragment and deny.[9]

By what must be an impossible paradox the unity of the poem is its disunity, its organising principle a consistent lack of organisation; impossible, because if *The Waste Land* offers as little purchase to the reader as this catalogue of negatives would assert how can anyone read it at all? It would tend to remain wholly self-sufficient so that, to borrow a metaphor from Jeremy Hawthorn, it would be like a sardine tin with the key contained inside.[10] And this is surely not what it feels like to read this most widely read of modern poems.

Outside the consensus the poem has also been under attack from the left. An essay by David Craig published first in 1960 began with the stern conclusion:

> T.S. Eliot's *The Waste Land* is one of the outstanding cases in modern times of a work which projects an almost defeatist personal depression in the guise of a full, impersonal picture of society.[11]

For Craig the poem contrasts older 'organic' ways of life, typified in the eighteenth century village, with the rootlessness of modern urban society. But since this view is incorrect or at least historically onesided, and since the poem in any case exhibits symptoms of Eliot's sexual disgust and snobbery, *The Waste Land* deals dishonestly with its reader, concealing a subjective view 'in the guise of' an objective statement. On similar grounds Terry Eagleton has objected to the use of myth in the poem since it 'smuggles private attitudes into what postures as impartial wisdom'.[12] Both writers, it should be noted, share the consensus assumption that the poem has a meaning to be read out in some way as an impersonal or impartial statement.

Whether it was to these later accusations or to earlier exegesis or simply to some higher authority that Eliot addressed himself in the epigraph to the manuscript published in 1971 we cannot know. Its effect was to dismiss altogether the poem's claim to an impersonal meaning: it might have been interpreted as 'an important bit of social criticism' but to the author it had been 'only the relief of a personal and wholly insignificant grouse against life'.[13] As Bernard Bergonzi summed up the situation after publication of the manuscript:

> ... the poem is, at bottom, an anguished reliving of subjective experience, and not the 'impersonal' meditation of cultural decline that so many commentators—whether sympathetic or unsympathetic—have assumed it to be.[14]

I take it that this question, the extent to which the poem is personal or subjective, must now be the point of departure for any discussion. I shall argue that *The Waste Land* is unified *in the first place* as the voice of a single unnamed speaker identifiable within an area of psychological consistency whose consciousness develops through definable phases. My thesis, then, is that the poem is at this level mimetic; and that it stands in relationship to a conventional genre, the dramatic monologue. This established, we can return to other considerations afterwards.

The Speaker

While *The Waste Land* was read as impersonal statement, the problem of its 'voice' or *persona* did not need to be taken too seriously. Critics said there was a variety of different speakers, or were content to identify the speaker casually as Eliot himself or Tiresias or, in a strange mixture of genres, as the 'protagonist' or as some central 'consciousness'. In any case, there were always two initial obstacles to reading the poem as a sustained monologue, the presence of *different* voices, and Tiresias.

The Waste Land does appear to contain distinct voices, usually set off as such by quotation marks: Marie, the 'hyacinth' girl, Madame Sosostris, the cockneys, the three Thames-daughters. This in itself is not incompatible with dramatic monologue—Browning's Andrea del Sarto hears or imagines the voices of several other people. So does Prufrock for that matter. The juxtaposition of scenes and voices is an appropriate technique for rendering urban life and corresponds to cinematic editing, as Pound noted in 1922: 'In a city the visual impressions succeed each other, overlap, overcross, they are cinematographic'.[15] The question is the use made of this technique, whether it is aimed objectively to give the impression of the city or subjectively the observer's impression. Clearly *The Waste Land* does not offer an objective context in which these impressions (scenes, voices) can be read as documentary report; each is intensively mediated through the speaker's consciousness to become what he thinks, remembers, wishes, imagines, fantasises. The external sensations, one may say, have become private to the self they express.

Tiresias—or rather the authority conferred on him in the note to line 218[16]—has been a continual source of difficulties. Some critics have followed this note to the letter, for example, Grover Smith, who speaks of 'the actions in the poem' as being 'only memories in the mind of Tiresias, the Proust of this inquiry'.[17] Others, such as Graham Hough, have remained emphatically unconvinced:

> Who was Tiresias? A man who had also been a woman, who lived for ever and could foretell the future. That is to say, not a single human consciousness, but a mythological catch-all, and as a unifying factor of no effect whatever.[18]

The note to 218 points accurately to the method of the poem, for what its speaker sees 'is the substance of the poem'. But it is misleading both by claiming that Tiresias is detached, 'a mere spectator', and by naming him as the speaker of the *whole* poem. The intention may have been to help the reader of a difficult new poem but without the note, as the poem was originally published,[19] the situation is somewhat clearer. The speaker of *The Waste Land* has no name, any more than does that of Beckett's novel *The Unnameable*, nor more relevantly, the hero of Tennyson's *Maud*. Tiresias does *not* speak the whole poem: on the contrary, its speaker assumes the role of Tiresias at this point and only for this section, a tactic ancitipated in the earlier poem where Prufrock sees himself variously as John the Baptist, Lazarus and Polonius. The nameless voice of *The Waste Land* thinks himself within a number of roles, some of which last briefly, from Ezekiel to Iachimo in Imogen's bedroom, from Phlebas the Phoenician to a Vedic seer. Of these Tiresias is only one, a *persona* of apparently unassailable detachment adopted at this point for reasons the context makes clear, as I shall argue later.

The first person singular ('I' twenty-nine times, 'me' twice) is used throughout *The Waste Land* to identify a single voice and a single consciousness. Pound dissuaded Eliot from prefixing *Gerontion* to the poem to give it a speaker and also from using the epigraph from Conrad:

> Did he live his life again in every detail of desire, temptation and surrender during that supreme moment of complete knowledge? He cried in a whisper at some image, at some vision—he cried out twice, a cry that was no more than a breath—'The horror! the horror!'[20]

Eliot thought this would be 'somewhat elucidative'.[21] It would have been, though it would not have changed the body of the text as it now stands for us. Kurtz is imagined to have re-experienced his life in the moment of death, just as a drowning man is supposed to re-live his whole life, as in Golding's *Pincher Martin* and possibly the last Act of *Peer Gynt*. *The Waste Land* is inserted into this exceptional but psychologically plausible space, a state of madness or dream for which, as Graham Hough says, the imagist technique is literally appropriate. Its obvious poetic precedent is Tennyson's *Maud* (from which incidentally Eliot borrowed the phrase 'a handful of dust'). In Part II, V, the speaker, confined to an insane asylum, imagines himself to be dead and buried alive but still thinking. 'And the wheels go over my head'. Kurtz is actually dying but imagines himself between life and death—the further striking precedent for rendering the kind of extreme experience is *The Ancient Mariner*. After shooting the albatross the Mariner experiences death-in-life until he is won by 'The Night-Mare LIFE-IN-DEATH' and crosses into her power. We may now begin to put *the Waster Land* in a somewhat less original position than it is usually allocated. If we are prepared to step outside it as I think we must once its power to impose itself on a generation is broken, then it can be read in the first instance as a not wholly untraditional dramatisation of a consciousness at the edge of oblivion, either dying or in madness imagining itself so. *Within* this dimension it lives over its life again, so that there is in *The Waste Land* a definite narrative consequence. But this is accompanied by a deterioration in the subject's control, a development by which one might say the first three sections correspond to Death-in-Life, the fourth is a death, 'Death by Water', and the fifth is Life-in-Death.

The Burial of the Dead

The note to line 218, as I.A. Richards pointed out soon after the poem was published, 'is a way of underlining the fact that the poem is concerned with many aspects of the one fact of sex'.[22] If all the women in the poem 'are one woman' and all the men are one man, then the main preoccupation is not sexuality in general but a sexual relationship. In the first line of the poem the speaker, feeling himself and wishing himself dead, is forced back into a form of life by an unwished for surge of consciousness, 'Memory and desire'.

Before the movement begins in earnest he dons the mantle of Ezekiel ('Son of man') to give us the conclusion won from the process of desire, temptation and surrender that he calls 'stony rubbish'. He offers a moment of complete knowledge, 'I will show you fear in a handful of dust'. What follows is the crux of the poem, the experience which brought the speaker to his present state of being neither living nor dead; in different images it recurs throughout; and it is also its conclusion in that the speaker cannot progress from this vision in which his eyes failed and were turned to pearl. Framed by quotations from Wagner, the passage begins with a girl recalling the beginning of a relationship. Crucially what happened in the hyacinth garden is displaced in the speaker's mind by his experience *after* the act of love, 'when we came back'. He has encountered something ultimate, transcendent:

> *. . . I could not*
> *Speak, and my eyes failed, I was neither*
> *Living nor dead, and I knew nothing,*
> *Looking into the heart of light, the silence.*

In his essay on Baudelaire Eliot distinguishes the spiritual from the animal:

> Baudelaire has perceived that what distinguishes the relations of man and woman from the copulation of beasts is the knowledge of Good and Evil . . . Having an imperfect, vague romantic conception of Good, he was at least able to understand that the sexual act as evil is more dignified, less boring, than as the natural, 'life-giving', cheery automatism of the modern world.[23]

With the hyacinth girl the speaker has found only 'the copulation of beasts', a mere encounter of bodies in which he experiences the *positive* absence of a spiritual dimension, Good and Evil. He *knew* nothingness itself and felt what Dante felt when he saw the Devil (*Inferno* XXXIV, 23 ff.):

> *. . . I write it not*
> *Because all speech would fail to tell,*
> *I did not die, and did not remain alive . . .*

Looking into what should have been 'the heart of light' he found a brilliant and silent void, '*Oed' und leer*', waste and empty, more like a heart of darkness.

Memories continue. In the next paragraph the speaker hears Madame Sosostris, whom we may suppose he consulted in trying to re-establish the spiritual dimension his experience has negated. Clairvoyantly her words touch on his state of mind as they return insistently to eyes which failed (turned to pearl), death and capital punishment. In context with 'The Hanged Man' the crowds 'walking round in a ring' suggest prisoners in an exercise yard, just as in *The Ballad of Reading Gaol* the condemned man walks in one yard while other prisoners walk 'Within another ring' (stanza four). On London Bridge the speaker sees himself as Dante among the damned, a

Early Poems and *The Waste Land*

living man among the dead. Meeting Stetson, seemingly a murderer who has planted a corpse in his garden, he admits complicity with him, recognising him as his likeness, 'mon semblable'.

Such references to death, murder and capital punishment have led Hugh Kenner to argue for a kind of plot to *The Waste Land*:

> In *The Waste Land* as in *The Family Reunion*, the guilt of the protagonist seems coupled with his perhaps imagined responsibility for the fate of a perhaps ideally drowned woman.[24]

The poem does owe something to such dramatic monologues as *My Last Duchess* and *Porphyria's Lover*, both case histories of psychopathic men who 'do a girl in'. But in *The Waste Land*, in the way indicated by Eliot's essay on Baudelaire, the speaker's state of mind arises from some general insight, what he saw in the sexual act, not from some crime he committed or imagined he had done. What he came to know might be put thus: if in the sexual act a woman is treated as only a body in what is thus indistinguishable from the 'copulation of beasts', then the act of love is equal to murder, the total reduction of a person to a body. Each man does kill the thing he loves exactly in so far as he treats her as a thing. For the speaker of *The Waste Land* a woman 'undone' (sexually betrayed) is like one 'undone' by death (see lines 63, 252, 294); 'White bodies naked on the low damp ground' (line 193) may be either copulating or rotting; he may have seduced the hyacinth girl's body 'a year ago' (line 35) but he also feels guilty as though he has treated her as a corpse 'planted last year' (71). Having discovered nothingness, the absence of Good and Evil in human sexuality, the living for him are as the dead, the living body is 'a handful of dust' in which he finds fear, and life in the modern world is a routine of meaningless automatism.

A Game of Chess

It is not difficult to complete a narrative context for 'A Game of Chess': the speaker fantasises while watching the woman brush her hair, she speaks to him and we have his unvoiced responses; she threatens to rush out and 'walk the street' but it seems to be he who leaves her for a pub where he overhears (presumably from the private bar) cockney voices in the public bar. In the first paragraph the elaboration of the description makes us aware of the consciousness which *is* describing. By specifying objects the speaker tries to conceal from himself what is on his mind, yet evoked excessively each object becomes a fetish, even the ascending perfumes suggesting sexual climax. His literary self-consciousness also hides its real object, for by picturing the woman as Cleopatra, Imogen, Dido, he enters unwittingly the roles of Antony, Iachimo, Aeneas. The sexual drift becomes overt in the idea of Philomel, 'So rudely forced'. At the thought of rape, which is complete reduction within the sexual act of a woman to a mere body, the speaker loses control, breaking into the present tense and into crude monosyllables:

> . . . *yet there the nightingale*
> *Filled all the desert with inviolable voice*
> *And still she cried, and still the world pursues,*
> *'Jug Jug' to dirty ears.*

The paragraph ends in images of horror, guilt and with the woman's accusing voice.

This vividly dramatic scene re-enacts the moment after the hyacinth garden and shows its consequence for the speaker. Shrilly neurotic, the woman accuses him of not speaking, not loving, not sympathising with her, so making her prey to the anxieties for which she reproaches him. Her jagged questions are answered only by his unspoken thoughts which reveal to us, not her, the vacancy on which his mind dwells. As Hamlet sees the Ghost his mother does not ('Do you see nothing there?'), so this man sees the nothing he first knew after the hyacinth garden, his life now fixed on this single memory:

> *I remember*
> *Those are pearls that were his eyes.*

Moving out among the cockneys he finds that what the world pursues is what he already knows: male insistence and female acquiescence following each other in a mechanical circle without spiritual meaning.

The Fire Sermon

The link between closing time, the goodnights, Ophelia's words and women seduced and abandoned beside the 'Sweet Thames' is developed in the speaker's mind. It is he who sees himself momentarily as Israel in exile, departed into another country ('By the waters of Leman I sat down and wept . . .') so identifying himself with the casual seducers who have departed leaving no addresses. From this follow thoughts of love and death inextricably related. The idea of joyful and ceremonious love in the refrain of Spenser's *Prothalamion* leads to an antithesis, 'But at my back . . .'. In the original context, the most famous poem of seduction in the language, the phrase urges a motive for intercourse but here it introduces images of the skull beneath the skin. In the next paragraph the speaker thinks the same ideas in reverse order; death leads to love and then to thoughts of rape. A Dickensian waterfront landscape of slime, rats, disused buildings and death by drowning (recalling *Bleak House*, Chapter LVII) expresses his horror of 'White bodies naked'. Now the antithesis, 'But at my back . . .' (line 196), enacts a movement of sexual desire, Sweeney, Mrs. Porter and her daughter, a movement which as in 'A Game of Chess' breaks down at the idea of rape:

Twit twit twit
Jug jug jug jug jug jug
So rudely forc'd
Tereu

Two different Elizabethan sources seem to fuse together here, one linking spring, lovers and birdsong, the other giving the cry of 'the ravish'd nightingale'.[25] The speaker feels them together since for him horror at the fact of physical copulation immediately supervenes on feelings of desire. And this set of mind is the context for the Tiresias passage.

The detached *persona* of Tiresias and the impersonal, Augustan style here cannot be taken at face value, for they enact the speaker's *need* to keep a maximum distance between himself and the object of his consciousness. The mythological neutrality of Tiresias, impotent and bisexual, is compromised if its immediate context is recognised, for the speaker has just thought (lines 212–14) of being the object of Mr. Eugenides' homosexual proposition. The mask fits in another respect since the speaker feels himself to be spiritually blinded, his eyes failing at the vision of the hyacinth garden. In fact the assumed impersonality enables the speaker to make a partial confrontation with the natural if not particularly cheerful automatism of the modern world, an act of copulation by the typist and clerk, which in the re-living becomes his own action. At the moment of climax they are displaced as he interposes himself to say he has 'foresuffered all', as indeed he has, not at Thebes, but in the hyacinth garden when like Dante at the end of the *Inferno* he 'walked among the lowest of the dead'.

The speaker repeats in his imagination the automatic act of the typist in the stories of the three Thames-daughters. It is really one story, the same story as before, since each is a woman 'undone' in an act of mechanical impassivity. The first is seduced not so much by a man as by the city:

'Trams and dusty trees.
Highbury bore me. Richmond and Kew
Undid me. By Richmond I raised my knees
Supine on the floor of a narrow canoe.'

Love and death are again equated in these lines for she speaks in the words of La Pia (*Purgatorio* V, 133 ff), apparently done to death by her husband at Maremma. In the second story the man is remorseful while she remains unmoved:

'. . . After the event
He wept. He promised "a new start."
I made no comment. What should I resent?'

The third is victim of what used to be called a dirty weekend at Margate, like that to which the speaker was invited at Brighton. Afterwards she sits on the beach emotionally destroyed, totally disabused:

> 'On Margate Sands.
> I can connect
> Nothing with nothing . . .'

Without the note to line 307, 'To Carthage then I came', we would not think of St Augustine but of a more famous visitor to Carthage whose history has already featured in the poem. When Aeneas left Dido she killed herself after ordering her body to be burned on the shore so that Aeneas in his departing ship might see the flames. The word 'burning' which concludes this section thus runs the fires of male desire into the thought of a woman destroyed. Again, the speaker 'kills' the thing he loves.

Death by Water

Although the stage for the whole poem is the speaker's own mind at no defined juncture in time or space, in the first two sections he re-lives his experience as a linear narrative, most clearly in the hyacinth garden passage and the bedroom scene in 'A Game of Chess'. There is a progression into 'The Fire Sermon' as he calls up surrogate figures, the clerk, the typist, the Thames-daughters, to represent himself and the hyacinth girl. But this attempted confrontation precipitates a new and deeper crisis showing itself in a changed quality in the speaker's consciousness in and after 'Death by Water'. Since his vision of the hyacinth garden he has always been the drowned Phoenician sailor with pearls for eyes but as he now imagines himself as Phlebas, forgetting and sinking, images of fire give way to water, the tension relaxes in an even and limpid tone as he 'goes under'.

What the Thunder Said

The sexual theme disappears for the first seventy odd lines of this section, and even such recognisable reality as we had before is dissolved into phantasmagoria. The voice which addresses us speaks with the fluency and bland repetitive insistence of someone at the remote edge of sanity: obsessive images (water, rock), hallucination ('Who is the third . . .?'), imaginary noises ('What is that sound . . .?'), explosions, ('Falling towers'). The reality of this psychological rendering is apparent if we put it alongside this account by a victim of PIDE in Portugal of the effects of sleep deprivation:

> All I recall of the sixth, seventh and eighth days is a hazy memory of hallucin-

ations, pains in the head, the permanent buzzing in my ears. I began to see very refined machines, complicated gadgets for torture, great heaps of electric cables all tangled up, beams of strong light directed at my eyes, the cries of people being tortured, the voice of my wife, my daughter's cries, deafening sirens, explosions that blackened the walls of my room.[26]

The 'I' of the first three parts of the poem spoke with some self-possession: 'I will show you fear', 'I think we are in rat's alley . . .'. He was conscious of—indeed unable to forget—what he had seen. Now the voice speaks unself-consciously in the present tense from within that memory itself. The landscape is seen as though through the mineral eyes of Phlebas, for now life is as death, stony rubbish, a handful of dust, a desert of rock, stone, sand, mountains. The speaker has crossed a frontier, 'He who was living is now dead' (line 329).

The crowing of the cock (line 392) brings on a passage of weird lucidity. In the persons of a Hindu prophet or perhaps Jehovah speaking to Job he regains some control over the contents of his mind. Though not free from delusion his portentous pronouncements seem to carry references back to himself and the woman still in the sexual knot as before. The first, 'The awful daring of a moment's surrender', could be spoken of the hyacinth garden, the second, 'each in his prison', of their alienation from each other in 'A Game of Chess', the third again unites love and death. It appears to evoke a moment of sexual fulfilment, the boat responding to the sailor as the woman to the touch of her lover.

> *Gaily, when invited, beating obedient*
> *To controlling hands*

But the lines say only that she 'would have responded', not that she did, and possibly the girl is 'undone', like the first Thames-daughter in her *alter ego* as La Pia. The heart might beat obedient to 'controlling hands' on the jugular vein and windpipe. Again, finally, a dead body is seen superimposed on a naked body, and the break at this thought is abrupt and unpunctuated.

It is usual to read the last paragraph as some kind of conclusion or summing up of the poem. Overimpressed perhaps by the range of cultural and linguistic reference (which includes Sanscrit) we are led away from the natural response. But read aloud the effect is unmistakable: the speaker collapses into incoherence and true madness. The antiquity and remoteness of the words in the last two lines encourage us to find some primordial wisdom. But they are primitive in quite another sense, that is, almost infantile. There is reference to Hieronymo being 'mad againe' and then three deep-throated cries: 'Datta. Dayadhvam. Damyata'. These are fully compatible with seizure of throat and jaw in a fit, as is 'Shantih shantih shantih', which is close to mad Lear's 'Sa sa sa sa'. The speaker of the poem has entered a peace which is past understanding in quite another sense to that implied by the note to the last line.

Some Conclusions: The Rhetorical Strategy

This account has tried to substantiate that we must read *The Waste Land* in the first instance as a dramatic monologue and so unified as a psychological continuity. Further it seems *necessary* for the poem to be one man's voice if it is to give a vivid rendering of modern experience, and particularly the urban experience. On this we may refer to one of the earliest and most famous accounts of city life, that of Engels in 1844. He discusses the crowd flowing through the streets as epitomising the structure of modern urban society; he recognises there a common humanity ('are they not all human beings with the same qualities and powers?') but one divided into separated individuals who notice each other only to avoid walking into each other:

> And, however much one may be aware that this isolation of the individual, this narrow self-seeking, is the fundamental principle of our society everywhere, it is nowhere so shamelessly barefaced, so self-conscious as just here in the crowding of the great city. The dissolution of mankind into monads, of which each one has a separate principle and a separate purpose, the world of atoms, is here carried out to its utmost extreme.[27]

As Steven Marcus has recently suggested,[28] Engels' capacity to make sense of the city depends on an abstract conceptualisation deriving from Hegel. Engels' analysis is external and objective: *The Waste Land* aims to give the experience of living in the modern city and it therefore must be radically subjective. Its point of view has to be located *inside* one of these 'monads', an individual who has 'a separate principle and a separate purpose' so that (in the words of F. H. Bradley given in the note to line 411) 'the whole world for each is peculiar and private to that soul'. Engels may be said to present an impersonal picture of society: *The Waste Land* explicitly offers itself as one man's consciousness: 'I will show you fear', 'I had not thought . . .', 'I saw one I knew . . ., 'I remember . . .', 'I Tiresias' . . ., 'I sat upon the shore . . .'.

This is a personal poem not only in that its point of view is situated within an individual consciousness but also because the content of this consciousness reinforces the speaker's peculiarity and tendency to solipsism. It is noteworthy that so many writers on the poem have responded to what others have seen only as an unrepresentative limitation. Long before David Craig complained of the sexual disgust in *The Waste Land* Edmund Wilson rejected in it what he saw as:

> the peculiar conflicts of the Puritan turned artist . . . the ascetic shrinking from sexual experience and the distress at the drying up of springs of sexual emotion.[29]

And F.R. Leavis came to revise his earlier judgement and to write that the distinctive feeling about sexual relations that dominated the poem was 'the highly personal one we know so well from the earlier poems'.[30] A work of literature should aim to be typical and generally representative. But Eliot

Early Poems and *The Waste Land*

recognised that in the divided, varied and complex conditions of modern society the writer could count no longer on creating a character an audience would receive as typical, and the essay of 1919, 'Tradition and the Individual Talent', is partly addressed to this issue. Although not formulated programmatically, this essay suggests that a technical solution to the problem might be found in a development of the dramatic monologue Eliot had used previously in *Prufrock* and *Gerontion*. The form could be exploited so as to circumvent an audience's now unreliable response to the specific psychological crisis of the monologue's speaker. As C. K. Stead has shown, in the famous essays published just before completion of *The Waste Land* Eliot was wrestling with 'the problem of conscious direction and unconscious process in the writing of poetry'.[31] The poet must engage his conscious attention with the personal, with 'emotions', and with problems of form, so that unconsciously the real meaning of the poem may unfold itself at the level of the 'impersonal'. So, in 'Tradition and the Individual Talent', Eliot writes that the business of the poet 'is not to find new emotions, but to use the ordinary ones' so that poetry may 'express feelings which are not in actual emotions at all'.[32] This distinction applies directly to a fictional character represented in a dramatic monologue. To the degree that the speaker within the monologue is self-conscious he is aware of his own 'actual emotions'; but the reader, situated outside the poem and beyond the speaker, necessarily sees and responds to more than can ever be present to the speaker's self-consciousness, responds therefore to 'feelings' not in the speaker's 'actual emotions'. This contrast corresponds to Robert Langbaum's authoritative characterisation of the genre:

> It can be said of the dramatic monologue generally that there is at work in it a consciousness beyond what the speaker can lay claim to.[33]

The reader's transcending awareness may be knowledge of the speaker's situation (Tennyson's Ulysses does not know he is voyaging to death) or of forces in the speaker's mind (Porphyria's lover is unaware that he is mad) though Eliot's conception of 'feelings' does not make this demarcation. The strategy of *The Waste Land* is to create a speaker with emotions—a special form of sexual obsession—and in so doing open up a shadowy space between the speaker's self-awareness and the reader in which—to repeat a series of Eliot's well-known formulations—the poem will do its work on the reader, unconscious may respond to unconscious, swarms of inarticulate feelings may be aroused, all beneath the surface in a third dimension where the words have 'a network of tentacular roots reaching down to the deepest terrors and desires'.[34]

Studies of *The Waste Land* and poems

Mimetic and Textual

The Waste Land opens itself to expression of feeling in quite another sense. So far, to show that the poem may be read as sustaining the continuity of a single consciousness, my commentary has addressed itself exclusively to the poem as representation, as mimesis. But this reading is only a partial one possible on the basis of a deliberate limitation. It must foreground the obviously narrative sequences of the poem; fill gaps left between scenes; and above all offer a psychological rationale for the fragmentation, namely that it enacts incoherences in the speaker's state of mind. The argument can now discard its tactical limitation and recognise (as must have been apparent throughout the commentary anyway) that *The Waste Land* goes far beyond any traditional dramatic monologue. How far can be indicated if we distinguish between the *mimetic* and the *textual*, between the poem as imitation of an action and the poem as poem, 'words on a page', an opposition contained ambiguously in Eliot's own programme of 'feelings' which seem to arise both from what is represented *in* a poem and from the work of the poem *itself*. *The Waste Land* is fissured with isolated quotations, half-lines, broken phrases, interjections, truncated dialogue, unexplained juxtapositions, uncompleted scenes, and in sum disruptions and *lacunae* of all kinds. These are not simply mimetic, a rendering of a mind on the edge of disintegration, but textual. They act as stops or pauses in the poem interrupting the speaker's voice and penetrating his words even while he speaks. A space is formed behind the speaker's voice in which his words become unfixed from a precise context and so release a swarm of suggestions, overtones, connotations, resonances. It is thus that, in an effect widely noted, almost any line or image is freed to associate with almost any other in the poem through a network of synaptic connections, floating fragments, the 'feelings' of the poem.

From many lines and images which might stand as examples we may consider two. In 'A Game of Chess' the line 'I think we are in rats' alley' (line 114) has a mimetic context as the speaker's silent response to the woman's demand to be told what he is thinking. At the same time the references of the first personal plural is opened so it may mean (for example) the 'we' of educated Europe after 1918. Significantly, this possibility is closed in the manuscript which refers unequivocally to the speaker's relationship: 'I think we met first in rat's alley'.[35] Or again, 'Falling towers' (line 373) may express the speaker's hallucinatory state of mind. But beyond this it may be felt as a reference to the devastated Europe of 1918, the Somme, and the then novel effects of high explosive on masonry (nor are further connotations precluded, phallicism for example). The *lacunae* in the text of *The Waste Land* anticipate the pauses in the theatre of Beckett[36] and Pinter; they are textual silences which amplify the connotations of the surrounding words.

The crucial quality of *The Waste Land* occurs because of the unique state of mind imagined for its speaker, on the edge of oblivion, dying, or in madness imagining itself so. On one side the breaks in the poem imitate the lapses and fragmentation of this consciousness; on the other they are marks in the text. The particular fiction allows these two possibilities to be held in the closest conjunction.

We may now summarise the rhetorical strategy by which the poem contrives to be a general representation of modern experience. Its success in a divided society derives from the degree to which the poem prevents the origin of its meaning coming into question and so, possible rejection. The poem has been accepted casually as a voiceless 'realisation' or an 'awareness' or voice of a vaguely conceived 'protagonist'. This unconcern has been a positive achievement, for the poem aims to communicate without appearing to do so. If its origin as impersonal truth is threatened (as it is by David Craig), the poem has a ready alibi: it is only a dramatic monologue spoken by someone with a 'personal grouse against life' who makes no general affirmation and demands no assent. If the speaker's narrow sensibility is rejected as unrepresentative (as it is by Edmund Wilson and the later Leavis) the poem's origin continues in residence but *behind* the speaker's limited self-consciousness. Nor can this in turn be located as the source of the poem's authority, for these 'feelings' cannot confidently be assigned to the speaker at all. Because of the close adhesion between the mimetic and textual in the poem such 'feelings' may have another source, that is, one apparently emanating from the silences of the text. *The Waste Land* insinuates its meaning in a way which precludes all facile rejection; its success is above all a rhetorical success.

Notes

1. See F.R. Leavis, *New Bearings in English Poetry* (London, 1932); F.O. Matthiessen, *The Achievement of T.S. Eliot* (London, 1935); Cleanth Brooks, *Modern Poetry and the Tradition* (Chapel Hill, 1939).
2. *New Bearings*, p. 93.
3. 'Precipitating Eliot', *Eliot in His Time*, ed. A. Walton Litz (Princeton, 1973), p. 130.
4. *The Achievement of T.S. Eliot*, p. 42.
5. *New Bearings*, p. 93.
6. C.K. Stead, *The New Poetic* (London, 1964), p. 152.
7. *Image and Experience* (London, 1960), p. 24.
8. *Image and Experience*, p. 27.
9. 'Eliot In and Out of *The Waste Land*', *Critical Quarterly* XVII (Spring, 1975), p. 14.
10. See the discussion of the claim that poetry may be only 'self-referential' by Jeremy Hawthorn, *Identity and Relationship* (London, 1973), p. 49.
11. 'The Defeatism of *The Waste Land*', *Critical Quarterly* II (Autumn 1960), p. 241.
12. *Exiles and Émigrés* (London, 1970), p. 159.
13. *The Waste Land: A Facsimile and Transcript of the Original Drafts*. ed. Valerie Eliot (London: Faber, 1971), no page number given.
14. 'Maps of *The Waste Land*', *Encounter* XXXVIII (April 1972), p. 81.
15. Cited in Helen Williams, *T.S. Eliot: The Waste Land*, Studies in English Literature, No. 37 (London, 1973), p. 15.

Studies of *The Waste Land* and poems

16. *Collected Poems, 1909–1962* (London, 1963), p. 82. All line references are to this edition.
17. *T.S. Eliot's Poetry and Plays* (Chicago, 1956), p. 58.
18. *Image and Experience*, p. 25.
19. Eliot's account of the making of the notes is in *Poets and Poetry* (London, 1957), pp. 109–10.
20. *Facsimile*, p. 3.
21. *The Selected Poems of Ezra Pound, 1907–1941*, ed. D.D. Paige (London, 1971), p. 171.
22. 'The Poetry of T.S. Eliot', *Principles of Literary Criticism*, 2nd ed. (London, 1926), p. 292 (an Appendix added in this edition).
23. *Selected Essays* (London, 1966), pp. 428–9. For another linking of Eliot, Baudelaire and *The Waste Land* see Yvor Winters, *In Defense of Reason* (London, 1960), where Eliot is accused of having 'surrendered to acedia which Baudelaire was able to judge' (p. 500).
24. *The Invisible Poet: T.S. Eliot* (New York, 1959), p. 162.
25. In Nash's *Spring, the sweet spring* the birds sing 'Cuckoo, jug-jug, pu-we, to-witta-woo', while in the song from Lyly's *Campaspe*, Act V, *What bird so sings*, the 'ravish'd nightingale' cries 'Jug, jug, jug, jug, tereu'.
26. *The Sunday Times* (London), 14 July 1974, Magazine, p. 20.
27. Frederick Engels, *The Condition of the Working Class in England in 1844*, in Karl Marx and Frederick Engels, *Collected Works* (London, 1975), Vol. IV, p. 329. The words 'and a separate purpose' are added in the German editions of 1845 and 1892.
28. See *Engels, Manchester and the Working Class* (New York, 1974).
29. *Axel's Castle* (New York, 1931), p. 105.
30. F.R. and Q.D. Leavis, *Lectures in America* (London, 1969), p. 41.
31. *The New Poetic*, p. 127.
32. *Selected Essays*, p. 21.
33. *The Poetry of Experience* (New York, 1957), p. 94.
34. *Selected Essays*, p. 155.
35. *Facsimile*, p. 11.
36. For an account of Beckett's use of pauses, see my own 'Hamm, Clov, and Dramatic Method in *Endgame*', *Twentieth Century Interpretations of Endgame*, ed. Bell Gale Chevigny (New Jersey, 1969).

116
A Handful of Words: The Credibility of Language in *The Waste Land**

◆

JONATHAN BISHOP

'No one is likely to dispute that *The Waste Land* is one of the most important poems written in English in the twentieth century.' writes David Ward, a recent commentator. 'It is something of a mystery that this should be so.'[1] Other recent readers must have entertained the same disquieting thought. The world has long since accepted Eliot's poem as the master work of a major poet without ever quite being able to agree on what exactly it was a classic of. 'Post-war' disillusion? The rise and fall of civilization? The soul of the poet—whatever that would be? The various interpretive options have successively contributed to our habitual readings without quite achieving a decent hermeneutical security.

Meanwhile, Eliot's overall reputation has, of course, declined. This does not prevent us from continuing to teach the poem, for there it still is in all the big anthologies, complete with notes on the Notes. And teaching will sometimes revive curiosity. But this in turn is apt, I suspect, to settle for whatever quick help may be found in the standard commentaries. We do not ordinarily feel compelled to think the poem through again.

A review of these somewhat overfamiliar 'sources' can in any case leave behind an impression that this work too has fallen back into the limbo of historical irrelevance. The critical impulse that once sought to transmit Eliot's special authority has long since become a period piece in itself. Reinforced by a once pressing need to reinforce the claims of literature against the philistine left, this initial apostleship was in due course normalized for the classroom. The pieties, eccentricities, or hesitancies of later critics would not interrupt the succession, which can now seem to have dribbled out in casebooks and collections. Eliot has become, of all things, a project for provincials. Such a conventionalization can, of course, only reinforce the assumption that no one need take him quite seriously.[2]

**Texas Studies in Language and Literature*, vol. 27, no. 1 (Spring 1985), pp. 154–77.

More up-to-date commentary has indeed emerged in response to the Death in 1965 and the Facsimile in 1971. A list of instances so occasioned would include a variety of more or less comprehensive studies.[3] But this work, however thorough, has not penetrated the general intelligence so as to make a difference to the place the poem holds in any contemporary equivalent of 'the mind of Europe.' For insiders the most satisfying recent studies have either been closely textual, as with those scholars who have pressed back from the Facsimile to the MSS in the hope of establishing a plausible chronology of composition, or else biographical, in partial assuagement of a curiosity that has prompted a variety of irregular contributions toward the as yet impossible Big Book. Here we have had a choice of scandal: T. S. Matthews for vulgarity, James Miller for homosexuality, and Robert Sencourt for piety. The best so far are still Lyndall Gordon on the *Early Years* and Herbert Howarth on background *Figures*: modesty is usefulness, as usual.[4] But textual studies merely postpone the task of determining how to read the final text. And biographical speculation can only prejudge this question by building in the assumption that meaning coincides with origin. Too much criticism, New and *nouvelle*, has sufficiently shown us what ought to seem wrong about that—especially for Eliot, who notoriously put final above efficient causes.

The eventual task is made both harder and easier by certain features of our current literary predicament. It is harder now that Eliot's work has long ago ceased to be instinctively comprehensible as a model for living artists. The time is past when *The Waste Land* could visibly recur in *The Sun Also Rises* and *The Sound and the Fury*, or even in such works of the Modernist decline as *Let Us Now Praise Famous Men* or *Invisible Man*. In poetry this precursive authority lasted somewhat longer: it is still presumed in the later as well as the earlier work of Jarrell or Berryman or Lowell and continues in the deep background of Sylvia Plath. But the poetic revolution of the middle 1950s that has since prevailed as a universal norm restored the romantic presumptions which Eliot had once seemed to have invalidated forever. From the same moment we can accordingly date that separation of criticism from poetry that has since generated such entirely distinct academic cultures. But the fact of this schism might also prompt us to appreciate anew the extent to which Eliot's poetry is as critical as it is 'creative.' And to realize as much might not only make us feel what is missing in contemporary poetry but also see the likeness between the theoretical obsessions of our day and the 'problematic' of *The Waste Land*. Eliot can now be read as raising in the concrete some of the same questions which have been preoccupying recent critics in the abstract. To that extent the task of understanding the poem might be easier than ever.

Such a connection would, of course, have to be worked out by way of language—in which case one could propose that the credibility of discourse has all along been the real subject matter of *The Waste Land*, whatever else it might also be 'about.' In that case too whatever was therein demonstrated might also supply a reason why the poem has persisted as a classic. For that rank is assigned to messages which can bear to be repeated within any situation in the confidence that they are sure to prove relevant. To 'interpret' a classic is to show that relevance, and what should be easier, if the example repeated should in fact have to do with the dependability of language in general? For whatever our situation, it is bound to include some doubt as to the trustworthiness of the language employed. And at no time have we been more painfully self-conscious about just this issue than in these days, which should make it plausible to reread *The Waste Land* as an experiment devoted to determining just how far any mode of discourse may be trusted. Contemporary poetry has become accustomed to answering this question for itself in the affirmative, somewhat too easily. Contemporary criticism has seemed equally busy denying that any such thing as credible language could possibly exist at all. *The Waste Land* recovers the issue as a set of specifics, and therefore, tentatively—which is to say, neither in hopeful innocence nor dogmatic refusal. One might accordingly be brought to suspect that the poem is still ahead of wherever we have got to along either line. We may not in fact have caught up with it yet—much less be free to abandon it to the limbo of the taken for granted.[5]

If the credibility of language is *the* persistent issue of the poem, we might begin to appropriate the argument apparently enacted by putting into some order the various modes of discourse which seem to obtain within it. For the famous collage effect is due not just to the plurality of materials assembled but to the different kinds of language deployed. The most elementary of these would be that thoroughly Eliotic mode, quotation. This species of discourse would include most obviously the epigraphs from Petronius (or Conrad, or Dickens); the snatches of Wagnerian song; the lines from Baudelaire and Spenser and Verlaine and Augustine; most emphatically that repeated Shakespearanism, 'those are pearls that were his eyes'; and eventually the terminal cluster of 'fragments' at the close of the poem. The various references to Chaucer, Ezekiel, Dante, Goldsmith, Luke, and the rest would then amount of a subspecies of indirect quotation, each with its own burden of allusion. It has been usual to assume that the wholes from which these parts are taken should all be somehow significant. This may not be so; Eliot appears in any case to have had a tag line sort of memory. He may simply have presumed a reader who could identify each item as what our generation has learned to call a 'trace.' For they all testify to some value already lost as such, though still repeatable in remembered words. Thus quotation illustrates the problem of poetry in miniature—and so the credibility of language in general.

So far, almost so obvious. We may notice too that it is not only the high tradition that passes on these recollections of a last presence in a universe of absence. For Eliot, the unconscious rhythms of popular speech exhibit the

Studies of *The Waste Land* and poems

same poignant power. So the music hall side of him appreciates cockney talk and soldier song as a communal analogue to the recollection of traditional verses. We may observe as well that discourse by quotation would also include mute images as well as verses and idioms. The private analogue to fragments from other poems or the dialect of the folk are those glimpses into moments of value in the past which recur so prominently throughout the poem. The conversation in the Hofgarten or the recollection of the Hyacinth girl are a kind of psychic quotation. A familiar reference here would recall that often repeated passage from the later criticism asking why 'for all of us . . . certain images recur'—which incorporates two examples which in fact do appear in the poems. Such memories, Eliot writes there, 'represent the depths of feeling into which we cannot peer.'[6] Thus individual unconscious and private past are linked to their public equivalents, popular custom and the cultural inheritance. But the linguistic reflection of them all, we are obliged to realize, is (in the nature of the case they share) untrustworthy. Verbal or imagistic repetition is always implicitly elegiac. If this mode of discourse is all there might be, no word could finally be believed, for none would truly bring back what had been lost—or never been enjoyed at all.

This vulnerability of even the most ecstatic past to the mere present of a verbal repetition that cannot recreate it is still more obvious when the 'images' are aural rather than visual. The 'water-dripping song' of the hermit thrush is, as the Note repeats, 'justly famous.' But the 'inviolable voice' of the nightingale deteriorates immediately into 'jug jug,' as the song of the Rhine Maidens deliquesces into a meaningless ripple of syllables, and the cock crows ridiculously in French. Music of all kinds is more important to the economy of the poem than is perhaps ordinarily realized. Those bells and mandolins ought to be dependable, whatever they *say*. So it seems an injurious anomaly that the final stroke of nine sounds 'dead' at St. Mary Woolnoth's. And creaturely or other natural sounds ought to emerge from a source even deeper than music and so feel that much more trustworthy. But the moment any such prelinguistic sound is translated into human words, 'dirty ears' can hear only one more reminder of their own limits. Bodily sounds, like memories, lose their restorative power in the very words which 're-present' them.

If so, it would probably be a mistake to seek the key to the poem in any reminiscent image of this kind. A.D. Moody, for instance, asserts that the Hyacinth girl is the 'centre from which the entire poem radiates.'[7] It is not hard to agree that this moment and its equivalents through the whole body of Eliot's writings must reflect a biographical occasion for the situation so repeatedly depicted within them. But the poem, like the passage it includes, commences at a conscious distance from any such point of origin. 'You gave me hyacinths a year ago'—and ever since, this speaker has been unable to understand what did or did not happen. It would be too Wagnerian to suppose that whatever is admitted as lost here could ever be recaptured in even the truest voice of feeling. And with that realization the poem as it is may properly be said to begin.

What these figments of inarticulacy can provide is a silent means of communication, as indeed occurs within the Hyacinth episode when flowers are passed from one person to another, or Mme. Sosostris 'reads' the pictures on the arbitrarily arranged tarot cards, or the chessmen take the place of other modes of intercourse. An impression builds that these mute emblems function within the different episodes as the episodes themselves do within the poem as a whole, where they occur as 'images' passed, as it were, from poet to reader. So they are produced to represent at least the presumption underlying all discourse, however tongueless and abused, that someone is with someone else. It is not irrelevant in this connection to recall that the strictly poetical dimension of Eliot's own achievement is confined to this nostalgic level of language. Here alone can we be sure of picking up an audible play of words. Within the next dimension up, that of speakers in situations, Eliot offers us only masks. His human voices are entirely unsupported. But the passage of time has served the poem well. *The Waste Land* has become mixed with the tradition out of which so many of its parts came, and we now remember lines and cadences from it as 'fragments' of virtually the same kind as those assembled within it. To that extent we very nearly experience the poem in the mode of quotation alone. But if we yield too readily to this advantage, we will be prevented from reading, precisely, the rest of the poem.

II

We take in more of that uncertain entity with the second mode of discourse the poem exhibits, the speech of speakers. At this level *The Waste Land* reads as a discontinuous sequence of theatrical moments through which a human predicament is rehearsed until it has almost become a dramatic situation—for which some denouement might be expected. Quotations, verbal or imagistic, have to remain 'fragments'; the various failed exchanges, though, overlap almost as a multiple plot. This is plainer in part 2 than at the ambiguous beginning of the poem. If one were to move directly from the Sibylline epigraph to the first episode of 'A Game of Chess,' the display of language as performance would be more obvious. That section of the poem presents a wealthy couple who are irritating each other as they prepare, apparently, to go out: the lady's jewel cases are open on her dressing table, and she has tried out more than one perfume while still brushing her hair. We take in this domestic occasion from the acutely limited perspective of the man, who exposes himself as well as the predicament they share. This is Eliot almost as Browning, in the manner of 'Prufrock' or *Gerontion*. So it has

Studies of *The Waste Land* and poems

seemed reasonable to connect the exceptionally elaborate pentameters with late Jacobean drama. It has not proved quite so obvious that the allusion is apparently meant to imply a negative judgment on both styles. Overwriting shows up writing (and so *this* kind of speech). Eliot enjoys the spurious luxury of such talk while at the same time inviting us to see through it. And his literally mute (for this is interior speech) protagonist may be assumed to share the ironic attitude of the author whose literary tastes he thus reproduces. Pound had trouble grasping his friend's satiric intention, as his notes on the typescript show; whereupon Eliot changed the language here and there to exaggerate its grandiloquence.[8] The husband in this marriage, we may gather, is unable to talk with his wife; instead he goes on inside his head for too long about things which do not matter in language which cannot be believed. So his introverted fustian is necessarily at his own expense—and that of language as self-affirming discourse in general.

The interior described is in any case an environment for a Bradleyan solipsist, or the girl telegraphist of James;s 'In the Cage,' which once provided a title for this part of the poem, or the Sibyl, with whom the whole now begins. The recollected alternative to such imprisonment is indicated within the scene by the picture showing 'the change of Philomel.' This *un*described image is a visual quotation repeating its aural equivalent, the voice of the nightingale, which this speaker, though, can hear only in a vulgar opposite to his own overly elaborate style. His derisory reference to 'other withered stumps of time' is a further bit of jug-juggism, flattening what may be equally nostalgic images. The 'Shakespearean Rag' which coarsens his reverie is another variant of the same despairing vandalism. These alternatives can offer no more than so many traces refracted through legend, art, or popular culture of an original speech anterior to the self-canceling excess with which they passively contrast. 'I remember, 'he says, and then does not mention what he recalls: presumably some episode equivalent, in his private past, to the story of Philomel in the mythology of the West. In the typescript, 'the Hyacinth garden' is supplied to complete the line, which would incidentally allow us to identify the husband of this scene with the speaker of the corresponding section in 'The Burial of the Dead.' But Eliot dropped this half line. What his character now remembers instead is the properly Shakespearean 'Those are pearls that were his eyes,' a formula which might suggest that the life lost should long ago have been converted into a genuine word—a word, perhaps, of love. But this has *not* happened. Such a speaker cannot do so much. When he tries, he becomes portentous: 'I think we are in rat's alley / Where the dead men lost their bones.'

Meanwhile, the woman's hair, brushed hard, 'glowed into words,' as if she were herself a living tree of the sort that might once have risen from those withered stumps. But she is no Daphne either. In this world the male is apparently held responsible for failing to convert reminiscent myth into current fact. 'Why do you never speak,' she asks, but he answers only her trivial questions. Her best effort to provoke a more genuine response is the threat to rush out as she is, hair down, and walk the streets, like a whore. What would he say then? But he does not rise to this either. All he promises is the usual routine, including a game of chess which, as we have seen, makes a mute figure for an unachieved exchange.[9]

Meanwhile, 'footsteps shuffled on the stair,' and the woman is frightened. If that unseen presence were ever to make itself evident, it would have to do or say—something. The *un*heard knock anticipates a judgment that would silence all spurious talk. On the far side of this scene, then, is still another kind of discourse whose authority would match the antecedent burden of the nightingale. But in the midworld there is evidently nothing more to be said.

The same point is made over again for another social context in the second section of part 2—which incidentally gives teachers a chance to practice their cockney. The draft allows us to oversee how Eliot's ear, assisted perhaps by Vivienne or Pound, was able to improve what he had written first. 'When Lil's husband got demobbed, I said' is much better than either 'was coming back out of the Transport Corps' or its intermediate alternative, 'was discharged out of the army.' One can indeed hear the final version as a species of bird song—though not of no nightingale.[10] But the pastoral pleasure we can take after him in this play of dialect at the primary level of discourse is distinguishable from our estimate of the character and the state of affairs she betrays. Evidently she has already broken up the marriage between Lil and Albert and is trying to justify her conduct to another friend (perhaps Lou or May), for the benefit of whom she is now rehearsing the story from the beginning. She is interrupted before we can learn what happened, which must have started over that famous gammon with spinach. Her interlocutor, like Prufrock's companion, remains enigmatically mute. If this silent Other were to speak, her words too might amount to an exposure of whatever is unbelievable in the speaker's language. But in this context also no critical voice is raised; instead we hear only the pubkeeper's call. 'HURRY UP PLEASE ITS TIME' can, to be sure, do almost too allegorically well as a substitute: the end of an evening's entertainment will stand for the end of the world to just this extent. The first time the warning is heard, it cuts off the speaker's claim that she 'didn't mince [her] words.' In fact she can do nothing else, for as long as she does not admit her crime she has no truth to express. At the close of the scene, still another voice comes in to repeat the colloquial 'good nights' of the dispersing company in a quieter and more literate tone. 'Good night, sweet ladies,' this person says, recalling Ophelia, another victim of helpless love, who died by water long ago in some play. The range of reference and melancholy tone recall the husband of the previous episode, who in turn might be identified, as we have seen, with the principal protagonist of part 1. This intermittent character might accordingly be called the Poet. Unfortunately, the only character that has so far appeared who could reasonably be imagined as able to listen in on a conversation in a pub could scarcely be this painfully limited individual. We would have to assign the privilege of ubiquity to another and more ghostly identity, the Prophet who speaks the threatening 'son of man' passage in part 1. The difficulty here is that this personage cannot be heard as saying such gentle words.

Even part 2, then, where dramatic situations are most readily distinguishable, presents problems when read as a display of discourse as theater, in which language functions to demonstrate self-affirming persons in relation to each other. It can indeed be disconcerting to discover how often critics disagree about the speakers in the poem as soon as they come down to cases. We are, in fact, less certain than we suppose about who is speaking at a given moment, where he or she begins and leaves off, whether the language is literal or hallucinatory, straight or ironic, and even whether we are listening to persons at all or just disembodied 'voices.' Some obscurity apparently follows from the style of Eliot's imagination, which in this context is theatrical to an unusually passive degree. He is inclined rather to listen to, almost to 'quote,' the words of others than to put them clearly on stage.[11] But we are also entitled to understand such local uncertainties as manifestations of a general readiness to encourage doubt about the right of persons to authorize their own language. If selves are fictional, permeable, ventriloquistic, and in any event almost always false, 'the self' is obviously devalued as an attestation for discourse. And the failure to communicate that marks so many of these situations would further expose the undependability of the language used.[12] For a self alone, however sincere, cannot validate its own words.

Such doubts need not, however, prevent a return from the comparative clarities of part 2 to 'The Burial of the Dead' with some degree of assurance that the opening lines had better be heard as spoken by the individual we have just called the Poet. It must be he, then, who winces from the hopefulness of the season and whose fastidiousness accounts for the falling rhythms and enjambments which qualify the tetrameter of these verses—a meter interrupted, in a sudden change of mood, by the end-stopped pentameter, 'Summer surprised us . . .' In which case too it must be the Poet who listens, on that unexpectedly agreeable occasion, to the recollections of Marie. As a character in an interrupted dialogue, Marie is less impressive than her memory of sledding downhill, as her affected boast of freedom in the mountains presently indicates. As a child she was and remains innocent; as a person asserting 'herself,' she is, the commentaries repeat, alienated from the truth of things. Still, this couple shares sunlight, coffee, and a memory which repeats the value of a lost past. 'Summer' has indeed 'surprised us.' No pair in the poem do better than these two at its inception.

Then comes an abrupt shift of scene: 'What are the roots that clutch?' The Poet, or 'son of man,' is no Ezekiel. He cannot answer the rude questions addressed to him. *You*, says this counter voice, cannot *say*: you know only 'a heap of broken images'—which the poem will continue to prove all too true. The biblical wilderness is a traditional antiimage to all possible images. Fear of such negativity is already implicit in that handful (or even a fingertip's worth) of the dust which predicts the fate of all flesh in the ritual of Ash Wednesday. So much this speaker knows—which makes him a Prophet indeed.

But his appearance here is brief. We are returned to a pair of quotations from *Tristan*, embracing a second episode in which the Poet listens as a woman speaks. He has just given her hyacinths, and she recalls an occasion the anniversary of which seems to have prompted the gift. But he does not enter into the banter that might be expected to follow. Instead he is carried away into an interior repetition of the original moment, when he could no more speak than he does now. He was blinded by the vision she then made, arms full, hair wet, as if he were looking into 'the heart of light, the silence.' *Words* have failed between them then and since. The flowers remain an image, a quotation from the past; like the beauty of the woman, they resemble music. But like Wagner's sailor's song, they cannot affirm the eternity of love.

The Poet reappears as the silent interlocutor of Mme. Sosostris, that shopworn Sibyl. The dramatic difficulty here is to imagine an occasion on which he might be telling the story of his encounter with this personage to someone else. Either interiorly at the time or audibly afterward he calls her pack of cards 'wicked' in a double sense. But she does all the talking; her chatter, though, is merely an accompaniment to the laying out of the cards, which make one more arrangement of images. Thus she 'quotes' from her tradition, which is no worse, on that scale, than any other. Her voice becomes a performance in the final instructions: 'If you see dear Mrs. Equitone . . . .' But since this self is already comic, there is no need for criticism, mute or explicit.

Finally, the Poet speaks again. As he crosses London Bridge, he remembers Dante. The abrupt 'Stetson!' is followed by a sequence of images gone loose, like grains of dust. The protosurrealism of these lines recovers dramatic plausibility with a final turn toward the reader as Poet and poet alike take refuge in Baudelaire. The voice is for the moment out of control: madness is the superlative of incoherence.

Part 1 then offers instances of three kinds of discourse: quotations, which is to say any *literal* repetition of word or image from the tradition or its private equivalent; arabesques of individual assertion, interior or exposed, and in either case self-annihilating; and third, the apparently conclusive word of a Prophet. This last possibility makes for a powerful yet unstable presence. Is Eliot really entitled to dramatize the judgment already implicit in the failures of discourse of the second kind to do more than pass on instances of the first?

III

If the poem in fact completed itself within the second mode of discourse on the scale of an individual speaker, *The Waste Land* would be a displaced autobiography—which some readers have insisted on reading it as. The Poet's voice would then render the last word, as it does in most poetry of that time or since. If the poem completed itself within the second mode but with several speakers, we should have an auditory collage or instance of mental theater, which as a boundariless assemblage might then be taken to represent the way of the world. The easiest way to teach the poem is as if it were no more than just this, for students can be trained to listen for voices and estimate predicaments. An enjoyable time is had by all. But Eliot does not quite leave us with this result either. The space for a third species of discourse does in fact open out, to be inhabited now and again by the figure we have called the Prophet.

The problems that arise in connection with this figure are most pressing in the third section of the poem, with which Eliot not coincidentally seems to have had the most trouble. The obscurities of 'The Fire Sermon' are already complicated by the number of passages which Pound helped his friend cut away. An unfortunate pastiche of Pope was once the first of these; in the draft this preceded the passage beginning 'The river's tent is broken,' to which no exception was then or need since be taken. After a sufficiently appropriate allusion to Augustine at Carthage, there once stood an uncomfortably positive description of 'the' sailor in patronizing quatrains, always a weak form for Eliot. This in turn was followed by a tedious first-person narrative in Victorian verse of a Grand Banks fishing voyage which ended in an implausibly phantasmagoric encounter with an ice floe. Eliot claimed he had Dante's Ulysses in mind; it reads rather as if he were remembering Poe's *Arthur Gordon Pym*, a dubious pre-text for any modern author. The poetic gist of these maritime excursions is salvaged in the concentrated lines devoted to Phlebas, conveniently translatable from the author's French. There were also brief but painfully overexplicit attacks on London and its supposedly phantasmal or mechanical inhabitants which Pound rightly dismissed as 'B—S.' All these excesses and uncertainties betray a problem which even the reduced text has not altogether avoided or solved: how to give explicit expression to a species of discourse in which authoritative judgments might at last be made.

'The Fire Sermon,' as the title implies, was apparently meant to provide just such an interruption of all the other voices as would sum up the preceding possibilities, personal, sexual, or verbal, as convincingly as the Buddha had once done for his world or Augustine for his. Some prophetic figures of the Old Testament are already evoked in part 1. The New Testament analogue would be John the Baptist, who does *not* appear. Instead we have Tiresias, now positively so named. But his language too proves unconvincing—unfortunately not on purpose.

Until this becomes evident there is, to be sure, nothing in the reduced text to cause disquiet. It is clearly the Poet who formulates the meditation on the bank of the abandoned river, which Pound labeled 'Echt.' The one unpleasant phrase, 'the loitering heirs of city directors,' may be taken dramatically as repeating the note of fastidiousness we are already familiar with in this character. The slightly fantastic picture of such a person fishing in a canal behind a gashouse may be understood as neurasthenically allegorical in the same self-contemptuous style as the conversation with the woman in part 2 or the hallucinatory challenge to Stetson in part 1. This Poet likes to exaggerate his own disorder. And as usual he can recall more authentic voices than his own, whether from some older poet or a bawdy ballad. A line from Verlaine, in another language altogether, is almost a shock: that voice of children singing in the dome makes for a quotation so utterly protological as virtually to become eschatological as well, like the moment in the Hyacinth garden. If a fish were ever to be caught, and a true Word spoken, it would surely rhyme with just such as these—or with the song of the nightingale, evoked once more, though still in a parodic 'jug jug.'

The Eugenides episode could also be assigned to the Poet if it were not followed by the very similar Tiresias passage, where the Prophet finally names himself. This presents, in what used to be quatrains, an episode between a typist and her bepimpled young man. The style brings this narrative nearer the rejected Popean pastiche than can be at all comfortable for readers who are now in a position to realize the likeness. The diction ('Endeavours to engage her in caresses') has been justified as satirically illustrative of the lingo a house agent's clerk might be expected to use in writing, if not as speech.[13] But such an intention, legitimate when the person exposed is the speaker, cannot be allowed in the voice of someone whose judgment, if it is to be accepted at all, must seem thoroughly trustworthy. An unreliable Poet may be not merely tolerable but informative, as Henry James had long since shown, but an unreliable Prophet is a contradiction in tone. The attitude manifested in this passage, though, is not just snobbish and brutal but inaccurate. Tiresias, who should know all, is apparently ignorant of contemporary styles of underwear.[14] Something nearer a recognizably prophetic manner may be picked up in a brief parenthesis ('And I Tiresias have foresuffered all'). If this note had prevailed throughout, there would be no objection. A real recovery, though, only begins as Tiresias repeats a fragment from Goldsmith, which in turn leads to the beautifully ordered lines in praise of 'the pleasant whining of a mandoline' and St. Magnus Martyr's 'inexplicable splendour of Ionian white and gold.' But here at the close of the passage, the Prophet has fallen back into the impressionable solitude of the Poet. The larger problem has been abandoned by a retreat into a merely dramatic identity which does not raise it.

The remaining portions of part 3 give less trouble. Only the Prophet could *see* both the Thames barges downstream and Elizabeth and Leicester by the Tower while *hearing* not only Wagner's Rhine Maidens but an English middle-class girl's version of a parallel submission.[15] If Tiresias had been allowed to pronounce on the fate of this young person or persons, he would doubtless have betrayed what ought not to be his attitude as inevitably as with the typist earlier. But this time he simply listens. As a detached consciousness, he need not commit himself to any explicit judgment. The reader, into whom he thereby disappears, will do this for him, silently: the images presented and the tales implied can be trusted to 'speak for themselves.' Such a reticence offers the best clue to the real solution for Eliot's problem: prophecy without authority becomes trustworthy precisely when it has nothing to say. For then it assimilates to criticism; and criticism, in poetry, manifests itself not as speech but in silence.

This generic overlap between prophecy and criticism on their negative sides allows us to connect the problem raised by the third mode of discourse with the Notes which Eliot was in due course to add to the poem. These are, in the first place, supplied by Eliot-the-scholar, identifying the sources of his own work. Thus he solemnly unwrites the poem, replacing his quotations in their original contexts. To be sure, the humor with which this academic function is qualified ensures that theatricality will sometimes undermine anonymity.[16] Whenever a personal speaker can be heard, he not surprisingly resembles the Poet of the poem. This figure is modest about Jessie Weston and arrogant about the tarot. In the second most interesting Note, the quotation from F. H. Bradley, the question of personality is put in general terms: 'My experience falls within my own circle, a circle closed upon the outside.' This is the Poet criticizing himself in philosophic terms, as Eliot had already done more literally, though still more indirectly, in his dissertation.

The *most* interesting Note is the highly equivocal claim that 'what Tiresias *sees*, in fact, is the substance of the poem.' A first generation of readers was inclined to take this observation straight. The young F.R. Leavis, for instance, applauded it as '*the*' clue to the poem on the ground that it reveals *The Waste Land* as an effort to 'focus an inclusive human consciousness.'[17] Over the years doubts have grown that there can be any such thing, and with good reason; to consent uncritically to Tiresianism would seem equivalent to confirming Eliot's defenses against his own insight into the inadequacies of all personal centers, psychic or linguistic.[18] This is not to say that the ostentatiously untranslated lines from Ovid are not indeed of considerable psychological (rather, surely, than 'anthropological') interest for the ideal biographer of the historical Eliot. But the truth of Tiresias would have to be found in Anyone's ability to enter into other lives in imagination—which the poem has already proved can be done without obtrusive mythological intervention. We are obliged to agree with the now common conclusion that Eliot-the-Note-maker is no more entitled to oversee his own poem than his overly privileged character is to articulate a judgment within it.[19]

Which is not to say, either, that these Notes do not offer their own version of the hint we have already picked up toward a happier solution to the problem. The final Note to part 3 informs us that the 'collocation' of Augustine and the Buddha is not accidental. We are thereby encouraged to work out for ourselves that asceticism, Western or Eastern, might prove a practical way of dealing with the unreliable ego. An intellectual equivalent would be represented by any sufficiently plausible solution to the problem of solipsism. Bradley's own *Appearance and Reality* is one such; Eliot's thesis on Bradley another. In literary criticism a solution of sorts is already mimed by the posture adopted in *The Sacred Wood*, with its assured dismissals of romantic hubris. Within that context, judgment can afford to be as arrogant as it pleases without moral embarrassment. But Eliot has to take poetry more seriously than prose. And in poetry the equivalent of ascesis, skepticism, or disenchantment is not some authoritative impersonation but silence. In the midst of discourse, silence becomes irony, which exposes the *in*sufficient word. So the prophetic function is best served by merely listening, the better to enact the detachment toward which any mixed sequence of voices cannot help but in any case invite a reader. The structure of the poem is in this way already a judgment of the predicaments dramatized within it, and so an implicit rebuke to whatever is still superfluous in its author's claims for his surrogate.

In which case what remains truly inviolable about Tiresias is simply his omnipresence, which can do without a name. Whatever he rightly stands for then disperses into all the other personages so as to share their suffering without necessarily crediting their claims. As sheer consciousness, he thereby unites with the reader, who is, after all, in principle speechless too, however much he or she may afterward have to say. A remaining share in the author may then be limited to the power of juxtaposition, still another variety of irony. That author, it is always worth recalling, is dispersed already: his ear to supply the dialect of the tribe, his bad luck for the facts of marriage, his tastes for the descriptions and allusions. His consciousness, though, has to be impersonal, like that of any reader who will join him. Sympathy is accurate in proportion to its disinterestedness.

The Notes can thus assist us toward a more radical reading of the poem than its author could quite permit himself at the time. Imaginatively disencumbered of whatever it still contains that parodies its own best implication, *The Waste Land* could then be read as demonstrating the absolute untrustworthiness of human language in all its modes. It would thus become a poem 'about' the end of poetry—including therefore all the other poems which have been written since in imitation of or reaction to it. All flesh is not only grass but dust; all voices are invaded by silence, which must prevail in the end. So throughgoing a deconstruction could only convince in proportion to its universality—and must therefore be allowed to disassemble whatever figure is got up to 'represent' the very judgment deployed. In that case too the poem could fulfill the possibility not just of poetry but of criticism as well—which should bring it altogether up to date. For its self-annihilating witness would then coincide with the typical insight of our generation, the work of which could easily be read as repeating the Eliotic enterprise on another scale as well as in another genre. The past is lost, we might summarize again; the present is damned, most thoroughly out of its own mouth. That leaves, if anything at all, only the future.

IV

'There is danger lest multiplied allusions, adventitious or not, should defeat meaning,' wrote Grover Smith, who ought to know; his work remains a type of that kind of commentary which completes itself in the discovery of some antecedent context.[20] We have seen how the poem promotes a realization that any such anteriority is 'always already' literary in virtually our current style and, therefore, useless if something beyond language is what one hopes to mean by meaning. Eliot is as antiromantic as any poststructuralist. But just as clearly he would still share Grover Smith's 'valorization' of the idea of meaning as such, which would put him on the other side in more recent wars. His notion, though, of where it might be looked for is not naive. It cannot ground the first mode of discourse from beneath, for the reason just mentioned. And theatricality and irony combine to disestablish all possible presences in the second mode of discourse. An ideal third kind, divested of all specious positivity, dwindles into silence—which is meaning only in the negative. Just this might suit the Buddhist in Eliot. But Eliot does not remain merely a Buddhist. If a true Word which should embody its own credibility is conceivable at all, it would have to obtain as an instance of what we must accordingly call a fourth species of discourse, which is to say, the language of the future, or voice of God.

To an exploration of this possibility the fifth section of the poem is devoted.[21] 'OK from here on I think,' wrote Pound, reasonably enough, at the beginning of 'What the Thunder Said.' Eliot himself was well pleased with this portion of the poem, which he reported afterward came easily and 'justifies the whole.'[22] Such assurance contrasts decisively with the hesitations and implausibilities of part 3. The differences may be explained generically as well as biographically. Hugh Kenner has recently pointed out that if we had only the first three sections of the poem to argue from, we should suppose that Eliot intended a Drydenesque satire on modern urban life.[23] In other words, Tiresianism very nearly conquered the poem. If it had, we should have to place *The Waste Land* rather nearer the other poems of the Gautier phase, and fewer readers would be left to call it a persisting classic.

Early Poems and *The Waste Land*

The famous breakdown, and still more the shift from Margate to Lausanne, may have helped rescue Eliot from such a fate. A more securely establishable factor would be his reading of Jessie Weston's book, which came out in 1920. This seems to have prompted a recasting of what might otherwise have continued to accumulate as a 'sophisticated' satire into the current poem, complete with title, direction, and appropriate ending. For the Weston influence, made normative by the Notes, really only prevails in part 5. With her help there emerges at least an antiromance—and perhaps even a gospel *manqué*. The speech and confidence with which the last section was written is a sign of this recasting of the intention.

Among the helpful changes is the emergence of a plot. Somebody is on the way somewhere, to an inn or a chapel, and something is almost said—which provides an occasion to end the poem. We are brought very near, that is, to the moment when if ever a trustworthy Word might be pronounced from which all previous acts of language might recover their due degree of credibility. The traditional context for such a demonstration is of course the Christian story. So part 5 begins in the aftermath of the crucifixion. The speaker is one of the disciples: 'We who were living are now dying / With a little patience.' If this identity is the applicable version of the Poet, as his tone suggests, then his companion must be the Prophet, the second of a pair who, according to Luke, are on their way to Emmaus. An early draft of part 5 included a more elaborate description of their journey through a region of 'sunbaked houses' which focused explicitly on the insufficiency of human discourse and the hope for an ultimately credible because supernatural speech. The 'concatenated words from which the sense seemed gone' are there contrasted with the 'This-do-ye-for-my-sake' of the Eucharist.[24] But this thematically useful material was dropped, to be replaced by the evocative 'Who is the third who walks always beside you?' For the pair are accompanied, according to Luke, by a stranger whom they do not recognize. To him they must explain the events that have just transpired in Jerusalem. This third person proceeds to expound the Scriptures to them. In Eliot's version, however, the stranger is a hooded illusion with whom no conversation takes place. The Shackleton reference supplied by the Note would confirm his *non*-existence. The same negative emphasis appears in the hallucinatory extremity of the wilderness through which this Poet and Prophet pass, so much more threatening than the commonplace highway of Cleopas and his companion.

But the issue dramatized remains the same. In Luke it is resolved: the disciples arrive at their destination and 'constrain' the stranger to stay with them, 'for it is toward evening, and the day is far spent.' Whereupon, as they are about to eat together, the third man 'took bread, and blessed *it*, and brake, and gave to them. And their eyes were opened, and they knew him; and he vanished out of their sight.'[25] In the poem, of course, no such denouement occurs. But for once a major pre-text is narratively indispensable. We

Studies of *The Waste Land* and poems

can realize from it what *ought* to have happened and measure what does in the light of that.

Prophet and Poet seem to alternate through the passages following. To the former may be assigned the summary judgment on 'Jerusalem Athens Alexandria,' not to mention 'London'; to the latter the private vision of 'bats with baby faces' and upside-down towers. It is also clearly this disturbed individual who reaches the height of the adventure in the 'decayed hole among the mountains,' where a chapel stands empty. Jessie Weston is here as useful as Luke was before, since in the romance version as she retells it the climax would be a vision of the Grail, which in Eliot's story does not take place either. This omission thus runs parallel to the Emmaus result: as that ends in a Eucharistic sharing of the blessed bread, so the medieval tale concludes in an encounter with the cup from which the corresponding wine might be drunk. An eschatological Word, should it ever be articulated, would have to be coincident with the risen body of Jesus: that is, with flesh and blood together once more—but now in another set of terms.[26] In the poem we have instead a cock's crow, which itself must be translated as usual into juggish before it can be heard: 'Co, co rico. . . .'

Still, a cock traditionally announces dawn as well as once reminded a disciple of his disloyalty, and it is still possible to hope that the expectations raised by the two parallel stones might yet be fulfilled. What we are given, though, is the voice of the Thunder, which is not quite the same thing. In the relevant Upanishad, which commentators have since had time to look up, this voice offers divine instruction to gods, men, and demons, each of which hears a different version of the fundamental command. The bare sound is syllabled as 'DA'; the word heard becomes severally '*Datta . . . Dayadvam . . . Damyata.*' These verbal concentrates are themselves translated by the Poet into as many distinct memories. 'Give' evokes a recollection of 'the awful daring of a moment's surrender.' This instruction at least has been obeyed. The command to 'sympathize' provokes a protest in general terms: 'I have heard the key / Turn,' he claims, in the tower of the solipistic self. But so much is presumably not enough, for the other association, beside Ugolino locked to starve, is to a Coriolanus 'broken' without restoration. We may take it that this speaker has *not* exercised compassion. And the memory associated with the command to 'control' is of an opportunity to advance toward a beloved whose heart, like the boat in which they were sailing, 'would have' responded if invited. But this did not happen either. The protagonist finds himself, that is, repentantly aware that he has most incompletely obeyed the divine instruction as that applies to him.

He confesses, then—but is *not* forgiven; which allows us to realize that the moral equivalent of the Eucharist within the situation depicted would have to be some revelation of mercy offered and received. In the light of this we can now assess the scope of that otherwise impressive 'DA.' Anticipation might well lead us to suppose that this enormous voice should be understood as a sufficiently ecumenical version of the last Word indeed, of a sort that might well appeal to the old Harvard student of Sanskrit. It is important, though, not to draw this conclusion too hastily. The Christian and para-Christian stories do indeed lead toward a correspondingly Christian conclusion. But this does *not* take place, nor does what happens instead amount to a cosmic equivalent. The voice of the thunder is better appreciated as an oriental analogue not to the Christian sacrament but the Jewish Law. It does not embody the presence of divinity but offers instruction from a distance. And therefore, as Paul once observed of its equivalent, it serves to expose sin but not yet to forgive it. The thunder had best be placed therefore in the third mode rather than the fourth. That 'DA' is a bird's song on a colossal scale, converted through sad experience from original trace into applicable criticism. It thus makes, as it were, an inarticulate version of that prophetic rebuke of which the overly explicit attitudes of Tiresias have been an unjustified anticipation.

We may notice too that the speaker at the close of the poem shows no disposition to obey the triple instruction for the future, though he has admitted its application to his past. Unforgiven, he lacks the necessary hope. Instead he declares himself no better than a Poet indeed, able, like some king after a defeat, to assemble fragments of that tradition which amounts for him to an equivalent of a scattered demesne. The compressed quotations which follow are ostentatiously no more than just that. 'These fragments,' he admits, 'I have shored against my ruins.' The Facsimile has shown how far this was the condition of the author as well. These lines report an *un*resolved predicament. But so it should be: the poem can only remain consistent with its own negativity as long as it omits any positive answer to the questions posed respecting the species of discourse employed.

Which does not prevent it from looking beyond itself toward that ambiguous 'peace which passeth understanding' with which the Note so discreetly glosses the triple *Shantih*. Unalienated from its archaically 'original' language, this expression might even be a rendering of the true Word indeed. But this is *not* pronounced here. It is (under this protological disguise) only repeated—in the mode of quotation. So at the very end the poem reverts to its own first mode of discourse, as the most constant type of the general problem, as well as the safest place to break off for the time being.[27]

In his fine biographical study, Herbert Howarth quotes Alain Fournier quoting Laforgue on the ideal of 'le style' to which the young Eliot, then a student and friend of one of these figures and already a follower of the other, would have been exposed during his formative period in Paris before the war. This style, these men agreed, would be simply 'du français de Christ.'[28] It is an arresting expression, upon which Howarth does not dwell. What then would be the *English* of Christ? The last section of the poem offers, as it were, the Sanskrit of Krishna. We have seen that this is not quite the same thing. The English of Christ would have to be in English, at least—or some other language even more immediately assimilable. And it would have to embody what it signified without alienation. It would therefore have to be 'spoken' out of the future, eschatologically, rather than merely remembered from the past or dramatized in the present.

To appreciate more exactly what the poem invites us to anticipate but does *not* supply, we might usefully revert once more to the New Testament. The long speeches which distinguish the Gospel according to John are placed in Jesus' mouth. But they cannot be understood as passed down through the tradition, like the *logia* we are accustomed to in the synoptics. Nor are they dramatic elaborations of these, though each is of course plausibly situated within the narrative. They must rather be understood as instances of that rather unusual species of discourse, *written* prophecy—and prophecy not as judgment but as salvation, words inspired by the Spirit to manifest the Word. As such they might count, we could say, as the Greek of Christ.

The Waste Land moves toward an equivalent for this in the mode of leaving space for it. In this way the poem accomplishes what Eliot was at the same time arguing criticism could do when, as he proposed in 'The Function of Criticism,' it raised the 'possibility of arriving at something outside of ourselves, which may provisionally be called truth.' But if (this virtually contemporaneous argument continues) 'anyone complains that I have not defined truth, or fact, or reality, I can only say apologetically that it was no part of my purpose to do so, but only to find a scheme into which, whatever they are, they will fit, if they exist.'[29]

So Eliot never claims to be inspired, as it is necessary to understand John to be doing in order to read him at all. For a fastidious traditionalist like Eliot, this possibility would no doubt have seemed impossible for any postapostolic figure anyway. Instead he joins the Church, where forgiveness may be obtained and food and drink consumed by way of words which can be allowed to mean what they say—for the believer.

Most commentary on *The Waste Land* has been untheological even when it has been avowedly Christian. So evidence is still lacking to support a hypothesis which nonetheless looms as the end of the poem is considered. This might be that, as Eliot personally drew near to the sacraments, he was freed to realize that the problem of an absolutely trustworthy Word had already been taken care of by Another. Confession and the Eucharist would then have shown themselves to be the 'English of Christ' for all practical purposes—especially within the Anglican liturgy, where that language was used and both bread and wine supplied, advantages that could have been determining for a convert of the period. If so, Eliot would then have been left to explore what remained to be done by somebody who had come to believe just this—in a world of readers who had not.

Early Poems and *The Waste Land*

Notes

1. David Ward, *T.S. Eliot between Two Worlds* (London: Routledge, 1973), p. 68.

2. The point would surely be that we do *not* need documentation for Leavis, Wilson, Brooks, Matthiessen, Drew, Kenner, Miller, Bergonzi, et al. There the books stand, a little worn, on the shelves of the graduate reading room. Subordinate authorities of a similar status might include Rajan, Unger, Smidt, and Langbaum.

3. These new respectables would include, in alphabetical order, Eloise Knapp Hay, *T.S. Eliot's Negative Way* (Cambridge: Harvard University Press, 1982); A.D. Moody, *Thomas Stearns Eliot* (Cambridge: Cambridge University Press, 1979); Derek Traversi, *T.S. Eliot: The Longer Poems* (London: Edward Arnold, 1973); and Ward, cited above. The valuable exception among these recent academic surveys seems to me Marianne Thormahlen, *The Waste Land: A Fragmentary Wholeness* (Lund: C.W.K. Gleerup, 1978), which does not appear as well known as it should be—perhaps because it is not shelved under a PS number?

4. A full reference *is* worth making here: Lyndall Gordon, *Eliot's Early Years* (New York: Oxford University Press, 1977), and Herbert Howarth, *Notes on Some Figures behind T. S. Eliot* (Boston: Houghton Mifflin, 1964), Ronald Bush, *T.S. Eliot: A Study in Character and Style* (New York: Oxford University Press, 1983), and David Spurr, *Conflicts in Consciousness: T.S. Eliot's Poetry and Criticism* (Urbana: University of Illinois Press, 1984), should also be counted as biographical studies, though at a discouragingly abstract distance from their subject.

Peter Ackroyd's prominently reviewed *T.S. Eliot: A Life* (New York: Simon & Schuster, 1984) brings together such units of information as now seem publishable. The recent flurry of protest surrounding the London production of Michael Hastings's play *Tom and Viv* would additionally illustrate a persisting curiosity about Eliot-the-man.

5. Other observers have naturally begun to entertain the same possibility. The most acute so far has been Denis Donoghue, with two rewarding pieces, a lecture reprinted in A.D. Moody, *The Waste Land in Different Voices* (York: Edward Arnold, 1974), pp. 185–201, and the somewhat more leisurely 'On the Limits of a Language,' *Sewanee Review*, 85 (1977), 371–91. Other recent essays which respond to this opportunity would include, in approximate order of interest for my purpose here, William Harmon, 'T.S. Eliot's Raids on the Inarticulate,' PMLA, 91 (1976), 450–59; Margaret Dickie Uroff, '*The Waste Land*: Metatext,' *Centennial Review*, 24 (1980), 148–66; Marianne Ryan, 'Retrieval of the Word in *Gerontion* and *The Waste Land*,' *Antigonish Review*, 20 (1974), 78–97; John Paul Riquelme, 'Withered Stumps of Time: Allusion, Reading and Writing in *The Waste Land*,' *Denver Quarterly*, 15 (1981), 90–110; Ruth Nevo, '*The Waste Land*: Ur-text of Deconstruction,' *New Literary History*, 13 (1982), 453–61; and William Stanos, 'Repetition in *The Waste Land*: A Phenomenological De-struction,' *Boundary* 2, 7 (1979), 225–85. Gregory Jay's *T.S. Eliot and the Poetics of Literary History* (Baton Rouge: Louisiana State University Press, 1984) is a book-length effort to assimilate Eliot to contemporary criticism. The general case would, of course, seem plausible in proportion to its current accessibility. My own hope is not simply to assert a connection between 'theory' and *The Waste Land* but show how this might be worked out by way of the poetical specifics.

6. T.S. Eliot, *The Use of Poetry and the Use of Criticism* (Cambridge: Harvard University Press, 1933), p. 148. Bush (pp. 57–58) traces some of these images back to Eliot's recent unhappy experience.

7. Moody, p. 81.

8. Obviously I am relying here on the Facsimile of *The Waste Land*, ed. Valerie Eliot (New York: Harcourt, 1971), as I shall be subsequently for similar observations. For the opening of 'A Game of Chess,' see p. 11. Stephen Spender has mentioned the curiously typical combination in this passage of real inventiveness with 'a sense of pastiche,' *as if* Eliot were quoting (see his *T.S. Eliot* [New York: Penguin, 1975], p. 110). In fact he almost is: Grover Smith has shown how closely the language of this episode reflects a pair of Poe stories in his new edition of *The Waste Land* (London: Allen & Unwin, 1983), pp. 123–25. It need not be news of course that the impulse toward burlesque which has produced so many parodies of the poem is already latent within it.

9. The first draft, it has often been observed, contains a line confirming as much: 'the ivory men make company between us,' The Facsimile tells us that Vivienne asked her husband to remove this verse. Eliot put it back as he copied the poem out by hand for a sale after her death

(Facsimile, pp. 13 and 126). It should presumably be restored to the canonical text.

10. Similarly, 'If you don't like it you can get on with it' is stronger than '"No, ma'am, you needn't look old fashioned at me," I said,' and '"It's them pills I took, to bring it off"' *sounds* better than '"It's that medicine . . . ."' Best of all, the splendidly insincere 'What you get married for if you don't want children?' replaces an inert 'You want to keep him at home, I suppose' (Facsimile, p. 13). Eliot is good at listening until he can hear the latent music of unguarded life.

11. Delmore Schwartz's 'T.S. Eliot's Voice and Voices,' *Poetry*, 85 (1955), 232–42, written while the plays were a topic for discussion, is shrewd about this characteristic. Eliot's special way of seeming merely to listen as others speak might also be linked with his special concern with the virtue of humility, of which this imaginative disposition could count as a dramatist's version. The problem of the speakers in general is well covered by Thormahlen, pp. 82–90.

12. Thormahlen summarizes as follows: 'Nowhere in the poem is there an instance of a message or a perception from one human being clinching with that of another on the same wavelength' (p. 110). She cites the monologues of Marie and Mme. Sosostris and Stetson's failure to answer the remarks apparently made to him in part 1; both sets of speakers in part 2; the absences of a social occasion for Tiresias' observation in part 3; and the unanswered questions in part 5. These are not all of the same weight; we *know* who is the third that walks always beside the first and the second, even if that figure does not speak. And the conversation in the Hofgarten seems pleasant. But in general she is clearly correct.

13. By Hugh Kenner in *The Invisible Poet* (New York: McDowell, Obolensky, 1959), p. 169.

14. It is distressing to find not only Kenner but F.O. Matthiessen, another longtime inhabitant of the graduate book shelf, positively admiring these lines as a masterful instance of Eliotic composition. See his *The Achievement of T.S. Eliot* (New York: Oxford University Press, 1947), pp. 31–32.

15. We can learn from the typescript that all three of the fragments here were once apparently intended as the continuous speech of a single young woman who recalls the trams of Highbury, the canoe at Richmond, and the sands at Margate. But the spacing naturally prompts most readers to assign them to different individuals. Pound found these verses 'Echt' too. See the Facsimile, pp. 51–53.

16. M.K. Blasing ('*The Waste Land*: Gloss and Glossary,' *Essays in Literature*, 9 [1982], 97–105) argues that the Notes undermine the authority of the poem by thematizing it. But this judgment underestimates the effect of humor and personal reference alike.

17. F.R. Leavis, *New Bearings in English Poetry* (London: Chatto & Windus, 1932), p. 95.

18. The growing skepticism about Tiresias is usefully summarized in Thormahlen, pp. 74–78. David Ward, with whom this essay began, is tarter than most; the prophetic voice is 'crickety, grumpy, and wilful, morally insecure and sometimes too clever by half.' Eliot's intention, legitimate in itself, is 'compromised' by 'the erratic individual note of spleen and anguish' (p. 70). In other words, though this is *not* said, Pound's cuts did not go deep enough. On the other hand, it is still possible for a comparatively recent academic critic like Elisabeth Schneider to call the poem an 'exhibition' of an 'ideal unity of culture' in her *T.S. Eliot: The Pattern in the Carpet* (Berkeley: University of California Press, 1975), p. 64. Evidently the need continues for some such focus in spite of all the evidence supplied in the poem and what we have come to know about the process of its composition that centerless*ness* is very much its (pen)ultimate upshot.

19. Eliot continued vulnerable to similar mistakes along a fault line that can be traced through a variety of contexts to the end of his career. The nastiness of the quatrain poems, the arrogance of the early criticism, the reactionary politics and establishment churchmanship, not to mention the solemnity of the public persona—all could be understood as variants of a disposition to overvalue some individual or collective posture within this world. Poetically he realized the *im*possibility of this quite early. And his religious practice could only have confirmed the intuition. But he never ceased to be susceptible to the temptation in one sphere or another. The *Quartets* and the later plays could accordingly be understood as strategies to evade its importunities one way or another.

20. Grover Smith, *T.S. Eliot's Poetry and Plays*, 2nd ed. (Chicago: University of Chicago Press, 1974), p. 79.

21. I assume nobody has any serious trouble with 'Death by Water.' In every myth silence, death, and water coincide. Part 4 thereby enacts the decision for which we have been trying to clear a space in reviewing part 3. For those still puzzled, a survey of the interpretive options may

be found in Paul Lewis, 'Life by Water: Characterization and Salvation in *The Waste Land*,' *Mosaic*, 11 (1978), 81–90.

22. Facsimile, pp. 71, 129.

23. Hugh Kenner, 'The Urban Apocalypse,' in *Eliot in His Time*, ed. A. Walton Litz (Princeton: Princeton University Press, 1973), pp. 23–49. The trendy *Oxford Anthology of English Literature*, ed. John Hollander and Frank Kermode (New York: Oxford University Press, 1973), adopts this argument in its introduction to the poem.

24. Facsimile, p. 113.

25. Luke 24:29–31 (King James Version).

26. This would also resolve the note of bodiliness so prominent earlier in the poem. Jay (pp. 149–55) rightly insists on this—without connecting the explicit negatives of burial or dismemberment with an anticipated positive of resurrection.

27. Milton Miller has proposed in 'What the Thunder Said,' *ELH*, 36 (1969), that the 'fragments' represent a Pentecostal speaking in tongues and so a successful end to the quest. This is ingenious but poetically as well as theologically impossible: we are back in this world, says the tone, making the best of a bad situation, not ecstatic at the commencement of a new (pp. 448–51).

28. Howarth, p. 156.

29. These are the final words of this important essay. T.S. Eliot, *Selected Essays, 1917–1932* (New York: Harcourt, 1932), p. 22.

117
The Waste Land A Sphinx without a Secret*

MAUD ELLMANN

In a fable of Oscar Wilde's, Gerald, the narrator, finds his old companion Lord Murchison so puzzled and anxious that he urges him to unburden his mind. Murchison confides that he fell in love some time ago with the mysterious Lady Alroy, whose life was so entrenched in secrecy that every move she made was surreptitious, every word she spoke conspiratorial. Fascinated, he resolved to marry her. But on the day he planned for his proposal, he caught sight of her on the street, 'deeply veiled', and walking swiftly towards a lodging house, where she let herself in with her own key. Suspecting a secret lover, he abandoned her in rage and stormed off to the Continent to forget her. Soon afterwards, however, he learnt that she was dead, having caught pneumonia in the theatre. Still tormented by her mystery, he returned to London to continue his investigations. He cross-examined the landlady of the lodging house, but she insisted that Lady Alroy always visited her rooms alone, took tea, and left as blamelessly as she had come. '"Now, what do you think it all meant?"' Murchison demands. For Gerald, the answer is quite simple: the lady was '"a sphinx without a secret."'[1]

Now, *The Waste Land* is a sphinx without a secret, too, and to force it to confession may also be a way of killing it. This poem, which has been so thoroughly *explained*, is rarely *read* at all, and one can scarcely see the 'waste' beneath the redevelopments. Most commentators have been so busy tracking its allusions down and patching up its tattered memories that they have overlooked its broken images in search of the totality it might have been. Whether they envisage the poem as a pilgrimage, a quest for the Holy Grail, an elegy to Europe or to Jean Verdenal, these readings treat the text as if it were a photographic negative, tracing the shadows of a lost or forbidden body.[2]

This is how Freud first undertook interpretation, too, but his patients forced him to revise his method, and his experience may shed a different

*From *The Poetics of Impersonality T.S. Eliot and Ezra Pound* (Brighton, 1987), pp. 91–113.

377

kind of light upon *The Waste Land*. In *Studies on Hysteria*, Freud and Breuer argue that 'hysterics suffer mainly from reminiscences' (and by this definition, *The Waste Land* is the most hysterical of texts).[3] Since the hysteric somatises her desire, enciphering her memories upon her flesh, Freud imagined that he could alleviate her suffering by salvaging the painful recollections. However, these archaeologies would leave her cold. For this reason, he shifted his attention from the past to the present, from reminiscence to resistance, from the secrets to the silences themselves (SE XVIII 18).

Now, *The Waste Land*, like any good sphinx, lures the reader into hermeneutics, too: but there is no secret underneath its hugger-muggery. Indeed, Hegel saw the Sphinx as the symbol of the symbolic itself, because it did not know the answer to its own question: and *The Waste Land*, too, is a riddle to *itself*.[4] Here it is more instructive to be scrupulously superficial than to dig beneath the surface for the poem's buried skeletons or sources. For it is in the silences *between* the words that meaning flickers, local, evanescent—in the very 'wastes' that stretch across the page. These silences curtail the powers of the author, for they invite the *hypocrite lecteur* to reconstruct their broken sense. Moreover, the speaker cannot be identified with his creator, not because he has a *different* personality, like Prufrock, but because he has no stable identity at all. The disembodied 'I' glides in and out of stolen texts, as if the speaking subject were merely the quotation of its antecedents. Indeed, this subject is the victim of a general collapse of boundaries. This chapter examines *The Waste Land* in the light of Freud—and ultimately in the darkness of *Beyond the Pleasure Principle*—to trace the poem's suicidal logic.

Throbbing between Two Lives

Let us assume, first of all, that *The Waste Land* is about what it declares—waste. A ceremonial purgation, it inventories all the 'stony rubbish' that it strives to exorcise (20).[5] The 'waste *land*' could be seen as the thunderous desert where the hooded hordes are swarming towards apocalypse. But it also means 'waste ground', bomb sites or vacant lots, like those in 'Rhapsody on a Windy Night', where ancient women gather the wreckage of Europe.[6] It means Jerusalem or Alexandria or London—any ravaged centre of a dying world—and it foreshadows the dilapidation of centricity itself. The poem teems with urban waste, butt-ends of the city's days and ways: 'empty bottles, sandwich papers, / Silk handkerchiefs, cardboard boxes, cigarette ends' (177–8). However, it is difficult to draw taxonomies of waste, because the text conflates the city with the body and, by analogy, the social with the personal. Abortions, broken fingernails, carious teeth, and 'female smells' signify the culture's decadence, as well as bodily decrepitude. The self is implicated in the degradation of the race, because the filth without insinuates defilement within.[7]

It is waste *paper*, however, which appals and fascinates the poem, the written detritus which drifts into the text as randomly as picnics sink into the Thames (177–8). Many modernist writers comb the past in order to recycle its remains, and Joyce is the master of the scavengers: 'Nothing but old fags and cabbage-stumps of quotations', in D.H. Lawrence's words.[8] Joyce treats the rubbish heap of literature as a fund of creativity ('The letter! The litter!'), disseminating writings as Eliot strews bones.[9] A funeral rather than a wake, *The Waste Land* is a lugubrious version of Joyce's jubilant 'recirculation' of the past, in which all waste becomes unbiodegradable: 'Men and bits of paper, whirled by the cold wind . . .' (BN III 15).[10] Indeed, *The Waste Land* is one of the most abject texts in English literature, in every sense: for abjection, according to Bataille, 'is merely the inability to assume with sufficient strength the imperative act of excluding abject things', an act that 'establishes the foundations of collective existence.'[11] Waste is what a culture casts away in order to determine what is not itself, and thus to establish its own limits. In the same way, the subject defines the limits of his body through the violent expulsion of its own excess: and ironically, this catharsis *institutes* the excremental. Similarly, Paul Ricoeur has pointed out that social rituals of 'burning, removing, chasing, throwing, spitting out, covering up, burying' continuously *reinvent* the waste they exorcise.[12]

The word 'abject' literally means 'cast out', though commonly it means downcast in spirits: but 'abjection' may refer to the waste itself, together with the violence of casting it abroad. It is the ambiguity of the 'abject' that distinguishes it from the 'object', which the subject rigorously jettisons (ob-jects). According to Julia Kristeva, the abject emerges when exclusions fail, in the sickening collapse of limits. Rather than disease or filth or putrefaction, the abject is that which 'disturbs identity, system, order': it is the 'in-between, the ambiguous, the composite.'[13] In the 'brown fog' of *The Waste Land*, for example, or the yellow fog of 'Prufrock', the in-between grows animate: and Madame Sosostris warns us to fear death by water, for sinking banks betoken glutinous distinctions.[14] In fact, the 'horror' of *The Waste Land* lurks in the osmoses, exhalations and porosities, in the dread of *epidemic* rather than the filth itself, for it is this miasma that bespeaks dissolving limits.[15] The corpses signify the 'utmost of abjection', in Kristeva's phrase, because they represent 'a border that has encroached upon everything': an outside that irrupts into the inside, and erodes the parameters of life.[16] It is impossible to keep them underground: Stetson's garden is an ossuary, and the dull canals, the garrets, and the alleys are littered with unburied bones. 'Tumbled graves' (387) have overrun the city, for the living have changed places with the dead: 'A crowd flowed over London Bridge, so many, / I had not thought death had undone so many' (62–3). *The Waste Land* does not fear the dead themselves so much as their invasion of the living; for it is the collapse of boundaries that centrally disturbs the text, be they sexual, national, linguistic, or authorial.

Kristeva derives her notion of abjection from Freud's *Totem and Taboo*, which was written ten years before the publication of *The Waste Land* and anticipates its itch for anthropology.[17] Like Eliot, Freud draws analogies between the psychic and the cultural, linking 'civilised' obsessionality to 'savage' rites. In both cases the ritual 'is ostensibly a protection against the prohibited act; but *actually* . . . a repetition of it' (SE XII 50). *The Waste Land* resembles this obsessive rite, because it surreptitiously repeats the horror that it tries to expiate. In particular, it desecrates tradition. The poem may be seen as an extended 'blasphemy', in Eliot's conception of the term, an affirmation masked as a denial. For the text dismantles Western culture as if destruction were the final mode of veneration. As Terry Eagleton argues:

> behind the back of this ruptured, radically decentred poem runs an alternative text which is nothing less than the closed, coherent, authoritative discourse of the mythologies which frame it. The phenomenal text, to use one of Eliot's own metaphors, is merely the meat with which the burglar distracts the guard-dog while he proceeds with his stealthy business.[18]

However, Eagleton omits a further ruse: for the poem uses its nostalgia to conceal its vandalism, its pastiche of the tradition that it mourns. Indeed, a double consciousness pervades the text, as if it had been written by a vicar and an infidel. The speaker is divided from himself, unable to resist the imp within who cynically subverts his pieties. Thus, Cleopatra's burnished throne becomes a dressing table, time's wingèd chariot a grinning skull (77, 186): but there are many subtler deformations.

Take, for example, the opening words. The line 'April is the cruellest month' blasphemes (in Eliot's sense) against the first lines of *The Canterbury Tales*, which presented April's showers as so sweet. At once a nod to origins and a flagrant declaration of beginninglessness, this allusion grafts the poem to another text, vaunting its parasitic in-betweenness. Only the misquotation marks the change of ownership, but the author's personality dissolves in the citational abyss. This is why Conrad Aiken once complained that Eliot had created '"a literature of literature" . . . a kind of parasitic growth on literature, a sort of mistletoe . . .'.[19] As blasphemy, *The Waste Land* is obliged to poach upon the past, caught in a perpetual allusion to the texts that it denies.[20] For it is only by corrupting Chaucer's language that Eliot can grieve the passing of his world:

> *April is the cruellest month, breeding*
> *Lilacs out of the dead land, mixing*
> *Memory and desire, stirring*
> *Dull roots with spring rain.*
> *Winter kept us warm, covering*

> *Earth in forgetful snow, feeding*
> *A little life with dried tubers.*
>
> *(1–7)*

Because these lines allude to Chaucer, they invoke the origin of the tradition as well as the juvescence of the year.[21] But words like 'stirring', 'mixing', and 'feeding' profane beginnings, be they literary or organic, provoking us to ask what 'cruelty' has exchanged them for uniting, engendering, or nourishing. Thus the passage whispers of the words *its* words deny, and sorrows for the things it cannot say. Most of the lines stretch beyond the comma where the cadence falls, as if the words themselves had overflown their bounds, straining towards a future state of being like the dull roots that they describe. They typify the way *The Waste Land* differs from itself, forever trembling towards another poem which has already been written, or else has yet to be composed.

This betweenness also overtakes the speaking subject, for the first-person pronoun roams from voice to voice.[22] The 'us' in 'Winter kept us warm' glides into the 'us' of 'Summer surprised us,' without alerting 'us', the readers, of any change of name or locus. At last, the 'us' contracts into the couple in the Hofgarten, after having spoken for the human, animal and vegetable worlds. What begins as an editorial 'we' becomes the mark of a migration, which restlessly displaces voice and origin. Throughout the poem, the 'I' slips from persona to persona, weaves in and out of quoted speech, and creeps like a contagion through the *Prothalamion* or Pope or the debased grammar of a London pub, sweeping history into a heap of broken images.

However, Eliot insisted in the Notes to *The Waste Land* that Tiresias should stabilise this drifting subject, and rally the nomadic voices of the text:[23]

> 218. Tiresias, although a mere spectator and not indeed a 'character', is yet the most important personage in the poem, uniting all the rest. Just as the one-eyed merchant, seller of currants, *melts into* the Phoenician Sailor, and the latter is *not wholly distinct* from Ferdinand Prince of Naples, so all the women are one woman, and the *two sexes meet* in Tiresias. What Tiresias *sees*, in fact, is the substance of the poem.[24]

But what *does* Tiresias see? Blind as he is, the prophet has a single walk-on part, when he spies on the typist and her lover indulging in carbuncular caresses.[25] In this Note, moreover, Eliot emphasises the *osmosis* of identities more than their reunion in a central consciousness. For Tiresias's role within the poem is to 'melt' distinctions and confuse personae:

> *I Tiresias, though blind, throbbing between two lives,*
> *Old man with wrinkled female breasts, can see*
> *At the violet hour, the evening hour that strives*
> *Homeward, and brings the sailor home from sea,*
> *The typist home at teatime, clears her breakfast, lights*

Her stove, and lays out food in tins.
Out of the window perilously spread
Her drying combinations touched by the sun's last rays,
On the divan are piled (at night her bed)
Stockings, slippers, camisoles, and stays.
I Tiresias, old man with wrinkled dugs
Perceived the scene, and foretold the rest—
I too awaited the expected guest.
He, the young man carbuncular, arrives....

(218–31)

Here the seer turns into a peeping Tom, the most ambiguous of spectators. 'Throbbing between two lives', Tiresias could be seen as the very prophet of abjection, personifying all the poem's porous membranes. A revisionary, he foresees what he has already foresuffered, mixing memory and desire, self and other, man and woman, pollution and catharsis. The Notes which exalt him are 'abject' themselves, for they represent a kind of supplement or discharge of the text that Eliot could never get 'unstuck', though he later wished the poem might stand alone.[26] Now that the manuscript has been released (1971), the poem throbs between two authors and three texts—the Notes, the published poem, and the drafts that Pound pruned so cunningly. The text's integrity dissolves under the invasion of its own disjecta. Just as its quotations confuse the past and present, parasite and poet, the poem leaks in supplements and prolegomena.

The typist symptomises this betweenness, too. Her profession parodies the poet's, demoted as he is to the typist or amanuensis of the dead. Too untidy to acknowledge boundaries, she strews her bed with stockings, slippers, camisoles, and stays, and even the bed is a divan by day, in a petit bourgeois disrespect for definition. She resembles the neurotic woman in 'A Game of Chess', who cannot decide to go out or to stay in, as if she were at enmity with their distinction. Eliot himself declares that all the women in *The Waste Land* are one woman, and this is because they represent the very principle of unguency. 'Pneumatic bliss' entails emulsive demarcations.[27] Yet the misogyny is so ferocious, particularly in the manuscript, that it begins to turn into a blasphemy against itself. For the poem is enthralled by the femininity that it reviles, bewitched by this odorous and shoreless flesh. In fact, woman is the spirit of its own construction, the phantom of its own betweennesses. In 'The Fire Sermon', Eliot personifies his broken images in a woman's bruised, defiled flesh; and it is as if the damsel Donne once greeted as his new found land had reverted to the old world and an urban wilderness:

'Trams and dusty trees.
Highbury bore me. Richmond and Kew

> Undid me. By Richmond I raised my knees
> Supine on the floor of a narrow canoe.'
>
> 'My feet are at Moorgate, and my heart
> Under my feet. After the event
> He wept. He promised "a new start".
> I made no comment. What should I resent?'
>
> 'On Margate Sands.
> I can connect
> Nothing with nothing.
> The broken fingernails of dirty hands.
> My people humble people who expect
> Nothing.'
>   la la
>
> To Carthage then I came
>
> Burning burning burning burning
> O Lord Thou pluckest me out
> O Lord Thou pluckest
>
> burning
>
>   (292–311)

The body and the city melt together, no longer themselves but not yet other. It is as if the metaphor were stuck between the tenor and the vehicle, transfixed in an eternal hesitation. Both the woman and the city have been raped, but the 'he' seems passive in his violence, weeping at his own barbarity. The victim, too, consents to degradation as if it were foredoomed: 'I raised my knees / Supine. . . . What should I resent?' (As Ian Hamilton observes, 'no one in *The Waste Land* raises her knees in any other spirit than that of dumb complaisance.'[28] 'Undone', the woman's body crumbles in a synecdochic heap of knees, heart, feet, weirdly disorganised: 'My feet are at Moorgate, and my heart / Under my feet.' But the city which undid her decomposes, too, in a random concatenation of its parts—Highbury, Richmond, Kew, Moorgate—and ends in broken fingernails on Margate Sands.

Itinerant and indeterminate, the 'I' slips from the woman to the city, and then assumes the voice of Conrad's Harlequin in *Heart of Darkness*, who apologises for a humble and exploited race. At last it merges with the 'I' who came to Carthage in St. Augustine's *Confessions*. As the last faltering words suggest, it is impossible to 'pluck' the speaking subject out of the conflagration of the poem's idioms. The I cannot preserve its own identity intact against the shrieking voices which assail it, 'Scolding, mocking, or merely chattering' according to their whim (*BN* V 18). In *The Waste Land*, the only voice which *is* 'inviolable' is the voice that does not speak, but only sings that phatic, faint 'la la.'

Early Poems and *The Waste Land*

These notes allude to the warblings of the nightingale, who fills the desert 'with inviolable voice' (101). In Ovid, however, the nightingale was born in violation. Tereus, 'the barbarous king' (99) raped his wife's sister Philomela, and cut out her tongue so that she could not even name her own defiler ('Tereu . . .' [206]). But Philomela weaves a picture of his crime into her loom so that her sister, Procne, can decode her wrongs.[29] In this way, her web becomes a kind of writing, a dossier to defend her speechless flesh. After reading it, Procne avenges Philomela by feeding Tereus the flesh of his own son. In *The Waste Land*, Eliot omits the web, and he ignores this violent retaliation, too. He alludes only to the ending of the myth, when the gods give both the sisters wings to flee from Tereus's wrath. They change Philomela into a nightingale to compensate her loss of speech with wordless song.[30] By invoking this story, Eliot suggests that woman is excluded from language through the sexual violence of a man. As Peter Middleton has pointed out, she is awarded for her pains with a pure art which is powerless and desolate—'la, la.'[31]

In *The Waste Land* as in Ovid, writing provides the only refuge from aphasia, but it is a weapon that turns against its own possessor. Rather than the record of the victim's wrongs, writing has become the very instrument of violation: and it invades the male narrator's speech as irresistibly as the 'female stench' with which it comes to be associated (*WL Fac* [39]). Although Eliot quotes Bradley to the effect that 'my experience falls within my own circle, a circle closed on the outside', this circle has been broken in *The Waste Land* (412n). Here no experience is proper or exclusive to the subject. Moreover, the speaker is possessed by the writings of the dead, and seized in a cacophony beyond control.

Prince of Morticians

> *Curious, is it not, that Mr. Eliot*
> *Has not given more time to Mr. Beddoes*
> *(T.L.) prince of morticians*
>
> Pound, Canto LXXX

In 'Tradition and the Individual Talent' Eliot celebrates the voices of the dead, but he comes to dread their verbal ambush in *The Waste Land*.[32] In the essay, he claimed that 'not only the best, but the most individual poetry' is that which is most haunted by its own precursors. Only thieves can truly be original. For any new creation gains its meaning in relation to the poems of the past, and writing is a voyage to the underworld, to commune with the phantasmal voices of the dead. Eliot published this essay immediately after World War I, in 1919, the same year that Freud was writing *Beyond the Pleasure Principle*. As Middleton has pointed out, they both confront the same material: the unprecedented death toll of the First World War. Like Freud's theory of repetition, Eliot's account of influence attempts to salvage something of a past that had never been so ruthlessly annihilated—however fearsome its reanimation from the grave. Whereas Freud discovers the death drive in the compulsion to repeat, *The Waste Land* stages it in the compulsion to citation.

In 1919 Freud also wrote his famous essay on the 'uncanny', which he defines as 'whatever reminds us of this inner compulsion to repeat.'[33] *The Waste Land* is uncanny in a double sense, for it is haunted by the repetition of the dead—in the form of mimicry, quotation and pastiche—but also by a kind of Hammer horror: bats with baby faces, whisper music, violet light, hooded hordes, witches, death's heads, bones, and zombies (378–81). According to Freud, 'heimlich' literally means 'homely' or familiar, but it develops in the direction of ambivalence until it converges with its opposite, *unheimlich* or uncanny.[34] Thus the very word has grown unhomely and improper to itself. The passage Eliot misquotes from *The White Devil* provides a good example of the double meaning of uncanniness:

O keep the Dog far hence, that's friend to men,
Or with his nails he'll dig it up again

(74–5)

Since the passage is purloined from Webster, the very words are ghostly revenants, returning as extravagant and erring spirits. This kind of verbal kleptomania subverts the myth that literary texts are private property, or that the author can enjoy the sole possession of his words. But Eliot writes Dog where Webster wrote Wolf, and friend where Webster wrote foe. Thus he tames the hellhound in the same misprision that domesticates the discourse of the past. Friendly pet and wild beast, the Dog becomes the emblem of the poem's literary necrophilia, and the familiar strangeness of the past that Eliot himself has disinterred.[35]

Quotation means that words cannot be anchored to their authors, and the fortune-tellers in the text personify this loss of origin. For prophecy means that we hear about a thing before it happens. The report precedes the event. The bell echoes before it rings. Tiresias, for instance, has not only foreseen but actually 'foresuffered at all', as if he were a living misquotation.[36] A fake herself, Madame Sosostris lives in fear of imitators ('Tell her I bring the horoscope myself'), nervous that her words may ago astray ('One must be so careful these days'). This anxiety about originality and theft resurges in the form of Mr Eugenides. A Turkish merchant in London, he also speaks demotic French: and the word 'demotic', Greek in etymology, alludes to Egyptian hieroglyphics. Being a merchant, he is not only the product but the sinister conductor of miscegenation, intermingling verbal, sexual and monetary currencies. Even his pocketful of currants could be heard as 'currents', which dissolve identities and definitions, like the 'current under sea' that picks the

Early Poems and *The Waste Land*

bones of Phlebas, his Phoenician alter ego.[37] His reappearances suggest that repetition has become a virus, unwholesome as the personages who recur. Indeed, the poem hints that literature is nothing but a plague of echoes: that writing necessarily deserts its author, spreading like an epidemic into other texts. Any set of written signs can fall into bad company, into contexts which pervert their meaning and their genealogy.

The worst company in *The Waste Land*, both socially and rhetorically, is the London pub where Lil is tortured by her crony for her bad teeth and her abortion. Here, the publican's cry, 'HURRY UP PLEASE IT'S TIME', becomes as vagrant as a written sign, orphaned from its author. Any British drinker knows its origin, of course, so Eliot does not identify the speaker, but sets the phrase adrift on a semantic odyssey. When it interrupts the dialogue, the two discursive sites contaminate each other.

> *You ought to be ashamed, I said, to look so antique.*
> *(And her only thirty-one.)*
> *I can't help it, she said, pulling a long face,*
> *It's them pills I took, to bring it off, she said.*
> *(She's had five already, and nearly died of young George.)*
> *The chemist said it would be all right, but I've never been the same.*
> *You* are *a proper fool, I said.*
> *Well, if Albert won't leave you alone, there it is, I said,*
> *What you get married for if you don't want children?*
> HURRY UP PLEASE ITS TIME
> *Well, that Sunday Albert was home, they had a hot gammon,*
> *And they asked me in to dinner, to get the beauty of it hot—*
> HURRY UP PLEASE ITS TIME
> HURRY UP PLEASE ITS TIME
> *Goonight Bill. Goonight Lou. Goonight May. Goonight.*
> *Ta ta. Goonight. Goonight.*
> *Good night, ladies, good night, sweet ladies, good night, good night.*
>
> *(156–72)*

This is the same technique that Flaubert uses in the fair in *Madame Bovary*, where Emma and Rodolph wallow in romance, while the voice of the Minister of Agriculture splices their sentiment with swine. In *The Waste Land*, the more the publican repeats his cry, the more its meaning strays from his intentions. Instead of closing time, it now connotes perfunctory and brutal sexuality: it means that time is catching up with Lil, in the form of dentures and decay, and rushing her culture to apocalypse. There is no omniscient speaker here to monitor these meanings, no 'pill' to control their pullulation. It is as if the words themselves had been demobbed and grown adulterous. When Ophelia's good-byes creep in, just as the dialogue is closing, the allusion dignifies Lil's slower suicide: 'Good night, ladies, good night, sweet ladies, good night, good night.' Yet at the same time, the text degrades Ophelia by suturing her words to Lil's, reducing Shakespeare to graffiti.[38]

In general, the poem's attitude towards Shakespeare and the canon resembles taboos against the dead, with their mixture of veneration and horror (SE XIII 25). As Freud says 'they are expressions of mourning; but on the other hand they clearly betray—what they seek to conceal—hostility against the dead . . .' (SE XIII 61). But he stresses that it is not the dead themselves so much as their 'infection' which is feared, for they are charged with a kind of 'electricity' (SE XIII 20–2, 41). The taboo arises to defend the living subject from their sly invasions. But strangely enough, the taboo eventually becomes prohibited itself, as if the ban were as infectious as the horrors it forbids. Prohibition spreads like a disease, tainting everything that touches it, 'till at last the whole world lies under an embargo' (SE XIII 27). A similar reversal takes place in *The Waste Land*, where the rituals of purity are perverted into *ersatz* desecrations of themselves. When Mrs. Porter and her daughter wash their feet in soda water, the ceremony of innocence is drowned, and the baptismal rite becomes its own defilement.

According to Freud, there are two ways in which taboo can spread, through contact and through mimesis. To touch a sacred object is to fall under its interdict. But the offender must also be tabooed because of 'the risk of imitation', for others may follow his example (SE XIII 33). These two forms of 'transference' work like tropes, since the first, like metonymy, depends on contiguity, the second on similitude like metaphor (SE XIII 27).[39] Freud adds that taboo usages resemble obsessional symptoms in that 'the prohibitions lack any assignable motive' and they are 'easily displaceable'. It is as if the spread of the taboo depended on the power of rhetorical displacement: and underneath the fear of the contagion is the fear of tropes, the death-dealing power of figuration (SE XIII 28).

Displacement is indeed the malady the poem strives to cure, but its own figures are the source of the disorder. Though Eliot condemns Milton for dividing sound from sense, it is precisely this dissociation which produces the semantic epidemic of *The Waste Land*. It is the rats, appropriately, who carry the infection. They make their first appearance in 'rats' alley'; but here a note refers us mischievously to Part III, where another rat peeks out again, like a further outbreak of the verbal plague:

> *White bodies naked on the low damp ground*
> *And bones cast in a little low dry garret,*
> *Rattled by the rat's foot only, year to year.*

However, Eliot seems to have forgotten one rodential apparition in between:

> *But at my back in a cold blast I hear*
> *The* rattle *of the bones, and chuckle spread from ear to ear.*
> *A* rat *crept softly through the vegetation*

> *Dragging its slimy belly on the bank*
> *While I was fishing in the dull canal*
> *On a winter evening round behind the gashouse*
> *Musing upon the king my brother's wreck*
> *And on the king my father's death before him,*
> *White bodies naked on the low damp ground*
> *And bones cast in a little low dry garret,*
> Rattled *by the* rat's *foot only, year to year.*
>
> *(III 185–95: my emphases)*

It is the sound, here, which connects the rattle to the rat, as opposed to a semantic link between them. And it is the rattle of the words, rather than their meaning, that propels the poem forward. Indeed, the sound preempts the sense and spreads like an infection.

Notice that the text associates the rattle of the rats with 'the king my brother's wreck' and 'the king my father's death before him.' For the contiguity suggests that it is these calamities that taint these signs, causing them to fester and grow verminous. Wrenched from their context in *The Tempest*, these deaths suggest the downfall of the father, as do the oblique allusions to the Fisher King, a figure Eliot derives from Jessie Weston's study of the Grail romance.[40] According to this legend, the King has lost his manhood, and his impotence has brought a blight over his lands. Eliot connects the Fisher King to 'the man with three staves' in the Tarot pack, as if to hint that both have failed to fecundate the waste land, to fish the sense out of its floating signifiers. Their emasculation corresponds to other injuries, particularly to the mutilation of the voice: as if the phallus were complicit with the Logos. Lacking both, language has become a 'waste of breath', a barren dissemination: 'Sighs, short and infrequent, were exhaled . . .'.

In the *Waste Land* manuscript, this anxiety about the Logos remains explicit. For here the pilgrim is searching for the 'one essential word that frees', entrammelled in his own 'concatenated words from which the sense seemed gone.'[41] In the finished poem, all that remains of the lightning of the Word is the belated *rattle* of the sign, the 'dry sterile thunder' of the desert (342). And this is why the poem is for ever grieving its belatedness: for not only does it come too late to establish an originary voice, but after the nymphs, after the messiah, after the tradition:

> *After the torchlight red on sweaty faces*
> *After the frosty silence in the gardens*
> *After the agony in stony places. . . .*
>
> *(322–4)*

The manuscript goes on at this point to lament the lateness of its own inditing: 'After the ending of this inspiration.'[42] For writing, in the waste land, is the 'wake' of voice—at once the after-image of the author and his obsequies.

Studies of *The Waste Land* and poems

If writing is in league with death, however, it is also in cahoots with femininity. In *The Waste Land*, the 'hearty female stench' converges with the odour of mortality—and both exude from *writing*, from the violated and putrescent corpse of speech. To use the text's sexology, writing and the stink of femininity have overpowered the priapic realm of voice. Eliot to some extent repressed this hearty female stench when he excised it from the manuscript: but it survives in the strange synthetic perfumes of the lady in 'A Game of Chess', which 'troubled, confused / And drowned the sense in odours'. ('Sense', here, may be understood as both semantic and olfactory: as if, under the power of the feminine, the sense of words becomes as unguent... or liquid' as her scents.) Now, the strange thing about smell, as opposed to vision for example, is that the subject smelling actually imbibes the object smelt, endangering their separation and integrity. And it is the fear of such *displacements* that Eliot's misogyny reveals, a terror deeper even than the dread of incest, which is merely the most scandalous offence to place. In *The Waste Land*, the fall of the father unleashes infinite displacements, be they sexual, linguistic or territorial. Even personal identity dissolves into the babble of miscegenated tongues.[43] As effluvia, the feminine dissolves the limits of the private body, and the boundaries of the self subside into pneumatic anarchy. It is as if the father's impotence entailed the dissolution of identity, imaged as asphyxiation in the body of the feminine.

At the end of the poem, Eliot demolishes the discourse of the West, petitioning the East for solace and recovery.

> *London Bridge is falling down falling down falling down*
> *Poi s'ascose nel foco che gli affina*
> *Quando fiam uti chelidon—O swallow swallow*
> *Le Prince d'Aquitaine à la tour abolie*
> *These fragments I have shored against my ruins*
> *Why then Ile fit you. Hieronymo's mad againe.*
> *Datta. Dayadhvam. Damyata.*
> *Shantih shantih shantih*
>
> *(426–33)*

Here at last the poem silences its Western noise with Eastern blessings. But ironically, the effort to defeat its own 'concatenated words' has only made the text more polyglot, stammering its orisons in Babel. It is as if the speaking subject had been 'ruined' by the very fragments he had shored. '"Words, words, words" might be his motto', one of Eliot's earliest reviewers once exclaimed, '" for in his verse he seems to hate them and to be always expressing his hatred of them, in words."'[44] Because the poem can only abject writing with more writing, it catches the infection that it tries to purge, and implodes like an obsessive ceremonial under the pressure of its own contradictions.

The Violet Hour

It is in another ceremonial that Freud discovers the compulsion to repeat, in the child's game he analyses in *Beyond the Pleasure Principle*. Here, his grandchild flings a cotton-reel into the abyss beyond his cot, and retrieves it with an 'aaaa' of satisfaction, only to cast it out again, uttering a forlorn 'oooo.' Freud interprets these two syllables as primitive versions of the German words 'fort' (gone) and 'da' (here), and he argues that the child is mastering his mother's absences by 'staging' them in the manipulation of a sign (SE XVIII 28). Indeed, Freud compares this theatre of abjection to the catharses of Greek tragedy, and he sees the child's pantomime renunciation as his first 'great cultural achievement.'

It is important, however, that the *drama* fascinates the child rather than the toy itself, for the bobbin belongs to a series of objects which he substitutes indifferently for one another.[45] While the cotton-reel stands for the mother, rehearsing her intermittencies, it also represents the child himself, who sends it forth like an ambassador. As if to emphasise this point, he tops his first act by staging his own disappearance. Crouching underneath a mirror, he lips, 'Baby o-o-o-o!' [Baby gone!], in a kind of abject inversion of Narcissus. By casting *himself* out, the child founds his subjectivity in a game that can only end in death. As Kristeva writes: 'I expel *myself*, I spit *myself* out, I *abject* myself within the same motion through which "I" claim to establish *myself*.'[46] By attempting to control his world with signs, the subject has himself become a function of the sign, *subjected to* its own demonic repetition.

In this scenario, Freud intervenes between the mother and the child, bearing the law of language. For it is he who transforms the oscillation of the child's vowels into intelligible speech. But he neglects the vengeful pleasure that the infant takes in their vibratory suspense and in the *rattle* of their sounds. It is significant, moreover, that the little boy never changed his 'o-o-o-o' into the neutral 'fort' when he acquired the command of language. Instead, he sent his bobbin to the trenches. 'A year later', Freud writes:

> the same boy whom I had observed at his first game used to take a toy, if he was angry with it, and throw it on the floor, exclaiming: 'Go to the fwont!' He had heard at that time that his absent father was 'at the front,' and was far from regretting his absence.... (SE XVIII, p. 16).

Like this child, *The Waste Land* is confronting the specific absence that succeeded World War I, and it evinces both the dread and the desire to hear the voices at the 'fwont' again.[47] In fact, the poem can be read as a seance, and its speaker as the medium who tries to raise the dead by quoting them. Its ruling logic is 'prosopopeia', as Paul De Man defines the trope:

> the fiction of an apostrophe to an absent, deceased, or voiceless entity, which posits the possibility of the latter's reply and confers upon it the power of speech. Voice assumes mouth, eye and finally face, a chain that is manifest in

the etymology of the trope's name, *prosopon poien*, to confer a mask or face (*prosopon*).⁴⁸

With the dead souls flowing over London Bridge, the corpses in the garden and the hooded hordes, *The Waste Land* strives to give a face to death. But it is significant that these figures have no faces, or else that they are hidden and unrecognisable:

> *Who is the third who walks always beside you?*
> *When I count, there are only you and I together*
> *But when I look ahead up the white road*
> *There is always another one walking beside you*
> *Gliding wrapt in a brown mantle, hooded*
> *I do not know whether a man or a woman*
> *—But who is that on the other side of you?*
>
> (360–6)

Here, these nervous efforts to reconstitute the face only drive it to its disappearance. Neither absent nor present, this nameless third bodies forth a rhetoric of disembodiment, and figures the 'continual extinction' of the self. For the speaker rehearses his own death as he conjures up the writings of the dead, sacrificing voice and personality to their ventriloquy. Freud compares his grandchild to victims of shell-shock, who hallucinate their traumas in their dreams, repeating death as if it were desire. This is the game *The Waste Land* plays, and the nightmare that it cannot lay to rest, for it stages the ritual of its own destruction.

Notes

1. Oscar Wilde, 'A Sphinx without a Secret', *Complete Writings*, Vol. VIII, pp. 121–32.

2. In fact the criticism reads more like a quest for the Holy Grail than the poem does. For the Holy Grail interpretation, see Grover Smith, *T.S. Eliot's Poetry and Plays: A Study in Sources and Meanings* (Chicago: University of Chicago Press, 1956), pp. 69–70, 74–7; and Edmund Wilson, *Axel's Castle: A Study in the Imaginative Literature of 1870–1930* (New York and London: Scribner's, 1931), pp. 104–5. Helen Gardner subscribes to this position with some qualifications in *The Art of T.S. Eliot* (London: Cresset Press, 1949), p. 87. George Williamson reconstructs *The Waste Land* ingeniously in *A Reader's Guide*, esp. pp. 129–30. For Jean Verdenal see John Peter, 'A New Interpretation of *The Waste Land*', in *Essays in Criticism*, 2 (1952), esp. p. 245; and James E. Miller, *T.S. Eliot's Personal Waste Land: Exorcism of the Demons* (University Park, Pennsylvania: Pennsylvania State University Press, 1977), *passim*.

3. Freud revises this formula, however, in *The Interpretation of Dreams*, where he states that 'Hysterical symptoms are not attached to actual memories, but to phantasies erected on the basis of memories.' The editor notes that in a letter to Fliess Freud explained that 'Phantasies are psychical facades constructed in order to bar the way to these memories' (SE V 491, 491n.). These facades both bar the way to memory and screen it as one screens a film: they *enact* what cannot be remembered. (Freud also uses the term 'facade' to describe the work of 'secondary revision' in the dream, which is discussed at further length in Chapter V.)

4. See *Hegel's Aesthetics: Lectures on Fine Art*, trans. T.M. Knox (Oxford: Clarendon, 1975), pp. 360–1.

5. Just as 'Ash-Wednesday' strives to be a prayer, *The Waste Land* aspires to the condition of ritual. This fascination with cathartic rites drew Eliot towards the theatre in his later work, but his poems also crave performance, incantation.

6. Suggested by Peter Middleton in 'The Academic Development of *The Waste Land*', forthcoming in *Glyph*.

7. Paul Ricoeur has pointed out that 'impurity was never literally filthiness' and 'defilement was never literally a stain', for the notion of impurity is 'primordially symbolic'. See Ricoeur, *The Symbolism of Evil*, trans. Emerson Buchanan (Boston: Beacon Press, 1967), pp. 35, 39.

8. Quoted by Jennifer Schiffer Levine in 'Originality and Repetition in *Finnegans Wake and Ulysses*', *PMLA*, 94 (1979), 108.

9. James Joyce, *Finnegans Wake*, p. 93, line 24.

10. *Ibid.*, p. 3, line 2.

11. Quoted in Kristeva, *Powers of Horror: An Essay on Abjection*, trans. Leon S. Roudiez (New York: Columbia University Press, 1982), p. 56.

12. Ricoeur, *Symbolism of Evil*, p. 35.

13. Julia Kristeva, *Powers of Horror*, p. 4; see also p. 9.

14. See *Waste Land*, 61, 208, etc.

15. Eliot originally quoted Kurtz's last words 'The horror! the horror!' from Conrad's *Heart of Darkness* as the epigraph to *The Waste Land*: see *WL Fac*, p. 3.

16. *Powers of Horror*, pp. 4, 3.

17. For contemporary interest in anthropology, see Kern, *The Culture of Time and Space*, pp. 19–20, 32, 34.

18. Terry Eagleton, *Criticism and Ideology*, pp. 149–50.

19. See Conrad Aiken, 'An Anatomy of Melancholy' (1923); repr. in *A Collection of Critical Essays on the Waste Land*, ed. J. Martin (Englewood Cliffs, New Jersey: Prentice Hall, 1968), p. 54.

20. Thus it could be said that writing *engenders* blasphemy, just as law is the prerequisite to crime.

21. See Chaucer, General Prologue to the *Canterbury Tales*, lines 1–4.

22. Alick West pointed this out long ago: see *Crisis and Criticism* (London: Lawrence and Wishart, 1937), pp. 5–6, 28.

23. For critics who see Tiresias as an omniscient narrator, see *inter alia* Grover Smith, *Eliot's Poetry and Plays*, pp. 72–6; F.O. Matthiessen, *The Achievement*, p. 60. For critics more sceptical of Tiresias's role, see Graham Hough, *Image and Experience: Studies in a Literary Revolution* (London: Duckworth, 1960), p. 25; Juliet McLaughlin, 'Allusion in *The Waste Land*', *Essays in Criticism*, 19 (1969), 456; Paul LaChance, 'The Function of Voice in *The Waste Land*', *Style*, 5, no. 2 (1971), 107ff.

24. *CPP* 52: my emphases, except for 'sees.'

25. Genevieve W. Forster takes the extraordinary view that the scene with the typist is therefore the 'substance of the poem' in 'The Archetypal Imagery of T.S. Eliot', *PMLA*, 60 (1945), 573.

26. See *PP* 110. For a summary of critical responses to the Notes, see Thormählen, *A Fragmentary Wholeness*, pp. 61–8. See also Eliot's own comments in 'The Art of Poetry I: T.S. Eliot, An Interview', *Paris Review*, no. 21 (1959); repr. in Donald Hall, ed., *Remembering Poets: Reminiscences and Opinions* (New York: Harper, 1978), p. 207. In *PP* 109, Eliot admits to including the Notes 'with a view to spiking the guns of those critics of my earlier poems who had accused me of plagiarism.'

27. See Eliot, 'Whispers of Immortality':

Grishkin is nice: her Russian eye
Is underlined for emphasis;
Uncorseted, her friendly bust
Gives promise of pneumatic bliss. (17–20)

28. Ian Hamilton, '*The Waste Land*', in *Eliot in Perspective*, ed. Martin, p. 109.

29. While Freud once said that weaving was woman's only contribution to civilisation, and that it originates in the 'concealment of genital deficiency' (SE XXII 132), Ovid makes women's weaving into the invention of the *text*.

30. See Ovid, *Metamorphoses*, VI, 412–674. Ovid juxtaposes her story to Arachne's, another weaving tattle-tale, who fraught her web with 'heavenly crimes', depicting Zeus in all the shapes

he took to ravish nymphs and mortal women: *Metamorphoses*, VI, 103–33.

31. Peter Middleton, 'The Academic Development of *The Waste Land*', forthcoming in *Glyph*.

32. Helen Gardner argues that *The Waste Land* is an 'exercise in ventriloquism', but she makes the dead the dummies, Eliot the ventriloquist. I suggest that the poem works the other way around. See Gardner, '*The Waste Land*: Paris 1922', in *Eliot in his Time*, ed. Litz, p. 78.

33. 'The "Uncanny"', SE XVII 238.

34. *Ibid.*, 222–6.

35. Curiously, Freud's word 'unheimlich' also alludes to property: for *heimlich* literally means 'homely', but it develops in the direction of ambivalence until it converges with its opposite, 'unhomely' (see SE XVII 222–6).

36. Even in *The Odyssey*, his prophecies make action a redundancy, for the deed becomes the mere mimesis of the word.

37. I owe this pun and some of the preceding formulations to my student John Reid at Amherst College, 1986.

38. Andrew Parker pointed out to me in conversation that 'degradation' in the poem always occurs through the association with the lower classes.

39. See 'Prufrock's Fixation', Chapter III.

40. See Jessie Weston, *From Ritual to Romance* (1920; Garden City, New York: Doubleday, 1957), Ch. 9, pp. 113–36.

41. *WL Fac* 109, 113.

42. *WL Fac* 109.

43. Lacan claims that the paternal law is 'identical to an order of Language. For without kinship nominations, no power is capable of instituting the order of preferences and taboos which bind and weave the yarn of lineage down through succeeding generations.' ('The Function of Language in Psychoanalysis', in *The Language of the Self*, ed. Anthony Wilden [New York: Dell, 1968], p. 40.) In *The Waste Land*, the phallus stands for these discriminations, but all three staves have detumesced, and the father has been shipwrecked on the ruins of his own distinctions.

44. Anon., review of *Ara Vos Prec*, *TLS*, no. 948 (1920), 184. See also Gabriel Pearson, 'Eliot: An American Use of Symbolism', in Martin, ed., *Eliot in Perspective*, pp. 83–7, for an illuminating discussion of 'the social as well as verbal logic' of 'the conversion of words into the Word.'

45. In the same way, Ricoeur argues that defilement is acted out through 'partial, substitutive and abbreviated signs' which 'mutually symbolise one another': *Symbolism of Evil*, p. 35.

46. Kristeva, *Powers of Horror*, p. 3.

47. See Middleton, 'The Academic Development of *The Waste Land*'.

48. Paul De Man, 'Autobiography as De-facement', *Modern Language Notes*, 94 (1979), 926: repr. as Ch. 4 in *The Rhetoric of Romanticism* (New York: Columbia University Press, 1984).